Liberalizing Foreign Trade

Volume 4

Liberalizing Foreign Trade

Edited by
*Demetris Papageorgiou, Michael Michaely, and
Armeane M. Choksi*

Volume 4

The Experience of Brazil, Colombia, and Perú

BRAZIL   *Donald V. Coes*

COLOMBIA   *Jorge García García*

PERU   *Julio J. Nogués*

Basil Blackwell

First published 1991

HF
1411
. L497
1989
v. 4

Basil Blackwell, Inc.
3 Cambridge Center
Cambridge, Massachusetts 02142, USA

Basil Blackwell Ltd
108 Cowley Road, Oxford, OX4 1JF, UK

British Library Cataloguing in Publication Data
A CIP catalogue record for this book is available from the British Library.

Library of Congress Cataloging in Publication Data

Liberalizing foreign trade/edited Demetris Papageorgiou, Michael Michaely, and Armeane M. Choksi.
p. cm.
Includes index.
Contents: v. 1. Liberalizing Foreign Trade. The Experience of Argentina, Chile, and Uruguay — v. 2. Liberalizing Foreign Trade. The Experience of Korea, the Philippines, and Singapore — v. 3. Liberalizing Foreign Trade. The Experience of Israel and Yugoslavia — v. 4. Liberalizing Foreign Trade. The Experience of Brazil, Colombia, and Perú — v. 5. Liberalizing Foreign Trade. The Experience of Indonesia, Pakistan, and Sri Lanka — v. 6. Liberalizing Foreign Trade. The Experience of New Zealand, Spain, and Turkey — v. 7. Liberalizing Foreign Trade. Lessons of Experience in the Developing World
ISBN 0–631–16666–1 (v. 1). ISBN 0–631–16669–6 (v. 4). ISBN 0–631–17595–4 (7 vol. set)
1. Commercial policy. 2. Free trade. 3. International trade.
I. Papageorgiou, Demetris, 1938—. II Michaely, Michael, 1928—.III. Choksi, Armeane M., 1944—.
HF 1411.L497 1989
382'.3–dc19   88–37455
                                                                                    CIP

Typeset in 10 on 12pt Times
by TecSet Ltd
Printed in Great Britain by T. J. Press Ltd., Padstow

Contents

About the Editors

Demetris Papageorgiou is the Chief of the Country Operations Division in the Brazil Department of the World Bank. He has served as a senior economist in the Country Policy Department and as an economist at the Industry Division of the Development Economics Department.

Michael Michaely is the Lead Economist in the Brazil Department of the World Bank. Previously he was the Aron and Michael Chilewich Professor of International Trade and Dean of the Faculty of Social Sciences at the Hebrew University of Jerusalem. He has published numerous books and articles on international economics.

Armeane M. Choksi is Director of the Brazil Department in the Latin American and Caribbean Region of the World Bank. He is co-editor with Demetris Papageorgiou of *Economic Liberalization in Developing Countries*, and has written on industrial and trade policy.

Editors' Preface

The General Objective

"Protection," said the British statesman Benjamin Disraeli in 1845, "is not a principle, but an expedient," and this pronouncement can serve very well as the text for our study of *trade liberalization*. The benefits of open trading have by now been sufficiently demonstrated and described by economic historians and analysts. In this study, we take them for granted and turn our minds from the "whether" to the "how."

The Delectable Mountains of open trading confront the pilgrim with formidable obstacles and there are many paths to the top. The direct route seldom turns out to be the best in practice. It may bring on rapid exhaustion and early collapse, while a more devious approach, skirting areas of excessive transition costs, may offer the best prospects of long-term survival.

Given the sharp diversity of economic background and experience between different countries, and indeed, between different periods in the same country, we should not expect the most favorable route to turn out the same for each country, except perhaps by accident. There are, however fundamental principles underlying the diversities and it is our thesis that a survey and analysis of a sufficiently broad spectrum of countries over sufficiently long development periods may serve to uncover them.

With this object in view, we set out to study as many liberalization experiences as possible and aimed at including all liberalizations in developing countries in the post-world war period. However, the actual scope of this study had three limitations. First, we restricted the study to market-based economies. Second, experiences with highly inadequate data had to be excluded. Third, to be an appropriate object of study, an experience had to be of some minimum duration. Applying these criteria, we were left with the study of liberalization experiences in the 19 countries listed at the end of this preface. This volume deals with three of these countries (Brazil, Colombia, and Perú). Five other volumes contain the rest of the country studies, and the seventh volume presents the synthesis of the country analyses.

Definitions

"Trade liberalization" implies any change which leads a country's trade system toward neutrality in the sense of bringing its economy closer to the situation which would prevail if there were no governmental interference in the trade system. Put in words, the new trade system confers no discernible incentives to either the importable or the exportable activities of the economy.

By "episode" we mean a period long enough to accommodate a significant run of liberalization acts terminating either in a swing away from liberalization or in a period where policy changes one way or another cease to be apparent.

The "episode of liberalization" thus defined is the unit of observation and analysis employed in each of our country studies.

Identification of Liberalization Episodes

There are three main indicators of a move in the direction of neutrality: (a) a change in the price system; (b) a change in the form of intervention; (c) changes in the foreign exchange rate.

Price system

The prices in question are nominal protection rates determining consumption patterns and, more importantly, effective protection rates affecting production activities. Any change which lowered the average level and distribution of rates of protection would count as a move toward neutrality. Typically, such a change would arise from a general reduction in tariffs, but it might also be indicated by the introduction, rather than the removal, of instruments of government intervention, or even, indeed, by the raising rather than the lowering of the incidence of government intervention. An instance of this might be the introduction of export subsidies in a protective regime previously biased against exports and favoring import substitution. Another instance might be the introduction or increase of tariffs on imported raw materials and capital goods in a regime where tariffs have previously escalated over the whole field, with the zero and lower rates applying on these imports.

Form of Intervention

The form of intervention may be affected by a change in the quantitative restriction (QR) system itself or by replacing QRs with tariffs. Although the actual changes might be assigned price *equivalents*, it is not feasible to assign price equivalents to their actual effects. Moreover, the reactions they induce are so different from responses to price signals that they are better treated as a separate category.

The Exchange Rate

A change in the level of a *uniform* rate of exchange, since it does not discriminate between one tradeable activity and another, is not of itself an instrument of intervention. A move from a *multiple* to a uniform rate would, however, be equivalent to a change in intervention through commercial policy instruments; changes in the rate would modify the effect of commercial policy instruments already in being, for example, where QR systems are operated through the exchange control mechanism itself or where tariffs effective at an existing rate become redundant at a higher rate. Failing detailed studies of the impact of exchange rate changes on QRs or tariffs we take as a general rule that a formal and real *devaluation* constitutes a step towards liberalization.

Policies and Results

We do not take the actual degree of openness of the economy as an indicator in itself of a liberalization episode. Liberalization policies may commonly be expected to lead to an increase in the share of external trade but this is not an inevitable result. For instance, if, starting from a state of disequilibrium, liberalization is associated with a formal devaluation imports may actually fall. Therefore attempts to detect liberalization by reference to trade ratios rather than to policy *intentions* would be misleading. Exceptionally, however, the authors of the country studies have used trade performance as an indication of liberalization, particularly where actual changes in imports can be used to measure the degree of relaxation, or otherwise, of QRs.

Measurement of Degrees of Liberalization

In each country study we have attempted to indicate the degree of liberalization progressively attained by assigning to each year a mark for performance on a scale ranging from 1 to 20. A mark of 20 would indicate virtually free trade, or perfect neutrality, a mark of 1 would indicate the highest possible degree of intervention. These indices are subjective and peculiar to each country studied and in no way comparable between countries. They are a rough and ready measure of the progress, or otherwise, of liberalization as perceived by the authors of the country study in question. They reflect, for instance, assessments of nominal and effective rates of protection, the restrictiveness of QRs, and the gap between the formal exchange rate and its equilibrium level.

Analysis of Successful Liberalization Exercises

To arrive at criteria of what makes for success in applying liberalization policies, the following questions might be asked in our studies.

1   What is the appropriate speed and intensity of liberalization?
2   Is it desirable to have a separate policy stage of replacement of nonprice forms of trade restrictions by price measures?
3   Is it desirable to treat productive activities during the process of trade liberalization uniformly or differentially?
4   If uniform treatment is indicated, how should it be formulated?
5   On what pattern of performance of the economy is the fate of liberalization likely to hinge?
6   Is it desirable to have a stage of export promotion? If so, what should its timing be in relationship to import liberalization?
7   What are the appropriate circumstances for the introduction of a liberalization policy?
8   How important are exogenous developments in deciding the sustainability of liberalization?
9   Finally, what *other* policy measures are important, either in their existence or absence, for a successful policy of trade liberalization?

Lurking behind many of these issues are the (potential) probable costs of adjustment of a liberalization policy and, in particular, its possible impact on the employment of labor.

Scope and Intention of our Study

The general purpose of our analysis is to throw up some practical guidance for policymakers and, in particular, for policymakers in developing countries where the economic (and political) climate tends to present the greatest obstacles to successful reform. It is for this reason that (as already explained) we have based our studies on the experience of a wide spread of countries throughout the developing world. All country studies have followed a common pattern of inquiry, with the particular analytical techniques left to the discretion of the individual authors. This approach should yield inferences on the questions raised above in two distinctly different ways; via the conclusions reached in the country studies themselves, and via the synthesis of the comparative experience of trade liberalization in these countries.

The presence of a common pattern of inquiry in no way implies that all country studies cover the same questions in a uniform manner. Not all questions are of equal importance in each country and the same quantity and quality of data were not available in all countries. Naturally, the country studies differ on the issues they cover, in the form of the analysis, and in the structure of their presentation.

The country studies are self-contained. Beyond addressing the questions of the project, each study contains sufficient background material on the country's attributes and history of trade policy to be of interest to the general reader.

The 19 countries studied, classified within three major regions, are as follows.

Latin America

Argentina	by Domingo Cavallo and Joaquín Cottani
Brazil	by Donald V. Coes
Chile	by Sergio de la Cuadra and Dominique Hachette
Colombia	by Jorge García García
Perú	by Julio J. Nogués
Uruguay	by Edgardo Favaro and Pablo T. Spiller

Asia and the Pacific

Indonesia	by Mark M. Pitt
Korea	by Kwang Suk Kim
New Zealand	by Anthony C. Rayner and Ralph Lattimore
Pakistan	by Stephen Guisinger and Gerald Scully
Philippines	by Florian Alburo and Geoffrey Shepherd
Singapore	by Bee-Yan Aw
Sri Lanka	by Andrew G. Cuthbertson and Premachandra Athukorala

The Mediterranean

Greece	by George C. Kottis
Israel	by Nadav Halevi and Joseph Baruh
Portugal	by Jorge B. de Macedo, Cristina Corado, and Manuel L. Porto
Spain	by Guillermo de la Dehesa, José Juan Ruiz, and Angel Torres
Turkey	by Tercan Baysan and Charles Blitzer
Yugoslavia	by Oli Havrylyshyn

Coordination of the Project

Demetris Papageorgiou, Michael Michaely, and Armeane M. Choksi, of the World Bank's Latin American and Caribbean Region, are the directors of this research project. Participants in the project met frequently to exchange views. Before the country studies were launched, the common framework of the study was discussed extensively at a plenary conference. Another plenary conference was held to discuss early versions of the completed country studies, as well as some emerging general inferences. In between, three regional meetings in each region were held to review phases of the work under way. An external Review Board consisting of Robert Baldwin (University of Wisconsin), Mario Blejer (International Monetary Fund), Jacob Frenkel (University of Chicago and Director of Research, International Monetary Fund), Arnold Harberger (University of Chicago and University of California-Los Angeles), Richard Snape (Monash University), and Martin Wolf (Chief Economic Leader Writer, Financial Times), contributed to the reviewing process of the country studies and of the synthesis volume.

Brazil, Columbia, and Perú are presented in this volume. The series' other publications are the following:

Volume 1: Liberalizing Foreign Trade. The Experience of Argentina, Chile, and Uruguay;

Volume 2: Liberalizing Foreign Trade. The Experience of Korea, the Philippines, and Singapore;

Volume 3: Liberalizing Foreign Trade. The Experience of Israel and Yugoslavia;

Volume 5: Liberalizing Foreign Trade. The Experience of Indonesia, Pakistan, and Sri Lanka;

Volume 6 : Liberalizing Foreign Trade. The Experience of New Zealand, Spain, and Turkey;

Volume 7: Liberalizing Foreign Trade. Lessons of Experience in the Developing World.

Demetris Papageorgiou, Michael Michaely, and Armeane Choksi

Part I
Brazil

Donald V. Coes
Department of Economics
University of Illinois

Contents

List of Figures

List of Tables

Acknowledgments

I would like to thank Paulo André, Helson Braga, Armeane Choksi, Sergio de la Cuadra, Jorge García García, Arnold Harberger, Ian Little, Michael Michaely, and Demetris Papageorgiou for their helpful comments on earlier drafts. The final draft has benefited from the comments of an anonymous referee. This study was undertaken for the Country Policy Division of the World Bank. The views and interpretations are those of the author and do not necessarily represent the views and policies of the World Bank or of its executive directors or the countries they represent.

1

Introduction

At the end of March 1964 Brazil's military officers ended the government of President João Goulart, replacing it with an authoritarian government that was to last for over two decades. Far-reaching changes in economic policy made in the first year of the regime ushered in a period of unprecedented economic growth that persisted until the oil shock of 1973–4.

Notable among these changes was the marked departure, in both commercial and capital account policies, from the inward-looking orientation of the preceding decade. These new policies, which may be loosely characterized as "liberalizing," included measures to encourage both exports and larger net capital inflows, as well as a general tariff reduction in 1967 and partial easing of import restrictions over the next six years.

Brazil's international economic policies since World War II have included a complex collection of commercial and exchange rate policies,[1] encompassing both microeconomic or allocational goals and macroeconomic aims, among them external balance and stabilization. The evolution and interactions of these policies with external economic conditions over the last four decades have resulted in substantial variation in the openness of the Brazilian economy to foreign trade on both the export and the import side.[2] Among these changes, the trade regime in the decade following the 1964 coup stands out as the most open that Brazil has experienced, before or since: by the early 1980s Brazilian external economic policies had reverted to their normal pattern of restrictiveness interspersed with occasional outward excursions.

---

[1] Among the former were import quotas, specific and *ad valorem* tariffs, linking schemes, prior deposits, export taxes, quotas, and subsidies, as well as a variety of fiscal and credit policies with trade objectives. Exchange regimes included fixed nominal rates, direct exchange allocations, multiple exchange rates, and, after 1968, virtually fixed real rates under a crawling peg.

[2] Although "openness" might be defined and measured in a variety of ways, it is useful in the Brazilian context to interpret it as the degree to which internal and external prices are linked.

The present study focuses on this "liberal trade episode," from 1964, when the move to greater openness began, to 1976, when the process of reversal triggered by the 1973 oil shock was complete. An examination of the Brazilian experience sheds light on some important questions about the timing and the sequencing of a trade liberalization policy. In particular, because it included significant changes in export policies and in capital account policies, the Brazilian experience is useful for understanding the interactions between trade liberalization and simultaneous capital account liberalization through their effects on the real exchange rate.

Principal Issues in the Brazilian Experience

To draw useful inferences about timing and sequencing of trade liberalizations from the Brazilian case study, several questions need to be resolved. Obviously, the question of whether the 1964–72 reforms constituted a genuine trade liberalization should be first on the list. Some of the changes in commercial policy, particularly on the import side in the 1967 tariff reductions, were more apparent than real, owing to a high level of redundancy in the existing protective system. Our analysis of import penetration by sectors, however, suggests that import coefficients increased significantly after 1967, even if some of the measured tariff level before then was redundant. A narrow focus on *ad valorem* tariffs, moreover, ignores profound changes on the export side, which had far-reaching effects on the Brazilian economy and survived many of the post-liberalization reversals in import policy.

A second issue central to the analysis of any episode of trade liberalization is the question of its costs and benefits. This question may be usefully divided into long-run and short-run effects. Even if we believe, as most economists do, that the net long-run effects of greater trade openness are positive, the short-run costs of temporary unemployment of productive factors and other disequilibrium effects may be large enough to dissuade policymakers from embarking on a program of trade liberalization. The Brazilian experience is interesting in this respect, since its short-run costs seem surprisingly small: few cases of economic loss, in terms of unemployment, business failures, or other measures of sectoral loss, can be identified as casualties of the 1964–73 policies. This is partly due to the greater emphasis, in the Brazilian experience, on export promotion than on the tariff reductions that would be central in a more orthodox trade liberalization episode. In terms of costs, the Brazilian experience should therefore be judged relatively more successful than those of several other nations, including some Latin American countries, that have embarked on trade liberalizations. On the benefit side, the greater openness of the

Brazilian economy after 1967 was an important contributor to the expansion of production and trade.

Why, in view of this apparent success, was the trade liberalization program not sustained? As the effects of the rise in petroleum prices on the Brazilian current account became apparent in 1974, several policies might have been essayed to restore external balance. Instead of using exchange rate policy to deal with the problem, policymakers began a general retreat from many of the liberalizing trade policies of the preceding years. There are several reasons for the retreat, particularly on the import side. Exchange rate policy, both in the favorable balance-of-payments period before 1973 and in the difficult times afterward, was not viewed as a sufficient or adequate tool for external balance. Commercial policies were regarded as such a tool, which may explain why policymakers turned quickly to import restrictions in the post-1973 period, while justifying the extension of export promotion policies of questionable allocational efficiency on balance-of-payments grounds.

The question then arises as to what kinds of economic circumstances are conducive to a durable trade liberalization program. Adverse international payments may force a reform in trade policies; conversely, they may be used as an excuse to avoid liberalization. The evidence from Brazil on this issue is mixed. Export liberalization and promotion, which began sooner and lasted longer than did import liberalization in Brazil, appears to have been fostered by the need to alleviate balance-of-payments constraints to growth both in the 1964–8 period and once again in the post 1973–4 period. Although import liberalization pre-dated the high growth and favorable balance-of-payments period from 1968 through 1973, it appears to have been strengthened by favorable external trends, particularly in the capital account. It may therefore be useful in the Brazilian case to distinguish between the initiation of a trade liberalization program and its maintenance; adverse external economic circumstances in the mid-1960s were critical in forcing a change from the earlier emphasis on import substitution, while favorable export and capital account trends after 1968 permitted import liberalization to continue.

A fifth issue raised by the Brazilian experience is the question of what type of political regime is most conducive to trade liberalization. One possibly disturbing hypothesis is that trade liberalization is more likely under authoritarian regimes. A superficial analysis of the Brazilian experience appears to support this hypothesis, since the Brazilian trade policies instituted between 1964 and 1973 were not the product of any widespread political consensus, and coincided with the most politically repressive period in modern Brazilian history. However, the same authoritarian regime abandoned much of the liberalization effort, with equal ease, after the oil shock. In other words, the Brazilian experience suggests that although a centralized authoritarian government may have greater free-dom to make significant economic policy changes, these policies do not necessarily have deep roots, and may be easily reversed by other authoritarian policymakers (or even by the same policymakers). The issue may therefore be more correctly understood in terms of credibility rather than centralized authority: although more difficult to implement, economic policies endorsed by a wide spectrum of society may have better long-run prospects of survival than those imposed by policymakers accountable to authoritarian rulers.[3]

One of the principal questions in the general analysis of a trade liberalization program, and more specifically in the analysis of its timing and sequencing, is the role played by the capital account in the liberaliza-tion process. The Brazilian case again is valuable for analyzing this question, since the trade liberalization process occurred concurrently with an opening to greater capital inflows. The latter trend has effects on the exchange rate that may undercut the exchange rate effects of import liberalization. A conventional model of trade liberalization suggests that a reduction in import restrictions forces a real depreciation, with consequent positive effects on exports, if external balance is to be maintained. This view implicitly ignores the capital account, or at least assumes it to be unchanged. This was definitely not so in Brazil. Beginning in the late 1960s, a number of policy changes, as well as external supply changes, led to massive capital inflows. Any effects which increasing import liberaliza-tion might have had in inducing a real depreciation were more than offset by the real appreciation induced by these capital account developments.

Finally, we must ask how much Brazil's opening to greater trade and investment after 1964 was conditioned by characteristics peculiar to Brazil. A country's attitude towards trade is naturally conditioned by its size and resource endowment. Import substitution policies, for instance, are more likely to enjoy wide support in a large economy than in a smaller market. Self-sufficiency in a wide range of activities, despite often high costs in terms of allocational efficiency, thus remains a far more alluring and attainable objective in Brazil than it would in Sweden, Singapore, or Israel.

Another aspect of the Brazilian experience, which stands in contrast with those of smaller economies with fewer regional disparities, is the differential impact of trade policy in a regional context. Import substitution and subsequent export-oriented industrial growth were concentrated in the southeast, especially in the state of São Paulo. As changes in the degree of protection also imply a degree of geographical redistribution of income,

---

[3] Brazilians sometimes express surprise at the slowness with which major changes in tax or commercial policies are made in the United States, in contrast with Brazil during the authoritarian period when executive decision faced little prospect of legislative opposition or modification.

trade policies had a definite regional bias. Many studies of Brazilian policies have concluded that agricultural activities, many of which are located in the northeast, have paid some of the price of protection afforded to the industrial southeast. A more conventional process of trade liberalization, which works primarily on the import side, would have redressed the balance in favor of the agricultural sectors at the cost of the formerly highly protected manufacturing activities. The Brazilian emphasis on export liberalization and promotion policies, however, appears to have maintained the bias in favor of industrial activities in the southeast, simply switching them from import substitution to exporting.

As a background to more detailed analysis of the principal issues described above, the next chapter describes the pattern of economic policies since the war, highlighting against that background the antecedents and motivations for some of the post-1964 policy changes and the motivations for their timing and sequencing. The principal policies of the liberalization period and the subsequent retreat from them are the focus on chapter 4. In chapter 5 Brazil's export promotion policy in both its liberalizing and protective aspects is examined. Capital account policies and trends in Brazil are considered in chapter 6. Some of the issues raised by the timing and sequencing of the liberalizing policies are analyzed in chapter 7. The response of the Brazilian economy during the liberalization period is discussed in chapter 8, which examines some of the potential costs of liberalizing policies. The study concludes in chapter 9 with an interpretation of the Brazilian experience and the general conclusions about the timing and sequencing of trade liberalization policies that may be drawn from it.

2

The Policy Background before 1964

The attitudes of the policymakers who initiated the modest trade liberalization of 1964–74 had been conditioned by a long and varied history of intervention in trade. In the absence, at that time, of developed economic theory on the complexities of commercial and exchange policy in a context of chronic external imbalance and high inflation, the policymakers' approach to trade reforms was naturally colored by their perceptions of apparent successes and failures before 1964, in particular the import substitution industrialization of the preceding decades and the exchange crises of the early 1960s. These experiences with external economic policy provide a partial explanation of the timidity of the post-1964 liberalization and the reluctance to continue the liberalizing trend after 1974.

To discuss the liberalization episode usefully, the context of earlier policy development thus needs to be sketched in; this chapter's brief review of the major developments of commercial and exchange rate policy before the 1964 coup is included for that purpose. By 1964, Brazilian external economic policy had already evolved significantly in both complexity and sophistication. The use of commercial policy as an instrument of industrial development had begun almost inadvertently before World War II, under the constraints imposed by the sharp fall in import capacity, and was consciously adopted and extended in the mid-1950s. Exchange rate regimes which provided a degree of protection to favored domestic activities were used throughout the post-war period, evolving from relatively simple exchange controls to a unified rate in conjunction with an *ad valorem* tariff system by 1957. The pre-1964 period may be conveniently divided into (a) the pre-World War II period, in which may be found some of the antecedents of subsequent commercial policies, (b) the immediate post-war period of exchange controls, followed by (c) the multiple exchange rate system adopted in 1953, and (d) the unified rate and *ad valorem* tariff system of 1957–64.

Pre-World War II Antecedents

Intervention in trade has a long tradition in Brazil, dating from colonial times when Portugal monopolized trade and forbade commerce with other nations. With independence (1822) and the opening of the ports, the British were granted preferences which helped ensure their dominant position in Brazil's trade throughout the nineteenth century.

Despite its status in the years before World War II as a primary producer on the periphery of the international economy, Brazil was not a low tariff country. The motivation for tariffs, however, was not to protect domestic activities but rather to finance government expenditure. Until World War I, tariff collections accounted for over two thirds of the government's receipts. The tariff-induced import substitution that occurred, therefore, was a byproduct and not an objective of policy. Trade intervention also occurred on the export side, as Brazil became the dominant world supplier of coffee. The Taubaté *valorização* (price support) plan begun in 1906 was a sophisticated effort to exploit Brazil's monopoly power in this market. The system worked well until 1929, when the combination of bumper crops and the retraction of international capital markets, from which Brazil borrowed to finance its stockpiles, forced a change in policy.

The precipitous fall in Brazil's import capacity after 1929, in conjunction with the government's partial maintenance of income in the coffee sector through an expansionary fiscal policy and domestic credit expansion, created conditions favorable for industrial growth in the 1930s. In marked contrast with the highly industrialized countries, in Brazil the macroeconomic effect of the Depression was moderate, with gross domestic product (GDP) regaining its 1928 level by 1932, and growing more rapidly in the 1930s than it had in the 1920s.[1]

Although some industrialization had occurred earlier, especially in the textile sector, stimulated in part by import constraints during World War I, most Brazilian economic historians regard the decade of the 1930s as the first major phase of Brazilian industrial growth. By 1939, import substitution in most consumer nondurables was virtually complete, with imports less than a tenth of total supply. In other sectors, imports provided a higher percentage of total supply, ranging from about a quarter in many intermediate goods to about two thirds in capital goods and some consumer durables. There were no major sectors in which there was not some local

[1] The macroeconomic effects of Brazilian coffee policies and the impact of the world depression were first analyzed by Furtado (1963), and have been reviewed by Baer (1983). Parallel experiences in other Latin American economies in this period have been noted by Díaz-Alejandro (1983).

production, however, and by 1939 Brazilian industrial production was well diversified (see Fishlow, 1975).

The effect of World War II on Brazilian trade was to continue to constrain imports. In contrast with the decade of the 1930s, however, this was due to supply-side constraints and limitations on shipping rather than to import capacity generated by Brazil's exports. Brazilian exports in fact increased sharply during the war, with coffee accorded a priority by the United States and a number of lesser exports also stimulated by wartime demand. As a result, Brazil emerged from World War II with over half a billion dollars in reserves and the Depression-era constraint on its import capacity effectively eliminated.

Exchange Controls, 1946–1952

The favorable balance-of-payments position enjoyed by Brazil at the end of World War II was short lived. Despite a near doubling of the domestic price level between 1939 and 1945, the nominal exchange rate had remained fixed at 18.7 (old) cruzeiros to the US dollar. The resulting overvaluation, once wartime supply-side limitations were past, rapidly worsened the Brazilian trade balance. The resumption of post-war growth in Brazil, together with the fact that many of the currencies acquired during the war remained inconvertible, thus accelerating the rate at which convertible reserves were spent, further aggravated the situation.

The immediate policy response, taken in February 1946, was to simplify the previous exchange regime established in 1939. The pre-1946 system had consisted of three markets: official, free special (*livre especial*), and free. The first two operated with exchange allocated from certain categories of exports by the Banco do Brasil and were intended to provide exchange for government services as well as capital account items. The 1946 reform abolished the free special category and effectively eliminated the official category; it also eliminated special exchange charges on certain categories of imports. As the principal aim of the new policy was to simplify the exchange regime, it did not eliminate the real overvaluation of the cruzeiro.

The combination of overvaluation and relatively unrestricted access to foreign exchange soon forced a change in policy. In June 1947, priorities in exchange allocations were re-established, with 30 percent of export receipts acquired by banks authorized to operate in the exchange market required to be turned over to the Banco do Brasil. The import–export division of the Banco (CEXIM) then allocated available exchange, giving priority first to "essential goods" and those of "national interest," then to exchange required for capital and debt servicing, lower priority goods and services, and finally to transfers and other items. The policy had a limited effect and did little to stem reserve losses in 1947.

Exchange controls were further tightened in February 1948, with 75 percent of exchange required to be turned over to the Banco do Brasil. Unless explicitly exempted, all imports and exports were subject to prior licensing, which was controlled by CEXIM. Criteria for licensed imports included domestic availability, relative domestic and international prices, and "essentiality," as well as the possibility of using inconvertible currencies. By the end of 1948 the trade balance had improved, with the current account for the year nearly in equilibrium. These developments are illustrated in table 2.1, which shows the principal items in the Brazilian balance of payments from 1947 to 1981.

One of the consequences of the system in its early stages was the development of a "parallel" market, with exchange coming both from extra-official sources and from that portion of receipts which authorized banks were allowed to retain. The government responded with further exchange controls, requiring the banks to turn over balances of exchange not used within 48 hours and eliminating exchange sales for travel, transfers, and related categories of transactions.

In the second half of 1949, in an attempt to stimulate noncoffee exports, severely affected by exchange rate overvaluation, the government instituted a policy of "linked operations" (operações vinculadas), which permitted exporters to sell exchange directly to an importer approved by CEXIM. Since the transaction was made at the official rate plus a negotiated premium, it was a de facto devaluation for certain categories of transactions. For the importer it had the advantage of circumventing the licensing restrictions otherwise applicable. By 1950, the linked operations accounted for almost 20 percent of the exchange transactions arising from merchandise trade. In early 1951, however, they were suspended, primarily because they had led to substantial increases in imports not considered essential by the government.

The Korean War led to renewed concerns by policymakers about the adverse consequences for the domestic economy of import shortages like those of World War II. In late 1950, CEXIM authorized the import of a large number of items judged essential, through the concession of import licenses which were issued without an expiration date and which temporarily set aside quota and origin criteria previously imposed. With increasing overvaluation and the relaxation of import controls, the current account worsened dramatically in 1951 and 1952, setting the stage for the next policy changes.

Multiple Exchange Rates, 1953–1957

In January 1953 a new exchange policy permitted the use of a "free" market (mercado livre) for a number of nontraditional exports. Compared with 1946, however, the market was less free; prior licensing for imports was maintained, and services and capital account transactions continued at the official rate (about half that of the "free" rate) administered by CEXIM.

A more fundamental change was made in October 1953. Direct quantitative restrictions via exchange allocations administered by CEXIM were replaced by an auction system. CEXIM itself was eliminated and its functions were transferred to a new division of the Banco do Brasil, the Carteira de Comércio Exterior (CACEX).

The exchange auction system consisted of five separate categories of transactions. On the import side, potential importers bid in public auctions for rights to buy exchange at a particular price and quantity (*promessas de venda de câmbio* or PVCs). On the export side, exchange was still offered at the official rate, but to it were added premia (*bonificações*), which were distinguished between coffee (intially set at Cr$5.0 per US dollar) and other exports (Cr$10.0 per US dollar). The premia offered by importers bidding at the weekly auctions were used to pay the exporters' *bonificações*, with the surplus directed to agricultural imports. Certain "essential" imports were exempted from PVC requirements.

The auction system was in a sense a variable tariff, with exchange administratively allocated among the five categories and allocated by the market within categories. In the first category were essential medical and pharmaceutical supplies, petroleum and some of its derivatives, and agricultural inputs. The second and third categories included chemicals, minerals, and most capital goods and intermediate inputs. The fourth category was primarily consumer goods, with the fifth and lowest priority category used for residual demands.

The auction system in effect permitted a progressive and long overdue devaluation of the cruzeiro over the 1953–7 period. Compared with the preceding regime, it was a step forward in terms of both economic and administrative efficiency, but it did not end overvaluation. A worsening of the trade balance, accompanied by a negative net capital account in 1954, led to efforts to stimulate exports beginning in early 1955. Exchange premia were extended and increased, with exports other than coffee, cotton, and cacao receiving the highest premia.

On the import side, Instruction 113 of the monetary authority (Superintendência da Moeda e do Crédito, or SUMOC), put into effect in January 1955, permitted imports of capital goods without exchange coverage if the investment was to produce goods in the first three exchange categories, provided that the investment was officially approved and financed externally. The measure both encouraged direct investment in Brazil and relieved some of the demand pressures on the exchange auction market.

Despite its superiority to the system existing before 1953, the multiple rate system had several disadvantages. It was administratively complicated, requiring weekly auctions to be conducted simultaneously in a

Descript ... v. ... ill. ; 24 cm

Note   Includes bibliographical references and index

Contents   v. 1. The experience of Argentina, Chile, and Uruguay.--v. 2. The experience of Korea, the Philippines, and Singapore.--v. 3. The experience of Israel and Yugoslavia.--v. 4. The experience of Brazil, Colombia, and Peru.--v. 5. The experience of Indonesia, Pakistan, and Sri Lanka.--v. 6. The experience of New Zealand, Spain, and Turkey.--v. 7. Lessons of experience in the developing world

Subject   Commercial policy
Free trade
International trade

Alt author   Choksi, Armeane M, 1944-
Michaely, Michael
Papageorgiou, Demetris

ODYsseus - Catalog of the St. Lawrence University Libraries

PREVIOUS RECORD | NEXT RECORD | RETURN TO BROWSE | ANOTHER SEARCH | START OVER | MARC DISPLAY

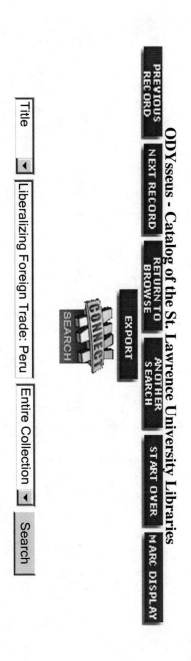

EXPORT

SEARCH CONNECT

Title ▾ | Liberalizing Foreign Trade: Peru | Entire Collection ▾ | Search

Title   **Liberalizing foreign trade / edited by Demetris Papageorgiou, Michael Michaely, and Armeane M. Choksi**

Imprint   Oxford, OX, UK : Cambridge, Mass. : B. Blackwell, <1991- >

LOCATION	CALL #	STATUS
ODY Upper Level	HF1411 .L497 1991 v.1	AVAILABLE
ODY Upper Level	HF1411 .L497 1991 v.2	AVAILABLE
ODY Upper Level	HF1411 .L497 1991 v.3	AVAILABLE
ODY Upper Level	HF1411 .L497 1991 v.4	AVAILABLE
ODY Upper Level	HF1411 .L497 1991 v.5	AVAILABLE
ODY Upper Level	HF1411 .L497 1991 v.6	AVAILABLE

number of Brazilian cities. Classification of a good in a particular category was sometimes arbitrary and not easily modified in response to the development of new sectors of the economy. Partly because of these problems, Brazil terminated the multiple exchange auction system in August 1957.[2]

Ad Valorem Tariffs, 1957–1964

The commercial and exchange policies adopted in 1957 were a significant departure from the past in several respects. First, they moved the Brazilian exchange regime closer to a unified rate, with divergences due primarily to the *ad valorem* tariff. Second, the structure of protection became more modern, in the sense that a number of quantitative and administrative trade restrictions were replaced with a tariff. Finally, the adoption of an *ad valorem* tariff in effect indexed the protective system from the effects of domestic inflation.

Since the Tariff Act of 1934, Brazil had maintained specific duties on many items, but after the war inflation had made these duties increasingly irrelevant. The Lei das Tarifas de Alfandega (Law 3244) of 1957 established two major categories of duties: the general and the special. Most capital and intermediate goods were covered by the former, with a number of consumer goods and a few domestically available producer goods in the latter, for which the exchange rate was usually more than double that of the general category. The relative importance of the special category was limited, and by 1960 the quantity of imports in this category was small.

Exchange auctions in the general category set the basic rate for most imports. To this was added the new *ad valorem* product-specific tariff instituted by the 1957 law. Concomitant with the tariff, the government created a new policymaking body, the Conselho de Política Aduaneira (CPA) or Customs Policy Council, charged with setting and revising the tariffs on individual items. Among its responsibilities was the administration of the Lei de Similaridade Nacional, which had existed since 1911 but was not effectively activated until the 1957 reforms. Under the law, domestic producers could petition the CPA to register their good as a similar. If successful, government agencies were required to purchase the domestic similar, and imports of the good were reclassified to the special category.

On the export side, an exchange premium system continued in operation, with some changes introduced in the different categories. Financial transactions were made at the "free rate," with the exception of a number

---

[2] The multiple exchange system of this period is analyzed by Kafka (1956) and Von Doellinger et al. (1977).

of government-guaranteed operations which received exchange at cost (the official, or basic export, rate).

The 1957 reform was not so much a liberalization of the preceding trade and exchange regime as it was a modernization and rationalization. Import costs were more or less maintained, with tariff categories broadly paralleling the previous exchange auction categories. As before, the system favored noncompeting capital and intermediate goods imports, now subject to duties from 0 to 50 percent, and penalized imports of goods available locally, with tariffs from 50 to 150 percent or higher. Some luxury consumer goods were transferred to the special category, in effect imposing the equivalent of a duty of 200 percent or more.[3]

Like the preceding system, the policies instituted after 1957 worked primarily on the demand side and did little to encourage export supply. As may be seen in table 2.1, poor export performance and the worsening of the trade balance between 1957 and 1960 aggravated the balance-of-payments deficit, which was also adversely affected by a deterioration in the capital account.

Several significant changes were made in 1961, when the exchange rate was progressively unified. SUMOC Instruction 204 in early 1961 transferred most transactions to the free market, introducing a degree of exchange rate realism. The cruzeiro was devalued by about 40 percent, and special rates for financial transactions were eliminated. The policies succeeded in improving Brazil's capital account, as private and official loans were obtained. Exports increased and the trade balance deficit incurred in 1960 was reversed.

The improvement in Brazil's external accounts was short lived, however. For reasons which were never fully explained, Jânio Quadros, who had been elected to the presidency by the largest vote in Brazilian history, resigned unexpectedly in August 1961. He was succeeded by João Goulart, a former Labor Minister and populist protégé of Getúlio Vargas.

With the entrance of Goulart, attempts at monetary and fiscal restraint ended. The shift to a more expansionary policy, as well as the effect of the earlier devaluation, led to accelerating inflation, which was not matched by accompanying exchange rate adjustments. Exports fell between 1961 and 1962, and preferential import rates for wheat and petroleum were reinstated. One result of the increasing real appreciation of this period was the appearance of the *boneco*, a kind of premium charged by exporters for foreign exchange and tolerated, although not officially sanctioned, by the government. The *bonecos* lasted until early 1964, when most transactions were again allowed at the "free" rate.

---

[3] The broad outline of the system on the import side may be seen in the first column of table 3.9 which reproduces Fishlow's estimates of the effective protection rate in 1958.

Table 2.1 Balance of payments, 1947–1981 (million US dollars)

Year	Exports	Imports	Trade balance	Net services	Current account	Capital account	Balance of payments
1947	− 1,027	1,157	130	− 257	− 151	12	− 182
1948	− 905	1,183	278	− 273	− 2	− 51	− 24
1949	− 947	1,100	153	− 232	− 82	− 74	− 74
1950	− 934	1,359	425	− 283	140	− 65	52
1951	− 1,703	1,771	68	− 469	− 403	− 11	− 291
1952	− 1,702	1,416	− 286	− 336	− 624	65	− 615
1953	− 1,116	1,540	424	− 355	55	59	16
1954	− 1,410	1,558	148	− 338	− 195	− 18	− 203
1955	− 1,099	1,419	320	− 308	2	3	17
1956	− 1,046	1,483	437	− 369	57	151	194
1957	− 1,285	1,392	107	− 358	− 264	255	− 180
1958	− 1,179	1,244	65	− 309	− 248	184	− 253
1959	− 1,210	1,282	72	− 373	− 311	182	− 154
1960	− 1,293	1,270	− 23	− 459	− 478	58	− 410
1961	− 1,292	1,405	113	− 350	− 222	288	115
1962	− 1,304	1,215	− 89	− 339	−389	181	− 346
1963	− 1,294	1,406	112	− 269	−114	− 54	− 244
1964	− 1,086	1,430	344	− 359	40	82	− 96
1965	− 941	1,596	655	− 362	368	− 6	331
1966	− 1,303	1,741	438	− 463	54	124	153
1967	− 1,441	1,654	213	− 527	− 237	27	− 245
1968	− 1,855	1,881	− 26	− 556	− 508	541	32
1969	− 1,993	2,311	318	− 630	− 281	871	549
1970	− 2,507	2,739	232	− 815	− 562	1,015	545
1971	− 3,245	2,904	− 341	− 980	− 1,307	1,846	530
1972	− 4,235	3,991	− 244	− 1,250	− 1,489	3,492	2,439
1973	− 6,192	6,199	7	− 1,722	− 1,688	3,512	2,179
1974	− 12,647	7,951	− 4,690	− 2,433	− 7,122	6,254	− 936
1975	− 12,210	8,670	− 3,540	− 3,162	− 6,700	6,189	− 950
1976	− 12,277	10,130	− 2,147	− 3,919	− 6,062	6,867	1,192
1977	− 12,023	12,120	97	− 4,134	− 4,037	5,269	630
1978	− 13,683	12,659	− 1,024	− 6,037	− 6,990	11,891	4,262
1979	− 18,084	15,244	− 2,840	− 7,920	− 10,742	7,717	− 3,155
1980	− 22,955	20,132	− 2,823	− 10,152	− 12,807	9,679	− 3,471
1981	− 22,091	23,293	1,202	− 13,135	− 11,734	12,773	625

Source: Banco Central, *Boletim*, various issues

The Goulart government, which was viewed with suspicion by conserva-
tives and many of the Brazilian military, adopted an increasingly national-
ist and populist posture in its approach to Brazilian economic development. The resulting political tension and radicalization of the discussion of
economic policies in the 1962–4 period had significant consequences for the
balance of payments. Overvaluation was in part justified as a means of

keeping down the cost of basic necessities, notably wheat and petroleum. Imports of capital goods without exchange coverage, previously allowed under Instruction 113, were subjected to tightened control, partly in response to nationalistic concerns that the measures had been overly favorable to foreign investors. The passage of Law 4131, limiting profit remittances, provided some temporary relief for the service account, but this was offset by its opposite effect on the capital account, which turned negative in 1963 for the first time since 1954. Instruction 263 in February 1964, transferring most transactions to the free market, was the last major balance-of-payments policy measure implemented by the Goulart government before its fall at the end of March.

3

The Background to Reform

The sequence of policies that Brazil followed in the years after 1964 and their timing appear to have been important determinants of their success in the intermediate run and their eventual demise after 1974. In this chapter the way in which the development of these policies was affected by domestic economic changes is discussed first. The political background of the early liberalization period is then considered and the political ideologies, personalities, and public attitudes are examined in turn. The chapter is concluded with a discussion of some of the motivations for the timing and sequencing of trade liberalization in the immediate post-coup period between 1964 and 1967.

The Economic Background of the Early Liberalization

At the time that the government of President João Goulart was overthrown by the military at the end of March 1964, inflation was perceived to be the single most serious economic problem. Prices were increasing in the first quarter of 1964 at unprecedented rates of over 100 percent. Internal disequilibrium was paralleled by external imbalance. Exports had stagnated since the early 1950s; the 1954 level of US$1.5 billion was not in fact surpassed until 1965. Despite substantial real exchange rate overvaluation, the low level of exports had been sufficient to maintain positive but declining trade balances through the decade of the 1950s, but in 1960 a small trade deficit and a large service account deficit led to a current account deficit of nearly half a billion dollars, forcing a devaluation of 40 percent in March 1961, and renegotiation of external debt as a precondition for new credits.

The temporary improvement in the balance of payments in 1961, obtained in part through an increase in net capital inflows, was soon overturned by real appreciation through 1961 and early 1962. A small (15 percent) devaluation in May 1962 did not restore competitiveness. Through 1962 and 1963, Brazil's capital account worsened, as net capital inflows fell in response to increasing political and economic uncertainty. Brazil ended 1963 with a current account deficit of US$114 million and a capital account deficit of US$54 million. The former would probably have been considerably worse, given the degree of exchange rate overvaluation, had the trade balance not been favorably affected by increases in world prices for several of Brazil's major exports and by the fall in internal demand.

Trends in income growth were equally serious. Annual growth rates of GDP had averaged about 7 percent from 1950 to 1963, with industrial output accounting for about a third of GDP by the early 1960s (tables 3.1 and 3.2). GDP and per capita GDP trends are shown in figure 3.1. In 1963 the growth rate fell to 1.5 percent, with per capita income falling by 1.3 percent, the largest decline since the war. Brazil's population had grown rapidly in the preceding decade. More and more people were concentrated in urban areas, especially the southeast, which was the principal destination of impoverished migrants from the northeast. These trends, which may be seen in more detail in tables 3.3–3.5, exacerbated the tensions created by the slowdown in growth.

From 1964 to 1968 Brazil's terms of trade deteriorated (see tables 3.6 and 3.7). This was due primarily to declines in coffee prices, although even

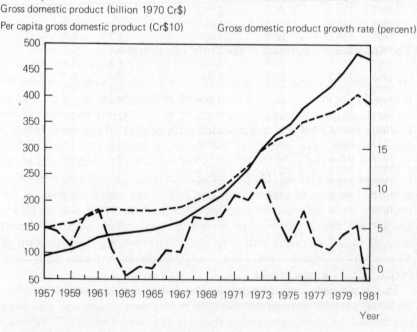

Figure 3.1   Gross domestic product (———), per capita gross domestic product (---), and gross domestic product growth rate (– – –).
Source: FGV, *Conjuntura Econômica,* various issues

Table 3.1 Real per capita gross domestic product, 1947–1981

Year	GDP (billion 1970 Cr$)	Population (millions)	GDP per capita (1970 Cr$)	GDP growth rate (%)	GDP per capita growth rate (%)
1947	49.8	48.5	1,027	—	—
1948	53.4	49.6	1,077	7.2	4.9
1949	57.0	50.8	1,122	6.7	4.2
1950	60.7	51.9	1,170	6.5	4.2
1951	64.3	53.5	1,202	5.9	2.8
1952	69.9	55.2	1,266	8.7	5.4
1953	71.7	56.9	1,260	2.6	− 0.5
1954	89.9	58.6	1,346	10.0	6.8
1955	84.3	60.4	1,396	6.8	3.7
1956	87.0	62.2	1,399	3.2	0.2
1957	94.1	64.1	1,468	8.2	5.0
1958	101.3	66.1	1,533	7.7	4.4
1959	107.0	68.1	1,571	5.6	2.5
1960	117.4	70.2	1,672	9.7	6.4
1961	129.5	72.2	1,794	10.3	7.3
1962	136.3	74.3	1,834	5.3	2.3
1963	138.4	76.4	1,812	1.5	− 1.3
1964	142.4	78.6	1,812	2.9	0.0
1965	146.2	80.9	1,807	2.7	− 0.3
1966	153.7	83.2	1,847	5.1	2.2
1967	161.1	85.6	1,882	4.8	1.9
1968	176.0	88.0	2,000	9.2	6.3
1969	191.9	90.5	2,120	9.0	6.0
1970	210.1	93.1	2,257	9.5	6.4
1971	235.3	95.5	2,464	12.0	9.2
1972	261.6	97.8	2,675	11.2	8.6
1973	298.2	100.3	2,973	14.0	11.1
1974	326.5	102.8	3,176	9.5	6.8
1975	344.8	105.3	3,274	5.6	3.1
1976	378.2	107.9	3,505	9.7	7.0
1977	398.8	110.6	3,606	5.4	2.9
1978	417.9	113.4	3,685	4.8	2.2
1979	445.9	116.2	3,837	6.7	4.1
1980	482.0	119.1	4,047	8.1	5.5
1981	472.0	122.1	4,866	− 2.1	− 4.5

—, not applicable.
The average 1970 cruzeiro–US$ exchange rate was Cr$ 4,594 per US dollar.
Source: GDP and population, Fundação Getúlio Vargas (FGV), Instituto Brasileiro de Economia, as published in Conjuntura Econômica, various issues

Table 3.2 Sectoral shares of total gross domestic product, 1939–1980 (percent)

Year	Industry						Services						
	Agriculture	Mining	Manufacturing	Public utilities	Construction	Total	Commerce	Financial	Transport and communica-tions	Government	Rents	Other	Total
1939	25.8	0.2	16.8	1.1	1.4	19.5	20.4	5.1	6.5	6.9	4.0	11.8	54.7
1947	27.6	0.5	16.2	1.3	1.9	19.9	19.4	4.7	7.1	7.3	3.2	10.9	52.5
1948	27.7	0.4	18.3	1.2	1.5	21.4	18.8	4.5	7.0	7.4	3.3	9.9	50.9
1949	26.4	0.4	19.9	1.3	1.7	23.2	18.5	4.6	7.2	7.5	3.4	9.2	50.4
1950	26.7	0.3	20.5	1.1	1.5	23.5	18.0	5.1	6.6	7.5	3.8	8.9	49.9
1951	26.1	0.3	19.5	1.0	1.7	22.5	19.0	5.4	6.4	7.5	3.6	9.4	51.4
1952	25.0	0.3	20.9	0.9	1.6	23.8	17.8	5.3	6.3	7.0	3.7	11.2	51.3
1953	26.0	0.4	20.9	0.8	1.6	23.7	16.5	5.4	6.3	7.5	3.9	10.6	50.3
1954	25.3	0.4	22.1	0.8	1.4	24.7	17.0	5.6	5.6	6.4	3.8	11.7	50.0
1955	25.1	0.3	21.7	1.0	1.4	24.4	16.3	5.6	6.3	7.0	3.5	11.7	50.5
1956	22.9	0.3	21.8	1.2	1.5	24.7	15.4	5.6	7.2	8.5	3.5	12.1	52.3
1957	22.8	0.3	21.3	1.4	1.5	24.4	15.2	5.9	7.0	8.2	4.0	12.6	52.8
1958	21.7	0.3	21.5	1.6	1.6	25.0	14.9	6.6	6.8	8.0	4.2	12.7	53.3
1959	22.6	0.4	21.3	1.7	1.8	25.3	15.4	6.3	6.7	8.6	3.7	11.5	52.1
1960	22.5	0.4	21.6	1.7	1.5	25.2	15.1	6.8	6.5	8.2	3.0	12.8	52.3
1961	21.2	0.4	21.7	1.6	1.5	25.3	14.5	6.8	7.2	9.0	2.7	13.4	53.5
1962	23.2	0.3	21.5	1.6	1.3	24.7	14.4	7.2	6.8	9.1	2.0	12.5	52.1
1963	19.8	0.3	23.3	1.7	1.4	26.8	14.9	7.1	6.8	9.9	2.6	12.2	53.4
1964	21.5	0.3	22.0	2.0	1.4	25.7	13.8	7.5	6.4	10.1	2.4	12.7	52.8
1965	22.3	0.3	20.9	2.1	1.1	24.4	13.5	8.5	6.6	9.5	1.9	13.4	53.3
1966	19.1	0.3	23.2	2.5	1.1	27.1	13.2	9.0	6.0	9.7	2.1	13.8	53.8
1967	19.2	0.3	22.2	2.5	1.2	26.2	12.8	9.3	6.3	10.0	2.3	13.9	54.5
1968	17.7	0.3	24.2	2.5	1.4	28.5	13.1	9.1	5.9	9.6	2.7	13.4	53.8

1965	15.9	0.8	24.8	1.7	5.3	32.5	15.1	4.4	6.3	8.5	7.0	10.4	51.5
1966	13.3	0.8	25.6	1.8	5.4	33.5	15.2	5.0	5.5	8.9	7.9	10.6	53.2
1967	12.8	0.7	24.3	1.9	5.6	32.5	14.8	5.1	6.0	9.4	9.1	10.4	54.7
1968	11.7	0.7	26.2	1.8	5.9	34.7	15.3	5.0	5.5	8.8	8.9	10.0	53.6
1969	11.1	0.7	26.8	1.9	6.3	35.8	15.5	5.6	5.4	8.8	8.2	9.7	53.2
1970	10.2	0.8	27.4	2.1	5.9	36.3	15.7	5.8	5.2	9.2	8.1	9.6	53.5
1971	10.7	0.8	27.7	2.1	5.6	36.2	15.8	6.2	5.0	9.0	8.0	9.1	53.1
1972	10.4	0.8	28.6	2.3	5.7	37.3	15.9	6.4	5.1	8.8	7.4	8.7	52.3
1973	11.0	0.7	29.5	2.1	5.7	38.1	16.1	6.5	5.2	8.2	7.0	8.0	50.9
1974	11.2	1.3	30.6	2.0	6.0	39.8	16.3	6.2	5.1	7.6	6.2	7.6	49.0
1975	10.5	1.4	30.2	2.2	5.7	39.4	15.9	6.9	5.1	8.0	6.8	7.3	50.0
1970	10.1	0.8	26.7	2.5	5.9	35.9	15.6	5.7	5.7	9.5	8.0	9.5	54.0
1971	10.4	0.7	26.9	2.6	5.5	35.7	15.8	6.1	5.5	9.4	7.9	9.2	53.9
1972	10.5	0.6	27.4	2.5	5.6	36.1	16.1	6.3	5.6	9.2	7.3	8.9	53.5
1973	11.3	0.4	28.2	2.4	5.5	36.6	16.6	6.3	5.5	8.6	6.8	8.3	52.0
1974	11.5	0.6	29.4	2.2	5.7	37.9	17.3	6.0	5.4	7.9	6.0	8.1	50.6
1975	11.0	0.6	28.8	2.3	5.4	37.1	17.1	6.5	5.5	8.5	6.4	7.9	51.9
1976	12.8	0.5	27.9	2.1	5.2	35.7	16.8	7.6	5.3	8.3	5.9	7.6	51.6
1977	14.9	0.5	26.8	1.9	5.1	34.2	16.7	8.1	5.3	7.7	5.6	7.5	50.9
1978	13.5	0.4	26.3	1.7	5.0	33.4	16.1	8.4	5.1	8.0	8.1	7.4	53.1
1979	13.3	0.4	25.8	1.2	5.0	32.4	15.6	9.0	5.0	7.8	9.5	7.2	54.2
1980	13.0	0.5	26.6	1.1	5.8	34.0	16.1	8.6	5.1	7.5	8.3	7.4	53.0

Sources: calculated from national accounts data prepared by the FGV, Instituto Brasileiro de Economia. The 1939–68 series was published in *Conjuntura Econômica*, September 1971; the 1965–75 series in *Conjuntura Econômica*, December 1979, and the 1970–80 series in *Conjuntura Econômica*, December 1981. The original data are in thousands of current cruzeiros at factor cost

Table 3.3 Population, labor force, and growth rates, 1920–1980

	1920	1940	1950	1960	1970	1980
Total population (millions)	30.64	41.24	51.94	70.19	93.14	119.07
Labor force (millions)	n.a.	14.76	17.12	22.75	29.56	43.8
Labor force as a percentage of population (%)	n.a.	35.8	33.0	32.4	31.7	36.8
Growth rate of population (%)	n.a.	1.5	2.3	3.1	2.9	2.5
Growth rate of labor force (%)	n.a.	n.a.	1.5	2.9	2.7	4.0

n.a., not available.
Source: population and labor force, IBGE, *Anuário Estatístico*, various issues

Table 3.4 Urban population by region, 1950 and 1960

	1950		1960	
Region	Population	Percent	Population	Percent
North	580.9	31.5	957.7	37.4
Northeast	4,744.8	26.4	7,516.5	33.9
Southeast	10,720.7	47.5	17,460.9	57.0
South	2,313.0	29.5	4,360.7	37.1
Central-west	423.5	30.0	1,007.2	43.4
Total urban	18,782.9	36.2	31,303.0	44.7

Urban refers to residents of Census districts with a population of 20,000 or more.
Source: IBGE, *Anuário Estatístico*, various issues

Table 3.5 Net internal migration

	To north	To northeast	To southeast	To south	To central-west
From north	—	− 156,220	62,067	− 1,576	− 9,162
From northeast	156,220	—	2,335,531	365,787	617,613
From southeast	− 62,067	− 2,335,531	—	1,041,390	712,800
From south	1,576	− 365,787	− 1,041,390	—	40,429
From central-west	9,162	− 617,613	− 712,800	− 40,429	—
Total	104,891	− 3,475,151	643,408	1,365,172	1,361,680

—, not applicable.
Entries correspond to net migration from the row region to the column region. The data are based on the aggregation of 1970 Census respondents' answers to a question asking about the respondent's state of birth.
Source: IBGE, *Anuário Estatístico*, various issues

when coffee is excluded the terms of trade worsened between 1964 and 1966. Although the increased importance of manufactured exports later made Brazil less vulnerable to falling prices for its primary commodity exports, in the early and mid-1960s manufacturing still enjoyed too small a share of total export values to diversify Brazil's export list adequately. Exports by major groups over the 1962–76 period are shown in table 3.3.

Brazil's import structure in the early 1960s reflected the effects of the import substitution industrialization of the preceding decade, with consumer goods less than a tenth of import value. (The share of imports of consumer goods in total imports actually increased slightly over the 1962–76 period, as may be seen in table 3.8). The study of Brazilian trade policies in the 1960s by Fishlow (1975) provides a reasonably good picture of the structure of protection in the mid-1960s, before the general reduction in *ad valorem* rates in March 1967. Estimates of the effective protection rates for 1958, 1963, and 1966 were made by Fishlow (table 3.9). Over the 1958–66 period, which begins shortly after the replacement of the multiple rate cum exchange auction system by a unified rate and an *ad valorem* tariff in 1957, effective rates in almost all industrial sectors increased substantially between 1958 and 1963, before receding almost to 1958 levels by 1966. Throughout the period, the consistently higher level of effective protection for consumer goods relative to intermediate and capital goods is evident.

These estimates of effective protection and other estimates such as those of Bergsman (1970, 1971) must be treated with caution, as Fishlow himself has noted. By the mid-1950s, and even earlier in some sectors, import substitution industrialization had proceeded so far in many consumer goods sectors that nearly the entire supply was domestic, with many goods in effect converted to what might be termed "pseudo-nontradeables." For this reason, tariff levels provide a rather imprecise guide to the effects of commercial policy on the divergence of relative prices in Brazil from world-market prices.[1]

Despite the difficulties in interpreting estimates of effective protection rates, there is little question that the distribution of rewards among factors would have been substantially different had trade been freer. The distortions had both factor (capital versus labor or land) and geographic (urban versus rural or northeast versus southeast) incidences. The estimates of

---

1 The high level of redundancy in many of the tariffs becomes more apparent when direct price comparisons are made. Estimates by Fishlow, using 1962 Economic Commission for Latin America (ECLA) data, show prices in Brazil to be considerably less for a number of commodities than would be indicated by the tariff; US retail prices are used as a proxy for world prices. This general pattern has been corroborated by more recent research at the Instituto de Planejamento Econômico e Social (IPEA), the research division of the Planning Secretariat.

Table 3.6 Exchange rates and foreign trade prices, 1964–1976

Year	Quarter	Buy rate (Cr$ per US$)	Sell rate (Cr$ per US$)	Import price index (Dec 1970 = 1; US$)	Export price index including coffee (Dec 1970 = 1; US$)	Export price index excluding coffee (Dec 1970 = 1; US$)
1964	I	0.600	0.620	0.857	0.859	1.184
1964	II	1.160	1.200	0.867	0.890	1.065
1964	III	1.550	1.610	0.846	0.869	1.053
1964	IV	1.820	1.850	0.867	0.890	1.086
1965	I	1.820	1.850	0.909	0.901	1.038
1965	II	1.820	1.850	0.920	0.911	1.053
1965	III	1.820	1.850	0.846	0.901	1.136
1965	IV	2.200	2.220	0.930	0.924	1.171
1966	I	2.200	2.220	0.878	0.767	1.192
1966	II	2.200	2.220	0.920	0.783	1.148
1966	III	2.200	2.220	0.867	0.822	1.322
1966	IV	2.200	2.220	0.890	0.809	1.266
1967	I	2.700	2.715	0.867	0.791	1.254
1967	II	2.700	2.715	0.930	0.799	1.361
1967	III	2.700	2.715	0.909	0.791	1.598
1967	IV	2.700	2.715	1.015	0.814	1.491
1968	I	3.200	3.220	0.927	0.821	1.086
1968	II	3.200	3.220	0.918	0.829	1.086
1968	III	3.675	3.700	0.902	0.821	1.029
1968	IV	3.805	3.830	0.901	0.799	1.019
1969	I	3.975	4.000	0.945	0.782	0.990
1969	II	4.025	4.050	0.991	0.797	0.990
1969	III	4.125	4.150	0.972	0.821	1.009
1969	IV	4.325	4.350	0.936	0.902	1.067
1970	I	4.460	4.490	0.972	0.902	1.114
1970	II	4.530	4.560	0.991	0.927	1.057
1970	III	4.690	4.720	0.982	0.976	1.009
1970	IV	5.000	5.030	1.000	1.000	1.000
1971	I	5.080	5.110	1.003	0.859	1.088
1971	II	5.250	5.280	1.003	0.885	1.182
1971	III	5.470	5.505	1.003	0.869	1.121
1971	IV	5.600	5.635	1.003	0.908	1.058
1972	I	5.810	5.845	0.945	1.146	1.229
1972	II	5.880	5.915	0.936	1.341	1.190
1972	III	5.990	6.025	1.018	1.472	1.086
1972	IV	6.180	6.215	1.009	1.496	1.257
1973	I	6.995	6.030	1.193	1.146	1.391
1073	II	6.060	6.100	1.257	1.341	1.638
1973	III	6.120	6.160	1.385	1.472	1.848
1973	IV	6.180	6.220	1.642	1.496	1.924
1974	I	6.145	6.445	1.930	1.496	1.863
1974	II	6.775	6.815	2.103	1.854	2.381
1974	III	7.090	7.130	1.852	1.918	2.515
1974	IV	7.395	7.435	2.113	2.101	2.815
1975	I	7.695	7.735	2.238	1.945	2.567
1975	II	8.020	8.070	2.306	1.532	1.977
1975	III	8.470	8.520	2.045	1.780	2.298
1975	IV	9.020	9.070	1.901	1.899	2.401
1976	I	9.885	9.935	2.016	1.890	2.319
1976	II	10.600	10.650	2.200	2.285	2.556
1976	III·	11.300	11.370	2.171	2.156	2.526
1976	IV	12.275	12.345	2.113	2.844	2.650

Sources: cruzeiro buy and sell rates, Banco Central, *Boletim do Banco Central*, various issues; import and export prices, FGV, *Conjuntura Econômica*, various issues; 1971 data from IMF tape

Table 3.7 Price indices and terms of trade, 1964–1976

Year	Quarter	CPI Rio (Dec 1970 = 1)	IGP-DI[a] (Dec 1970 = 1)	Terms of trade (including coffee)	Terms of trade (excluding coffee)
1964	I	0.139	0.159	1.003	1.383
1964	II	0.160	0.178	1.027	1.229
1964	III	0.179	0.203	1.028	1.245
1964	IV	0.210	0.240	1.027	1.252
1965	I	0.249	0.275	0.991	1.142
1965	II	0.271	0.289	0.990	1.144
1965	III	0.292	0.308	1.065	1.343
1965	IV	0.305	0.323	0.993	1.259
1966	I	0.346	0.365	0.874	1.358
1966	II	0.379	0.398	0.851	1.247
1966	III	0.411	0.432	0.948	1.525
1966	IV	0.431	0.448	0.909	1.423
1967	I	0.469	0.488	0.912	1.447
1967	II	0.500	0.513	0.859	1.463
1967	III	0.523	0.537	0.870	1.757
1967	IV	0.535	0.557	0.803	1.469
1968	I	0.565	0.601	0.886	1.172
1968	II	0.611	0.642	0.904	1.183
1968	III	0.639	0.670	0.910	1.141
1968	IV	0.665	0.698	0.887	1.131
1969	I	0.703	0.724	0.827	1.048
1969	II	0.735	0.758	0.804	0.999
1969	III	0.781	0.807	0.844	1.038
1969	IV	0.827	0.838	0.964	1.140
1970	I	0.863	0.878	0.928	1.146
1970	II	0.901	0.914	0.935	1.067
1970	III	0.965	0.970	0.994	1.028
1970	IV	1.000	1.000	1.000	1.000
1971	I	1.048	1.055	0.856	1.084
1971	II	1.093	1.115	0.882	1.178
1971	III	1.144	1.159	0.866	1.117
1971	IV	1.181	1.195	0.905	1.054
1972	I	1.239	1.258	1.213	1.300
1972	II	1.276	1.297	1.434	1.272
1972	III	1.325	1.348	1.445	1.066
1972	IV	1.346	1.382	1.482	1.246
1973	I	1.398	1.442	0.961	1.116
1973	II	1.437	1.492	1.067	1.303
1973	III	1.476	1.539	1.062	1.334
1973	IV	1.531	1.597	0.911	1.171
1974	I	1.701	1.764	0.775	0.966
1974	II	1.849	1.958	0.881	1.132
1974	III	1.949	2.040	1.035	1.358
1974	IV	2.049	2.149	0.995	1.332
1975	I	2.188	2.282	0.869	1.147
1975	II	2.330	2.426	0.664	0.857
1975	III	2.523	2.605	0.870	1.124
1975	IV	2.688	2.780	0.999	1.264
1976	I	3.039	3.095	0.937	1.150
1976	II	3.345	3.409	1.039	1.162
1976	III	3.626	3.811	0.993	1.164
1976	IV	3.893	4.066	1.346	1.254

[a] IGP-DI, índice geral de preços – disponsibilidade interna (general price index).
Sources: Rio de Janeiro consumer price index and IGP-DI, FGV, Conjuntura Econômica various issues; terms of trade, calculated from table 3.6

Table 3.8 Import composition, 1959–1976 (percentage shares of total imports)

Year	Consumer goods	Fuels	Other intermediates	Capital goods
1959	7.4	15.3	31.8	45.5
1960	6.8	13.1	31.9	48.2
1961	6.0	16.3	31.4	46.3
1962	6.4	14.3	31.9	47.4
1963	7.0	14.1	33.7	45.2
1964	10.7	17.3	44.4	27.6
1965	10.9	17.4	46.5	25.2
1966	11.8	13.8	46.3	28.1
1967	14.1	11.4	42.6	31.9
1968	13.6	11.5	41.2	33.7
1969	13.1	11.5	38.1	37.0
1970	14.3	11.0	37.0	37.7
1971	7.8	10.4	40.5	41.3
1972	11.0	9.0	39.0	41.0
1973	11.6	11.7	42.1	34.6
1974	7.6	22.4	45.2	24.8
1975	6.8	23.9	37.0	32.3
1976	8.1	31.0	30.7	30.2

Sources: 1959–67, Tyler, 1976, p. 42; 1968–76, CACEX, Brasil–Comércio Exterior, Série Estatísticas, various issues

Bergsman (1970, 1971) and Fishlow (1975), after appropriate exchange rate adjustment, show effective protection for agriculture to have been negative, especially before 1967. Thus, in the sense that industry as a whole received net positive protection relative to agriculture, the Brazilian protective structure favored capital and urban labor at the expense of land and rural labor. Within industry, however, the factor incidence of protection was more complex. Some of the most highly protected sectors, for instance furniture, tobacco, and clothing and footwear, appear to be among the most labor-intensive sectors. Conversely, protection for relatively capital intensive sectors such as mining, metals, paper, and chemicals was lower.

Although the geographic incidence of protection has not been measured explicitly for the 1960s, as it has been in recent years, there is little question that the import substitution process of the 1950s, partly induced by high levels of protection for industrial activities, discriminated in favor of the southeast, primarily the urban areas of São Paulo and Rio de Janeiro, and against the rural areas, particularly the northeast. This point has long been recognized by northeastern politicians and writers, some of whom have

Table 3.9 Effective rates of protection by sector, 1958–1967

Sector	1958	1963	1966	1967[a]	1967[b]
Agriculture					
Vegetable products	− 47	− 15	− 13	− 14	− 14
Animal products	24	12	16	18	n.a.
Mining	− 5	34	24	13	9
Nonmetallic mineral products	73	130	72	45	48
Metals	61	124	63	35	33
Machinery	22	68	30	32	31
Electrical and communications					
equipment	83	169	112	67	57
Transportation equipment	82	147	103	84	81
Wood products	138	176	120	81	44
Furniture	221	367	251	90	92
Paper products	86	169	91	43	42
Rubber products	139	221	158	126	182
Leather products	248	405	174	127	84
Chemicals	56	146	56	29	20
Pharmaceuticals	17	60	1	10	10
Perfumes and cosmetics	279	453	281	121	74
Plastic products	281	489	332	133	117
Textiles	239	298	232	162	88
Clothing and footwear	264	481	321	107	154
Food products	502	6,778	423	252	71
Beverages	171	243	183	104	76
Tobacco products	273	469	299	114	79
Printing and publishing	139	305	142	4	8
Miscellaneous industries	88	175	95	47	45
All sectors (weighted by 1959					
value added)	29.7	75.2	43.7	24.2	13.9
Industry	106.1	183.5	108.0	63.3	47.8
Consumer goods	242.0	359.9	230.1	122.2	65.7
Intermediates	64.9	130.6	68.0	40.3	38.5
Capital goods	53.0	112.5	69.1	55.7	52.4

n.a., not available.
[a] Based on 1959 input–output table.
[b] Based on 1971 input–output table.
Source: Fishlow, 1975

suggested that the costs of Brazilian industrial growth have been dispropor-
tionately borne by the northeast.

Adequate statistics on employment and unemployment at a national
level do not exist for the 1960s. Some information on available labor,
although not on trends in actual employment, can be gathered from the
censuses of 1960 (the results of which were not published in full) and 1970
(see table 3.3), and some information exists on industrial employment

since the early 1960s. The reported annual growth of the labor force over the 1950–60 period was 2.9 percent, declining slightly to 2.7 percent in the succeeding decade. With the slowing of growth in the early 1960s, following the rapid rates of GDP growth until 1961, there seems little question that the employment situation in 1963 and 1964 had worsened. Since the fall in growth rates was most pronounced in industry, the effects of the slowdown on employment were particularly severe in this sector.

The rates reached by inflation in the early 1960s, whether measured by wholesale or consumer prices, were unprecedented. Rates approaching 100 percent would be considered targets in Brazil in the mid-1980s; two decades earlier they were grounds for military intervention. Appearances, however, given the much lower degree of indexation in the early 1960s, may be deceptive: the real effects of inflation at the time may in fact have been more severe than those of contemporary Brazil in the early 1980s. Not only was inflation at a record high, but it was accelerating. Between 1960 and 1961, as measured by the Rio de Janeiro consumer price index, it was 33.1 percent. In succeeding years it was 51.5, 70.8, and 91.4 percent, respectively, with the rate in the first quarter of 1964 over 100 percent at annual rates.

The Political Background of the Early Liberalization

The economic policies instituted after 1964 were made in a profoundly different political setting from the preceding years. Both ideologies and personalities were important in shaping the political context. Public attitudes towards economics were muffled by authoritarian rule, but they were nevertheless important in the longer run. In this section some of the political positions and their proponents in the post-1964 period are reviewed, and an examination of public attitudes during the trade liberalization experience is given.

Political Ideologies and Personalities

The three-year presidency of João Goulart that preceded the military coup of March 31, 1964 was marked by increasing tensions and divisions within Brazilian society. These strains were exacerbated by the combination of accelerating inflation and falling per capita income. The basic structural reforms (*reformas de base*) advocated by the Goulart regime were viewed initially with suspicion and increasingly with alarm by the conservative opposition, which included businessmen, most of the military, and large segments of the urban middle class, as well as rural landowners and some elements in the church.

Neither the government nor its conservative opponents favored a continuation of the status quo, but in contrast with the populist interventionism of Goulart, or more radical policies supported by some of his allies, the position of his critics was markedly more orthodox, with a general consensus that the most immediate concerns of Brazil were inflation and the balance of payments. Associated with these short-run goals was a belief among the conservative opposition that the path out of the impasse of the early 1960s required a reduction in government intervention and greater reliance on markets in allocating resources.

The military government that assumed power in 1964 firmly supported the conservative position. During the presidency of General Castelo Branco from 1964 to 1967, the dominant economic policymaker was the Planning Minister, Roberto Campos, supported by Finance Minister Octávio Gouvea de Bulhões. Their orthodox stabilization measures were strongly backed by the president and the military, although the restriction of credit provoked protests from many of the businessmen who had supported the overthrow of Goulart.

The repressive measures adopted after 1964 stifled any overt political opposition that might have been aroused by a strongly and severely orthodox stabilization program that included wage limitations, monetary and fiscal restraint, the elimination of subsidies, and increases in tax collections and the prices of public services. The military government dissolved the former political parties and stripped most of the important political figures, including several of the civilian ex-presidents, of their political rights. The press was censored, and a series of "institutional acts" (Atos Institucionais) or decrees effectively suspended constitutional guarantees.

Economic policymakers were consequently relatively free to pursue measures that probably would not have been politically viable in the more open society of Brazil in the 1950s or today. If there were divisions in the military over the direction or the efficacy of the government's economic policies, they were muffled by the high command's insistence on unity and by a belief, correct or not, that the choice was between adherence to orthodox stabilization policies or a return to the tension and confusion of the immediate pre-1964 period. There was thus no serious challenge to the government's policies in the 1964–7 period from the dominant force in Brazilian politics, the military. Economic policymaking was in effect delegated to a limited group of technically competent and politically sheltered planners and higher-level public servants or *tecnocratas*.

In these circumstances, major changes in commercial or economic policy were unlikely to be subjected to public scrutiny or discussion. Campos and others often argued for their policies outside the bureaucracy itself, in the printed media and in public appearances, but such statements were motivated more by a desire to explain the policies than by any necessity of mobilizing public support. Such public discussion of the principal economic issues as there was focused on inflation and the balance of payments as a whole, particularly the capital account and international lending and direct investment, rather than on commercial policy and the structure of protection.

Support for the Campos–Bulhões stabilization policies from international agencies, notably the US Agency for International Development (USAID) and the International Monetary Fund (IMF), was influential during the early years of the new regime, since there was little new private lending and therefore public lending from USAID and other sources was more important.[2] External support alone, however, was not sufficient to account for the durability in subsequent years of many of the features of the 1964–7 economic policies, among them the emphasis on export expansion and more realism in pricing. Despite the support such policies received from outside Brazil, they were home-grown rather than imported.

A change in leadership in 1967, when General Costa e Silva, the former army minister, succeeded Castelo Branco as president, brought some significant differences in the direction and emphasis of policy. The new Planning Minister was a lawyer, and the center of economic policymaking soon shifted to the Ministry of Finance, now headed by one of the most politically astute economists of the post-1964 period, Antonio Delfim Neto. Delfim was less committed than Campos to orthodox stabilization policies and remained open to more heterodox solutions, then and later, as Planning Minister and as Finance Minister in subsequent governments.

Delfim's more eclectic approach, distinctly more expansionary than that of Campos, might today be labeled "supply side," since it implicitly denied an automatic link between greater output growth and inflation. Its success, however, is at least partly attributable to external influence, notably the resumption and rapid increase in large net private capital flows to Brazil.

Meanwhile, the ideology of the political leadership was also shifting. The new president was more closely allied than his predecessor with hard-line (*linha dura*) conservative elements of the military. After 1967, the repressiveness of the regime increased, culminating in December 1968 with Institutional Act 5 (AI-5), which in effect repressed what little political opposition had survived after the 1964 coup.

In August 1969 President Costa e Silva became seriously ill, and in early September the US ambassador to Brazil was kidnapped by urban guerril-

2 Although US officials have hinted that the large and relatively flexible level of program lending to Brazil was instrumental in the formation of macroeconomic policies, especially in the 1964–7 period, it is probable that many of the policies followed by the Brazilian government after 1964 would have been pursued without international endorsement. On this point see Díaz-Alejandro (1971).

las. Following his exchange for political prisoners, the military responded harshly, imprisoning or killing a number of opponents. In October, General Emílio G. Médici assumed office, and political repression escalated.

This state of affairs remained largely unchanged until the end of the Médici government in 1974, when, with the succession of General Ernesto Geisel to the presidency, some limited steps were taken towards redemocratization; some forms of press censorship were gradually relaxed and discussion of future political evolution became more open. The political system between 1964 and 1984, and most markedly between 1968 and 1974, could nevertheless be characterized as basically authoritarian, with little organized or effective opposition to the policies of the federal government. Modifications in policies, or changes in the timing or emphasis of particular programs, were therefore likely to result from discussions within the bureaucracy itself, or from the pressure of economic events, rather than from organized opposition or criticism.

Public Attitudes during the Liberalization Experience

Under a powerful authoritarian regime changes in economic policies are clearly more likely to result from initiatives within the government itself, or from the pressure of economic events, than from any organized political opposition. During the liberalization period opponents of the regime in any case concentrated their criticism on noneconomic political issues such as repression. In fact, even these critics tended to regard economic policies after 1968 as a success, perhaps because the high annual rates of GDP growth (more than 10 percent between 1968 and 1974) may have muffled much potential criticism. The fact that many of Brazil's poor shared very little in the *milagre*, or "miracle," was not widely recognized at the time. Evidence that income distribution had worsened between 1960 and 1970 did not surface until 1972, and even then had negligible impact.

The bureaucracy was not impervious to outside influences, however, despite its repression of public criticism of its policies through press censorship and other means. Businessmen, particularly those in the manufacturing sectors, maintained close contact with the major policymakers, especially Delfim. Communication was both informal and organized. Among the major associations with a voice in policymaking were the Federação das Indústrias do Estado de São Paulo (FIESP), a parallel association in Rio de Janeiro, and the Confederação Nacional da Indústria, as well as the exporters' association, the Associação dos Exportadores Brasileiros. There were in addition several sectoral groups. One of the more important ones, especially in the mid-1970s and later, was the association of producers of capital goods. As the government became more activist in its industrial policy, seeking to encourage growth in specific sectors, potential producers were often involved with government planners in formulating sectoral development policies, an approach that goes back at least to the 1950s when the government of President Juscelino Kubitschek established *grupos executivos* for sectoral planning. Such groups were active in the automotive industry, chemical production, and a number of other activities.

A second important influence on government policy was that of professional economists. The Planning Minister in the first post-1964 government, Roberto Campos, was an economist, as was Delfim Neto, the principal economic policymaker after 1967. Under them, an influential group of generally young, politically inexperienced but technically competent economists served in key positions in most of the important ministries. As many of these *tecnocratas* were recent students or academics (Delfim had been a professor at the University of São Paulo), they may have been in closer touch with both theory and empirical research in the relevant areas of economics than most of their bureaucratic counterparts in other countries. Their influence and prestige in the late 1960s and early 1970s was one of the reasons for the substantial increase in the number of Brazilians studying economics at a graduate level, both in Brazil and overseas.

The influence of professional economists on attitudes and policies in many areas of the bureaucracy was important, but it should not be exaggerated. In a number of institutions, for example CACEX, the foreign trade division of the Banco do Brasil and the organization responsible for the execution of most commercial policy, a degree of innocence of many elementary concepts of economic efficiency in international trade remained the rule throughout the 1970s. CACEX placed much emphasis on bilateral trade balances and even on balanced trade at a microeconomic or firm level. In the late 1970s, for instance, individual firms and public enterprises such as the federal railroad system were singled out for public scolding because they were net importers.

Outside a small group of economists, the idea that exchange rate policy could compensate for the potential effects of trade liberalization on the balance of payments was not (and is not) widely understood. With a few exceptions, economists themselves rarely made this point in public discussions of policy, although in some studies of Brazilian trade (see for instance Pastore et al., 1979) it was suggested that import-substitution-induced overvaluation of the exchange rate penalized exporters who were not favored by export subsidies.

Some of the bureaucratic preference for commercial policy rather than exchange rate adjustment as a tool for attaining external balance may have arisen from the greater discretionary power afforded by the former instrument: more reliance on exchange rate adjustment, even if arguments for it had been understood and accepted, would have entailed a loss of control by the bureaucracy. Resistance to the use of exchange rate policy may also have been strengthened by some earlier studies of Brazilian trade, which generally found rather low price elasticities in demand for imports and supply of exports. (See, for example, Von Doellinger et al., 1973, who concluded that most Brazilian primary product export price elasticities were not significantly different from zero.)

A related idea that had a widespread influence on discussions of exchange policy arose from the growing external debt. Since a depreciation, unlike import restrictions, directly increases the cruzeiro value of a debt denominated in foreign currency, commercial policy was often viewed as a more appropriate external adjustment tool. At a macroeconomic level, the argument implicitly ignores that fact that a real depreciation is intended to improve the current account and so reduce the debt denominated in foreign currency. From a microeconomic point of view, however, the argument was compelling, since most external borrowing by Brazil in the post-1964 period required exchange risk to be borne by the ultimate borrower. When the cruzeiro was finally depreciated sharply in real terms in the late 1970s and early 1980s, many such borrowers were severely squeezed.

Chronic inflation and widespread indexation may also have influenced public attitudes toward the efficacy of exchange rate policy. Advocacy of exchange rate policy to deal with external imbalance presumes that a real depreciation can be maintained by sufficient control of the price level, so that the nominal adjustment is not simply offset by price change. Despite Brazil's continental size and relative restrictiveness to foreign trade, the exchange rate, particularly the cruzeiro to US dollar rate, has long been one of the most visible prices in the Brazilian economy, partly because of the erosion of the cruzeiro's function as a store of value. A rise in the cruzeiro cost of a dollar therefore creates pressures for corresponding increases by those who are affected by the more expensive dollar. Indexation permits part of this increase to be included in the price level, so that a given nominal depreciation is not likely to produce an equal real one.

Despite the importance of commercial policies in affecting prices in the Brazilian economy, surprisingly little attention was paid to the question of the relative economic efficiency of alternative policies. Economists have long argued that if the society's objective is to increase the production of a particular sector above its level under a free-trade or no-intervention situation, this objective is attained at the lowest welfare cost if production subsidies and/or taxes are used. Tariffs and other forms of intervention in trade are less desirable, even if they provide the same level of protection for the producer, since they unnecessarily distort the prices faced by consumers of the product.

The proponents of protection for specific activities in Brazil have generally identified protection purely with trade intervention, ignoring the fact that, if their objective is specifically a production one, the more efficient form of intervention is a production subsidy or tax. Discussions of trade policy in Brazil have therefore tended to characterize the choice as one between tariffs or free trade. Although this was hardly surprising in the 1940s, in the debates over industrial policy between the São Paulo industrialist Roberto Simonsen and the economist Eugenio Gudin, the assumed limitation of the choice was also implicit in much of the public discussion of policy even 30 years later.

Motivations for the Timing and Sequencing of Trade Liberalization in the 1964–1967 Period

One of the central questions posed by a move towards greater openness to trade such as that observed in Brazil after 1964 is why policymakers attempt a degree of liberalization in a period of balance-of-payments difficulties. The Brazilian episode suggests that periods of external payment constraint may in fact be more conducive to fundamental changes in trade policy than more favorable conditions. This conclusion, which is consistent with the argument that the continuation and maintenance of a liberalization policy is facilitated by an easing of balance-of-payments pressures, rests on a variety of evidence about the performance of the Brazilian economy in the decade preceding the 1964 changes in government.

By the time the new government took power in 1964, the opportunities for further growth via import substitution were largely exhausted and the external payments problems increasingly severe. Between 1961 and 1963 the growth rate of the GDP fell sharply, resulting in negative per capita income growth in 1963 (table 3.1).

Import substitution does not appear to have lessened Brazilian dependence on the foreign sector, and the shift in import composition toward a larger share of capital and intermediate goods may have narrowed the latitude of policymakers to respond to balance-of-payments pressures by reducing imports. This problem was aggravated, moreover, by the probability that reductions in an import bill which was largely for intermediate and capital goods by the early 1960s would harm industrial output more than they would have done a decade before.

Some formal evidence of the decline in growth induced by import substitution has been provided by Tyler (1976), who used an approach originally developed by Chenery (1960) and modified by Morley and Smith (1970), to measure the sources of Brazilian industrial growth since the war. The Chenery approach breaks observed growth down into three categories: (a) growth attributable to domestic demand, (b) growth due to export expansion, and (c) growth induced by import substitution. The Morley–Smith and Tyler modifications allow for indirect as well as direct effects of changes in aggregate demand on total product through the use of input–output coefficients. Tyler, using a 32-sector input–output table based on the 1959 industrial census, estimated the growth sources for three periods – 1947–64, 1964–7, and 1967–71 – for Brazilian industry disaggregated into 21 sectors. His results are summarized in table 3.10, which shows the share of industrial growth attributed to each source in the three periods: individual sector estimates have been weighted by the sector's share in total value added.

Table 3.10 Sources of demand growth in Brazilian industry

	1947–64	1964–7	1967–71
Domestic demand	0.744	1.030	1.019
Export expansion	0.021	0.039	0.059
Import substitution	0.235	– 0.069	– 0.078
Total	1.000	1.000	1.000

Source: Tyler, 1976, p.74

Although Tyler's measurement does not permit a comparison of the effects of different sources of growth in the periods before 1960 and between 1960 and 1964, the pronounced decline in the contribution of import substitution to Brazilian industrial growth had evidently set in at least as early as 1964. The net contribution of import substitution to growth after 1964 was actually negative, even before the liberalization in imports of March 1967, suggesting that by this date there was little prospect for further expansion of aggregate demand as a result of import substitution.

The exhaustion of import substitution possibilities by the early 1960s appears to have been evident not only to policymakers in the post-1964 government but also to a number of outside observers. Notable among these were Tavares and Lessa who expressed this view in studies for the Economic Commission for Latin America (ECLA), an institution that had hitherto been a prominent advocate of import substitution policies in Latin America (see Tavares, 1964; Lessa, 1964). Brazil's turn to a more open external economic policy was consequently less controversial than some of the other changes in economic policy made by the new government.

The perception among policymakers in 1964 that import substitution possibilities were largely exhausted is the principal explanation of the decision to move to a more liberal outward-oriented trade policy at that time. In addition to helping to explain the timing of Brazilian trade liberalization, moreover, the pessimism about the prospects for further import substitution sheds light on the subsequent sequencing of trade policies.

Import substitution in the 1950s had often been viewed as a way of decreasing Brazilian dependence on the external sector and of alleviating the alleged shortage of foreign exchange resulting from slow export growth (see Von Doellinger et al., 1973). The recognition by 1964 of the limit to the foreign exchange savings that could be realized from import compression, in conjunction with the decline in net capital inflows in the early 1960s, left export expansion as the only viable means of assuring the rising level of imports necessary for future economic growth. For this reason, the reorientation towards a more open economy emphasized export growth much more heavily than import liberalization. Measures to increase exports were adopted almost immediately after the coup in early 1964. A number of official pronouncements about the necessity of export expansion were made within a few months of the entrance of the new government and gained credibility with the Imposto sobre Produtos Industrializados (IPI) exemption, the drawback, and other export incentives noted above.

No corresponding official statements were made about import policy, and there is no evidence that import liberalization was a high priority in the first year of the new government. The decree law to liberalize imports was not passed until late 1966 and went into effect in March 1967, well after the export incentives had begun.

Although one may question whether export expansion should precede import liberalization (an issue examined in more detail in chapter 6), or even whether export promotion of the type engaged in by Brazil after 1964 can be legitimately considered as trade liberalization, it is improbable that any other sequence of policies would have been followed in Brazil in the immediate post-1964 period. The order followed by the Brazilian authorities in 1964–7 suggests that early export liberalization and promotion, accompanied only later by import liberalization, is a natural response by policymakers facing severe balance-of-payments constraints.

4

Policies in the Post-1964 Period: Timid Liberalization and Subsequent Retreat

The change in Brazil's international economic policies that began after 1964 took the form of an extended sequence of measures aimed at imports, exports, and the capital account. Different phases of separate policies sometimes overlapped and the sequencing of the policies that are identified in this study as "liberalizing" did not follow a completely predetermined path. In this chapter the policy changes that immediately followed the assumption of power by the new government are examined first, and in the next two sections some of the adjustments made in commercial and exchange rate policies after 1967 and the partial reversal of import liberalization in late 1968 are discussed. The effects of the 1973–4 oil shock and Brazil's retreat from trade liberalization are then studied, and the chapter concludes with an attempt to represent in a simplified form the degree of trade restrictiveness over the whole post-war period.

The 1964 Coup and Short-run Policy Changes

The immediate priorities of the military government that assumed power in April 1964 were primarily domestic, with control of inflation paramount. The stabilization policies implemented in the 1964–7 period were strongly and sometimes harshly orthodox (see Lara Resende, 1982).

The cruzeiro was devalued sharply in May, and measures were taken to simplify and streamline the administration of trade on both the import and the export side. Compulsory deposits for imports were reduced, and exporters were allowed to retain half their exchange earnings if these were to be used to import capital goods or intermediate inputs for their own production. Capital goods and used equipment imports were liberalized, and measures were taken to finance exports of consumer durables and capital goods. The former tariff structure, however, was not immediately changed by the new government.

The record trade balance and current account in 1965 were the result of the increase in exports, stimulated in part by the above measures and in part by favorable external conditions. The sharp fall in imports to their lowest level in more than a decade was primarily due to the stabilization program. The capital account, however, actually worsened, as amortizations postponed from 1964 were made and as foreign investors waited for the outlines and results of the new regime's economic policies to become clearer.

Although major changes in commercial policy did not occur until 1967, several modest but significant steps in the direction of greater trade liberalization were taken between 1964 and 1967, primarily in the area of export promotion. With Law 4502 of November 1964, exports were exempted from the IPI, or tax on manufactured products (examined in more detail in chapter 5).

A second export incentive created by the government in this period was a corporate income tax incentive for manufactured exports. Overall corporate tax was reduced in proportion to the share of the firm's sales that were exported. A third measure, formally existing at least since the 1957 tariff reforms, but not effectively implemented, was the "drawback," or import duty exemption for inputs into goods produced for export. In June 1964 the policy was reformed, allowing firms to claim an exemption for a variety of inputs, although not for capital goods imports.[1]

In 1966, with continued growth in exports and a significant improvement in the capital account, the government undertook a substantial reform in the *ad valorem* tariff, basically unchanged since 1957, despite the addition and subsequent removal of surcharges and prior deposits. The new schedule was enacted in March 1967 and effectively cut *ad valorem* rates to about half their previous level for most manufactures, with the reductions somewhat larger for some consumer goods sectors. Even after the reforms, however, the characteristic hierarchy of higher protection for consumer goods than for intermediates and capital goods remained. Brazilian trade policy did not eliminate discrimination with the 1967 reform.

The fall in effective protection rates by sector between 1966 and 1967 may be seen in several estimates of the effective protective rate. Table 4.1 presents the earliest such estimates, made by Bergsman in 1969 using a 1959 input–output table (Bergsman, 1970). Corresponding estimates by

---

[1] The imposition of surcharges, prior deposits, and other restrictive measures on imports in the early 1960s and their subsequent reduction in the 1964–6 period is reflected in the pattern of effective protection rates shown in table 3.9. By 1966 the level of effective protection for industry as a whole was back down to the 1958 level, established after the 1957 general reforms.

Table 4.1 Effective rates of protection by sector, 1966–1973

Sector	Jun 1966	Apr 1967	Nov 1973
Agriculture	n.a.	n.a.	25
Vegetable products	35	8	n.a.
Animal products	164	17	n.a.
Mining	25	13	14
Nonmetallic mineral products	86	39	46
Metals	58	36	35
Machinery	41	32	32
Electrical and communications equipment	215	97	61
Transportation equipment	151	75	34
Wood products	45	25	68
Furniture	239	124	74
Paper products	118	59	50
Rubber products	136	116	66
Leather products	117	85	81
Chemicals	59	42	19
Pharmaceuticals	39	35	17
Perfumes and cosmetics	8,480	3,670	46
Plastic products	183	58	41
Textiles	379	162	118
Clothing and footwear	337	142	293
Food products	87	40	83
Beverages	447	173	114
Tobacco products	313	124	83
Printing and publishing	142	67	30
Miscellaneous industry	128	72	37
Average, industry	181	76	47

n.a. not available.
Sources: 1966 and 1967, Bergsman, 1970; 1973, Tyler, 1973

Fishlow (1975), shown in table 3.9, also use the 1959 matrix but are generally lower owing to the weighting of sectoral value added by world prices, which tends to diminish proportionately the effect of the higher tariff sectors. Despite problems of comparability, the estimates are consistent in their indication that effective protection levels shifted downward substantially as a result of the 1967 reform.

The late 1950s were a period of rapid output growth, partially induced by the import substitution industrialization policies of the Kubitschek government (1955–60). Import substitution in this relatively mature stage did not have a pronounced effect on the trade balance, since the decline in consumer goods imports was offset by a rise in capital goods imports and some intermediate goods imports, while the value of aggregate exports declined not only as a share of GDP but absolutely.

Since some of the import substitution industrialization was externally financed, moreover, the capital services component of the current account became increasingly negative, with the current account as a whole moving from approximate balance in the mid-1950s to a deficit of about 20 percent of aggregate export value by the early 1960s. Although the increase in net capital inflows easily financed the growing current account deficit in the early years of the Kubitschek government, these flows leveled off and declined after 1961, with a net capital outflow occurring in 1963.

Adjustments in Commercial Policy and Exchange Rate Policy after 1967

Following the tariff reforms in the early 1967 came an important shift in macroeconomic strategy, caused primarily by changes at the ministerial level. Roberto Campos, the Planning Minister and chief architect of the 1964–7 stabilization policies, was replaced by a lawyer, Helio Beltrão, and economic policymaking was soon centered in the Finance Ministry, now headed by Antonio Delfim Neto. From today's vantage point Delfim's policy approach might be labeled "supply side," in contrast with Campos's more conventional emphasis on contractionary monetary and fiscal policies to restrain inflation. The new policies emphasized output growth, rather than demand restriction, as a means to reduce inflation, which was already much below its 1963–4 levels. Excess capacity in much of the Brazilian economy, particularly the industrial sector, favored this shift in strategy, as did favorable balance-of-payments developments over the 1964–6 period.

One of the first major changes in external economic policy undertaken by the new economic leadership was the adoption of a crawling peg exchange rate regime in August 1968. The small but frequent adjustments or *minidesvalorizações* were approximately linked to internal inflation in Brazil and its major trading partners, particularly the United States. Although the policy was primarily intended to reduce short-term speculative pressure on the capital account, it appears to have had a marked effect in making the economy more open to trade, by reducing uncertainty about the real exchange rate.[2]

The increase in imports induced by more expansionary policies beginning in 1967, in conjunction with a fall in exports also partially induced by rising domestic demand, led to a deterioration in the trade balance and the current account in 1967. Although exports resumed their growth in 1968,

[2] In an earlier study (Coes, 1979), it was concluded that this impact of the crawling peg after 1968 may have had as strong an incentive effect on the ratio of exports to production in some sectors as did a number of more conventional export incentives.

this was not sufficient to check the fall in the trade balance through 1968. Concern about this decline, as well as pressure from producers who had lost protection, appear to have been the motives for a partial retreat from the 1967 tariff reforms.[3]

In December 1968 rates were again raised. With a few exceptions, however, they did not attain the levels prevailing before the 1967 tariff reforms. The retreat from liberalization was substantial for consumer nondurables but rather moderate for producer goods, including both capital and intermediate inputs. The change in protection in 1968 moved Brazil closer to its traditional position of discriminating most heavily against consumer goods imports, while taxing producer goods more lightly.

The external balance pressures on policymakers were relieved beginning in 1969. Although some of the improvement in balance of payments was due to strong export growth, the primary reason was the sharp rise in both financial capital flows and net foreign direct investment in Brazil. The policies and external factors that led to this increase in net capital inflows are discussed further in chapter 8. These developments permitted a period of gradual and selective import liberalization which continued through 1973. Tariff concessions for imports of capital goods and intermediate goods were frequently granted through the Conselho de Desenvolvimento Indústrial (CDI, Industrial Development Council) as well as by the CPA. Regional development agencies, particularly the Superintendência para o Desenvolvimento do Nordeste (SUDENE), responsible for the northeast, and the Superintendência para o Desenvolvimento da Amazonia (SUDAM), with a corresponding regional responsibility in the Amazon basin, were also able to grant tariff concessions for development-related projects. Also important in this context was the expansion of the duty-free region in Manaus, which allowed producers to assemble a number of consumer durables and other products with inputs available at world prices.

Since many of these *de facto* reductions in tariffs did not affect posted rates, the fall in effective protective rates between 1967 (after the already significant reduction in March) and late 1973 may actually understate the true degree of liberalization. Even without allowance for this potential downward bias in the estimates of the change, however, the level of protection appears to have declined in most sectors after 1967. Tyler's estimates for sectors at the two-digit level in November 1973, at the end of the period of rapid GDP growth before the first oil shock (table 4.1), indicate a significant degree of liberalization over the 1967–73 period, after the original tariff reduction and despite the partial retreat in December 1968.

[3] The reasons for this partial retreat from the 1967 tariff liberalization are examined in more detail in chapter 5.

Table 4.2 The Brazilian opening to trade after 1964: a summary

Question	Characteristic
Broad nature	Export promotion, tariff reduction and exemption, capital account opening, exchange rate correction for inflation
Size, duration	Large and extended
Stages and targets	Not explicit

Economic circumstances before the episode

Balance of payments	Worsening deficits
Prices of major exports	Sharp decline 1960–4
Inflation	Accelerating
Rate of GDP growth	Low
Openness to trade	Low
Shocks	No major external shocks
Agricultural output	Stagnant

Political circumstances during the episode

Stability of government	Strongly authoritarian military regime
Ideological shift	Sharp rightward shift from populist and radical rhetoric
Public perception and debate	Little public discussion
Administering arm of government	Planning and finance ministries
International influence	Strong US backing for new government

Accompanying policies

Exchange rate	Crawling peg (after 1968)
Export promotion	Extensive, with shift from tax to credit incentives over episode
Export taxes	Sharp reduction for manufactures, little change for traditional exports
Monetary policy	Contractionary 1964–7, then loosening
Fiscal policy	Sharp increase in tax collection and other public revenues
Capital account policy	Significant relaxation, with encouragement of capital inflow

Implementation

Stages	Gradual, with export promotion preceding import liberalization
Departures from the trend	Partial reversal in 1968, with resumption in succeeding years

Economic performance

Employment	No negative effect of greater trade openness; strong employment growth after 1968
Inflation	High, but declining after 1964
Growth	At historically unprecedented rates after 1968 (10–12%); slowed after first oil shock
Imports and exports	Grew both absolutely and as a percentage of total supply in most sectors
Capital account	Massive capital inflow after 1968
Real wages	Fall in early part of period during stabilization program, recovery after 1968 with tightening labor markets
Business failures	No noticeable trends; no evidence of link to trade policies

The liberalization trend in Brazilian external economic policy is characterized in summary form in table 4.2. Although it is difficult to characterize the episode between 1964 and 1974 as a full-scale trade liberalization, the policies adopted during this period were significantly different from those of preceding years. The timing of these policies is summarized in table 4.3.

Table 4.3 Major events in the post-1964 episode of greater trade openness

Date	Principal policy or government change
Apr 1964	Military regime installed; Marshal Castelo Branco as President, Roberto Campos as Planning Minister and principal economic policymaker
Jun 1964	"Drawback," or tariff exemption on imported inputs into manufactured exports implemented
Aug 1964	Reformulation of Law 4131, facilitating capital inflows
Apr 1965	Exemption of manufactured exports from IPI (tax on manufactured products)
Nov 1965	Devaluation of cruzeiro of 21%
Feb 1967	Exemption of manufactured exports from ICM (state value-added taxes); income tax refund for manufactured exports; large cruzeiro devaluation (23%)
Mar 1967	Generalized reduction in tariffs, with cuts half former levels in many sectors
Mar 1967	General Costa e Silva assumes presidency; Delfim Neto new Finance Minister and principal economic policymaker
Aug 1967	Central Bank Resolution 63, encouraging foreign borrowing through commercial banks
Jul 1968	Subsidy for manufactured exports based on IPI
Aug 1968	Crawling peg exchange rate policy begun; nominal rate indexed to domestic and foreign (US) inflation
Dec 1968	Institutional Act (AI-5) increases political repression, opposition figures arrested
Dec 1968	Partial reversal of earlier tariff cuts
Oct 1969	General Emílio G. Médici assumes Presidency following serious illness of Costa e Silva; Delfim Neto continues as Finance Minister
Sep 1971	Subsidy for manufactured exports based on ICM tax
Mar 1974	General Ernest Geisel assumes presidency; Finance Minister Mario Henrique Simonsen
Jun 1974	Elimination of import financing for goods paying tariffs over 55% (Resolution 289) and increase in tariff rates (Decree Law 1334)
Nov 1974	Decree 74.908, restricting public sector imports
Feb 1975	Import financing prohibited for goods paying tariffs over 37%
July 1975	Prior deposit of 100% for 6 months required for most imports
Dec 1975	Decree Law 1427 extended prior deposit to 1 year
Apr 1976	Increase in restrictions on purchases by Brazilian tourists abroad
Jun 1976	Compulsory deposit for Brazilian tourists abroad

Reactions to Trade Liberalization and the 1968 Retreat

The most obvious departure from the general trend of trade liberalization that began in 1964 was the increase in most *ad valorem* tariffs in December 1968, less than two years after the significant 1967 liberalization. Although nominal rates did not reach pre-1967 levels, many of the increases were in consumer goods sectors, resulting in effective rates of protection in early 1969 that in some sectors were only slightly below the pre-liberalization levels.

There is little evidence that the 1968 reversal was motivated by basic policy difference between the government that entered in March 1967, at the time of the tariff reductions, and the preceding government, which was largely responsible for the 1967 reduction. It appears instead to have been motivated by an attempt to restrict the rapid rise in imports that began with the resumption of higher rates of GDP growth in late 1967 and early 1968. The reaction presaged the response of Brazilian policymakers to the first oil shock: in both cases, import restriction via commercial policy, rather than real depreciation, was apparently seen as a more rapid and effective way to deal with external imbalance.

An alternative explanation of the 1968 reversal is that sectors that lost protection in 1967 put pressure on the government to restore at least part of what had been lost. There is no way to evaluate the relative weight of these influences conclusively, but some circumstantial evidence is available from an analysis of the pattern of import response by sector after the initial reductions and the subsequent reversal. If the reversal was undertaken primarily to improve the trade balance, sectors in which imports grew most rapidly after liberalization would be the most likely targets for tariff increases. If the intention was to placate sectors that had lost relatively more protection in the original cuts, the reversal would be concentrated in those sectors. It should be noted, however, that the two explanations are not mutually exclusive, if imports grew most rapidly in the sectors subject to the largest initial cuts.[4]

Bergsman (1971) estimated nominal and effective rates of protection for 51 sectors, for dates corresponding to the pre-liberalization period, the post-liberalization and pre-reversal period, and the post-reversal period. Import data that can be reasonably matched with Bergsman's estimates are available for about 20 sectors. Under the assumption that imports in 1965 and 1966 could be identified with the tariff structure in the pre-liberalization phase (until March 1967), and that imports in the next two years could be associated with the liberalization, the average rates of

---

[4] A further complication arises from the existence of tariff redundancy, which implies that measured reductions in rates do not correspond to the relevant reduction in protection.

growth for each two-year subperiod were calculated and compared. The differences between effective rates in February and April 1967, and between April 1967 and January 1969, were also calculated.

A simple correlation of the growth rate of imports by sector with the size of the reversal, as measured by the tariff increase from April 1967 to January 1969, yielded a coefficient of 0.18. Although positive, as would be expected if the reversal were motivated by a desire to cut imports in those sectors in which they had grown most rapidly after the initial cuts, the coefficient was not significant (prob $H_0 = 0.207$). This suggests that other factors besides a desire to diminish the trade deficit may have been important in the reversal.

If one of these factors was pressure on authorities to restore some of the protection lost in early 1967, we would expect the reversals to be largest in those sectors that had lost the most protection in 1967. This hypothesis received somewhat stronger support from the data. The correlation between the fall in protection by sector between February 1967 and April 1967 and its subsequent rise as a result of the December reversal is 0.35, which is moderately significant (prob $H_0 = 0.055$).

Yet another explanation of these same results may be bureaucratic convenience. If policymakers themselves used the pre-liberalization tariff levels as a rough guide in the December 1968 reversal, the pattern of the reversal would not in fact be due to external pressures from sectors which had lost protection but simply to the existence of a convenient precedent.

Conclusions of this type, based on imprecise measures and data, must be tentative. The sectors are not a random sample of Brazilian tradeable activities, since sectors in which imports were negligible, owing either to Brazilian comparative advantage or to their conversion to pseudo-nontradeables by high protection, do not appear on the import list. In addition, the correspondence between Bergsman's classification and the official import classification (the Nomenclatura Brasileira de Mercadorias, NBM) is only approximate. Despite these difficulties in interpreting the data, it does appear that the pre-1967 protection system provides a rough guide to the pattern of protection resulting from the partial retreat in late 1968.

Finally, cuts and subsequent restorations of tariffs may not be symmetric in their effects. A tariff cut, in the absence of redundancy, is more likely to have stronger short-run effects on production that will an increase, unless surplus capacity in the sector is easily available to respond to the increase. Reliable sectoral data on capacity utilization in the late 1960s do not exist, but data for industry in the aggregate show little unused capacity in the Brazilian industrial sector from 1968 onwards.

External Shocks and the Retreat from Liberalization after 1974

The response of Brazilian policymakers to the sharp deterioration in Brazil's terms of trade with the first oil shock effectively ended the decade-long trend toward greater trade openness. Although the response was both delayed and initially confused, in the long run it marked the end of any serious attempt to liberalize Brazilian trade.

Initial Reactions: External Borrowings

The first oil shock did not evoke an immediate response from Brazilian policymakers, apparently because they thought at the time that it would be briefer and less profound than it was. The initial strategy was to finance the resulting current account deficit, which began to widen rapidly as early as the beginning of 1974, with external borrowing. Brazil was well situated to pursue this strategy in the short run, however harmful it may have been in the long run, since it was one of a privileged group of developing countries with excellent access to international capital markets. The initial effect of the increase in international liquidity resulting from Organization of Petroleum Exporting Countries (OPEC) surpluses may actually have facilitated Brazilian borrowing.

The consequences of the oil crisis for the balance of payments were more promptly apparent than the responses of the economic policymakers. As may be seen in table 2.1, the approximate balance between imports and imports in 1973 became a historically unprecedented 4.7 billion dollar deficit in 1974, with the current account deficit of 7.1 billion more than four times greater than any earlier one. Although record capital inflows in 1974 provided most of the immediate financing, the need for adjustment was obvious as the new administration of General Ernesto Geisel replaced that of President Emílio G. Médici in March 1974.

Commercial Policy Adjustments: Import Restriction and Export Expansion

The response of policymakers to the pressures to adjust primarily took the form of adjustments in the commercial policy rather than the exchange rate. Although the crawling peg policy was continued, the level of the real exchange rate was not altered significantly, despite the sharp deterioration in the terms of trade.

The first steps were taken in June 1974, when the government suspended all forms of import financing for products subject to a nominal tariff of 55 percent or higher, allowing their import only if the tariff was paid in full. Accompanying this measure, embodied in Resolution 289 of the Banco

Central, was Decree Law 1334, which doubled the tariff rates of nearly 900 products considered to be superfluous. This list was further expanded over the course of the year. Import duty reductions on capital goods, previously granted by the CPA, were suspended.

The balance-of-payments results of 1974 brought further restrictive policies in 1975. In February, imports already subject to a duty of 37 percent or higher were made subject to prior payments, with no financing available. In July of that year, a 100 percent prior deposit, refundable six months after the transaction without interest or monetary correction, was imposed. With the inflation rate near 30 percent, the prior deposit, applicable to most imports, was a significant restriction. In October 1975, tariffs on a series of intermediate goods were raised. The government reduced its own import budget, applicable to state enterprises, and Decree Law 1427, issued late in 1975, extended the prior deposit to a period of one year before refunding.

On the export side, the existing incentive system was further extended, with fiscal incentives linked to investment that would follow an approved export expansion plan negotiated with the government. The principal program of this type was the BEFIEX (Fiscal Benefits for Exporting) plan, which assumed increasing importance after 1975. Although export expansion was clearly preferable to import restraint, as appears to have been recognized by the government, it would be wrong to consider all the steps taken to increase exports as moves in a liberalizing direction. In the earlier stages of the post-1964 period, export promotion was clearly a move toward greater liberalization, since the incentives only partially offset the anti-export bias produced by restrictive commercial policy and exchange rate overvaluation. By 1975, however, this anti-export bias had been largely eliminated, at least for highly processed and manufactured products, which were the largest beneficiaries of the policies. If the choice is viewed as export promotion via incentives and subsidies instead of through exchange rate adjustment, it is clear that export promotion in the last decade was not necessarily synonymous with increasing liberalization. The distinction between liberalizing and protective export promotion is discussed further in chapter 6.

Attempts to reduce the balance-of-payments deficit, primarily through the visible trade balance, continued through the next few years. In January 1975, a special program for export financing for manufactured products was implemented. Financing at favorable terms in amounts up to 100 percent of the preceding year's export increase was offered. Later in the month the government announced a reduced import budget for all the federal ministries. Despite its preoccupation with the overall trade balance and current account, however, the government often acted to protect its own capacity to import on relatively favorable terms. CPA resolutions in March 1976 reduced import duties for a large number of public investment activities, provided that no domestic similar was determined by CACEX to exist.

This period was also marked by an attempt to reduce the invisible or service account deficit, which had been a relatively neglected target of policymaking in earlier years. In April 1976, restrictions on imports brought back by returning Brazilian tourists were severely tightened. In June tourist expenditures were restricted even further, with a Cr$12,000 compulsory deposit (approximately equal to US$1,100 at the time) for a passport or exit visa, returnable after a year without interest or monetary correction. (These measures, which in a low tariff economy might be trivial, were much less so in Brazil, since Brazilian tourists abroad had a greater incentive to purchase relatively cheap consumer goods.)

Several steps were taken to create greater incentives for the export of services. In late 1977, income tax incentives like those applicable to manufactured exports were extended to Brazilian tourist enterprises, provided that the exchange earned was surrendered at the official rate. An earlier policy, implemented in September 1975, had also aimed at increasing service account receipts by extending tax and credit facilities to firms supplying goods as part of an engineering project abroad. On the expenditure side, Brazilian flag restrictions on vessels used for import shipments were revised and tightened in October 1975.

Restrictions on visible trade were further extended in March 1976, with a complete ban on all automobile, pleasure craft, and toy imports, as well as on several other consumer goods imports judged to be luxuries. Earlier restrictions were adjusted a number of times with import deposit requirements extended for some items, but they were eliminated for several industrial and intermediate goods imports in September 1977.

The Exchange Rate

Despite the piecemeal, often *ad hoc*, policies that attempted during 1975–9 to manipulate various parts of the current account, little use was made of exchange rate policy. The crawling peg continued, but it was increasingly apparent that adjustment in the real exchange rate was desirable, given Brazil's external balance problems beginning in 1973. Only in late 1979, however, did the government finally shift its stance, devaluing the cruzeiro by 30 percent against the US dollar (in addition to the regular crawling peg devaluations guided by a rough purchasing power parity rule). Travel deposit requirements were eliminated at the same time, as were some tax incentives for manufactured exports. In April 1980 a further step was taken in the form of a disguised partial devaluation. The Imposto sobre Operações Financeiras (IOF), a tax on financial transactions, was extended to purchases of exchange for imports of goods and services. It was initially set at 15 percent, but at the end of 1980 was raised to 25 percent.

Early in 1981 importers were required to submit an annual import program to CACEX, on the basis of which import licenses for individual transactions were to be approved. Although no explicit policy was announced, CACEX made frequent use in the post-1979 period of deliberate administrative delays in the granting of import licenses as a means of controlling imports. Christened by the market *operações tartaruga* (turtle operations), part of their function may have been to discourage potential importers from even applying for an import license. On the export side, major potential exporters were directly pressured to negotiate target levels of exports, which were periodically revised upward. Sanctions for failure to meet the target included denials by CACEX of import licenses for necessary imported inputs.

Measures such as these may have contributed to the fall in imports from 1981 to 1982. A more important factor, however, was the complete halt in GDP growth, which began with a 2.1 percent decline in 1981, following real growth rates that had averaged more than 6 percent even after the oil shock. As may be seen from table 3.1, this was the sharpest fall in income in Brazil's post-war history. The fall in the level of Brazilian economic activity resulted not only from government efforts to maintain access to international capital markets through the adoption of a sharply contractionary stabilization policy, but also from a fall in private sector investment as uncertainty about future payments difficulties deepened.

Despite the containment of imports, the trade balance worsened in 1982, as exports fell in response to the recession in Brazil's major trading partners. The most severe pressures arose from the service account, however, as capital servicing costs nearly doubled from their 1980 level. Brazil closed 1982 with a balance-of-payments deficit of nearly US$9 billion and its ability to borrow in international capital markets severely restricted. In early 1983, the cruzeiro was sharply devalued in real terms, and the rate of crawl was accelerated, reducing and possibly eliminating the overvaluation which had characterized exchange policy and indirectly conditioned commercial policy in the preceding decades.

A Profile of Trade Restrictiveness, 1947–1982

The gradual evolution of Brazilian commercial and balance-of-payments policy, from quantitative allocations of foreign exchange in the late 1940s, through multiple rates and *ad valorem* tariffs after 1957, to the 1964–74 episode and its reversal, is depicted in an approximate and synthetic form in figure 4.1. Although a single series cannot portray the complexities of Brazilian external economic policymaking over a third of a century, some major trends can be represented. Over time there has been a gradual move toward greater liberalization. The movement has not been smooth or

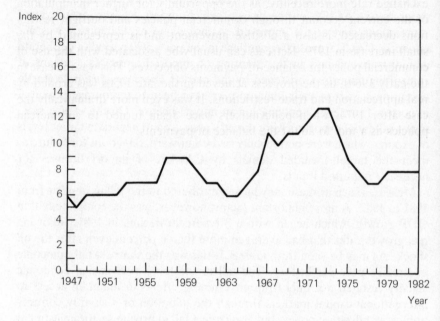

Figure 4.1   Index of trade liberalization for Brazil, 1947–1982

continuous, and it is still too soon to tell whether the ground lost after 1974 will be regained.

Given the arbitrary nature of any characterization of a policy as "more liberal" or "less liberal," the graph does not distinguish between small changes (less than a unit on the vertical scale from 0 to 20). A gradual move over several years may therefore appear as a jump. Events are reflected in the year in which they occurred; thus the scale may be interpreted as an estimate of the situation at the end of the year. Exchange rate policy is given less weight in the construction of the index than is commercial policy; thus there is a fall in the index from 1967 to 1968, due to the increase in tariffs in late 1968, even though the crawling peg may have been an important (and positive) step in the liberalizing direction. Export promotion has been considered, but more weight is given to the incentives in earlier years, when they offset the anti-export bias of exchange and tariff policies, than to those in later periods.

The most important liberalization episode in the post-war period is clearly that from 1964 or 1965 through 1972 or 1973. Several other events, however, are notable. The transition from simple administrative allocation of exchange to auctions in 1953 was a move towards greater efficiency.

Similarly, the evolution of policies from quantitative controls to an *ad valorem* tariff in 1957 was also a step forward. Relatively greater use of the exchange rate more recently, as the opportunity for further manipulation of the current account through commercial policies and outright restrictions decreased, is also a positive movement and is represented by the small increase in 1979. Retreats can usually be associated with the use of commercial policy for balance-of-payments objectives. This was the case in the early 1960s, as the progress achieved in the late 1950s was eroded by real appreciation and trade restrictions. It was even more dramatically the case after 1974, when policymakers once again turned to commercial policies as a tool to adjust the balance of payments.

5
Export Promotion in the Post-1964 Period

Of the liberalizing measures instituted between 1964 and 1973 only the export promotion policies survived the first oil shock. Although export promotion, rather than import liberalization, was pivotal to Brazil's move to greater trade openness, many features of the Brazilian export promotion measures suggest that their liberalizing effects were incidental; the policies were not so much an integral part of a trade liberalization program as a complex sequence of individual incentives, combining both liberalizing and protective features.

Export incentives were concentrated in the manufacturing sector and were created with little concern for economic efficiency. Some of them encouraged exports of products for which there is little evidence of Brazilian comparative advantage, in either a static or even a dynamic sense. In their later stages, several of the incentives operated indirectly, primarily in the form of credit programs, and may have made distortions in Brazilian factor markets larger than they would otherwise have been. However, the incentives to export did have the effect of integrating a number of formerly autarkic economic activities into the international economy. Many producers with little previous external economic contact became more export oriented and more responsive to opportunities in world markets.

This chapter distinguishes between liberalizing and protective export incentives. A progression from policies that were basically liberalizing to signficantly more protective measures is clearly discernible in Brazilian export policy between 1964 and 1976. The major fiscal incentives, with the approximate dates of their implementation, are listed below. Since credit incentives existed from the late 1960s but only became important after 1970, their effect cannot be dated precisely.

1   "Drawback" – exemption from import duties on imported inputs into manufactured exports (June 1964)

2   IPI exemption – refund of value-added tax paid on inputs into manufactured exports and exemption of IPI on export sales (April 1965)

3   ICM exemption – similar refund and exemption of the state value-added tax (ICM) (February 1967)

4   Income tax credit – tax refund granted to exporters of manufactured products proportional to the share of total output which is exported (February 1967)

5   IPI credit – a subsidy for manufactured exports based on the product's IPI rate (July 1968)

6   ICM subsidy – parallel manufactured export subsidy similar to the above subsidy (September 1971)

The Liberalizing Early Phases: 1964–1967

Few relative price incentives to export from Brazil existed in the early 1960s. Fixed nominal exchange rates and high inflation resulted in a highly overvalued cruzeiro by early 1964, reflected in a black-market rate that was nearly three times the official rate. The real exchange rate, or ratio of prices of tradeables to nontradeables (using the official exchange rate), was lower than at any later date (see tables A1.1–A1.3).

In addition to simple overvaluation, which discriminated equally against all exportables, the structure of protection in the early 1960s discriminated against those potential exporters who had to acquire inputs at tariff-distorted domestic prices. This was most serious in manufacturing sectors in which the import component was higher than in the primary product sectors. Table 5.1 shows various components of the cost of a cruzeiro of output from Brazilian producing sectors, disaggregated to the two-digit level. The import column shows the total percentage share of imports, both direct and indirect, per unit of product. The total component ranges from less than a percent (tobacco products) to about 19 percent (chemicals), with the share of inputs in a unit of agricultural output about 3 percent.[1]

Although the structure of effective protection in Brazil both before and after 1967 favored manufacturing activities at the expense of primary sectors, particularly agriculture, this was a result of output protection, since input protection had a larger negative effect on the heavy users of

[1] The total import component was calculated by Savasini et al. (1974), who also calculated labor and capital input shares, using the 1971 Conselho Interministerial de Preços (CIP, Interministerial Price Council)–Finance Ministry input–output table. It should be noted that even the inclusion of indirect imported inputs may underestimate the impact of tariffs on input costs, since a number of producers of domestic inputs which are partially substitutable for imports may be able to raise their prices as a function of tariffs on the import.

Table 5.1 Total direct plus indirect input shares by sector, 1970 (percent)

Sector	Imports	Labor
Mining	9.30	51.28
Nonmetallic minerals	5.55	25.48
Metals	11.46	36.87
Machinery	13.66	39.13
Electrical and communications		
equipment	15.21	29.96
Transportation equipment	9.69	31.92
Wood products	5.17	37.72
Furniture	5.11	48.19
Paper	8.01	27.87
Rubber	9.11	32.02
Leather	7.12	30.73
Chemicals	18.89	18.15
Pharmaceutical products	16.14	40.75
Perfumes and cosmetics	9.04	21.59
Plastics	13.98	27.76
Textiles	9.45	37.01
Clothing and footwear	8.52	42.23
Food products	6.94	19.07
Beverages	5.33	29.39
Tobacco products	0.60	4.07
Printing and publishing	7.00	25.62
Miscellaneous	14.07	43.15
Construction	5.50	41.40
Agriculture	3.12	36.41

Source: Savasini et al., 1974

imported inputs such as the chemical industry or the electrical and communications equipment sector. Relative to a hypothetical free-trade situation, Brazilian manufacturing sectors received positive effective protection, owing to tariffs on their outputs. From the point of view of export competitiveness, however, the structure of protection discriminated against exports, owing to the tariffs on their relatively higher level of imported inputs. In 1964 most manufacturing sectors of the Brazilian economy were oriented almost exclusively to domestic sales, with some sectors exporting less than 0.5 percent of their output.[2]

The first incentive in Brazil's export promotion program, the 1964 import "drawback," addressed this anti-export bias by exempting from tariffs those inputs used in exports of manufacturers. Though relatively

[2] Export shares of output by sector in 1964 ranged from 0.001 (clothing) to 0.043 (food products), averaging 0.02 for Brazilian industry as a whole.

modest in both intent and impact, this policy was clearly "liberalizing" in the sense that it moved the costs of production closer to international levels.

In contrast with the import drawback, the IPI exemption that followed it in 1965 had a significant effect on the relative profitability of exports. Since it provided a refund of the value-added tax paid on inputs into manufactured exports and exempted export sales from the tax, its effect varied by sector.[3] Like the drawback, the exemption had the effect of reducing the difference between the price received by the Brazilian producer and the world price, since this tax had formerly been applied to the producer's gross export revenue based on the percentage rates prevailing for the product and those inputs subject to the IPI. In this sense, the IPI exemption could also be considered "liberalizing," since it reduced the anti-export bias of the pre-1967 price structure.

The other major fiscal incentive for exports established before 1969 was the ICM exemption, which was a refund of the state value-added tax formerly charged. Its mechanism was similar to that of the IPI exemption, and it also tended to reduce the anti-export bias by removing taxes incident on both the output and purchased inputs for manufactured exports. Its quantitative effect was on the order of three times as great as the effect of IPI exemption in the first few years of its operation.

The three preceding fiscal incentives may all be characterized as "liberalizing," since they resulted in a price for exports closer to that which would prevail in a free-trade situation.[4] In this sense they reduced a distortion in the Brazilian export price structure and parallel the border-tax adjustments that have been used in the Common Market countries. Starting from an initially tax-distorted situation, however, they were not neutral in their effect on the change in profitability of exporting by sector, since the existing tax and duty system had penalized some activities more than others.

Thus sectors in which imports were an important input, for example, received a greater stimulus from the drawback than did ones with few imported inputs. Similarly, sectors in which the IPI rates were high received a relatively greater stimulus. It is more difficult, however, to ascribe a liberalizing effect to subsequent fiscal incentives and to the credit incentives, which assumed increasing importance after 1970. The fourth fiscal incentive listed above is the income tax credit. This tax refund, which was granted to exporters in proportion to the share of their output exported, was created in 1967. Although it clearly increased the return

---

3 Musalem (1981) estimated its effect in its early years of operation between 1965 and 1970 to be about 5–7 percent, defined as a percent of a unit export price.

4 The effect of tariff reduction on the equilibrium exchange rate, which would tend to depreciate, would provide an additional stimulus not considered here.

from exports relative to domestic sales, it is not clear that it moved Brazilian export prices in a free-trade direction.[5]

The Transition to Export Protection: 1968–1971

The two additional incentives introduced after 1967 – IPI credit, created in 1968, and the ICM credit, created in 1971 – cannot be characterized as "liberalizing" in the same sense as the earlier incentives. Both were subsidies, rather than exemptions from taxes, and were based on the taxes that would have been payable on the product if it were sold domestically. Since they added a fixed percentage amount per unit of export sales to the price received by the exporter, they were true subsidies and not simply adjustments that reduced anti-export bias.

The progression of Brazilian export promotion policies from simple measures that moved export prices closer to the world price to policies that may actually have moved prices beyond these levels is represented synthetically in table 5.2. For simplicity only one produced input, which is assumed to be imported, is represented. The first three policies, which are shown above the broken line, had the cumulative effect of moving value added per unit of output to the level that would prevail under free trade, ignoring any induced exchange rate changes. This is represented by the level of $1 - a_{ij}$ shown on the third line which prevailed between 1965 and 1967. The table's simplified representation of the Brazilian export incentive program shows clearly the movement of exports from the earlier "liberalizing" phase to a more protected phase in which the subsidies

Table 5.2 Liberalizing and protective export incentives

Year	Taxes, tariffs	Unit value added
1963	Tariffs, no exemptions	$(1 - t_{vj}) - a_{ij}(1 + t_{vi} + t_i)$
1964	Drawback	$(1 - t_{vj}) - a_{ij}(1 + t_{vi})$
1965–7	Drawback and IPI and ICM exemptions	$1 - a_{ij}$
1968–71	Above incentives plus IPI and ICM credits	$(1 + s) - a_{ij}$

t_{vj} is the IPI and ICM tax on output, a_{ij} is the unit input–output coefficient, t_{vi} is the IPI and ICM tax on the input, t_i is the tariff on the ith input, and s is the IPI and ICM credit (subsidy).

[5] The net effect of this incentive depends on the share of corporate profits in total sales, and on the degree to which the exemption is passed on. For these reasons, quantification of this incentive is more arbitrary and less precise than for the others.

pushed the export price structure beyond the simple elimination of anti-export bias.

In comparison with a free-trade situation, the relative price incentives to exports may have been low even after the IPI and ICM subsidies of 1968 and 1971, not because subsidies should have been higher but because of continued protection in the domestic market. True liberalization, in the sense used here of alignment of domestic with international relative prices, would have implied a reduction in the protection for importables rather than the extension of the export subsidies.

Consolidation of Export Protection: 1971–1974

The export credits introduced in the later stages of the export promotion program made their first appearance in 1968 but were inconsequential before 1970. Their subsidy element arises from the fact that the export financing loan is granted at a rate generally below prevailing market rates. With the acceleration of Brazilian inflation after the first oil shock the net subsidy increased, because the spread between market interest rates and export credit rates widened. Consequently, this type of export promotion policy became much more important after 1973.[6]

One of the first attempts to measure the effect of this incentive was made by Musalem (1981), who estimated the net credit subsidy per unit of manufactured exports as the spread between the market rate and the subsidized rate times the proportion of exports that received such financing. His estimates for manufactured exports as a whole are given in table 5.3, which shows the gradual rise in the subsidy value of export credits over the decade after 1968.

The aggregate series estimated by Musalem masks rather sharp differences in the level of subsidized financing available to different activities. Although no full accounting of allocations of export financing by sector has been published or made available by CACEX to outside researchers, its 1973 Relatório presents a partial breakdown of manufactured export financing by major product groups. Most of this financing was made through the Resolution 71 facility, which provided production loans for manufactured exports with a production cycle up to 180 days. Longer-cycle products, primarily durables and capital goods, received financing under separate facilities, among them Resolution 43 loans. This financing was heavily concentrated in the transport equipment, machinery, and electrical and communications sectors, according to the CACEX Relatório, while the Resolution 71 financing gave priority to textiles, shoes, and a number of processed foods.

---

[6] Credit incentives are ignored, for example, in the study by Savasini et al. (1974).

Table 5.3 Incentives for manufactured exports (percentage of unit value)

	Exemptions			Tax credits			Financial subsidies		
Year	ICM	IPI	Drawback	IPI	ICM	Income tax	Credit	Prior deposit	Total
1964	–	0.4	–	–	–	–	–	–	0.4
1965	–	5.0	–	–	–	–	–	–	5.0
1966	–	5.0	–	–	–	–	–	–	5.0
1967	16.1	5.2	–	–	–	–	–	–	21.3
1968	19.6	6.0	–	–	–	–	0.6	–	26.2
1969	20.5	6.8	0.7	4.3	–	–	1.7	–	34.0
1970	20.5	7.0	1.9	6.0	5.1	–	3.3	–	43.8
1971	19.8	7.5	2.4	6.4	5.9	1.3	4.2	–	47.5
1972	19.1	8.1	2.6	6.9	6.6	1.3	3.9	–	48.5
1973	18.3	9.8	3.5	7.0	7.0	1.3	3.6	–	50.5
1974	17.7	10.0	2.8	8.5	8.5	1.8	3.2	–	52.5
1975	17.0	10.0	4.6	10.1	10.1	1.7	5.6	3.2	62.3
1976	16.3	10.9	4.4	13.2	13.2	1.3	9.7	5.0	74.0
1977	16.3	12.0	2.9	11.2	11.2	1.5	12.3	4.1	71.5
1978	16.3	12.3	4.0	12.0	12.0	1.5	10.5	4.4	73.0

–, negligible.
Source: Musalem, 1981

The increase in the relative importance of export credits in the 1970s and their concentration in particular sectors in Brazil intensified the growing protective emphasis of the program. The earlier tax incentives and subsidies, which worked by changing the relative price of production for export in relation to the domestic market price for the same product, had been in effect *ad valorem* subsidies (or in the earlier stages, tax reductions). They were thus neutral with respect to the rate of inflation. In addition, they altered the relative price of different outputs but did not alter relative factor prices.

Export credits were not neutral in either sense. First, their value to a potential recipient increased with inflation for a given subsidized credit rarte. Nominal interest rates on the Resolution 71 loans in the early 1970s were 8 percent, with no monetary correction. Other types of financing were only slightly more expensive. Rates of inflation, as measured by the general price index (IGP-DI), were of the order of 20 to 30 percent in the early 1970s before their sharp increase following the first oil shock. For this reason, they became increasingly attractive during the 1970s, making it worthwhile for firms to expend resources to lobby for access to subsidized export credits. Although there is no obvious way to measure this cost, deeply negative real rates of interest for a number of export-related activities in the 1970s guaranteed a high private return on this form of rent seeking.

Second, the export credits tended to lower the relative price of capital, particularly in the case of the Resolution 43 credits. Most loans were in principle authorized for the financing of stocks of inputs into manufactured exports, and varied in duration between six months and two and a half years. Their effect, particularly as their real rate became more negative, was to lower the cost of working capital well below market levels. At negative real rates of interest there was little incentive to economize in the use of capital, which thus became a factor allocated administratively rather by credit markets.

The effects of this type of factor market distortion are in principle well known, and have been extensively discussed in the international trade theory literature. Although there has been little investigation of the effects of the Brazilian export credits in this context, theory suggests that a factor price distortion that lowers the price of capital relative to labor in some sectors results in a deadweight loss to the economy from factor misallocation, as well as the creation of a differential between the marginal rate of transformation in production and market prices. In general, for a given degree of stimulus for a favored activity, such as manufactured exports, this type of market intervention entails a higher welfare loss than would either direct subsidy or tax policies in either product or export markets.

These welfare costs, moreover, are simply those that would arise in a static context. Over time, the effects of credit subsidies for selected activities are less predictable, but they are not necessarily more likely to promote welfare. In a study of Brazilian export promotion by the Fundação Centro de Estudos do Comércio Exterior (Pastore et al., 1979)[7] exports from the least labor intensive sectors were at once the most highly protected and expanded most in the period from 1970 to 1975. This may be one of the reasons why industrial employment grew more slowly than did either industrial production or exports after 1964.

The Brazilian export program in the period after 1965 is probably not a model for other trade liberalization programs. The initial stages, as argued earlier, were useful in focusing on the basic problem of anti-export bias inherited from the preceding era of import substitution, and could arguably be characterized as successful from the point of view both of allocation and of balance of payments. Subsequent policies, particularly in the later stages of export promotion via subsidized credit for selected manufactured exports, inevitably led the economy away from the efficiency that might

---

[7] In this study it was also concluded that, within sectors receiving similar levels of protection, those activities using relatively more labor expanded more. The authors interpret this as evidence of Brazilian comparative advantage in more labor intensive exports.

well have been attained had the early policy changes been reinforced by a more competitive real exchange rate. Virtually all examinations[8] of the sectoral effects of the export incentive program suggest that such an alternative policy would have generated the same or a higher level of exports at a significantly lower cost in domestic resources.

[8] In addition to Pastore et al. (1979), this point was made earlier by Savasini et al. (1974) and Mendonça de Barros et al. (1975).

6
Capital Account Policies and Trends in the Trade Liberalization Episode

Brazil's increased openness to the world economy in the decade after 1964 was as much a change in the capital account as it was a conventional trade liberalization; the country's entrance into world capital markets on an unprecedented scale occurred contemporaneously with the modest import liberalization of the late 1960s and the more sustained export drive that began in 1964. Brazilian external economic experience in this period was in fact dominated by the capital account, which gained increasing importance from 1968 onwards. Because capital account trends interfered with and in the end dominated the effects that trade liberalizing policies might otherwise have had on the real exchange rate, the Brazilian experience is instructive for an analysis of the timing and the sequencing of liberalization policies. Although the interaction of capital inflows with current account developments through the effect of the former on the real exchange rate was less dramatic than in Argentina or in Chile, Brazil also appears to be a case in which capital inflows prevented the emergence of the exchange rate changes which otherwise would have occurred.

In this chapter the relationship of the major capital account policies and trends with Brazilian commercial policy is examined. Our primary focus is on the capital account as it relates to trade liberalization; other interesting issues, such as its relationship with the level of external debt, or the impact of capital account policies on domestic financial markets, are not considered here. The first section examines the contrast between trade liberalization in the absence of capital account changes and the actual experience of Brazil. In the next section some of the factors and policy changes that led to the massive capital inflows after 1968 are discussed. The chapter concludes with an examination of the relationship of capital account trends with the real exchange rate.

Theory versus Brazilian Experience

The policymakers who formulated the economic reforms of the post-1964 period had an ambitious program for change. Opening the economy was just one of a number of "liberalizing" objectives. Indeed, as was argued earlier, there is little evidence that import liberalization was regarded as a central goal in the immediate post-1964 years: both export growth and diversification and a resumption of positive net capital inflows were considered more pressing objectives. These priorities were understandable, given the balance-of-payments constraints facing policymakers in 1964. On the domestic side, early attention was given to the reduction of distortions in both capital and labor markets.

In retrospect, Brazil's policies in the 1964–70 period cannot be regarded as having had a clear sequence of domestic factor market reform, then trade liberalization, and finally opening of the capital account, either in that order or any other, since they were really related parts of a larger reform package. The delay until 1967 in the implementing of the import liberalization part of these reforms, coupled with the more prompt attention that policymakers paid to the resumption of significant net foreign lending to Brazil, made trade liberalization and capital account liberalization approximately contemporaneous.

The obvious difficulty with this collapsing of the sequence is that if capital account reforms lead to an increase in net inflows, as was both the aim and eventual achievement of Brazilian economic policymakers, the real depreciation that would otherwise be forced by a significant liberalization of imports is lost. Although there was no discussion of this problem at the time, it has recently been the focus of considerable attention. First raised by McKinnon (1973), this issue has been addressed by Dornbusch (1983) and Frenkel (1983), who have both argued that the capital account should not be liberalized until the necessary real depreciation has been achieved. One persuasive argument for such a delay is that asset markets will respond more rapidly than goods markets to new price signals.[1]

Conventional theory suggests that import liberalization like that of Brazil in the 1967–73 period would lead to a real depreciation if current account balance were maintained. Export response to the real depreciation, even if delayed, would absorb those factors released by the contraction in importable production. Engaging in a capital account liberalization at approximately the same time, however, could easily upset this pattern,

---

[1] In Brazil, however, private international capital flows responded relatively slowly to the change in regime in 1964, and did not assume major importance until 1968. This was partly due to the uncertainty of potential private lenders in the immediate post-1964 period about the ability of the new government to implement its program.

especially if (a) the import liberalization is modest, (b) part of the trade liberalization is on the export side, through the reduction of anti-export bias, or (c) capital inflows are large in relation to the current account. All three of these conditions obtained in Brazil in the late 1960s. The conventional model of trade liberalization, which identifies trade liberalization with import liberalization and implicitly assumes no significant capital account changes, thus has limited applicability in a case like the Brazilian one. As is shown in tables A1.1–A1.3, there was no marked change in the level of real exchange rates, under a variety of different measures, in the late 1960s. The institution of the crawling peg policy in 1968 in effect pegged the real exchange rate (rather than the nominal one, as had been done previously), but not at a more competitive level – principally because of the sharp increase in international capital inflows to Brazil in the late 1960s.

Brazilian Capital Account Policies and Trends in the Post-1964 Period

Brazilian policy towards both direct foreign investment and foreign borrowing is a complex system that mixes a degree of economic nationalism with a pragmatic recognition of the supplementary role of capital inflows in increasing the resources available for investment. Although official rhetoric since 1964 has welcomed foreign direct investment, the structure of policies has tended to favor foreign borrowing over direct foreign investment, which in the post-1964 period has rarely exceeded 20 percent of gross borrowing.

Since 1946, Brazil has required the registration of foreign investments and loans with the Banco Central (or its predecessor). Registered loans and investments may then be serviced, using authorized banks, at the official exchange rate. In 1953 the majority of remittances of profits and interest, as well as repatriation of capital, were freed from earlier restrictions. This situation continued until 1962, when the Profit Remittance Law was promulgated. The law prohibited reinvested earnings from being added to the registered capital base which was used in determining profit remittances, and limited the remittances to 10 percent of registered capital, with repatriation also limited to 10 percent. As a result, direct foreign investment fell sharply (see table 2.1). In the political and economic climate of the 1962–4 period, however, this might have happened in any case even without the 1962 law.

One of the first important capital account policies of the new government in 1964 was to replace these restrictions with a progressive supplementary income tax on remittance that exceeded 12 percent. Registration of an investment either in currency or in kind in capital goods was permitted. Intangible properties, such as patents and technology, however, were more difficult to register, and the 1964 reforms did little in this area.

Although the investment registration system corrected for internal Brazilian inflation, it made no allowance for inflation in the counry of origin of the direct investment. Even though inflation rates in all Brazilian creditor countries were low by Brazilian standards, they were not negligible, particularly for foreign investment registered in US dollars in the late 1960s and the 1970s. If it is assumed that nominal interest rates on external debt denominated in foreign currency include an inflation component, that is, a premium for expected purchasing power loss over the duration of the loan, then the Brazilian investment registration system was biased against direct investment, since it did not permit an inflation adjustment for direct investment analogous to that provided by nominal interest rates on variable rate loans. This feature of the Brazilian system may well explain why the portfolio rather than direct investment predominated in the post-1964 period.

Subject to the registration requirement, loans to private sector banks or corporations (*pessoas jurídicas*) in Brazil were basically unrestricted, although the Banco Central often monitored the interest rate and the amortization schedule. In addition to medium- and long-term foreign loans, the Banco Central also approved trade financing for terms over two years. Private individuals (*pessoas físicas*) in Brazil were not authorized to borrow abroad, nor could the proceeds of a loan be used by a firm to purchase Brazilian securities.

Foreign borrowing in Brazil was regulated primarily by Law 4131, passed in September 1962 and amended in August 1964 by Law 4390, and by Resolution 63 of the Banco Central, issued in August 1967. Under Law 4131, the borrower dealt directly with the foreign lender. After authorization by the Banco Central, which conditioned approval on characteristics of the loan such as the interest rate, the spread over relevant international rates (the US prime rate or the London interbank offered rate (LIBOR), the minimum grace period, and the amortization schedule, the principal would be deposited in an authorized commercial bank, which would then pass the cruzeiro equivalent on to the borrower. Exchange risk in this case was borne by the final borrower.

Resolution 63 loans allowed a Brazilian bank or authorized subsidiary of a foreign bank to obtain a loan abroad and, after registration with the Banco Central, to reloan it to one or more local firms, at possibly differing terms and rates. Commercial risk, arising from nonpayment by the local firm, was borne by the bank. Like the 4131 loans, however, exchange risk was borne by the ultimate borrower. The availability of exchange cover for registered loans was guaranteed by the Banco Central. Criteria similar to those used for 4131 loans were employed in the approval of Resolution 63 loans.

On occasion in the post-1964 period the Banco Central required that a stipulated percentage of the foreign private loans entering under Law 4131 or Resolution 63 rules be deposited with the Banco Central without interest. Although Brazilian law provided for the conversion of foreign loans into registered equity investment, this provision of Brazilian capital account policies was virtually ignored until the aftermath of the debt crisis in 1982.

Capital outflows from Brazil, other than amortization of debt, were much less important than inflows. Outward transfers required individual approval by the Banco Central. Although private capital outflows were not explicitly prohibited, approval by the Banco Central was unusual, except for trade financing and some limited Brazilian direct investment.

The sharp increase in net capital inflows to Brazil after 1968 is shown in table 2.1. Until 1968 Brazil's net capital inflow had never exceeded 300 million dollars, and averaged about 100 million annually from 1954 through 1967, and only 35 million annually in the 1963–7 period.

Net capital inflows in the billions, unprecedented in Brazil's history and approached by few other developing countries, were far in excess of the current account deficit in the 1969–73 period. Before the first oil shock, inflows averaged 2.15 billion dollars annually, compared with average current account deficits of 1.07 billion. As errors and omissions in the balance of payments were on average positive during this period, Brazil's reserves increased even more rapidly over the five-year period than the gap between the positive capital inflow and the current account deficit would indicate.

The high level of net capital inflows into Brazil in the post-1968 period thus cannot be explained simply as a passive demand-induced response to the need to finance a current account deficit. Capital account liberalization, which began with the repeal of the remittance limitations in 1964 and was reinforced by the creation of the administratively simplified mechanisms of Law 4131 and Resolution 63, effectively opened the Brazilian account. The surge in capital inflows to Brazil in the 1968–73 period, which also coincided with the highest levels of trade openness in recent Brazilian economic history, can be explained convincingly in an asset or stock-adjustment framework.

Before 1964 or 1965, the level of foreign borrowing was effectively constrained; with the capital account reforms of the post-1964 period, the gap between the desired capital stock and the actual stock was closed by the massive inflows of the late 1960s and early 1970s. In this sense, the rapid increase in capital flows in the late 1960s may be regarded as earlier flows that had been postponed by both the restrictions and the uncertainties of the early 1960s. Capital flows in the late 1960s and early 1970s thus "overshot" their long-run level.[2]

Despite the importance of the post-1964 capital account measures, the increase in capital inflows cannot be entirely attributed to these policy changes and other demand-side factors in Brazil. The episode of trade and capital account liberalization in Brazil coincided with several supply-side changes in international capital markets; in particular, Brazil was one of the early and principal borrowers using variable rate loans.

These loans, which first became important in international financial markets in the mid-1960s, in effect indexed interest payments to inflation in the principal creditor countries by their provision for automatic resetting of the interest rate at current international rates (LIBOR or US prime) at periodic intervals over the duration of the loan. From the lender's point of view, such loans reduced the risk of inflation loss at fixed nominal rates as well as potential capital loss from such loans if they were resold on a secondary market, since the income stream they generated was expected to accompany inflation in the currency of the loan, assuming that nominal interest rates incorporate an inflation premium. Although they were not perfect hedges, in that the principal of the loan was fixed, they were well suited for international financial intermediation, since they permitted multinational banks to accept short-term deposits at fixed nominal rates and make longer-term loans at variable rates without exposing themselves to the risk that interest rates on their liabilities would exceed those on their assets.

Brazil was one of the major international borrowers using variable rate loans, and the perfection and widespread acceptance of this form of international lending in the late 1960s may be the single most important supply-side factor behind the large increase in net capital flows to Brazil. At the time, both Brazilian policymakers and the banking community appeared to regard the variable rate loan as a kind of international counterpart of the indexed loans instituted domestically in Brazil after 1964, although the latter type of loan allowed for indexation of principal as well. The perceived reduction in interest rate risk thus cleared the way for Brazilian borrowing on a scale that would have been unimaginable a decade earlier.

Also important in explaining the increase in capital flows was the large increase in Brazilian international borrowing, either by government entities or by private borrowers with "full faith and credit" backing from the government for specified investment projects. Borrowing of this type was

[2] A simple model of this kind of overshooting resulting from capital account liberalization is given by Edwards (1984). Explicitly related to such episodes in Argentina, Chile, and Uruguay, it is implicitly applicable to the Brazilian experience in the late 1960s as well.

favorably treated by international banks, which regarded such loans as less risky since they were made to a sovereign borrower and in principle could be serviced through the taxing capacity of the borrower, or of the borrower's guarantor. However precarious these assumptions may appear from the vantage point of the 1980s, they were little questioned in the late 1960s and early 1970s.

The Capital Account and the Real Exchange Rate

An important consequence of capital inflows well in excess of the current account deficit and the resulting accumulation of reserves was the removal of pressure on economic policymakers to maintain exchange rate competitiveness. Although some of the increased spending permitted by a net capital inflow falls on tradeable goods, and is reflected in a corresponding current account deficit, the net inflows to Brazil after 1967 far exceeded this deficit, implying that a part of the increased spending fell on nontradeable goods. Clearance of excess demand in this market then implies a rise in the price of nontradeables relative to tradeables.

The rise in net capital flows to Brazil after 1967 and the magnitude by which they exceeded the current account deficit can be seen clearly in figure 6.1, which shows the current account, the capital account, and the difference between both accounts from 1957 through 1976. Since the absolute values of all three variables rose substantially over this period, figure 6.1 shows them as a percentage of exports in the corresponding year rather than as absolute levels.

If net capital inflows to Brazil had simply financed excess domestic demand for tradeables, the full line in figure 6.1, which shows the ratio of the difference between the net capital inflow and the current account deficit to exports, would lie close to zero. From 1961 through 1967, this ratio fluctuated around zero, averaging 0.6 percent of export value in the period and exceeding 20 percent only in 1965 when the recessionary effects of the stabilization program resulted in a significant current account surplus. In the period from 1968 through 1973, however, the excess of net capital inflows over the current account deficit averaged 23.7 percent of exports.

When the real exchange rate is defined as the ratio P_T/P_{NT} of the price of tradeables to the price of nontradeables, it is clear that capital flows like those received by Brazil in the post-1967 period can result in a substantial real appreciation. As is shown in tables A1.1–A1.3, the real exchange rate P_T/P_{NT} shows a marked fall in this period. This conclusion is robust to a variety of ways of measuring P_T/P_{NT}, and does not appear to be sensitive to the particular variables used to calculate the P_T/P_{NT} series.

Percent of export value

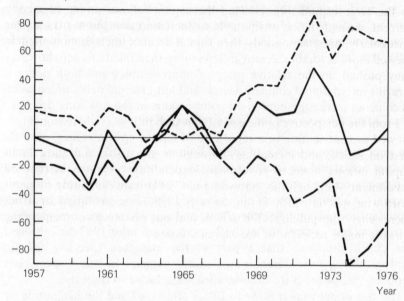

Figure 6.1   Capital and current account relative to exports: – – –, ratio of the current account to exports; ---, ratio of the capital account to exports; ——, ratio of the capital account minus the current account to exports

It is difficult to separate demand-side and supply-side influences in explaining the sharp increase in net capital inflows to Brazil in the late 1960s. It is nevertheless clear in retrospect that the capital account liberalization measures undertaken by the new government in the post-1964 period contributed to the real appreciation observable in this period.

Real appreciation, which was an inevitable consequence of capital inflows of the magnitude experienced by Brazil, undercut the effects that trade liberalization might otherwise have had. Had capital account liberalization been delayed, and the level of capital inflows in this period substantially reduced, the increase in the current account deficit, especially after the resumption of high rates of product growth after 1968, could not have been financed as it was. Although Brazil's export promotion program might have made some contribution in reducing a current account deficit, the principal adjustment that would have to have occurred in the absence of the capital flows would have been a depreciation of the real exchange rate. That the depreciation did not occur is due primarily to the change in the capital account.

A more favorable interpretation of Brazil's capital account experience in the years after 1967 might link the high rates of GDP growth in those years to the large capital inflows. Had the capital inflows simply financed a current account deficit attributable to increased demand for tradeables, particularly investment goods, then capital account liberalization might be viewed more favorably. As the inflows more than filled this gap, however, they pushed up the relative price of nontradeables and both undercut Brazil's international competitiveness and left external debts which would become an increasing burden on policymakers in the following decades.

From the perspective of the early 1970s such inflows could reasonably be viewed as contributing to a rapid rate of output growth. Later, after the first oil shock, and increasingly throughout the 1970s and early 1980s, capital inflows financed government expenditure as much as they did investment. Although this "crowding out" of private borrowing by public borrowing was only incipient in the early 1970s, in succeeding years it was increasingly the public sector deficit, and not private investment, which was the major recipient of the capital inflows.

7

The Timing and Sequencing of the Post-1964 Trade Reforms

The trade policies followed by Brazil after 1964 were one part of a larger set of external and domestic economic policies which affected each other. In this chapter first the links between trade policies and the real exchange rate, a key variable in trade liberalization, are discussed. Then the question of the sequencing of export promotion policies and import liberalization is studied. The concluding section examines trade policy in the context of domestic macroeconomic policies.

The Coordination of Commercial and Exchange Rate Policy, 1964–1976

The Official Exchange Rate System

The Conselho Monetário Nacional, created at the end of 1964, was officially responsible for Brazil's exchange rate policy. Actual execution of the policy was delegated to the Banco Central, thus separating it from commercial policy, which was primarily administered by CACEX. During most of the post-1964 period Brazil had a unified exchange rate, to which were added import tariffs or export subsidies or from which were subtracted export taxes, as was the case with coffee exports which were subject to a *cota de contribuição* or tax. Brazil entered the liberalization period, however, with the vestiges of the multiple rate system of the preceding decade, which by the early 1960s had been reduced to a "general" and "special" rate. The special rate, which applied to exports of coffee and sugar and to imports of petroleum and wheat, as well as some specified government transactions, was abolished early in the new government in May 1964. In a formal sense, this exchange rate system has continued to the 1980s.

The market is operated by the Banco do Brasil and other banks authorized by the Banco Central to deal in foreign exchange, with buy and sell rates (table 3.6) periodically set by the Exchange Division of the Banco Central. Since the Banco Central does not offer to buy or sell unlimited quantities of foreign exchange at the stated prices, a variety of exchange controls exist, as does a *mercado paralelo* or black market. The black-market or "parallel" rate is shown on a quarterly basis over the 1964–76 period in table 7.1.

Although technically illegal, the market operates openly. (In recent years it has received tacit recognition from the government, which uses the parallel rate and international gold prices to determine the cruzeiro price at which it purchases gold from Brazilian miners.) Despite its long existence, the market appears to be of secondary importance in Brazil, since most visible trade occurs at official rates owing to the requirements of exchange cover for imports and the surrender of export proceeds to an authorized bank. For some service transactions, however, notably tourism, the parallel market is important, though the largest component of the service account, capital services, is transacted at the official rate, since foreign loans and investments registered with the Banco Central may be serviced at this cheaper rate.[1]

The Crawling Peg

Between 1964 and 1968, the exchange rate system continued to operate as it had earlier, with large but infrequent devaluations of a fixed nominal rate. An important policy change occurred in August 1968, however, when the crawling peg or *minidesvalorização* regime of frequent but small adjustments in the rate was adopted. Before this policy was adopted, the combination of infrequent adjustments in the nominal rate and continuous inflation in Brazil resulted in substantial fluctuations in the real exchange rate. Despite official statements about the need for exchange rate realism, overvaluation was frequent in the 1964–8 period as is argued in the following section. After a large devaluation in February 1964, shortly before the fall of the Goulart government, the cruzeiro was devalued three more times in 1964 by the new government. During 1965, however, the nominal rate was adjusted only once, by about 20 percent in mid-November, and did not change at all in 1966. Since inflation in 1965 and in 1966 was 35 and 39 percent respectively, real appreciation of the cruzeiro was substantial in this period. Some competitiveness was restored by a 23 percent devaluation in February 1967, but this was subsequently eroded by inflation of the same amount during the year.

The adoption of the crawling peg in principle could have permitted Brazil to effect a real depreciation of the cruzeiro from its overvalued levels of the 1964–8 period. Before 1968 the high rates of domestic price

---

[1] The Brazilian parallel market has been analyzed by Dornbusch et al. (1983).

Table 7.1 Black-market and official exchange rates and premium rate, 1964–1976

Year	Quarter	Sell rate (Cr$ per US$)	Parallel market rate (Cr$ per US$)	Premium rate (%)
1964	I	0.620	1.705	175.00
1964	II	1.200	1.305	8.75
1964	III	1.610	1.800	11.80
1964	IV	1.850	1.850	0.00
1965	I	1.850	1.845	− 0.27
1965	II	1.850	1.875	1.35
1965	III	1.850	1.870	1.08
1965	IV	2.220	2.230	0.45
1966	I	2.220	2.230	0.45
1966	II	2.220	2.220	0.00
1966	III	2.220	2.220	0.00
1966	IV	2.220	2.210	− 0.45
1967	I	2.715	2.725	0.37
1967	II	2.715	2.780	2.39
1967	III	2.715	3.150	16.02
1967	IV	2.715	3.320	22.28
1968	I	3.220	3.360	4.35
1968	II	3.220	3.700	14.91
1968	III	3.700	3.850	4.05
1968	IV	3.830	4.300	12.27
1969	I	4.000	4.300	7.50
1969	II	4.050	4.430	9.38
1969	III	4.150	4.500	8.43
1969	IV	4.350	4.650	6.90
1970	I	4.490	4.750	5.79
1970	II	4.560	5.020	10.09
1970	III	4.720	5.150	9.11
1970	IV	5.030	5.150	2.39
1971	I	5.110	5.450	6.65
1971	II	5.280	6.000	13.64
1971	III	5.505	6.300	14.44
1971	IV	5.635	6.300	11.80
1972	I	5.845	6.400	9.50
1972	II	5.915	6.700	13.27
1972	III	6.025	6.700	11.20
1972	IV	6.215	6.650	7.00
1973	I	6.030	6.450	6.97
1973	II	6.100	6.450	5.74
1973	III	6.160	6.750	9.58
1973	IV	6.220	6.950	11.74
1974	I	6.455	6.850	6.12
1974	II	6.815	7.150	4.92
1974	III	7.130	7.900	10.80
1974	IV	7.435	7.950	6.93
1975	I	7.735	7.800	0.84
1975	II	8.070	9.600	18.96
1975	III	8.520	9.600	12.68
1975	IV	9.070	12.300	35.61
1976	I	9.935	12.500	25.82
1976	II	10.650	13.400	25.82
1976	III	11.370	13.700	20.49
1976	IV	12.345	15.200	23.13

Source: Parallel rate, Pechman, 1984, table 6; official rate, Banco Central, *Boletim do Banco Central*, various issues

increase with a fixed nominal rate led to a loss of export competitiveness as well as speculative short-term capital movements.

Judged by comparison with other Latin American countries in the past two decades, notably Argentina and Chile, Brazilian exchange policy after 1968 might be considered a success since it avoided any prolonged periods of overvaluation. In retrospect, however, Brazil's crawling peg was not as successful a policy as it might have been. It did not in fact end overvaluation in a trend or average sense, but simply eliminated the extreme levels of overvaluation which had preceded the several large nominal devaluations before 1968. In relation to its early 1964 levels the real rate appears to have been stabilized around a considerably higher level.

Although there is little question that the reduction in real exchange rate uncertainty after 1968 had a favorable effect on exports, the rate may have been too stable. With the 1973–4 oil shock, Brazil's external terms of trade deteriorated significantly. A prompt real depreciation might have avoided some of the subsequent external disequilibrium which resulted. Policymakers appear to have preferred to maintain the real exchange rate, thus forcing the current account to be either financed by large capital inflows or reduced through commercial policies instead of real exchange rate depreciation.

Overvaluation

An assessment of the degree of overvaluation is fundamental in the analysis of exchange rate policy during the Brazilian trade liberalization episode. In principle, a fall in the "real exchange rate" could be identified with an increase in the degree of overvaluation. In practice, a series of difficulties arise in the definition of a real rate.

The fundamental difficulty which underlies any discussion of real exchange rates is that three goods prices, the price P_M of importables, the price P_X of exportables, and the price P_{NT} of nontradeables, affect external equilibrium, and implicitly define three relative prices P_X/P_M, P_X/P_{NT}, and P_M/P_{NT}. Defining the "real exchange rate" as a single relative price implicitly forces us either to ignore one price or to aggregate two of them.

The approach taken in this study was to aggregate exportable and importable goods prices into a single price, that of "tradeable" goods. This procedure in effect makes the terms of trade exogenous. This does not of course imply that they were constant. As table 3.7 shows, they varied significantly in Brazil between 1964 and 1976, deteriorating sharply in the early 1970s.

From a policy point of view, however, there is little that can be done about the external terms of trade, particularly if the country in question is a minor participant in world markets for its imports and most of its exports, as was the case in Brazil. This is not true for the ratio of tradeable prices, or internal terms of trade, which could vary with nominal exchange rate changes and other policy changes in the home country. A nominal depreciation, for example, would raise the domestic price of tradeables relative to nontradeables, other things being equal, while a domestic monetary expansion would lower P_T/P_{NT}.

At an empirical level, the major problem in implementing this procedure is that there is no readily available price series for nontradeables. Two broad approaches to resolving this problem might be considered. The first would use as a proxy for nontradeable prices in general some specific price index which might be assumed to be representative of all nontradeables prices. Examples might be construction costs, health services, or wages for unskilled labor since none of these goods or services could easily be arbitraged internationally. Although data of this type are available for Brazil for much of the post-1970 period, the main drawback to such an approach is that a nontradeable price series derived in such a way is highly vulnerable to market-specific price changes which may have little to do with overall trends in nontradeable prices.

An alternative approach, which was adopted in this study, is based on the availability of indices of tradeables prices and the fact that broadly based price indices like the consumer price index of Brazil's general price index include both tradeable and nontradeable prices. The nontradeables price series may then be derived residually from the general price index and the tradeables index, analogously to the way in which the implicit GNP deflator is derived once the nominal and real GNP series are known. Although this approach avoids the difficulties arising from the use of sector-specific price indices employed as proxies for nontradeable prices in general, it has some limitations of its own. As it is a residual, different definitions of either the general price index or the price index of tradeables will yield potentially different nontradeable series.

This feature of our approach is evident in tables A1.1–A1.3 which present a series of estimates of the real exchange rate over the 1964–76 period based on several different price series and definitions of the real rate. All the series shown represent the real rate as the price ratio P_T/P_{NT} of tradeable to nontradeable goods, so that a rise in this ratio implies an increase in Brazilian competitiveness. A common alternative definition of the real rate would define it as the nominal rate adjusted by foreign and home price levels, that is, eP^*/P, where e, P^*, and P are respectively the nominal exchange rate in units of home currency (cruzeiros) per unit of foreign currency, the world price level, and the home price level. Although theoretically distinct, the two definitions become statistically identical under some of the assumptions used to estimate them, as is shown in appendix 1 in which both the methodology used to derive the various P_T/P_{NT} series and the data sources used to calculate them are discussed.

Despite the differences in the underlying price indices and in the methods by which the P_T/P_{NT} series in tables A1.1–A1.3 were estimated, they all tell a basically similar story about the real exchange rate over the 1964–76 period. This is shown clearly in figure 7.1, which plots the various series over this period. Inflation combined with an infrequently adjusted nominal rate in the 1964–8 period resulted in a sharp fall in P_T/P_{NT}, or real appreciation, between 1964 and 1967. In addition, changes in the real rate were significantly greater in this period than they were subsequently. The adoption of the crawling peg in August 1968 in effect made overvaluation permanent, with the cruzeiro significantly overvalued between 1967 and 1973 relative to either earlier or subsequent periods.

Exchange Rate Policy and Growth

These results are of particular interest in the context of the trade liberalization that was going on at the time. The high export growth was clearly not due to exchange rate policy, since the relative remuneration to producing tradeables actually fell.[2] On the import side, the high real exchange rate may have contributed to high growth, along with declining rates of inflation, since it permitted a level of imports, particularly of intermediate inputs and capital goods, consistent with high rates of product growth. The real appreciation of the cruzeiro in this period also suggests that some of the increase in imports observed in the late 1960s was due to exchange policy rather than to import liberalization.

The use of commercial rather than exchange rate policy to promote exports in the post-1964 period is apparent in the large differences in the rates of growth of different classes of exports over the 1964–76 period. Table 7.2 shows these rates of growth, which averaged 35.4 percent at annual rates for manufactures versus 15.2 percent for exports as a whole.

Exchange rate policy in the post-1964 period may have had a positive effect on trade, however, through its effects in reducing real exchange rate uncertainty after the adoption of the crawling peg in 1968. Under the assumptions that potential exporters are risk averse and that production and exporting decisions must be made before the real rate is known, the diminution of uncertainty about the real rate after 1968 would be expected to increase the share of exports in total production. This appears to have happened, although it is difficult to separate the effects of commercial policies from the effect of reduced uncertainty.[3]

[2] The export incentive program, which is discussed in chapter 5, was responsible for much of the growth in manufactured exports.
[3] This argument is developed in Coes (1979). In 12 of 13 manufacturing sectors analyzed over the 1957–73 period, the ratio of exports to production was significantly related to a measure of exchange rate uncertainty.

Relative price: 1970, quarter IV = 1.0

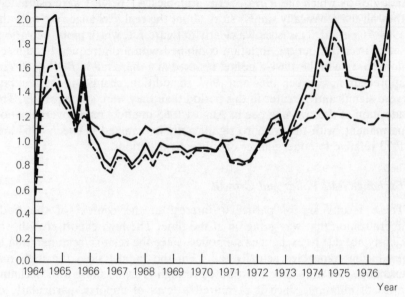

Relative price: 1970, quarter IV = 1.0

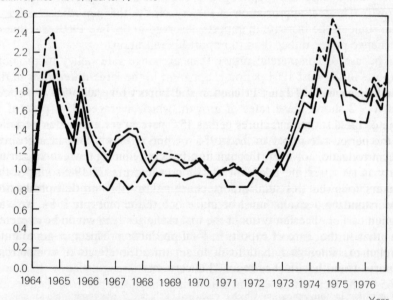

Figure 7.1   Ratio of tradeable to nontradeable prices: (a) using the consumer price index
with export price including coffee (——), the general price index with export
price including coffee (---), and method B with the consumer price index
(— — —); (b) using the consumer price index with export price including coffee
(— — —), the consumer price index with export price excluding coffee (---), and
the general price index with export price excluding coffee (——)

Table 7.2 Annual growth rates of exports by major groups, 1962–1976 (percentage change from previous year)

	Coffee	Noncoffee traditional exports	Minerals	Nontraditional and semiprocessed exports	Manufactures	Total
1962	− 9.4	− 18.2	2.9	− 34.3	25.0	− 13.5
1963	16.3	16.0	− 3.8	29.9	13.3	15.9
1964	1.6	− 6.9	5.9	− 9.2	86.3	1.6
1965	− 7.0	− 1.3	34.6	95.6	36.8	11.6
1966	8.1	24.2	− 0.7	− 11.0	16.9	7.4
1967	− 7.7	− 7.4	− 7.7	− 2.2	28.9	− 3.5
1968	9.9	20.7	11.4	23.4	3.1	13.7
1969	4.9	35.1	25.2	37.3	40.6	22.9
1970	15.5	− 11.5	46.2	33.1	46.5	18.5
1971	− 17.7	− 2.0	11.2	25.4	37.7	6.0
1972	27.9	47.0	− 5.4	44.2	56.7	37.7
1973	25.8	54.2	75.3	72.8	59.7	55.0
1974	− 30.5	78.9	55.8	7.1	57.8	28.3
1975	− 1.0	− 13.6	60.8	10.3	14.2	9.0
1976	154.2	− 50.4	8.4	32.4	7.4	16.8
Period average (1962–76)	12.7	11.0	21.3	23.7	35.4	15.2

Source: Calculated from data in table 8.2

The Sequencing of Export Promotion and Import Liberalization

One of the distinctive features of Brazil's move to greater trade openness in the period between 1964 and 1974 was the relatively long lag between the introduction of export promotion policies, some of which began as early as 1964, and the 1967 liberalization of imports. The reasons policymakers followed this sequence in changing Brazilian trade policies are understandable, given their perception of the choices in 1964, as was argued earlier. The consensus, both within the government and outside it, was that further import substitution offered little prospect of generating foreign exchange and that, to maintain an adequate level of imports, exports would have to increase. This view was strengthened in 1964 and 1965 by the fact that net capital inflows had fallen sharply from their levels of the early 1960s, and were actually negative in 1965, forcing any expansion of imports in the foreseeable future to be financed from within the current account.

Even if one accepts this diagnosis of the external situation, which does appear correct given the information available to policymakers in 1964, a question remains about the timing and sequencing of export promotion and import liberalization. Conventional trade theory oversimplifies the issue, since it implicitly assumes that trade balance or current account equilibrium is maintained. A liberalization of imports, such as that resulting from the 1967 tariff reductions, is assumed to result in an incipient trade deficit. If the nominal exchange rate is fixed, in the absence of financing via net capital inflows, it is assumed that current account equilibrium is maintained by a real devaluation which is attained by a rise in the relative price of tradeables. With flexible rates, the exchange rate is assumed to depreciate sufficiently to maintain equilibrium.[4] In this view, export expansion is an automatic consequence of import liberalization, and the issue of the timing and sequencing of export expansion and import liberalization has little meaning.

From a policymaker's point of view, there are several difficulties with this scenario. In a fixed exchange rate regime, like that of Brazil in the 1960s, or in many other episodes of trade liberalization, the appropriate real depreciation must be determined. Even under several simplifying assumptions, the appropriate real devaluation may range from zero to the full amount of the percentage reduction in the tariff, depending on the elasticities of export supply and import demand, as is shown in more detail in appendix 2. In a situation of high inflation such as that of Brazil in the early 1960s, moreover, the proper degree of nominal adjustment would be difficult to gauge even if the required real depreciation were known. As both the rate of inflation and the elasticities of export supply and import demand were quite uncertain in the immediate post-1964 period, the conventional assumption that the nominal exchange rate adjustment appropriate to maintain external balance could in fact be ascertained must be questioned.

The preceding analysis has several implications for trade and exchange rate policy. When import tariffs are significantly reduced early in a trade liberalization program, it may be easier for policymakers to allow the exchange rate to float to the level necessary to effect the required real depreciation than to attempt to set a new fixed rate.

There is no evidence that such a policy was considered in Brazil in the post-1964 period. The first major innovation in exchange rate policy, as mentioned above, was the institution of the crawling peg in August 1968, following a three and a half year period in which the fixed nominal rate had been devalued only three times, and even then only enough to offset internal inflation. This particular aspect of the Brazilian trade liberaliza-

[4] This argument is developed in Corden (1971). The calculation of "net effective protection" relative to an equilibrium exchange rate, like that of Bergsman (1970) for Brazil, explicitly assumes that such a depreciation occurs.

tion episode suggests that the theoretical link between tariff reduction and an induced exchange rate stimulus to exports simply did not exist.

A second implication of the import liberalization cum real depreciation argument for policy is more applicable to Brazil. Under the assumption that import liberalization would lead *ceteris paribus* to a worsening of the trade balance, the increase in imports could be financed through either an offsetting increase in exports or an increase in net capital inflows. There are elements of both approaches in the sequence of policies attempted by Brazil in the post-1964 period, although between 1964 and 1968 only the former were successful.

Net capital inflows to Brazil were interrupted in 1963 and were positive in 1964 only because amortizations were reduced through postponements. Over the 1963–5 period the net capital inflow averaged about US$7 million annually, or less than 0.7 percent of Brazil's import level. In the preceding six-year period, from 1957 through 1962, in contrast, the net capital inflow had averaged about 15 percent of the import level.

The prompt and determined attempts by Brazilian policymakers after 1964 to increase the net capital inflow, which are examined in more detail in chapter 8 and which only began to have an effect after 1968, were therefore designed simply to restore Brazil's earlier capacity to import and to maintain existing import levels, and not to finance any significant liberalization on the import side.

Export expansion was therefore the only way to finance any increase in imports in the mid-1960s. Given both the uncertainty about the response of potential exports to a general change in the exchange rate, and the difficulty of setting the appropriate real rate with the combination of nominal fixing and high inflation prevailing in Brazil before 1968, exchange rate policy does not appear to have been seriously considered as a tool of export promotion in this period. Export growth in the post-1964 period was attained almost entirely through fiscal and, later, credit incentives for specific exports.

From the point of view of allocative efficiency, one must question whether Brazil's reliance on providing incentives through commercial and credit policies, rather than through exchange rate policy, was appropriate. The approach is comprehensible in the context of the mid-1960s, when there was little evidence of a strong response by potential exporters to the type of general relative price incentive provided by exchange rate policy. Brazilian policymakers opted instead for a sector-specific, or even product-specific, program of export incentives. Their reliance on such incentives, which are examined in more detail in chapter 6, was partly based on the dominance of primary products on Brazil's export list at this time, and the presumption that the price elasticity of export supply from many of these sectors was low.

A related argument for the use of specific export incentives, rather than the general stimulus of a real depreciation, is based on the issue of policy credibility, a point which is usually ignored in simple models of export response. Conventional models assume that potential exporters respond to a relative price, which may be equally affected by (a) a rise in the world price P_i^* of the good, (b) a real depreciation, and (c) an export incentive s_i specific to the product; that is, the exports X_i in the ith sector are given by $f\,[eP_i^*(1 + s_i)]/P$, where P is a domestic price deflator. It is not clear, however, that the potential exporter would regard an increase in the local currency price of the export coming from each of these three sources as identical. Both changes in the world price P_i^* and a real depreciation may be regarded as transitory, particularly in an inflationary context like that of Brazil in the mid-1960s. An increase in net subsidies s_i specific to the sector, however, may be regarded as indicating a commitment by policy-makers to maintain the relative price incentives for exporting the particular product. If so, the elasticity of export supply with respect to s_i would be higher than that with respect to either P_i^* or to e, since the former represents a commitment which the latter do not.

Evidence that such a phenomenon existed and influenced the Brazilian export sector is difficult to obtain and interpret. But it is a plausible hypothesis that policymakers believed that sector-specific policy would be more understandable and credible than the general stimulus provided by a real depreciation induced by tariff reduction, and hence preferred to use export incentives rather than real exchange rate depreciation in the post-1964 period.

Coordination of Domestic Macroeconomic Policies in the Trade Liberalization Period

Monetary restriction was at the heart of the stabilization program implemented by the Castelo Branco government beginning in 1964. Statements of intent, however, did not always correspond to the policies actually executed, with the result that the degree of monetary restraint varied considerably from year to year, particularly in the early part of the post-1964 period.

Several important institutional reforms were made within the first few years. Monetary correction, or indexation of financial balances to adjust nominal assets for the effects of inflation, was formally introduced in mid-1964. Over succeeding years indexation of assets was extended, with correction applied to interest as well as principal. Another step was reform of the monetary authority, with the Banco Central assuming many of the functions of the former Superintendência da Moeda e do Crédito (SUMOC). Although the Banco Central did not have independent powers, and there were some ambiguities in the demarcation of its own responsibilities and those of the Banco do Brasil, this reform increased the government's control over monetary policy.

In July 1964 the government created indexed treasury bonds (Obrigações Reajustáveis do Tesouro Nacional, ORTNs), which were instrumental in permitting the domestic financing of government deficits. The nominal value of the ORTN was initially originally adjusted each quarter, usually in line with a moving average of the general wholesale price index of the Fundação Getúlio Vargas (FGV). Adjustments were monthly beginning in September 1965. Between 1964 and 1985, when indexation ended, the ORTN was one of the major standards for the indexation of assets.

Monetary policy in 1964, despite attempts at tightening, was fairly expansionary because of the expansion in the first quarter. In 1965 monetary growth exceeded targets, partly as a result of export receipts that were higher than expected. Monetary policy became harshly restrictive in 1966, with expansion of the means of payment (public holdings of currency plus demand deposits in commercial banks and the Banco do Brasil) limited to less than 14 percent. In no succeeding year was monetary growth so low, and from 1967 onwards rates of growth varied much less from year to year.[5] The principal trends in Brazil's money supply M1 in nominal and real terms between 1964 and 1976 are shown in table 7.3. The sharp fall in the real money supply in 1966 was followed by nearly a decade of increase, much of it accounted for by the rising demand for money during the boom years of high real product growth.

Fiscal policy in Brazil in this period is difficult to evaluate quantitatively owing to the way in which the government budget is presented. Data on the operating budget (*execução financeira*) do not give a complete statement of the impact of public sector expenditure on the economy because they exclude the operations of many public enterprises from the published budget. To the extent that in the aggregate these operations were in deficit, with the difference financed *ex post* by the monetary authorities, published budget data overstate the restrictiveness of the budget. Unfortunately, no adjusted or consolidated budget data are available for the period.

Some trends in fiscal policy are nevertheless discernible. Fiscal policy received fairly prompt attention from the new government in 1964. On the expenditure side, user fees were increased to reduce financing of the operating deficits of several public services, while public services were priced more realistically throughout the following decade. Reforms on the tax side were probably even more important. The federal income tax, previously rather ineffective, was indexed to domestic inflation, with tax

---

[5] Monetary policy in the stabilization period of the mid-1960s has been critically analyzed by Lara Resende (1982).

Table 7.3 Nominal and real money supply and rates of growth, 1964–1976

Year	Total M1 (million Cr$)	Annual growth rate (%)	IGP-DI (Dec 1970 = 1)	Real M1 rate (P = IGP)	Real growth (%)
1964	4,875	—	0.240	20,313	—
1965	8,750	79.5	0.323	27,090	33.4
1966	9,959	13.8	0.448	22,230	– 17.9
1967	14,513	45.7	0.557	26,056	17.2
1968	20,174	39.0	0.698	28,903	10.9
1969	26,735	32.5	0.838	31,903	10.4
1970	33,638	25.8	1.000	33,638	5.4
1971	44,514	32.3	1.195	37,250	10.7
1972	61,550	38.3	1.382	44,537	19.6
1973	90,460	47.0	1.597	56,644	27.2
1974	120,788	33.5	2.149	56,207	– 0.8
1975	172,433	42.8	2.780	62,026	10.4
1976	236,506	37.2	4.066	58,167	– 6.2

—, not applicable.
Sources: M1, Banco Central do Brasil, as reported in FGV, Conjuntura Econômica, March 1976, March 1977; IGP-DI, FGV, Conjuntura Econômica, various issues

brackets indexed as well. Tax debts were also indexed, and the tax collection system was strengthened legally and administratively. In addition, the IPI, a value-added tax on manufactured products, was increased for many products. As a result, tax revenues increased substantially, bringing down the apparent deficit as a share of GDP from about 4 percent in the first part of the decade to less than 1 percent in the late 1960s.

Equally important in this period was the government's strategy for financing its deficit by selling an increasingly large share of its new debt to the public rather than to the monetary authorities. Public financing of the federal deficit, which had been negligible in the early 1960s before the advent of indexation mechanisms like the ORTN, became more than adequate to finance the federal deficit by the end of the decade.

8

The Impact of the New Trade Policies on Brazilian Economic Structure

The commercial policy measures initiated after 1964 significantly changed the set of relative prices for producers. On the production side, these price changes altered both the profitability of producing for the home market, relative to exporting, and the profitability of some sectors relative to others. On the consumption side, whether for final use or as intermediates, the effects were less dramatic, but imports became relatively cheaper over the 1967–74 period, because of both the more open commercial policy and exchange rate overvaluation.

The key question for an assessment of trade liberalization raised by these relative price changes is how the economy responded to them in the short and long run. Since the program of export incentives for manufacturers meant that the most significant changes were on the export rather than the import side, the examination of the economy's response in this chapter begins with an evaluation of the aggregate response of manufactured exports. Econometric evidence is presented that suggests a high elasticity of export response to relative prices, a finding with important implications for the design of trade liberalization programs. We go on to look at the patterns of export and import response by industrial sectors in more deail, disaggregated to a two-digit level, and examine some of the potential costs of the trade liberalization episode, as indicated by sectoral employment trends, wages, and business failures. We conclude with some inferences about the winners and losers from Brazilian trade policies.

The Response of Manufactured Exports

Since the import substitution era of the 1950s, Brazilian commercial policies have notably emphasized industrial development. In this context, several econometric estimates have examined the response of manufactured exports to the export-oriented policies instituted after 1964.[1] Central to these efforts is the attempt to measure the impact on industrial activities as a whole of the various incentives created for manufactured exports during that phase.

The progression of export incentives over the post-1964 period from tax or fiscal incentives and exemptions that simply reduced anti-export bias to financial incentives in the form of credit subsidies has been described in the previous chapter. Since the financial incentives were of limited importance until the mid-1970s, earlier studies dealt only with the first type of export incentive. Cross sectional studies, such as that of Savasini et al. (1974), of the impact of the incentives on Brazilian industry at a two-digit level have attempted to measure the combined effect of the incentives at a particular date.

Most time series of export incentives have been constructed on the assumption that each incentive's effect could be added to that of existing incentives at the time it was effectively implemented.[2] As none of the incentives were removed over the 1964–76 period, such estimates are in effect increasing step functions, with each step corresponding to the introduction of a new incentive.

Musalem's (1981) estimates of export incentives for manufacturing build upon previous work by Cardoso (1980) and others. His estimates for the 1964–77 period are shown in table 5.3. In their 1980 study of Brazilian manufactured export response, Cardoso and Dornbusch used the series of net incentives estimated earlier by Cardoso (1980) as one of the components of a real exchange rate, together with nominal rates and international and domestic prices, to explain movements in the share of Brazilian manufactured output that was exported. A measure of capacity utilization was used as a second explanatory variable.

The Cardoso and Dornbusch estimates of the export coefficient in Brazilian industry are important in the context of trade liberalization. Earlier studies had generally found relative prices to have a significant but weak effect on export supply, implying that exchange rate policy or price incentives like those provided for manufactured exports in Brazil after 1964 would not be adequate tools for current account balance. This conclusion, a variety of "elasticity pessimism," lends support to bureaucratic arguments for import restrictions, possibly including direct controls like some of those used after 1974, to maintain or restore current account equilibrium.

[1] Among the first such studies were those of Von Doellinger et al. (1971, 1973, 1974). Others include Tyler (1976), Suplicy (1976), and Carvalho and Haddad (1980).
[2] As the date an incentive was formally granted and the date it becomes effective are not the same, there is some variation in the dating of changes in the export incentive time series estimated by different investigators.

Two forms of export supply were estimated by Cardoso and Dornbusch. The first was in the form

$$\ln x = a_0 + a_1 \ln p + a_2 y$$

where x is the ratio of exports of manufactures to total production, p is the world price of manufactures in cruzeiros, adjusted by the Cardoso export incentive series and home prices, and y is a measure which could be interpreted as either internal demand or excess capacity.[3]

The second form based on a "disequilibrium" or adjustment process in which $\ln x = \ln x_{-1} + w(\ln x^* - \ln x_{-1})$, with actual x approaching desired x^* over time, yields the form

$$\ln x = (1 - w) \ln x_{-1} + wb_0 + wb_1 \ln p + wb_2 y$$

Their ordinary least squares estimates, using data for the 1959–77 period, are shown in table 8.1.

Table 8.1 Manufactured export equation

Period	Constant	P	y	x_{-1}	R^2	Durbin–Watson coefficient
1959–77	0.08	0.88	− 0.016	—	0.78	1.60
	(0.14)	(7.46)	(− 3.87)			
1960–77	− 0.26	0.53	− 0.012	0.46	0.85	—
	(0.26)	(3.14)	(− 3.24)	(2.53)		

—, not applicable.
t statistics are shown in parentheses.
Source: Cardoso and Dornbusch, 1980

Even in the short run the price elasticity is high (0.88), and highly significant. In the long run the elasticity is $wb_1/(1 - w) = 1.15$. The capacity or income variable is also significant, as was the case in other studies of Brazilian export supply. The second model, in which the lag coefficient is significant, implies a mean lag of slightly less than a year ($(1 - w)/w = 0.85$).

From the point of view of exchange rate policy and trade liberalization, the Cardoso and Dornbusch results are encouraging, since they suggest that Brazilian exports of manufactures were responsive to price. As other Brazilian exports did not receive the incentives that manufactures did, their relatively poorer performance (table 8.2) appears consistent with these results.

[3] This variable is the percentage deviation of output from its trend.

Table 8.2 Exports by major groups, 1962–1976 (million current US dollars)

Year	Coffee	Noncoffee traditional exports	Minerals	Nontraditional and semiprocessed exports	Manufactures	Total
1962	643	287	105	134	45	1,214
1963	748	333	101	174	51	1,407
1964	760	310	107	158	95	1,430
1965	707	306	144	309	130	1,596
1966	764	380	143	275	152	1,714
1967	705	352	132	269	196	1,654
1968	775	425	147	332	202	1,881
1969	813	524	184	456	284	2,311
1970	939	508	269	607	416	2,739
1971	773	498	299	761	573	2,904
1972	989	732	283	1,097	898	3,999
1973	1,244	1,129	496	1,896	1,434	6,199
1974	864	2,020	773	2,031	2,263	7,951
1975	855	1,746	1,243	2,241	2,585	8,670
1976	2,173	866	1,347	2,966	2,776	10,128

Sources: 1962–72, Tyler, 1976; 1973–6, total, coffee, minerals, and noncoffee traditional exports, IBGE, *Anuário Estatístico*; manufactured exports (manufactures); World Bank, 1983; nontraditional exports calculated as a residual

We felt that the price responsiveness of manufactured exports to Brazilian incentives, or to the real exchange rate as a whole, was important enough to warrant a reestimation of the basic Cardoso and Dornbusch models, with several minor refinements. First, the "world price" series P^* used by Cardoso and Dornbusch appears to be a unit value index, at least in the earlier years of the series. This raises a potential estimation problem. If P^* is value of exports divided by quantity, then export quantity appears implicitly in inverse form as an explanatory variable, potentially biasing the estimate toward -1. To avoid this problem, the US price index for industrial products was used as a proxy for world price.

A second modification was the use of Musalem's reestimated series of export incentives, which included financial incentives. In the original Cardoso and Dornbusch estimate the bilateral cruzeiro-to-dollar exchange rate was used; in the reestimate of the present study a trade-weighted multilateral rate was used. Finally, the original published home price series for industrial products was used, rather than the rounded version of the original estimate, because although rounding makes no difference in a period of moderate price rises, it can misreport price levels in the early years of the series by as much as 20 percent.

The revised estimates are shown in table 8.3. As is clear from the price coefficient, the responsiveness of manufactured exports to relative prices

Table 8.3 Manufactured export equation (revised estimate)

Period	Constant	P	y	x_{-1}	R^2	Durbin–Watson coefficient
1959–77	− 3.78 (− 2.82)	1.67 (6.17)	− 0.018 (− 2.88)	—	0.74	1.92
1960–77	− 2.73 (0.26)	1.06 (3.14)	− 0.014 (− 3.24)	0.45 (2.53)	0.80	—

—, not applicable.

appears to have been even higher than was estimated by Cardoso and Dornbusch.

Their results appear to be basically corroborated by these estimates which suggest that, in addition to a high price elasticity (1.67 in the short run or 2.37 in the long run in our estimate), the excess capacity or domestic demand variable had a significant effect on manufactured export response. The mean lag is 0.80, little changed from the Cardoso and Dornbusch estimate.

At an aggregate level, Brazilian manufactured exports thus appear to have responded strongly to the increase in their relative price provided by the sequence of export incentives, especially when allowance is made for a lagged response. As our measure attempts to capture the entire change in the price of manufactured exports relative to the corresponding price for domestic sales, it reflects the effects of both commercial and exchange rate policy. The former was highly favorable to increased exports over this period, while the real exchange rate provided little incentive, since it was virtually unchanged between 1968 and 1973 (see tables A1.1–A1.3).

The strong response of exports of manufactures after 1967 supports the premise, inherent in the design of a successful trade liberalization program, that the effect of a real depreciation on relative prices will expand exports, thus offsetting the production and employment losses that may be induced by reducing the protection of importables. This is a critical condition for the success of trade liberalization; the reluctance of policymakers to rely on relative price changes may arise partly from uncertainty that they will produce the desired effect. Our analysis of Brazilian export response suggests that the elasticity of export supply is more than sufficient for the necessary expansion in exports to occur.

The question follows as to whether export response would have been as great had the relative price incentive come from a real depreciation rather than from commercial policy. The estimation procedure used above implicitly imposes the linear restriction that the elasticities of the export-to-production ratio with respect to the exchange rate b_{1r} be equal to the corresponding elasticity b_{1c} with respect to commercial policy incentives, that is, that $b_{1r} = b_{1c} = b_1$. Conventional microeconomic theory implies that these elasticities are equal, although it has been suggested by Tyler (1976) that the response to commercial policy incentives may be stronger.[4]

If export response to relative price changes in Brazil is as strong as the above econometric evidence indicates, there are important implications for the execution of a trade liberalization program. Brazil abandoned the move toward greater openness after the 1973–4 oil shock, and attempted to restore current account equilibrium through import restrictions and other administrative controls. A high responsiveness of exports to relative prices, however, suggests that a substantial real depreciation in 1973 or 1974 might have preserved the allocational gains of the preceding six years of greater trade openness while simultaneously restoring the current account equilibrium threatened by rising imported energy prices.

Sectoral Responses to Commercial Policies

The aggregate pattern of increasing openness on both the import and the export side of the Brazilian economy between 1964 and 1974 masks a degree of variation among individual sectors in industry. It is likely, moreover, that an even greater variation in export and import response might become apparent if data were available to analyze some of the nonindustrial tradeable sectors, notably agriculture.

In analyzing sectoral responses during the liberalization period, certain features need to be considered. First, some sectors were considerably more mature and developed than others. Import substitution had occurred earliest and proceeded furthest in the consumer goods sectors, among them food products, clothing and footwear, and textiles. The rates of growth of production would therefore be expected to be lower in such sectors over the post-1964 period. An examination of production trends suggests that this was in fact the case. At the other extreme, the less traditional sectors such as transport equipment, electrical and communications equipment, and machinery grew rapidly over the period.

A second and related feature of the post-1964 period is the contrast between the capital goods and intermediate goods sectors and those producing primarily consumer goods. Although import liberalization

---

[4] Tyler tested this hypothesis by estimating b_{1r} and b_{1c} separately. The difficulty with this procedure in the sample period of this study is that there is little variance in the real exchange rate but a sharp rise in the level of export incentives, so that export incentives and other commercial policy incentives show a significant effect while the real exchange rate does not. The argument that $b_{1c} > b_{1c}$ might be justified if changes in relative prices resulting from export incentives were regarded as having greater credibility and permanence than those resulting from changes in the real exchange rates.

occurred across a broad front in March 1967, the effective protective structure continued to discriminate most heavily against consumer goods. This tendency was reinforced from 1969 onwards, following the temporary liberalization reversal, by the policy of granting exemptions and reductions in protection for capital goods and for intermediate inputs. Effective rates for imports, which are based on posted tariff rates, consequently understate the dispersion in protection, since they do not capture the relatively greater importance of such exemptions in the capital and intermediate goods sectors.

Third, the degree of excess capacity in Brazilian industry varied substantially over the 1964–74 period, with some lesser but still important variations among sectors. As was shown above, the fairly sharp increase in exports during the 1964–7 stabilization period can be partially attributed to excess capacity. At a sectoral level, data on capacity utilization are unfortunately available only from 1968, and even afterwards are incomplete for several sectors. As the degree of capacity utilization increased, with excess capacity virtually disappearing in the early 1970s in many sectors, this reason for exporting was eliminated. On the import side, the low degree of excess capacity may have contributed significantly to the rise in imports of capital and intermediate goods.

To examine patterns of export and import response in the different sectors of industry in more detail, production, export, and import data were collected at the Instituto Brasileiro de Geografia e Estatística (IBGE) two-digit level. Most of these data were index numbers published by the Fundação Getúlio Vargas in various issues of the *Conjuntura Econômica*, supplemented by other sources. Indices of production, exports, and imports for the 1964–74 period for ten industrial sectors are given in table A3.1. For five other sectors, in which imports were negligible, production and export quantity indices for the same period are given in table A3.2. Data sources and the construction of the series are discussed in more detail in appendix 3.

In addition to these quantity series, import and export effective exchange rates were estimated (tables A4.1 and A4.2) for those sectors in which exports or imports were significant.[5] The calculations yielded 15 series of export indices and export effective rates, and ten corresponding import series for 1959–77.[6]

[5] The export effective exchange rate at a two-digit sectoral level was defined analogously to the aggregate effective exchange rate for manufactures used above. The subsidy rates by sector are shown in table 8.4. The data sources and methods used to obtain the effective exchange rates are discussed in more detail in appendix 3.

[6] The export series are nonmetallic mineral products, metals, machinery, transportation equipment, electrical and communications equipment, wood products, paper, rubber, leather, chemicals, textiles, clothing and footwear, food products, beverages, and tobacco products. The import series consist of the preceding sectors with the exception of wood products, leather, clothing and footwear, beverages, and tobacco products.

In 14 of the 15 sectors for which data on exports and production were collected, exports rose more rapidly than did production, even in sectors in which production itself was growing rapidly. The single exception was wood and wood products. This exception is not easily explained by our data, since the export effective exchange rate in this sector rose more than it did in many other sectors. Supply constraints including reduced availability of many types of higher grade wood in southern and southeastern Brazil, may have been a reason.

At the other extreme in terms of export response in industry was the clothing and footwear sector. The rapid growth of exports in this sector, largely concentrated in the shoe industry, which became an important supplier to the United States and some other markets during this period, can only partially be attributed to the rise in the effective exchange rate for this sector between 1964 and 1974. Some of the rapidity of export growth is more apparent than real, in that it began from a very low base in the early 1960s. In sectors, such as textiles, in which exports were already established by the mid-1960s, their growth appears lower.

Like the clothing and footwear sector's response to the new policies, transport equipment showed a rapid increase in exports. Here again the response appears to be related to a single product, motor vehicles, which became an important Brazilian export, especially to other Latin American countries, after 1968. The Brazilian automobile industry in this period moved successfully from the earlier import substitution phase of the 1950s and early 1960s to become a net exporter. Export subsidies and incentives were important for this sector; without them the export effective exchange rate for the sector would have fallen. On the supply side, an increase in exports may have been partially stimulated by the increasing scale of manufacturing in this sector. Most if not all automobile manufacturers were operating at a level of capacity below the cost-minimizing level in the mid-1960s. By the early 1970s they were lowering the average costs per unit and were narrowing the gap with competitors in the northern hemisphere, increasing their competitiveness in this market.

The pattern of export response of rubber and rubber products was rather different from that of other sectors. Despite a rise in the export effective exchange rate between 1963 and 1968, exports fell between 1964 and 1968 before recovering rapidly in 1969 and 1970. Some of this movement may be ascribed to a single product: tires. Since this is a subsector in which relatively few plants determine capacity, both lumpy investments and long lead times in building new capacity may be related to the fall, dominating trends in the sector as a whole.

Aggregate Trends and the Secondary Role of Trade Policy

It has been argued in earlier sections of this study that the liberalization of Brazilian trade between 1964 and 1973 was relatively modest and gradual in its effects on the economy as a whole. One interpretation of Brazilian experience over this period is that such liberalization as took place was more apparent than real, with the tariff reductions of 1967 primarily cosmetic, or serving mainly to reduce redundancy in the tariff schedule and not to promote any real opening of Brazilian industry to foreign competition.

There is some merit to this argument. The tariff cuts in many cases reduced posted rates from prohibitive levels, particularly in the consumer goods sectors, to levels in which many imports were still excluded. Direct price comparisons, moreover, suggest that some redundancy remained in the tariff structure for a number of products even after the reductions.

It is easy to overemphasize these aspects of the Brazilian experience, however. First, trade policies after 1964 encouraged greater openness not only via the conventional route of import liberalization but, perhaps less superficially, and certainly more durably, through export promotion. The production and export data discussed above for Brazilian industry leave little doubt that export promotion did lead to a larger share of exports in the production of almost all the industrial sectors.

Second, at a broad sectoral level liberalization on the import side appears to have been genuine, particularly in the capital goods and intermediate goods sectors. Import effective exchange rates fell between 1964 and 1968 in almost all sectors in which imports were significant. In some cases the fall was steep, as is shown in table A4.1. Although an elimination of redundancy alone could account for this movement in the import effective exchange rate, an examination of the behavior of imports over the period following the fall suggests that real imports increased more rapidly than before. Between 1966 and 1970, imports increased faster than production in seven of the ten sectors for which data were collected at the two-digit level. Only in the metals and metal products sector did the level of imports actually fall between 1966 and 1970, while the proportion of imports to total production was roughly constant in the transportation equipment and food products sectors.

When this period is extended over the next four years, until the end of the import liberalization episode in 1975, the conclusion is reinforced. From 1966 through 1974 imports rose more rapidly than production in all sectors except food products, with particularly large increases in the machinery, transportation equipment, and textiles sectors. After 1974 the majority of sectors show a significant drop in imports, not only relative to production, but absolutely. Although some of the drop may be attributed to both the slowing of the economy after the first oil shock and the imposition of administrative controls on some imports, the main cause appears to have been the sharp rise in the effective exchange rate for imports between 1974 and 1977. It seems difficult to conclude, therefore, that the Brazilian import liberalization between 1967 and 1974 was not genuine. The impact of the 1967 tariff cuts and further reductions between 1970 and 1974 may be overstated because of redundancy, but the available evidence at a broad sectoral level supports the view that the import liberalization was real and that the Brazilian economy in this period did become increasingly open on the import as well as the export side.

Costs: Employment and Business Failures

If the conclusion suggested by the preceding discussion, that the post-1964 liberalization was genuine in most sectors of industry, is accepted, the next question is whether the short-run costs of liberalization possibly outweighed the long-run benefits. Even if one accepts the premise, usually only implicit in this study, that any economy can in the long run increase its welfare through efficiency gains resulting from exposing both its producers and its consumers to world prices, it is possible that these benefits, while indisputable, may not be great enough to cover the possible short-run costs in terms of employment, lost production, potential business failures, and other temporary effects of the change in relative prices in the economy. Critics of trade liberalization might therefore argue that if these temporary costs are large and the future benefits of liberalization, discounted to the present, are small, then policies promoting a greater degree of trade openness are not justified.

Although there are no estimates of the aggregate costs of trade restrictions (and therefore of the benefits of their removal) for the Brazilian economy in the post-1964 period, indirect evidence suggests that they were substantial. The estimates by Mendonça de Barros et al. (1975) of the domestic resource costs of various export activities (table 8.4), for example, show significant resource costs in many protected manufacturing activities. These estimates, moreover, were made in the early 1970s, when the economy was already more open than it had been in the mid-1960s. In addition, they show only the static costs of trade restrictions and do not reflect potential long-run dynamic benefits from growth of more efficient sectors. Even using a high social discount rate, it therefore appears that the potential benefits to Brazil of trade liberalization in the late 1960s were large.

We now turn to the question of the short-run costs of the change in trade policies which began after 1964. Two obvious indicators of such possible

Table 8.4 Domestic resource cost per net dollar of exports

Activity	Cr$ per US$	Activity	Cr$ per US$
Oranges	2.17	Penicillin	8.95
Peanuts	2.14	Nylon fiber	4.14
Cotton (nonmech)[a]	4.10	Polystyrene	5.58
Cotton (mech)[b]	4.34	Rayon fiber	7.26
Corn (mech)[b]	5.27	Citric acid	5.24
Corn (nonmech)[a]	5.31	Tannic extract	5.67
Soybeans (nonmech)[a]	5.78	Tires	7.26
Soybeans (mech)[b]	6.24	Synthetic rubber	6.34
Manioc	2.17	Men's footwear	4.45
Soluble coffee	6.23	Women's footwear	4.56
Manioc flour	3.46	Bicycles	6.42
Peanut meal	4.65	Heavy tractors	7.66
Peanut oil	4.65	Pistons	3.78
Orange juice	4.74	Sewing machines	4.02
Soybean meal	7.53	Electrical refrigerators	4.69
Soybean oil	7.53	Kerosene refrigerators	4.84
Portland cement	3.72	Blenders	5.18
Diesel oil	6.47	Motorized grader	6.18
Kerosene	10.32	Lathe, 1,500 mm	7.33
Paraffin	11.08	Lathe, 2,200 mm	7.52
Sanitary ceramics	3.92	Lathe, 3,000 mm	8.08
Pig iron	4.51	Manual typewriters	13.00
Thin sheet (hot)	5.09	Radio receivers	5.94
Thin sheet (cold)	8.71	Calculators	6.71
Chrome steel	6.39	Televisions	6.86
Heavy steel sheet	6.51	Electric typewriters	15.05
Wire	7.49	Auto radios	18.82
Cellulose	4.55		

[a] Produced using traditional nonmechanized labor intensive technology.
[b] Produced using modern mechanized capital intensive technology.
Source: Mendonça de Barros et al., 1975, table 1

costs due to the increase in imports in the late 1960s and early 1970s are unemployment and the level of business failures.

Unemployment

Satisfactory data for either of the variables do not really exist, even in the industrial sectors. The data presented in previous sections, however, permit a partial answer. Although unemployment rates by sector are not available, the IBGE employment data discussed earlier and shown in table 8.5 may be regarded as an approximate indicator of employment or unemployment trends in the industrial sectors. The missing element is an

Table 8.5 Industrial employment, 1962–1976 (thousands)

Sector	1962	1965	1966	1967	1968	1969	1970	1971	1972	1973	1974	1976
Nonmetallic mineral products	146.0	120.7	137.3	135.1	147.0	153.6	155.8	160.4	172.2	211.0	226.2	264.7
Metals	231.7	231.2	210.5	215.6	233.5	228.4	249.1	266.1	283.4	355.0	405.3	455.5
Machinery	80.1	72.2	88.3	90.7	103.6	97.3	107.5	133.2	181.2	289.3	337.0	396.9
Electrical and communications equipment	88.3	72.5	94.9	105.4	114.8	106.3	106.8	124.5	133.4	175.1	195.6	193.6
Transportation equipment	138.5	132.1	134.1	131.2	150.6	153.2	154.3	184.4	185.5	214.1	204.4	221.9
Wood products	40.3	72.4	77.6	75.9	84.7	68.8	85.1	85.0	98.0	140.7	162.4	180.3
Furniture	58.0	44.0	55.1	56.1	58.1	61.8	64.0	65.0	72.1	105.7	108.2	128.7
Paper products	51.0	48.6	48.3	54.2	54.1	53.3	56.4	61.7	70.8	86.6	91.6	89.7
Rubber products	28.0	23.8	25.3	24.9	29.4	24.4	28.5	30.5	33.3	47.0	50.2	51.8
Leather products	21.5	22.2	20.5	22.4	23.8	22.4	23.0	24.4	25.4	29.5	28.6	37.8
Chemicals	90.5	77.8	100.1	98.5	104.2	97.9	103.0	117.3	116.6	137.1	139.0	134.0
Pharmaceuticals	33.1	34.1	37.7	39.4	35.8	34.8	35.2	36.8	41.0	45.2	47.0	45.4
Perfumes and cosmetics	13.9	12.3	15.6	15.9	15.9	16.9	17.8	18.7	19.9	24.1	24.2	24.9
Plastic products	19.5	18.5	20.4	26.6	30.3	30.1	32.5	37.7	43.3	73.3	76.0	86.9
Textiles	365.8	307.1	299.9	290.0	308.3	288.5	297.7	310.6	319.7	370.9	354.4	350.8
Clothing and footwear	99.8	91.6	104.3	107.1	109.4	111.0	122.1	133.1	138.3	221.0	239.1	308.6
Food products	239.7	246.8	233.7	232.6	239.9	259.6	272.5	278.5	314.4	399.2	412.1	448.8
Beverages	45.5	43.3	48.7	47.0	48.5	47.5	47.5	51.1	51.6	57.0	51.7	50.6
Tobacco products	16.0	17.4	19.4	18.9	16.6	16.1	15.1	16.2	16.6	19.5	19.7	23.1
Printing and publishing	62.7	57.8	67.3	69.9	74.5	77.2	80.6	86.9	84.5	112.3	111.8	127.6
Miscellaneous industries	40.7	33.6	46.0	45.1	43.1	42.4	43.2	47.8	68.0	77.6	122.8	87.8
Total	1,910.6	1,780.0	1,885.0	1,902.5	2,026.1	1,991.5	2,097.7	2,269.9	2,469.2	3,191.2	3,407.3	3,709.4

Source: IBGE, *Anuário Estatístico do Brasil*, various issues

accurate estimate of the available labor force; such estimates are not available for the 1964–76 period. Rates of capacity utilization in most sectors, however, reached record levels in 1973 or 1974, and it seems reasonable to assume that excess supply of labor was substantially reduced in most sectors at about this time or shortly afterwards. In addition, the rise in real wages at rates above those a few years earlier, even in the presence of a number of regressive indexing arrangements and the repression of open labor bargaining, supports the view that labor markets tightened considerably at this time. In the absence of either direct estimates of unemployment or adequate data on labor supply, such conclusions are tentative, but in comparison with periods either before or after the early 1970s the period may be regarded as one of low unemployment in a Brazilian context.

The reasons for a strong demand for labor were primarily domestic in origin, and derived in large part from the expansionary fiscal and monetary policies put in place after 1967.[7] The potentially unfavorable effects of import liberalization on employment were superimposed on this generally favorable employment situation, so that it is difficult to identify the adverse effects, if any, that the sharp rise in imports in most industrial sectors may have had.

Examination of the IBGE employment estimates by sector provides little or no evidence of any negative relation between imports and employment. Between 1967, the year in which *ad valorem* tariffs were reduced, and 1973, the year of the oil shock and the beginning of the slowdown in Brazilian growth, employment rose in each year in eight of the 15 sectors for which production and export data were obtained. In four more sectors, electrical and communications equipment, wood products, rubber products, and leather products, the upward trend in employment regressed only slightly, in a single year or two, most commonly in 1969, during the entire 1967–73 period.

In the remaining three sectors (chemicals, textiles, and tobacco products), the evidence that falls in employment were import induced is scanty or nonexistent. In tobacco, a sector in which Brazil has traditionally enjoyed a comparative advantage, imports were negligible throughout the period. In the chemical sector, employment generally rose over the 1967–74 period, although more slowly than in many of the other sectors: between 1968 and 1970 employment in the sector was relatively constant, as it also was from 1971 to 1972. However, since neither of these periods of slower growth of employment in the sector coincided with particularly rapid rates of growth in imports, it is difficult to make the case that employment trends in the sector were import related.

---

[7] Brazilian industrial product growth was not matched, however, by employment growth, as Bacha (1976) and others have shown.

Only in the textiles sector is there some suggestion of a relationship between imports and employment levels. Imports in the sector increased sharply after the March 1967 liberalization and remained relatively high in comparison with their depressed levels of the mid-1960s. Employment in this sector throughout the 1963–77 period was virtually flat, the only exception being an increase from 1972 to 1973. The slow growth of employment in this sector is not unequivocally related to imports, but the trends in both variables are more favorable to this hypothesis than they are in any of the other 14 sectors.

Wages

Data on wages and employment for the 1960s and 1970s are among the most deficient economic statistics in Brazil, perhaps reflecting the greater emphasis that governments since 1964 have placed on industrial growth and on financial markets and prices. The best-known nominal wage is the minimum salary (*salário minimo*), which varied slightly among regions during most of the period. The *salário minimo* for the Rio de Janeiro–São Paulo region is shown in table 8.6. This wage is not particularly helpful, however, for attempting to determine the course of real wages in the post-1964 period. Government spokesmen and supporters have noted that many workers, particularly the more skilled ones, earned considerably more than the minimum wage, especially in the years of high product growth between 1968 and 1973. Critics have noted, however, that mini-

Table 8.6 Nominal wages, 1962–1976

Year	Industrial sector: median monthly wage (Cr$ per month)	Rural day worker, São Paulo (daily wage × 30 days)	Minimum salary (Rio–São Paulo area)
1962	16.7	6.69	13.4
1963	27.0	10.86	21.0
1964	47.2	22.92	42.0
1965	79.1	41.1	66.0
1966	110.0	53.4	84.0
1967	158.0	74.7	105.0
1968	172.0	98.7	129.6
1969	216.0	119.0	156.0
1970	262.0	154.2	187.2
1971	317.0	193.5	225.6
1972	379.0	251.4	263.8
1973	469.0	340.5	312.0
1974	657.0	475.5	376.8
1975	879.0	619.5	532.8
1976	1,163.0	835.5	768.0

Sources: monthly and daily wages, Bacha, 1979; minimum salaries, FGV, *Conjuntura Econômica*, March 1976

mum wage legislation effectively extended only to the industrial sector, with rural workers and many workers in the service sector excluded.

Some alternative and partial evidence about the behavior of wages is presented in table 8.6, columns 1 and 2, estimated by Bacha (1979). The industrial sector median nominal wage was based on information from Labor Ministry questionnaires for the period 1965–73, supplemented by estimates from surveys of firms in Rio de Janeiro in earlier years and hourly wages in construction activities after 1973. The rural wage until 1970 is based on cattle ranchers' records from a sample of farms in the state of São Paulo, supplemented by data from the Agricultural Institute of São Paulo, which is the source after 1970. The real wage estimates shown in table 8.7 use these nominal wage series, with the Rio de Janeiro consumer price index as the deflator, while those in table 8.8 use the wholesale price index.

Despite their limitations, the evidence of the nominal wage series is sufficient to indicate that the "minimum" wage effectively applied only to the urban sector until 1973, when rural wages began to rise more rapidly. In the urban or industrial sector, real wages fell in the early part of the period, beginning their recovery in the late 1960s and rising until 1976.[8] Although the real minimum salary fell over the period, the behavior of

Table 8.7 Real wages, 1962–1976 (consumer price index for Rio de Janeiro as deflator; 1965–1967 = 100)

Year	Industrial	Rural	Minimum salary
1962	128.5	51.5	103.4
1963	121.6	48.9	94.6
1964	111.1	53.9	98.8
1965	112.2	58.3	93.6
1966	110.4	53.6	93.6
1967	121.5	57.5	80.8
1968	108.2	62.1	81.5
1969	111.3	61.4	80.4
1970	110.1	64.8	78.7
1971	110.8	67.7	78.9
1972	113.8	75.5	79.2
1973	125.1	90.8	83.2
1974	137.2	99.3	78.7
1975	142.2	100.2	86.2
1976	131.8	94.7	87.0

Source: FGV, Conjuntura Econômica, Indice de Preços ao Consumidor, March 1976

8 The high "real wage" shown for 1967 reflects the softening of prices as excess capacity resulted from the austerity program, and is not a good indicator of the urban standard of living relative to other years.

Table 8.8 Real wages, 1962–1976 (wholesale
price index as deflator; 1965–1967 = 100)

Year	Industrial	Rural	Minimum salary
1962	114.4	45.8	92.1
1963	105.1	42.3	81.7
1964	101.3	49.2	90.1
1965	110.5	57.4	92.2
1966	108.9	52.9	83.2
1967	123.4	58.4	82.0
1968	109.6	62.9	82.5
1969	115.5	63.7	83.4
1970	117.5	69.1	83.9
1971	117.0	71.4	83.2
1972	118.8	78.8	82.7
1973	127.4	92.5	84.8
1974	138.3	100.1	79.3
1975	144.8	102.1	87.8
1976	136.2	97.8	89.9

Source: FGV, Conjuntura Econômica, Indice de Preços
por Atacado, March 1976

both urban and rural wages suggests that the minimum wage became less relevant as an indicator of average wages.

Employment data are similarly limited in coverage. Such data as do exist are largely for urban employment in industry, with little known even today about employment in rural areas, services, and the informal sectors of the urban economy. Data from the survey of industry provide the basis for the estimates of industrial employment by sector shown in table 8.5. Employment data in this series for 1963 and 1964 and for 1975 were not published by IBGE.

Several points stand out from the data. The 1965–6 recession is evident, with total industrial employment in 1967 still below its 1962 level. The sharp growth in output beginning in 1968 is apparent, although employment did not increase as rapidly as did production. Some of the reported increase in employment in 1973, however, may be partially due to increased coverage by the IBGE survey.

At a sectoral level, employment trends paralleled production, with more rapid growth in the higher-technology and capital intensive sectors and in the capital goods sectors. Employment in the consumer goods sectors increased rather slowly, even in the "boom" years after 1967, and in several of them, including textiles, beverages, and tobacco products, was flat or falling in some years. Even in the sectors in which industrial employment grew more rapidly between 1967 and 1972, the absorption of labor by industry was probably well below the rate of growth of available labor. Adequate statistics on unemployment and underemployment during this period do not exist, but the IBGE data suggest that the high rates of product growth did not automatically lead to tighter labor markets in all sectors.[9]

Some further evidence on employment trends and several indicators of economic activity are provided by the quarterly *Sondagem Indústrial*, the industrial survey of the Fundação Getúlio Vargas, which began in 1966. Firms responding to the survey were asked to characterize four variables (production, demand, inventories, and employment) in their sector as having increased, remained unchanged, or decreased. Published survey results report a net response for each variable, defined as the number of positive (increase) responses minus the negative (decrease) ones, with no change responses excluded from the net response. Table 8.9 shows these quarterly data over the period from the beginning of the survey, the third quarter of 1966, through 1978. The four variables are plotted in figure 8.1.

Percent positive or
negative responses

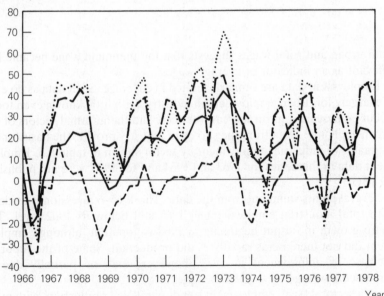

Figure 8.1 Levels of activity in manufacturing: – – –, production; . . . , demand; ---, inventories; ——, labor force (see table 8.9).
Source: FGV, *Conjuntura Econômica*, various issues

[9] Several Brazilian economists have investigated the relatively poor performance of the Brazilian industrial sector in providing employment despite high rates of product growth. For one such examination, see Bacha (1976): "O subemprego, o custo social da mão-de-obra e a estratégia brasileira de crescimento."

Table 8.9 Levels of activity in manufacturing[a]

Year	Quarter	Production	Demand	Inventories	Labor force
1966	III	18	− 4	18	4
1966	IV	− 4	− 16	35	− 22
1967	I	− 17	− 29	34	− 17
1967	II	21	22	3	1
1967	III	25	29	4	16
1967	IV	38	47	− 17	16
1968	I	39	43	− 7	17
1968	II	37	45	− 3	22
1968	III	43	43	− 4	21
1968	IV	39	45	7	22
1969	I	13	2	19	8
1969	II	17	7	28	3
1969	III	16	− 2	19	− 5
1969	IV	18	15	11	− 3
1970	I	6	2	9	3
1970	II	30	32	3	11
1970	III	36	44	3	16
1970	IV	39	49	− 7	20
1971	I	17	11	6	19
1971	II	22	19	7	19
1971	III	38	26	1	17
1971	IV	36	38	− 1	21
1972	I	27	19	− 1	16
1972	II	32	38	0	20
1972	III	47	50	− 2	28
1972	IV	45	53	− 8	30
1973	I	16	28	− 7	28
1973	II	48	57	− 9	37
1973	III	49	70	− 19	42
1973	IV	37	63	− 12	38
1974	I	6	19	− 3	30
1974	II	31	21	16	24
1974	III	26	10	21	11
1974	IV	7	16	9	7
1975	I	− 5	− 18	14	10
1975	II	29	26	2	15
1975	III	35	38	− 2	17
1975	IV	21	41	− 13	24
1976	I	6	15	− 5	27
1976	II	39	46	− 6	32
1976	III	42	44	5	21
1976	IV	16	20	3	14
1977	I	− 15	− 23	19	9
1977	II	29	25	7	12
1977	III	34	34	6	16
1977	IV	20	30	− 5	13
1978	I	6	12	9	16
1978	II	42	43	4	24
1978	III	46	46	4	23
1978	IV	33	44	− 12	18

[a] Entries are the percentage of positive (increase over the previous quarter)
responses in the *Sondagem Indústrial* minus the percentage of negative
responses with "no change" responses not counted.
Source: FGV, *Conjuntura Econômica,* July 1981

Inventories, which run countercyclically to the other three indicators, are entered negatively in the graph. Although there is considerable variation from quarter to quarter, the recovery from the 1965–6 recession is evident in all four series. There is no evidence of any adverse effects of any of the four indicators of the March 1967 import liberalization. The record levels attained by all four indicators in 1972 and 1973 in fact coincide with the period in which the Brazilian economy was most open to imports.

Business Failures

The general conclusion, based on examination of employment trends, that the temporary costs of the Brazilian import liberalization episode were low is reinforced by the data on firm failures. Brazilian law establishes two categories of failure: a firm facing payments difficulties but anticipating future recovery may seek judicial protection from its creditors under a *concordata*, or it may file or be required to file for bankruptcy, in which case *falência*, or bankruptcy, is declared. Data on *concordatas* and *falências* in São Paulo between 1962 and 1976 are shown in table 8.10.[10]

Table 8.10 *Falência* and *concordata* requests in São Paulo, 1962–1976

Year	Falências	Concordatas	Total	Firm population	Failure rate
1962	568	69	637	202,569	0.314
1963	552	104	656	209,969	0.312
1964	780	63	843	217,638	0.387
1965	1,154	156	1,310	225,589	0.581
1966	1,621	353	1,974	233,830	0.844
1967	2,184	259	2,443	242,372	1.008
1968	2,066	309	2,375	251,225	0.945
1969	2,340	295	2,635	260,403	1.012
1970	2,243	218	2,461	269,915	0.912
1971	2,025	187	2,212	290,465	0.762
1972	2,164	267	2,336	312,580	0.747
1973	2,767	116	2,883	336,378	0.857
1974	1,755	140	1,895	361,988	0.523
1975	2,157	99	2,256	389,548	0.579
1976	2,325	121	2,446	419,206	0.583

Sources: *Falências* and *concordatas* 1962–8, FGV, *Conjuntura Econômica*, various issues; 1969–76, Damiao, 1984; firm population in São Paulo in the industrial, commerce, and service sector, IBGE, *Censo Indústrial, Censo de Serviços*, and *Censo de Comércio*, 1959, 1970, 1975

10 The failure rate represented in table 8.10 is the ratio of failures to the relevant firm population, which nearly doubled between 1964 and 1974. Several earlier studies of macroeconomic trends in the post-1964 period, for example Lara Resende (1982), have used the absolute number of failures in this period, which would be expected to rise even under normal conditions in a growing economy like that of Brazil.

There are a number of limitations, geographical and temporal as well as conceptual, to these data, and conclusions based on them are at best tentative. They are available on a two-digit sectoral level only from 1969 onwards, so that differential effects between sectors resulting from the 1967 liberalization, if there were any, would not be apparent from the aggregate data. Furthermore, they refer to the city of São Paulo rather than to the economy as a whole. This is not a severe problem, however, since the city contains a large proportion of Brazilian manufacturing firms. Finally, there is a difficulty in interpreting the *concordata* and the *falência* data, since the former is in fact undertaken to avoid the latter. The degree to which the two series overlap is not clear, although examination of failure rates using both concepts suggests that they are closely related. A number of Brazilian publications, including *Conjuntura Econômica*, have treated them as virtually equivalent, occasionally summing them and presenting the total as an indicator of failure. For the purposes of this study, this approach is probably adequate, since both statistics reflect firm financial difficulties such as might in principle be induced by a sharp increase in import competition.

Examination of *falência* and *concordata* data from the Associação Comercial in São Paulo, which reported sectoral data beginning in 1969, shows no clear trend in either rate. Both the *concordata* and *falência* rates generally fall or are flat in most sectors between 1969 and 1974, corresponding to the period of greatest openness to imports. The rise in the failure rate between 1964 and 1967 is clearly attributable to the domestic stabilization program of the time, and not to import penetration. Possible exceptions to this pattern are wood products and leather products. As imports were negligible in both sectors, however, there does not appear to be any link between greater import openness and higher failure rates there.

There are sharp differences in both the average yearly rate and its variation by sector, with low and stable rates for rapidly growing sectors like machinery and clothing and footwear, and rather high and variable rates in several sectors, notably leather products and beverages. Imports were unimportant in the last two sectors, and there does not appear to be any link between failure rates and imports in these cases.

With the advent of the first oil shock in 1973–4, failure rates in most sectors turned up as Brazilian growth slowed. Examination of the Associação Comercial data for the post-1977 period shows the trend accelerating. Since the Brazilian economy became more closed to imports after 1974 than it had been for at least a decade, the failure rate data as a whole do not support any hypothetical positive relationship between import competition and business failures.

Some Inferences about Winners and Losers

Conventional trade theory suggests that trade liberalization would significantly affect the distribution of income among sectors and regions,
reducing the income of highly protected activities and reallocating
resources to the expanding export sectors, which are assumed to be
favored by the real depreciation of the exchange rate that theoretically
follows an opening up to imports. Implicit in this view is the assumption
that the principal changes in trade policies will be on the import side,
consisting of a significant reduction in tariffs and other import restrictions.
Trade liberalization in this interpretation would raise the relative prices of
the outputs of sectors with negative real protection, defined relative to a
"free trade exchange rate," and lower those of sectors receiving positive
real protection.

As may be seen from Fishlow's estimates of the net protective effect of
Brazilian commercial policy before the 1967 tariff reduction (table 3.9), a
number of manufacturing sectors, particularly those producing consumer
goods, enjoyed a high level of protection, in some cases well over 200
percent. In the primary sectors, for which such disaggregated estimates are
not available, net protection was negative in the most important sector,
agricultural crops and vegetables, and only modestly positive for livestock
and for mining. Removal of protection would therefore be expected to
benefit the primary sectors while moving resources out of the formerly
highly protected manufacturing sectors. In this interpretation, the
"winners" from Brazilian trade liberalization would be primarily those
factors – such as agricultural labor and landowners – and those regions
most closely associated with agricultural and other primary production.
Factors such as physical capital and highly skilled labor, much of it
concentrated in urban areas like São Paulo, would be negatively affected
by import liberalization.

The Brazilian move to greater economic openness in the 1964–74 period
does not fit this paradigm. One of the distinctive features of the Brazilian
experience, as described earlier, was the emphasis on export promotion,
which both preceded and outlasted the 1967 import liberalization and
continued longer. Real depreciation, which provides the stimulus to export
expansion in the conventional model, did not occur; the growth in exports
after 1964 was due primarily to export incentives.

Had the export promotion program favored those activities that were
relative "losers" during the import substitution phases, the winners and
losers in the 1964–74 trade liberalization episode might correspond approximately to those predicted by the conventional model. The available
evidence, however, suggests that this was not so.

In an attempt to assess the efficiency of the export incentives program, Mendonça de Barros et al. (1975) calculated the domestic resource cost (DRC) of generating a net dollar of foreign exchange in 1971 through different exports. Their estimates generally show a high DRC for a number of products from sectors which were relatively highly protected before 1964 (table 8.4). More efficient (low DRC) exports were more frequent in the agriculture sector, one of the "losers" from Brazilian trade policy both before and after 1964. The authors argue that part of the higher DRC was caused by policymakers' tendencies to favor a number of less efficient activities, particularly more sophisticated manufactures, at the expense of products in which Brazil enjoyed a greater comparative advantage. Furthermore, the Mendonça de Barros et al. estimates suggest that many of the activities for which export incentives were highest were also among sectors that had enjoyed a relatively high level of protection on the import side. The Brazilian export incentive program, which avoided a real depreciation and heavily favored manufactures, in effect prevented those sectors that might have been "losers" in the conventional trade liberalization model from actually losing.

This tendency can be seen graphically in figures 8.2 and 8.3, which plot two measures of export protection against the corresponding sectoral estimates of net effective protection in 1966 made by Fishlow, which are given in table 3.9. The first measure, used in figure 8.2, is the level of net export incentives by sector in 1969, which were estimated for this study and are given for the 1963–77 period in table A4.3. Four sectors – clothing and footwear, food products, beverages, and tobacco products – were excluded owing to difficulties arising from aggregation and tariff redundancy. The second measure, available for only nine sectors, is taken from the Mendonça de Barros et al. DRC estimates for 1971 discussed above.

The tendency for the sectors that were highly protected before 1967 also to benefit the most from the export incentives is clear from figure 8.2 and is confirmed by a regression of the net subsidy level by sector on the net effective protection level. The estimated regression was

NES = 1.240 + 0.135NEP
R^2 = 0.403   degrees of freedom, 15
standard error of coefficient, 0.042

where NES and NEP are respectively the net export subsidy level and net effective protection level by sector. The coefficient of the protection level is positive and the t statistic for the explanatory variable is significant at the $P(H_0) < 0.005$ level.

These results, together with studies like those of Mendonça de Barros et al. (1975), suggest that Brazil's trade liberalization program did not engender the same group of "winning" and "losing" sectors as those that would be predicted to emerge in a more conventional model of import

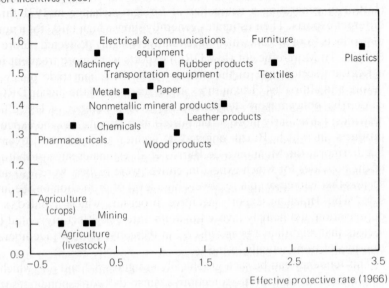

Figure 8.2   Import protection and export incentives

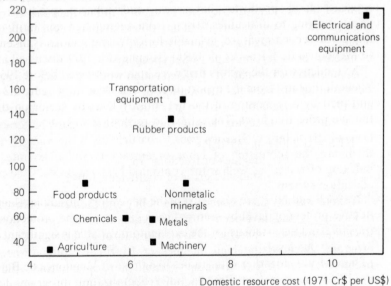

Figure 8.3   Import protection and export efficiency

liberalization. The unorthodox outcome is attributable to two factors. The first was the avoidance of real depreciation, due primarily to the capital inflows and secondarily to the export promotion. The second was the bias of the incentives in favor of a group of sectors and activities that had been most protected in the earlier phase of import liberalization.

Even allowing for the effect of the authoritarian political system, the changes in Brazilian trade policy between 1964 and 1972 encountered remarkably little opposition. The preceding examination of the "winners" and "losers" may help explain why. Had Brazil really moved to a more outward oriented trade policy via import-side liberalization, as the conventional model assumes, the shift in relative prices at a sectoral level might have been much greater, arousing correspondingly more opposition from losing sectors. By encouraging export development via incentives to sectors favored with high net protection in the past, Brazilian policymakers may have eliminated or at least reduced much potential opposition to the post-1964 trade policies. The price for this kind of policy was paid in economic efficiency. The favoring of manufactures by the export incentive program at the expense of other sectors, notably Brazilian agriculture, required more domestic resources to be expended in earning a given amount of foreign exchange than might have been required if Brazil's liberalization had placed more emphasis on import liberalization and exchange rate competitiveness.

We can also consider the question of "winners" amd "losers" from trade policy changes in the context of rich versus poor or, in other words, in terms of the personal distribution of income rather than the distribution among factors. Conclusions about any potential links between the greater openness of the Brazilian economy to trade and the personal distribution of income, however, must be rather speculative.

A superficial examination of this question would associate the apparent worsening of the personal distribution of Brazilian income between 1960 and 1970 with the shift toward greater trade openness. Such an interpretation is seriously misleading, however, since there are many better explanations of the failure of Brazil's poor to participate in the *milagre*. Among them are the repression of labor organizations and deliberate under-indexing of wages, as well as the continued backwardness of the primary education system.

If there was any link between trade policy and the personal distribution of income, it may have been the continuation of a high level of protection to capital intensive manufacturing activities through the export promotion program. Because the high incomes of Brazilian capital owners were protected, even while the economy became more open to trade, the effects of a more conventional trade liberalization in raising the demand for the products of the rural poor were forgone. Brazilian policymakers' preferences for an opening of the economy through export promotion rather than import liberalization and real exchange rate depreciation may therefore have incurred costs not only in terms of economic inefficiency but in terms of income inequality as well.

9

Liberalization: an Interpretation of the 1964–1976 Experience

Brazil's episode of increasing economic openness, which began shortly after the 1964 change of government and which ended within a few years of the 1973–4 oil shock, provides a number of useful lessons for both policymakers and students of trade policy. Its costs and benefits, the opportunities both seized and lost, and its impact on the structure of the Brazilian economy are relevant to future liberalization attempts, either in Brazil or in other countries. Because it was a rather heterodox and complex set of policies, many difficulties arise in interpreting the 1964–76 experience.

One legitimate question is whether there was a "trade liberalization" at all. The fall in nominal and effective tariff rates after the March 1967 cuts overstates the true degree of opening on the import side, since part of the decrease in *ad valorem* rates was due to the elimination of redundancy. The import liberalizing trend was interrupted, moreover, by the partial retreat in late 1968, when many tariffs were again raised. Although the trend was subsequently resumed, much of the increase in import openness from 1969 onwards was concentrated in favored capital and intermediate goods sectors.

Despite these features of the post-1964 experience, Brazil's experience between 1967 and 1974 was a liberalization, if only a timid and weak one. After successive years of decline or no change in the import coefficients in most manufacturing sectors in the early 1960s, this trend was reversed after 1967, as import growth outpaced production in the majority of the sectors examined in this study. Had the liberalization of imports which began in 1967 been primarily an elimination of redundancy, the import coefficient would not have increased as much as it did in most sectors. Brazil in 1973 was more open to imports than it had been at any time in the preceding two decades or was to be in the following one.

A conventional interpretation of trade liberalization would focus on the reduction in tariffs and other restrictions to imports. In this scenario, the economy would become more open on the export side indirectly, through the induced real depreciation necessary to maintain current account balance. This interpretation of trade liberalization implicitly assumes that there is no exogenous change in exports, due either to demand influences or policies which directly encourage exports, and that there are no exogenous changes in the capital account of the balance of payments.

A more complete characterization of the post-1964 Brazilian liberalization episode, however, requires more emphasis both on the export side of Brazil's foreign trade and on capital account trends. Export promotion began earlier, extended to more activities, and lasted longer than did import liberalization. Some indication of its relatively greater staying power is given by the fact that the 1974 oil shock in effect killed the timid import-side liberalization, while export promotion continued to flourish, and indeed gained support from policymakers who viewed it as a substitute for greater real depreciation of the cruzeiro.

This difference between import-side and export-side trade liberalization in Brazil raises a related issue, and a potential explanation of what went wrong after 1974. Commercial policy in Brazil has long been regarded both as an allocative tool, particularly as a complement to industrial policies, and simultaneously as a tool for aggregate external balance. The argument that exchange policy should bear the primary burden of aggregate external sector adjustment and that, in principle, it could free commercial policy for allocative functions was rarely, if ever, heard in Brazil in the 1960s or 1970s. As was shown in preceding chapters, there was little evidence or even belief among Brazilian policymakers that the trade balance would respond to a real depreciation of the cruzeiro.

This perception among policymakers and other participants in trade about the structure and price responsiveness of Brazilian trade flows, and a corresponding preference for direct controls of trade, manifested itself in two distinct phases over the post-1964 period. As Brazil received massive capital inflows beginning in the late 1960s, balance-of-payments pressures eased. In the absence of commercial policy changes, such a tendency could have been accommodated by exchange rate policy with real appreciation. Although this occurred to a limited degree in this period, a significant part of the adjustment was accomplished by the gradual import liberalization of the 1967–74 period. In this sense, the liberalizing trends observable on the import side in the 1967–73 period may have been regarded in part as a means of balance-of-payments adjustment rather than for the purpose of allocative efficiency.

The tendency for commercial, rather than exchange, policy to be the principal external adjustment mechanism may have been strengthened by Brazil's adoption of the crawling peg in 1968. In subsequent years the cruzeiro was virtually locked to the US dollar in real terms, with almost negligible deviations from a purchasing power parity path. The consequent real exchange rate rigidity which characterized Brazil in the 1968–74 period, despite the large capital inflows, was made possible by the progressive import liberalization.

With the 1974 oil shock and the sharp deterioration in Brazil's terms of trade, this situation was abruptly reversed. Given the severity of the shock, some real depreciation would have been an understandable and probably appropriate response. Real exchange rigidity continued, however, with only minor real depreciation. Commercial policy and a continuation of heavy external borrowing, rather than exchange policy, were the tools preferred by policymakers to respond to the sharp change in the external sector. From the policymakers' point of view, this approach had the attraction of appearing more certain and possibly more rapid than would exchange rate depreciation, since the level of imports could be directly controlled through an existing administrative mechanism, CACEX, the foreign trade and exchange division of the Banco do Brasil. As this bureaucratic structure was left intact over the 1967–73 liberalizing period, it appeared to policymakers as an obvious and relatively easy tool to use to control trade flows after the first oil shock.

Interpreted in this way, Brazilian exchange policy provides a clue as to why import liberalization appeared to work and yet was so easily aborted after the first oil shock. If commercial policy, rather than exchange policy, is assigned the primary responsibility for external adjustment, as appears to have been the case in this period in Brazil, then an episode of import liberalization such as occurred there after 1964 may be highly vulnerable to external reverses. In retrospect, the crawling peg policy which was instituted in 1968, and which was widely hailed both by market participants and by economists as an important innovation, may have had the undesirable effect of introducing a degree of real exchange rate rigidity into Brazilian trade and payments policy at a time when more flexibility would have been useful, especially after 1973.

A related group of issues in a study of the Brazilian experience in the 1964–76 period involve the depth of the "liberalization" and its potential costs. Measured in terms of either unemployment or business failures, variables which may be appropriate in other contexts, there is no noticeable effect of the 1967 tariff changes. This observation is consistent with a number of potentially conflicting interpretations of the 1964–74 "liberalization" episode. By itself, the absence of marked unemployment or business failure effects lends support to the view that litle true liberalization actually occurred. The principal difficulty with this interpretation is the implicit assumption, possibly rooted in an overly static model of trade liberalization, that other relevant macroeconomic trends can be ignored.

If, as is argued above, the liberalization is regarded as at least partially genuine, then the apparently low costs must have other explanations. Domestic macroeconomic trends clearly provide the most likely one. The shift to relatively more expansionary monetary and fiscal policies in 1967 under Delfim Neto, following the orthodox Campos–Bulhões stabilization program of 1964–7, marked the beginning of a period of high product growth which was only partially slowed by the first oil shock. If greater import liberalization resulted in any increase in unemployment or business failures in import-competing sectors, these effects are completely hidden, at least at the two-digit industrial classification level for which data are available, by the expansion in aggregate demand and employment. Trade liberalization in Brazil, in other words, was not a *ceteris paribus* experiment in which other policies, notably fiscal and monetary policy, are unchanged.

This interpretation of Brazilian experience in the post-1964 period thus treats the 1967 import liberalization and its subsequent extensions as genuine, but something of a sideshow in the larger economic arena. Inferences about the timing and sequencing of trade liberalization based on the Brazilian experience must consequently respect these particular features, which may not be repeated in other economies or again in Brazil. Both the expansion of output and the inflow of foreign capital were unprecedented in Brazilian economic history. The first trend required a substantial increase in imports, and the second helped to finance it.

Trade liberalization was as significant and extensive on the export side as it was in the more conventional import sense. As was shown in chapter 5, Brazil's export promotion program can be divided into two stages. In the earlier liberalizing phase anti-export bias was reduced, with relative prices for export activities moved closer to international prices. In the subsequent phase in which credit subsidies became relatively more important, policies went considerably further than simply eliminating price distortions, and may have created new distortions.

If there is a lesson in the Brazilian export promotion experience, it may be that policymakers may find it difficult to stop at an "optimal" level of export promotion, once such a process has begun. Since the export promotion program was in part advocated for balance-of-payments reasons, paralleling similar arguments made for import substitution in the preceding decades, little attention was given to the allocative efficiency of the export promotion program.

In early phases, the export promotion effort was a useful component of Brazil's greater openness to external goods and capital markets after 1964. There are a number of positive features of this type of policy in a trade liberalization package. The approach has the advantage that if export liberalization is deep and extensive, perhaps even preceding import liberalization, the costs of the latter, in terms of either the required exchange rate adjustment or employment and business failures, may be minor or even negligible.

A second less favorable feature of the Brazilian experience relevant to the design of liberalization programs was the excessive degree of real exchange rate rigidity and consequent external adjustment burden on commercial policy. While supporting a degree of liberalization during the 1967–74 period, as capital inflows relieved and then eliminated balance-of-payments pressures, it made the liberalization process vulnerable to an adverse external shock like the first oil shock.

One obvious question raised by Brazil's experience is the role that domestic macroeconomic trends played in either permitting the post-1964 program to be initiated or in allowing it to be sustained. It is useful in this context to distinguish between initiating and sustaining a trade liberalization policy.

The major reforms in commercial policy, on both the import and the export side, and in capital account policy, clearly preceded the post-1968 period of high rates of product growth. As was noted earlier, the crisis atmosphere and economic downturn of the early 1960s, as well as Brazil's external payment difficulties, convinced a number of policymakers and economists outside the government that the easy import substitution opportunities of the preceding decade were largely gone. In this sense, adverse economic conditions may have facilitated the initiation of a new set of economic policies.

The maintenance of the Brazilian liberalization program, however, was facilitated by a number of favorable macroeconomic changes which began after 1967. Among them were the rapid increase in the GDP growth rate and the move toward a balance-of-payments surplus in the late 1960s. The former reduced and perhaps even eliminated the employment and business failure costs which might have appeared in other circumstances.

The massive inflow of capital in the late 1960s, which arose both on the supply side and in response to Brazilian capital account policy changes in the mid-1960s, was reinforced by export growth. While it continued, it permitted policymakers to use commercial policies for external adjustment, in this case in a liberalizing direction. In the longer run, however, the capital inflows may have undermined the possibilities for a permanent trade liberalization. As the various measures of the real exchange rate used in this study all demonstrate, the real depreciation which is predicted by the conventional model of trade liberalization simply did not occur in Brazil. The primary cause was the positive capital account, with export growth due to the export incentive program playing a secondary supporting role.

As a result, liberalization of the current account was subordinated to capital account developments. Brazilian export growth was due to specific commercial policies, concentrated in manufacturing, and not to competitive exchange rate policy. In the period before the 1973–4 oil shock, when the capital account more than financed the growing current account deficit, an increasingly liberal commercial policy was viable, without any exchange rate adjustment. After 1974, however, policymakers turned to commercial policy as a means of balance-of-payments adjustment, in effect ending Brazil's experiment with greater openness.

Appendix 1

Calculation of the Tradeables-to-Nontradeables Real Exchange Rate

The real exchange rate, whose evolution in the 1964–74 period was critical in the course of the Brazilian trade liberalization episode, was defined in this study as the ratio P_T/P_{NT} of tradeable to nontradeable prices. This ratio is conceptually simple but less easy to estimate empirically, since price series which can be readily identified as representing a broad category of "nontradeables" do not exist. This study takes an indirect approach, defining nontradeables residually, using general price indices that include both tradeable and nontradeable prices.

Tradeable prices in this study were defined in two different ways, corresponding to methods A and B referred to in tables A1.1–A1.3. In the first method they were calculated as a weighted geometric average of cruzeiro import and export price indices. These indices were obtained by multiplying the dollar import and export prices by an index of the nominal exchange rate. The tradeable price shown in tables A1.1 and A1.2 assigns equal weights to imports and exports. As Brazil's export price index was heavily influenced by coffee price trends, particularly in the early part of the 1964–76 period, the tradeable price is calculated both with and without coffee prices in the export price index.

As is the case elsewhere, there is no price index in Brazil that can be readily identified with that of nontradeables. The nontradeables indices shown in all three tables were consequently derived indirectly, under the assumption that aggregate price indices like the consumer price index or the general price index are weighted averages of both tradeable and nontradeable prices. This may be represented by the definition of the overall price level P as $P = P_T{}^a P_{NT}{}^{1-a}$. The nontradeables price is therefore $P_{NT} = P^{1/(1-a)} P_T{}^{-a/(1-a)}$. The particular value of a, which is the weight of tradeable goods in the overall price index P used in tables

A1.1 and A1.2, was 0.4.[1] This value is based on the proportion of industrial and agricultural value added to GDP in the early 1970s. As is demonstrated below, however, its actual value is not important in the assessment of exchange rate policy.

Tables A1.1 and A1.2 show the tradeable and nontradeable price indices and their ratio, using export prices with and without coffee in the calculation of tradeable prices and both the Rio de Janeiro consumer price index and the general price index (IGP-DI) to define the aggregate price level P. As may be seen from the tables, there is relatively little difference in the four series derived in this way.

When P_{NT} is derived residually, as is done here, the resulting P_T/P_{NT} series is proportionately equivalent to the common definition of the real rate as ep^*/P. This may be seen by noting that $P_T/P_{NT} = eP^*/P_{NT}$. Since $P_{NT} = P^{1/(1-a)}(eP^*)^{-a/(1-a)}$, $P_T/P_{NT} = (eP^*/P)^{1/(1-a)}$. For a given value of a, the rates defined respectively as P_T/P_{NT} and eP^*/P will move together. As $a < 1$, movements of the P_T/P_{NT} rate will be larger than those of eP^*/P, but will always be in the same direction. Conclusions about real exchange rate trends will therefore be robust to varying assumptions about the value of the share a of tradeables in the general price index.

One consequence of the derivation of P_{NT} as a residual is that the different tradeable price series used give different nontradeable prices. In this particular case, the nontradeable series reflects the inclusion or exclusion of coffee prices in the tradeables index. An alternative definition, referred to in this study as method B, avoids this problem, although it involves potentially restrictive assumptions of its own. Using this approach, the tradeables price was assumed to be a weighted average of wholesale prices in the industrial sector, in agriculture, and of imports. These weights were based on the approximate relative shares of the three sectors in total domestic supply in the early 1970s.[2] The method excludes any direct effect of export prices, implicitly assuming that they would be reflected in the industrial and agricultural price indices. As a result, relatively little weight is given to the exchange rate compared with method A. Since imports are the least important of the three sectors in the definition of P_T, the nominal exchange rate e has relatively little effect on the P_T/P_{NT} series derived using method B.

[1] The assumption that a is constant implicitly denies the effectiveness of changes in P_T/P_{NT} in altering the share of tradeables to nontradeables in total product. If a rise in the ratio shifts expenditures toward nontradeables, the weight a will fall, thus dampening the elasticity of P_T/P_{NT} in relation to eP^*/P.
[2] The weights actually used in the estimates shown in table A1.3 were 0.6, 0.25, and 0.15 respectively for the industrial price index, the agriculture wholesale price, and the cruzeiro import price index. Similar estimates of this type for a more recent period have been made by Braga et al. (1985).

Table A1.1 Prices of tradeables and nontradeables, 1964–1976 (method A, using the consumer price index)

Year	Quarter	Cruzeiro import price index (Dec 1970 = 1)	Cruzeiro export price (including coffee) (Dec 1970 = 1)	Tradeables price index (equal weights)	Nontradeable price index (P = CPI, including coffee)	Tradeable to nontradeable price ratios
1964	I	0.106	0.103	0.104	0.169	0.618
1964	II	0.207	0.207	0.207	0.135	1.530
1964	III	0.271	0.269	0.270	0.136	1.984
1964	IV	0.319	0.324	0.321	0.158	2.039
1965	I	0.334	0.328	0.331	0.206	1.604
1965	II	0.338	0.332	0.335	0.236	1.422
1965	III	0.311	0.328	0.319	0.275	1.160
1965	IV	0.411	0.407	0.409	0.251	1.626
1966	I	0.387	0.338	0.362	0.337	1.075
1966	II	0.406	0.345	0.374	0.382	0.979
1966	III	0.383	0.362	0.372	0.440	0.846
1966	IV	0.393	0.356	0.374	0.473	0.790
1967	I	0.468	0.427	0.447	0.485	0.923
1967	II	0.502	0.431	0.465	0.524	0.888
1967	III	0.491	0.427	0.458	0.572	0.801
1967	IV	0.548	0.440	0.491	0.566	0.867
1968	I	0.593	0.525	0.558	0.570	0.980
1968	II	0.587	0.531	0.558	0.649	0.860
1968	III	0.663	0.604	0.633	0.642	0.985
1968	IV	0.686	0.608	0.646	0.678	0.952
1969	I	0.752	0.622	0.684	0.716	0.954
1969	II	0.798	0.641	0.715	0.749	0.956
1969	III	0.802	0.677	0.737	0.812	0.908
1969	IV	0.809	0.781	0.795	0.849	0.936
1970	I	0.868	0.805	0.836	0.882	0.948
1970	II	0.898	0.840	0.868	0.923	0.941
1970	III	0.921	0.915	0.918	0.997	0.921
1970	IV	1.000	1.000	1.000	1.000	1.000
1971	I	1.019	0.873	0.943	1.124	0.839
1971	II	1.053	0.929	0.989	1.167	0.847
1971	III	1.098	0.951	1.022	1.234	0.828
1971	IV	1.124	1.017	1.069	1.262	0.848
1972	I	1.098	1.332	1.209	1.259	0.960
1972	II	1.100	1.578	1.318	1.248	1.055
1972	III	1.220	1.763	1.466	1.238	1.185
1972	IV	1.247	1.849	1.519	1.243	1.222
1973	I	1.430	1.374	1.402	1.395	1.005
1973	II	1.524	1.626	1.574	1.352	1.164
1973	III	1.697	1.801	1.748	1.318	1.326
1973	IV	2.031	1.849	1.938	1.308	1.481
1974	I	2.476	1.838	2.134	1.463	1.459
1974	II	2.849	2.512	2.675	1.445	1.851
1974	III	2.626	2.719	2.672	1.579	1.693
1974	IV	3.123	3.108	3.116	1.550	2.011
1975	I	3.442	2.994	3.210	1.694	1.895
1975	II	3.700	2.458	3.106	1.962	1.537
1975	III	3.464	3.015	3.232	2.139	1.511
1975	IV	3.427	3.427	3.427	2.286	1.499
1976	I	3.983	3.737	3.858	2.593	1.488
1976	II ·	4.657	4.844	4.750	2.648	1.793
1976	III	4.907	4.874	4.890	2.970	1.646
1976	IV	5.186	6.981	6.017	2.913	2.066

CPI, consumer price index.
The tradeables price is an equally weighted geometric average of import and export prices. The nontradeables price is based on the assumption that tradeables have a weight of 0.4 in the aggregate price index.

Table A1.2 Alternative measures of tradeable to nontradeable price ratios, 1964–1976
(method A, with tradeables prices as the geometric average of export and import prices)

Year	Quarter	Tradeable to nontradeable price ratios (P = CPI, including coffee)	Tradeable to nontradeable price ratios (P = CPI, excluding coffee)	Tradeable to nontradeable price ratios (P = IGP-DI, including coffee)	Tradeable to nontradeable price ratios (P = IGP-DI, excluding coffee)
1964	I	0.618	0.808	0.493	0.644
1964	II	1.530	1.777	1.278	1.484
1964	III	1.984	2.329	1.609	1.888
1964	IV	2.039	2.406	1.625	1.918
1965	I	1.604	1.805	1.363	1.535
1965	II	1.422	1.605	1.280	1.444
1965	III	1.160	1.408	1.062	1.289
1965	IV	1.626	1.982	1.480	1.804
1966	I	1.075	1.551	0.984	1.420
1966	II	0.979	1.346	0.901	1.238
1966	III	0.846	1.256	0.780	1.159
1966	IV	0.790	1.147	0.740	1.075
1967	I	0.923	1.355	0.863	1.267
1967	II	0.888	1.384	0.851	1.327
1967	III	0.801	1.439	0.767	1.378
1967	IV	0.867	1.435	0.810	1.340
1968	I	0.980	1.236	0.883	1.115
1968	II	0.860	1.076	0.793	0.992
1968	III	0.985	1.188	0.909	1.097
1968	IV	0.952	1.166	0.878	1.075
1969	I	0.954	1.162	0.909	1.107
1969	II	0.956	1.146	0.907	1.088
1969	III	0.908	1.078	0.861	1.022
1969	IV	0.936	1.076	0.915	1.051
1970	I	0.948	1.130	0.922	1.099
1970	II	0.941	1.050	0.918	1.024
1970	III	0.921	0.948	0.912	0.939
1970	IV	1.000	1.000	1.000	1.000
1971	I	0.839	1.022	0.830	1.011
1971	II	0.847	1.078	0.819	1.042
1971	III	0.828	1.024	0.811	1.003
1971	IV	0.848	0.962	0.832	0.944
1972	I	0.960	1.017	0.936	0.992
1972	II	1.055	0.955	1.027	0.930
1972	III	1.185	0.920	1.150	0.893
1972	IV	1.222	1.057	1.169	1.012
1973	I	1.005	1.180	0.954	1.121
1973	II	1.164	1.375	1.093	1.291
1973	III	1.326	1.603	1.237	1.495
1973	IV	1.481	1.827	1.380	1.702
1974	I	1.459	1.752	1.373	1.649
1974	II	1.851	2.281	1.683	2.073
1974	III	1.693	2.122	1.568	1.966
1974	IV	2.011	2.565	1.857	2.369
1975	I	1.895	2.387	1.766	2.224
1975	II	1.537	1.901	1.438	1.778
1975	III	1.511	1.869	1.433	1.773
1975.	IV	1.499	1.822	1.417	1.723
1976	I	1.488	1.764	1.444	1.712
1976	II	1.793	1.969	1.738	1.908
1976	III	1.646	1.878	1.515	1.729
1976	IV	2.066	1.948	1.922	1.812

CPI, consumer price index; IGP-DI, indice geral de preços – disponibilidade interna (general price index)

Table A1.3 Prices of tradeables and nontradeables, 1964–1976 (method B, *P* equals the consumer price index)

Year	Quarter	Industrial price index (Dec 1970 = 1)	Agricultural price index (Dec 1970 = 1)	Import price index (Dec 1970 = 1)	Tradeables price index[a]	Non-tradeables index	Tradeable-to-nontradeable ratio
1964	I	0.159	0.175	0.106	0.153	0.131	1.174
1964	II	0.187	0.185	0.207	0.189	0.143	1.320
1964	III	0.209	0.216	0.271	0.219	0.156	1.403
1964	IV	0.257	0.250	0.319	0.264	0.180	1.465
1965	I	0.296	0.267	0.334	0.294	0.224	1.312
1965	II	0.315	0.269	0.338	0.306	0.250	1.224
1965	III	0.321	0.298	0.311	0.314	0.279	1.126
1965	IV	0.338	0.313	0.411	0.341	0.283	1.205
1966	I	0.386	0.347	0.387	0.376	0.328	1.146
1966	II	0.411	0.390	0.406	0.405	0.363	1.117
1966	III	0.426	0.435	0.383	0.421	0.405	1.039
1966	IV	0.446	0.446	0.393	0.438	0.426	1.027
1967	I	0.487	0.478	0.468	0.482	0.461	1.046
1967	II	0.521	0.474	0.502	0.506	0.496	1.020
1967	III	0.537	0.513	0.491	0.524	0.523	1.002
1967	IV	0.549	0.540	0.548	0.547	0.527	1.038
1968	I	0.628	0.564	0.593	0.606	0.540	1.123
1968	II	0.678	0.568	0.587	0.635	0.596	1.064
1968	III	0.715	0.595	0.663	0.675	0.615	1.098
1968	IV	0.740	0.630	0.686	0.703	0.641	1.095
1969	I	0.773	0.634	0.752	0.732	0.684	1.070
1969	II	0.814	0.658	0.798	0.769	0.713	1.079
1969	III	0.833	0.766	0.802	0.811	0.762	1.065
1969	IV	0.848	0.831	0.809	0.838	0.819	1.023
1970	I	0.894	0.877	0.868	0.886	0.848	1.044
1970	II	0.940	0.890	0.898	0.921	0.887	1.038
1970	III	0.986	0.960	0.921	0.970	0.961	1.009
1970	IV	1.000	1.000	1.000	1.000	1.000	1.000
1971	I	1.044	1.091	1.019	1.051	1.046	1.005
1971	II	1.110	1.161	1.053	1.114	1.079	1.032
1971	III	1.155	1.186	1.098	1.154	1.138	1.014
1971	IV	1.183	1.247	1.124	1.189	1.175	1.012
1972	I	1.238	1.344	1.098	1.241	1.238	1.002
1972	II	1.281	1.355	1.100	1.270	1.279	0.993
1972	III	1.326	1.459	1.220	1.341	1.314	1.021
1972	IV	1.361	1.523	1.247	1.382	1.323	1.044
1973	I	1.416	1.609	1.430	1.464	1.355	1.080
1973	II	1.462	1.663	1.524	1.519	1.385	1.097
1973	III	1.520	1.712	1.697	1.592	1.403	1.135
1973	IV	1.588	1.777	2.031	1.695	1.430	1.185
1974	I	1.736	1.996	2.476	1.896	1.582	1.198
1974	II	1.914	2.282	2.849	2.123	1.686	1.259
1974	III	2.026	2.224	2.626	2.156	1.821	1.184
1974	IV	2.153	2.332	3.123	2.322	1.885	1.232
1975	I	2.279	2.434	3.442	2.465	2.021	1.220
1975	II	2.457	2.517	3.700	2.628	2.150	1.223
1975	III	2.579	2.923	3.464	2.781	2.364	1.176
1975	IV	2.771	3.120	3.427	2.947	2.528	1.186
1976	I	3.019	3.559	3.983	3.279	2.889	1.135
1976	II	3.276	4.017	4.657	3.634	3.166	1.148
1976	III	3.646	4.855	4.907	4.095	3.343	1.225
1976	IV	3.884	5.205	5.186	4.364	3.608	1.210

CPI, consumer price index.
[a] Weighted average of the three previous indices.

Appendix 2

Import Liberalization and the Equilibrium Exchange Rate

The conventional model of trade liberalization assumes either implicitly or explicitly that, in the absence of external financing through the capital account, import liberalization will lead to an increase in exports through an induced depreciation, under flexible exchange rates, or through an appropriate devaluation, if the exchange rate is fixed. This model may be developed using an elasticities approach under several simplifying assumptions. First, under a small-country assumption, it is assumed that the elasticities of demand for exportable goods and of supply of importable goods are large enough to be treated as infinite. Second, cross-elasticities between exportables and importables in both production and consumption are assumed to be negligible. Finally, it is assumed that the income effects of changes in tariffs and exchange rates can be ignored. Under these assumptions, the appropriate percentage real depreciation or devaluation r can then be calculated.

The elasticity of supply of exports is

$$e_X = \frac{dX}{dp} \frac{p}{X} = \frac{dX}{X} \frac{1 + r}{r} \tag{A2.1}$$

since r is the increase in the price of exportables. The corresponding elasticity of demand for importables is

$$e_M = \frac{dM}{dp} \frac{p}{M} = \frac{dM}{M} \frac{1 + r}{t - r} \tag{A2.2}$$

since the net change in the price of importables is the percentage depreciation r minus the tariff t which is to be removed. Exports (X) and imports (M) are valued at the free-trade exchange rate. Maintenance of the trade balance requires that

$$dM = dX \tag{A2.3}$$

Combining (A2.1)–(A2.3) and solving for r yields the percentage depreciation or devaluation, which can be interpreted as the percentage rise in the price of traded goods when money prices are expressed in terms of the nontradeable numeraire:

$$r = \frac{t}{1 + e_X X / e_M M} \qquad (A2.4)$$

With balanced trade and for $e_X > 0$ and $e_M > 0$, equation (A2.4) implies that $0 < r < t$, so that the required real depreciation is less than the percentage tariff cut. If the elasticities of export supply and import demand are approximately equal, and the trade balance is in equilibrium at free-trade prices (equivalent to assuming no net external financing and no other net flows in the current account), the required depreciation r is $t/2$. If both elasticities are low in the short run but increase together over the long run, then it is possible that the required depreciation remains equal to $t/2$ throughout the adjustment period.

For a country whose export list is concentrated in primary products and their derivatives, however, as was the case in Brazil in 1964, it is quite possible that the initial elasticity of export supply is low and that it lags the increase in the elasticity of import demand. This would consequently require a larger initial exchange rate adjustment, since $dr/de X < 0$, followed by gradual appreciation as eX increases. Temporary surplus capacity in the export sector, in contrast, would raise the short-run elasticity, reducing the size of the initial devaluation required.

From a policy point of view, it is clear that the determination of the initial devaluation required to maintain the trade balance following an import liberalization depends on several factors of which none except t is known with much precision. In a broad trade liberalization with many importable goods, moreover, even the tariff rate t is uncertain, since it is a weighted average of many individual rates. Since the short-run elasticities of export supply and import demand may be affected by temporary excess capacity in their respective sectors, determination of the appropriate devaluation to offset the trade balance effects of import liberalization is likely to be considerably more difficult in practice than in theory.

Appendix 3

Production, Export, and Import Quantity Indices

Brazilian economic statistics are more extensive and complete for the industrial sectors of the economy than for other sectors. "Industry," however, is defined broadly, and includes several activities that involve the processing of primary products. Sawn lumber, or orange juice, for example, are included in many compilations of "industrial" exports. Under this broad definition of industrial activity, the share of "industry" in real GDP in 1970 was about 36 percent and rising, while the share of manufactured and semi-processed products in total export value in 1970 was nearly 25 percent and was also increasing.

Data on the sectors of manufacturing industry, or the Indústrias de Transformação, are most readily available at a two-digit level for 20 sectors.[1] The IBGE further subdivides the two-digit system to a three- and four-digit level, but many fewer data are published at these levels. At the two-digit level of aggregation a number of sectors are simultaneously producers of exportables and producers of importables. The implicit ambiguities in the classification of specific products, particularly in the larger and more heterogeneous sectors, require that caution be used in interpreting data at the two-digit level. Over the past two decades, moreover, the IBGE has reclassified some items from one industrial census to another. Although there have been sound reasons for doing so, the comparability of some series over time may be weakened.

A further problem arises from the increasing sophistication of Brazilian industry over the 1965–75 period, when many new products appeared both in production and on the export list. Most sectoral level data, like those used in this study and those provided by both the IBGE and the Fundação Getúlio Vargas, are in the form of index numbers, intended to represent quantity or price trends for the sector. Early (pre-1965) quantity indices are frequently direct fixed-base indices, formed by defining a "representa-

[1] Excluded from this list is *Diversos*, or miscellaneous industrial activities.

tive" group of items to approximate physical production trends in the given sector. Such measures are commonly constructed using Laspeyres indices. More recent series, including the quantity series used here for the period from 1965, have been constructed indirectly by Bonelli and Werneck (1980) by deflating a current value production series by a price index (Paasche). These investigators have argued that, at least for Brazilian production statistics, the latter procedure is more accurate.

Similar problems arise with quantity series for exports and imports. An additional difficulty is created by the change, between 1970 and 1971, in the Brazilian merchandise classification system. No official equivalence list or key was published, and some trade time series that cover this period may not be strictly comparable before and after the change.

The data presented in tables A3.1 and A3.2 are not complete for all 20 sectors at the two-digit level. Production series are not available before 1975 for pharmaceuticals or before 1970 for plastics. Published export quantity series are available for only eight sectors: metals and metal products, machinery, electrical and communications equipment, transpor-

Table A3.1 Production, export, and import quantity indices, 1964–1974 (1970 = 100)

Year	Production	Exports	Imports	Production	Exports	Imports
	Nonmetallic mineral products			Metals and metal products		
1964	68.2	12.69	12.3	57.5	12.00	51.6
1965	61.7	28.33	16.3	55.3	32.00	48.1
1966	66.4	34.24	31.5	71.4	23.20	117.5
1967	66.0	106.30	38.5	71.1	64.90	65.6
1968	83.3	97.92	160.8	88.3	47.00	75.6
1969	90.6	79.81	171.8	94.4	55.30	88.1
1970	100.0	100.00	100.0	100.0	100.00	100.0
1971	104.4	167.28	88.2	112.1	58.60	158.0
1972	118.6	152.19	90.7	129.6	100.00	160.0
1973	138.1	179.49	94.9	137.8	104.00	233.0
1974	158.5	271.59	114.1	144.9	100.00	450.0
	Machinery			Electrical and communications equipment		
1964	69.3	18.90	31.2	46.7	10.50	25.8
1965	53.7	35.30	23.2	54.1	24.60	22.8
1966	64.7	39.70	33.9	61.6	30.70	37.4
1967	62.9	58.20	46.4	68.6	34.90	46.7
1968	77.5	58.70	60.5	87.8	40.30	61.3
1969	85.8	75.70	73.3	95.7	62.30	78.0
1970	100.0	100.00	100.0	100.0	100.00	100.0
1971	123.0	102.00	150.0	116.4	136.00	85.1
1972	149.6	139.00	208.0	141.4	172.00	111.0
1973	189.7	167.00	192.0	181.9	293.00	158.0
1974	211.8	253.00	264.0	200.6	471.00	199.0

	Transportation equipment				Paper products		
1964	55.4	16.40	83.1	64.1	35.30	42.5
1965	55.0	26.00	39.7	63.9	132.70	33.1
1966	63.0	51.90	59.9	68.5	83.50	43.2
1967	59.4	18.00	65.4	77.8	38.10	57.9
1968	74.7	25.00	87.9	84.1	41.70	92.0
1969	90.9	39.40	84.1	95.1	96.70	88.9
1970	100.0	100.00	100.0	100.0	100.00	100.0
1971	124.3	113.00	179.0	107.0	121.20	134.0
1972	153.3	306.00	199.0	105.5	509.50	173.0
1973	194.3	365.00	313.0	161.2	795.80	182.0
1974	231.0	794.00	478.0	121.2	683.30	252.0

	Rubber products				Chemicals		
1964	54.9	78.30	78.5	55.5	45.70	31.2
1965	50.7	60.80	43.0	51.7	55.00	34.6
1966	65.2	32.10	65.4	62.7	56.30	41.9
1967	67.9	13.70	63.9	63.0	68.30	45.5
1968	81.5	10.70	114.6	74.2	59.80	74.4
1969	85.6	24.40	97.2	84.1	87.40	73.6
1970	100.0	100.00	100.0	100.0	100.00	100.0
1971	112.9	105.00	179.4	109.0	86.20	112.0
1972	138.9	72.00	160.3	127.2	116.00	136.0
1973	156.1	118.00	252.8	157.2	146.00	155.0
1974	184.5	183.20	364.2	165.7	149.00	184.0

	Textiles				Food products		
1964	102.4	58.90	13.0	68.2	22.10	70.7
1965	85.0	63.80	5.4	56.4	50.30	53.6
1966	84.0	73.60	4.7	67.7	55.90	72.4
1967	77.0	65.40	16.9	75.9	60.30	86.5
1968	95.9	73.00	125.9	81.6	74.30	83.7
1969	100.1	89.20	65.3	92.5	91.60	84.4
1970	100.0	100.00	100.0	100.0	100.00	100.0
1971	116.6	109.00	156.0	100.4	118.00	81.6
1972	120.9	205.00	194.0	118.1	187.00	77.3
1973	129.3	316.00	226.0	127.9	187.00	117.0
1974	124.7	343.00	353.0	134.9	196.00	87.8

tation equipment, wood products, chemicals, textiles and food products. Export quantity series for an additional seven sectors were constructed for this study using quantity data published in various issues of the *Anuário Estatístico*. These sectors were nonmetallic mineral products, paper, leather products, rubber products, clothing and footwear, beverages, and tobacco products. There are thus 15 sectors of the total 20 for which production and export quantity indices are available.

On the import side, published quantity indices are available for eight sectors: metals and metal products, machinery, electrical and communica-

Table A3.2 Production and export quantity indices, 1964–1974 (1970 = 100)

Year	Wood products		Leather products		Clothing and footwear		Beverages		Tobacco products	
	Production	Exports	Production	Exports	Production	Exports	Production	Exports	Production	Exports
1964	76.2	107.00	65.2	11.20	73.7	5.40	67.0	25.90	88.6	24.40
1965	60.3	117.30	84.5	67.90	70.1	6.20	74.0	11.70	84.4	14.70
1966	69.2	120.80	79.7	91.90	71.2	4.70	82.9	23.10	79.1	53.60
1967	67.0	103.00	85.1	78.60	71.7	9.20	77.9	48.70	84.9	62.90
1968	78.3	129.90	95.8	60.80	81.4	9.70	83.7	53.60	90.2	52.60
1969	91.4	103.60	96.2	111.40	84.8	31.90	91.2	61.60	94.1	86.90
1970	100.00	100.00	100.00	100.00	100.00	100.00	100.00	100.00	100.00	100.00
1971	92.4	115.00	105.2	114.80	94.3	256.00	111.3	91.60	104.9	172.20
1972	102.2	115.00	127.8	211.90	99.0	470.00	116.8	277.50	111.1	187.70
1973	160.4	137.00	139.8	183.40	113.0	801.00	137.5	179.00	118.2	280.40
1974	199.6	105.00	134.6	244.20	115.3	1,062.90	149.0	340.10	133.3	312.90

tions equipment, transportation equipment, paper, chemicals, textiles, and food products. In addition, import quantity series for two additional sectors, nonmetallic mineral products and rubber products, were constructed from the *Anuário Estatístico* data, yielding two sectors with import series. In the remaining five sectors for which export and production quantity indices were obtained, an examination of import statistics led to the conclusion that the few items that might be classified in any of these categories were of negligible quantity, so that an import quantity series in these cases would be meaningless. All these five sectors are either activities in which Brazil may be assumed to enjoy a strong comparative advantage, owing to relatively lower primary commodity input costs (that is, tobacco, wood, or leather products), or consumer goods sectors in which a long tradition of protection had reduced imports to a negligible share of total supply even before 1960 (that is, clothing and footwear or beverages). For the purposes of this study these five sectors were therefore treated as "nonimportable" sectors.

For most of the series shown in tables A3.1 and A3.2, production data are based on the Bonelli and Werneck series. For wood products and leather products the Bonelli and Werneck series ends in 1969. Indices for the post-1969 period were constructed by deflating the *valor da produção* (product value) in current cruzeiros, as reported for the two sectors in various issues of the *Anuário Estatístico*, by the respective wholesale price indices published in *Conjuntura Econômica*, from 1969 onwards.

Export quantity indices were taken from various issues of *Conjuntura Econômica* for eight of the 15 sectors. In the remaining cases (nonmetallic mineral products, paper and paper products, rubber products, leather products, clothing and footwear, beverages, and tobacco products) a direct quantity index was constructed from data in various issues of the *Anuário Estatístico*.

Import quantity series were also taken from *Conjuntura Econômica* data when available. In this group are metals and metal products, machinery, electrical and communications equipment, transportation equipment, paper products, chemicals, textiles, and food products. The remaining two import quantity series, nonmetallic mineral products and rubber products, were constructed from quantity data published in various issues of the *Anuário Estatístico*. The former series is heavily influenced by the behavior of Portland cement imports, particularly in the period of rapid economic growth after 1968 when domestic capacity was inadequate to supply total demand. In the latter series, imports of vehicle tires or materials used in their manufacture were an important component.

Clearly the indices presented in tables A3.1 and A3.2 must be regarded as approximations of general trends in the respective sectors and variables. Sharp changes in an individual year, as occur in several of the series, may therefore reflect as much the difficulties inherent in the construction of the indices as they do actual trends. The apparent degree of precision (usually to the unit or first decimal level) encountered in the published data has been preserved in conversion from one base year to another. In most cases the impression of precision conveyed is spurious. Although there is no easy way to circumvent this problem, these data nevertheless appear adequate for the general purpose for which they are used in this study.

Appendix 4

Import and Export Effective Exchange Rates

Tables A4.1 and A4.2 present sectoral estimates of effective exchange rates for imports and exports. It is assumed here that at the level of aggregation implicit in the classification at the IBGE two-digit level the "law of one price" would not hold, even if we assume a high degree of arbitrage in individual goods markets between the Brazilian economy and the rest of the world. Hence it would be possible to observe considerable divergence between an international price series for a given sector and the domestic price, even in the absence of tariffs, subsidies, or other instruments of commercial policies.

It is therefore meaningful to define the export effective exchange rate for a given sector i as $E_i = rP_i^*(1 + s_i)/P_i$, where r, P_i^*, s_i, and P_i are respectively the nominal exchange rate (in units of home currency per unit of foreign currency), the international price of the sector's product, net export subsidies (expressed as the proportional premium above the free-trade price, for which s_i would be zero), and the domestic price of the sector's product. The import effective exchange rate is defined analogously, with $1 + s_i$ substituted by $1 + t_i$, where t_i is the net tariff in *ad valorem* terms imposed on imports competing with the sector.

Most past studies of Brazilian trade that use an effective exchange rate approach have identified the nominal exchange rate r with the cruzeiro-to-dollar rate. In recent years trade-weighted nominal exchange rates for Brazil have been calculated by Lemgruber and Gouvea Vieira (1981). The nominal exchange rate used in the calculation of effective rates in this study is an index of the annual average cruzeiro-to-dollar rate, as given in various issues of *Conjuntura Econômica*, multiplied by the ratio of the Lemgruber–Vieira multilateral rate to the bilateral rate.

Several problems arise in the choice of an appropriate series for the "world" price P_i^*. Several studies of Brazilian prices have used the price indices for respective imports and exports published in *Conjuntura Econômica*. Although the way in which these indices are constructed and

Table A4.1 Effective exchange rates for imports, 1959–1977

Sector	1959	1960	1961	1962	1963	1964	1965	1966	1967	1968	1969	1970	1971	1972	1973	1974	1975	1976	1977
Nonmetallic mineral products	220.8	217.8	220.8	214.7	176.9	209.4	193.4	172.7	131.6	133.1	149.3	151.0	161.0	160.6	165.9	160.5	237.9	229.0	243.8
Metals	161.6	185.2	203.9	188.8	144.0	183.5	164.9	152.9	134.9	135.3	152.4	147.0	142.5	148.5	141.2	145.7	185.3	193.7	208.2
Machinery	158.8	156.7	157.7	169.1	138.1	166.5	151.6	135.6	127.9	128.7	142.5	144.0	140.3	138.6	143.1	134.8	167.5	159.8	167.7
Electrical and communications equipment	247.3	243.1	241.7	270.4	218.1	260.2	239.8	217.4	156.8	155.1	171.4	171.0	144.3	140.9	143.4	131.2	191.1	171.4	200.9
Transportation equipment	246.5	239.2	240.6	262.6	213.7	256.9	237.3	210.4	153.8	157.4	187.5	191.0	161.7	161.1	162.8	145.1	199.6	191.1	200.9
Paper products	241.6	239.7	234.9	238.8	193.7	231.3	215.1	195.6	145.3	143.7	157.7	158.0	148.7	148.3	159.6	163.1	256.8	243.4	249.8
Rubber products	256.2	252.7	245.3	247.9	203.8	240.3	222.5	201.1	174.2	176.0	195.2	194.0	162.8	157.6	162.2	161.6	212.2	202.5	210.5
Chemicals	446.3	255.1	267.3	236.8	164.9	159.5	143.3	158.0	124.3	158.7	131.5	129.0	121.5	112.6	116.4	117.0	174.9	162.9	158.7
Textiles	379.0	343.3	309.0	309.9	251.9	316.4	309.9	275.5	135.5	135.3	227.5	220.0	194.3	206.2	238.9	274.6	468.2	388.5	440.9
Food products	245.6	219.1	232.6	192.1	121.1	200.2	214.0	176.3	116.7	130.6	148.0	140.0	158.8	180.0	158.9	183.3	225.2	182.8	188.9

Table A4.2 Effective export exchange rates, 1959–1977

Sector	1959	1960	1961	1962	1963	1964	1965	1966	1967	1968	1969	1970	1971	1972	1973	1974	1975	1976	1977
Nonmetallic mineral products	122.65	121.00	122.66	119.97	97.52	117.18	110.66	106.26	121.35	130.01	140.37	142.56	153.44	159.52	164.75	159.16	172.75	167.53	178.08
Metals	106.33	121.81	133.98	122.57	93.50	120.01	111.43	108.62	128.41	137.43	148.75	145.58	151.77	165.77	175.38	172.75	182.31	183.14	203.20
Machinery	117.63	116.06	116.83	114.26	93.31	115.93	113.12	109.15	131.45	141.73	154.89	158.98	165.60	171.25	176.87	165.75	186.69	183.19	191.08
Electrical and communications equipment	134.39	132.14	131.34	126.37	102.30	125.12	123.21	120.14	138.08	145.39	154.84	156.17	160.76	163.72	166.65	151.92	164.98	158.02	163.19
Transportation equipment	132.53	128.61	129.35	126.23	102.75	125.13	122.14	117.28	132.15	144.67	149.77	154.23	163.74	172.16	174.00	154.0	166.84	162.88	170.49
Wood products	124.36	118.04	113.84	112.04	93.88	114.39	107.73	102.90	115.29	132.36	147.74	130.06	143.31	159.38	195.76	166.58	153.47	161.95	183.49
Furniture	114.62	113.81	116.12	114.68	94.56	113.85	112.15	113.64	130.80	142.80	157.61	157.28	162.64	171.67	180.07	164.26	167.83	159.51	166.16
Paper products	128.52	127.49	124.94	123.73	100.36	119.92	115.23	111.41	127.87	134.86	144.97	145.45	147.96	155.47	167.39	170.97	182.71	173.57	178.06
Rubber products	135.54	133.69	129.78	123.31	101.39	120.41	118.87	119.34	134.53	145.81	157.44	156.91	158.38	163.06	167.83	167.02	175.66	168.53	175.00
Leather products	147.46	98.72	115.07	115.64	102.94	142.09	141.63	130.34	134.19	158.36	170.40	140.48	136.96	139.60	124.73	124.42	143.63	142.38	149.99
Chemicals	249.02	122.65	140.85	111.17	82.82	97.88	104.46	108.55	88.04	106.09	113.41	136.14	136.03	113.19	225.65	228.05	157.53	137.52	146.46
Pharmaceuticals	150.30	148.64	147.28	140.57	113.91	136.81	128.33	118.10	130.63	132.46	135.79	132.78	133.10	133.12	134.47	119.78	127.74	121.76	126.15
Plastic products	135.54	133.69	129.78	123.31	101.39	122.06	121.03	119.74	137.23	148.20	158.74	158.36	158.97	160.98	165.69	164.83	173.63	166.91	173.25
Textiles	132.52	120.05	108.05	110.30	89.65	114.58	118.59	113.28	123.46	132.08	156.78	155.01	161.61	180.52	209.15	239.47	297.92	253.22	285.88
Clothing and footwear	117.41	104.52	97.41	98.66	81.58	108.11	115.01	110.23	122.38	128.81	158.20	159.77	161.42	166.14	169.18	172.84	203.36	187.40	203.16
Food products	124.67	111.20	118.10	105.54	65.66	110.07	119.54	101.35	112.81	131.99	138.81	132.49	123.03	123.87	151.23	144.45	149.74	123.71	123.61
Beverages	120.07	117.61	119.11	116.91	95.59	118.08	144.75	175.85	186.68	196.88	210.34	216.64	218.21	218.03	233.78	221.98	244.09	235.89	269.58
Tobacco products	112.90	111.13	112.13	109.67	92.06	111.84	124.53	112.36	127.95	137.06	152.34	147.04	161.57	168.11	176.33	165.59	173.17	157.84	163.59

derived is not fully explained in *Conjuntura Econômica*, several of them appear to be indices based on the unit value of imports or exports. Some difficulties arise in using such data as a measure of world prices. Among them is their sensitivity to modest changes in the composition of actual exports or imports, which may reflect trade decisions that have little to do with actual changes in the relevant international prices faced by exporters and importers. Examination of the *Conjuntura Econômica* price series suggests that this may have been a serious problem in the 1960s. Another problem arises from measurement error in the export or import quantity. Since this is used to calculate the unit value, which is total value of exports or imports divided by the quantity, econometric estimates of export or import response that use unit values as proxies for international prices will be biased.[1]

To avoid these problems, the "world" price used for a given sector in this study is taken from the most closely corresponding series published in the group of US wholesale price indices in the *Survey of Current Business*. In most cases, the correspondence at the aggregate two-digit level is close, since the US classification at the two-digit level and that of IBGE are similar.

Domestic price series P_i are available prior to 1970 for only six of the 18 industrial sectors for which export effective exchange rates were calculated. These indices, published in *Conjuntura Econômica*, are metals and metal products, leather products, chemicals, textiles and clothing, and food products. For the remaining 12 sectors, the wholesale price index for industrial products (series 18 in *Conjuntura Econômica*) was used to measure P_i. An alternative to this procedure for the period from 1970 through 1977 would be the use of individual sector indices available in *Conjuntura Econômica* beginning in 1970. This approach was not followed owing due to the potential discontinuity in the resulting series between 1969 and 1970.

The remaining elements in the effective rate calculations are the net subsidy s_i or net tariff t_i rates. The export subsidy rates by sector, which are shown in table A4.3 are derived under a number of simplifying assumptions, which should be noted. As was noted in chapter 6, the export incentives were introduced in stages over the 1964–70 period, beginning with measures that simply reduced the anti-export bias of Brazilian value-added taxes and gradually progressed to true subsidies. The approach used here parallels on a sectoral level that taken by Tyler (1976), Cardoso (1980), and Musalem (1981) for manufactured exports as a whole, and uses the work of Savasini et al. (1974) to obtain sectoral estimates. The

[1] In a simple bivariate model with only one explanatory variable the bias would be downward; in a more general specification the calculation of the bias becomes more complicated.

Table A4.3 Export subsidies and incentives, 1963–1977

Sector	1963	1964	1965	1966	1967	1968	1969	1970	1971	1972	1973	1974	1975	1976	1977
Nonmetallic mineral products	1.000	1.002	1.036	1.101	1.293	1.368	1.420	1.426	1.449	1.510	1.510	1.508	1.517	1.529	1.527
Metals	1.000	1.007	1.041	1.094	1.276	1.362	1.435	1.456	1.491	1.563	1.564	1.556	1.591	1.633	1.623
Machinery	1.000	1.031	1.105	1.192	1.378	1.475	1.565	1.590	1.629	1.705	1.705	1.697	1.738	1.789	1.778
Electrical and communications equipment	1.000	1.029	1.099	1.183	1.383	1.472	1.545	1.562	1.593	1.661	1.662	1.656	1.684	1.718	1.710
Transportation equipment	1.000	1.013	1.071	1.160	1.349	1.443	1.526	1.542	1.580	1.667	1.667	1.661	1.689	1.722	1.714
Wood products	1.000	1.000	1.017	1.051	1.233	1.279	1.295	1.301	1.309	1.323	1.323	1.321	1.331	1.343	1.340
Furniture	1.000	1.000	1.060	1.181	1.374	1.477	1.568	1.573	1.612	1.720	1.721	1.719	1.727	1.737	1.735
Paper products	1.000	1.001	1.034	1.099	1.303	1.389	1.453	1.455	1.482	1.563	1.563	1.562	1.565	1.569	1.568
Rubber products	1.000	1.007	1.074	1.193	1.375	1.475	1.564	1.569	1.606	1.707	1.707	1.706	1.714	1.723	1.721
Leather products	1.000	1.001	1.032	1.093	1.265	1.336	1.390	1.405	1.431	1.486	1.487	1.482	1.506	1.536	1.530
Chemicals	1.000	1.007	1.036	1.079	1.255	1.315	1.352	1.361	1.379	1.415	1.415	1.409	1.428	1.448	1.444
Pharmaceuticals	1.000	1.005	1.029	1.068	1.243	1.299	1.327	1.328	1.340	1.376	1.376	1.376	1.377	1.377	1.377
Plastic products	1.000	1.021	1.093	1.197	1.402	1.499	1.577	1.584	1.612	1.686	1.686	1.684	1.694	1.706	1.704
Textiles	1.000	1.018	1.075	1.155	1.348	1.445	1.530	1.550	1.589	1.672	1.672	1.666	1.699	1.740	1.731
Clothing and footwear	1.000	1.038	1.125	1.225	1.405	1.498	1.582	1.598	1.634	1.716	1.716	1.711	1.737	1.768	1.761
Food products	1.000	1.001	1.017	1.047	1.228	1.283	1.313	1.325	1.340	1.367	1.367	1.363	1.383	1.407	1.402
Beverages	1.000	1.035	1.312	1.798	1.983	2.078	2.161	2.166	2.169	2.198	2.283	2.282	2.290	2.300	2.298
Tobacco products	1.000	1.002	1.065	1.188	1.373	1.474	1.565	1.570	1.609	1.717	1.718	1.716	1.724	1.734	1.732

An entry in the table refers to the value of $1 + s_{it}$, where s_{it} is the net percentage subsidy in sector i and year t. Thus exports from the machinery sector in 1970, for example, enjoyed a 59 percent subsidy in relation to the price they would receive without subsidies and incentives.

Savasini group estimated the net reduction in taxes paid or net subsidy per cruzeiro of export by sector in 1971 for the six major fiscal incentives. The index for each sector thus starts at zero in the period before 1964 and increases in steps as each incentive was successively introduced, the height of each step being derived from the Savasini estimates. This information was supplemented with data on credit subsidies by sector for the last few years of the period, obtained from various issues of the Relatório CACEX and the Boletim do Banco do Brasil and the interest rates on 360-day *letras de câmbio*, as reported in *Conjuntura Econômica*.[2]

Nominal tariff estimates by sector were used to obtain the corresponding commercial policy measure for the effective import exchange rate estimates. Each set follows the two-digit industrial classification used throughout this study. It was assumed that the nominal tariff changed by a discrete amount at given times over the 1959–77 period, and that six sets of nominal tariff estimates could be used to approximate the behavior of $1 + t_i$ over time. For the period from 1959 through 1961, the source was Fishlow's estimate for 1958. Bergsman's estimates (1970) were used for the 1962–6 period and the 1967–8 period. The estimates for 1969 and 1970 were taken from a World Bank study, *Current Economic Position and Prospects of Brazil* (1973), which presented estimates for early 1969. The 1971–4 estimate is from Tyler (1976). The post-oil-shock rate after 1974 was taken from another World Bank study, *Política Indústrial e Exportação de Manufaturados do Brasil* (1983). The resulting $1 + t_i$ series for each sector is thus a step function, changing little over the first eight years of the period and falling in 1967. There was then a temporary rise for the 1969–70 period and a new fall in the early 1970s, followed by a steep rise in 1975.

2 In the absence of either published or even publicly available data about export financing by sector in this period, the estimates presented here are approximations. This type of incentive, which was ignored in other studies with the exception of Musalem (1981), became increasingly important in the 1970s and was definitely not neutral in an intersectoral sense.

References

Bacha, Edmar L. (1976) *Os Mitos de uma Década*, Rio de Janeiro: Paz e Terra.

Bacha, Edmar L. (1979) "Crescimento econômico e salários urbanos e rurais: o caso do Brasil." *Pesquisa e Planejamento Econômico*, 9 (3), December, 585–627.

Baer, Werner (1983) *The Brazilian Economy – Growth and Development*, 2nd edn. New York: Praeger.

Banco Central, *Boletim do Banco Central*, various issues, Brasilia: Banco Central.

Bergsman, Joel (1970) *Brazil – Industrialization and Trade Policies*. London: Oxford University Press for the OECD.

Bergsman, Joel (1971) "Foreign Trade Policies in Brazil." Mimeo. Rio de Janeiro: USAID.

Bonelli, Regis and Dorothea F. F. Werneck (1980) "Desempenho industrial: auge e desaceleração nos anos 70." In Wilson Suzigan, ed., *Indústria: Política, Instituições e Desenvolvimento*. Rio de Janeiro: IPEA.

Braga, Helson, Flavio Castelo Branco, and Pedro Malan (1985) "Balança comercial, preços relativos e a relação câmbio/salário no Brasil," *Pesquisa e Planejamento Econômico*, 15 (1) April, 73–106.

CACEX (Carteira do Comércio Exterior), *Brasil – Comércio Exterior*, various issues. Rio de Janeiro.

Cardoso, Eliana and Rudiger Dornbusch (1980) "Uma equação para as exportações Brasileira de Economia 34(2), April–June, 241–50.

Cardoso, Eliana and Rudiger Dornbusch (1980) "Uma Equação para as exportações brasileiras de produtos manufaturados." *Revista Brasileira de Economia*, 34(3) July–September, 429–37.

Carvalho, José Luis and Claudio Haddad (1980) *Estrategias Comerciais e Absorção de Mão-de-Obra no Brasil*. Rio de Janeiro: Fundação Getúlio Vargas.

Chenery, Hollis B. (1960) "Patterns of industrial growth," *American Economic Review*, 50, 624–54.

Coes, Donald V. (1979) *The Impact of Price Uncertainty: a Study of Brazilian Exchange Rate Policy*. New York: Garland.

Corden, Warner Max (1971) *The Theory of Protection*. London: Oxford University Press.

Damiao, Vitoria F. (1984) "A explicação de insolvencias num modelo macroeconômico." Masters thesis, COPPEAD, Rio de Janeiro, unpublished.

Díaz-Alejandro, Carlos F. (1971) "Some aspects of the Brazilian experience with foreign aid." In J. Bhagwati, R. W. Jones, R. Mundell, and J. Vanek, eds, *Trade, Balance of Payments and Growth*. Amsterdam: North-Holland.

Díaz-Alejandro, Carlos F. (1983) "Stories of the 1930's for the 1980's." In P. Aspe Armella, R. Dornbusch, and M. Obstfeld, eds, *Financial Policies and the World Capital Market: the Problem of Latin American Countries*, Chicago, IL: University of Chicago Press.

Dornbusch, Rudiger (1983) "Panel discussion on the southern cone." *IMF Staff Papers*, 30, March, 173–6.

Dornbusch, Rudiger, Daniel Valente Dantas, Clarice Pechman, Roberto de Rezende Rocha, and Demetrio Simões (1983) "The black market for dollars in Brazil." *Quarterly Journal of Economics*, 98, February, 25–40.

Edwards, Sebastián (1984) "The order of liberalization of the external sector in developing countries." Princeton, NJ: Princeton University International Finance Section, Essay no. 156.

Fishlow, Albert (1975) Foreign Trade Regimes and Economic Development: Brazil. Mimeo, summary for NBER series, vol. X.

Frenkel, Jacob (1983) "Panel discussion on the southern cone." *IMF Staff papers*, 30, March, 1964–73.

FGV (Fundaçao Getúlio Vargas), *Conjuntura Econômica*, various issues.

FGV, *Sondagem Industrial*, quarterly, various issues.

Furtado, Celso (1963) *The Economic Growth of Brazil*. Berkeley, CA: University of California Press.

IBGE (Instituto Brasileiro de Geografia e Estatística), *Anuario Estatístico*, various issues. Rio de Janeiro: IBGE.

IBGE (1959, 1970, 1975) *Censo de Comércio*. Rio de Janeiro: IBGE.

IBGE (1959, 1970, 1975) *Censo Industrial*. Rio de Janeiro: IBGE.

IBGE (1959, 1970, 1975) *Censo de Serviços*. Rio de Janeiro: IBGE.

Kafka, Alexandre (1956) "The Brazilian exchange auction system." *Review of Economics and Statistics*, 38, August, 308–22.

Lara Resende, Andre (1982) "A política brasileira de estabilização." *Pesquisa e Planejamento Econômico*, 12 (3), December, 757–806.

Lemgruber, Antonio Carlos and José M. Gouvea Vieira (1981) "Taxas efetivas de câmbio – o caso brasileiro, 1973–1978." In Paulo Nogueira Batista Jr et al., eds, *Ensaios sobre o Setor Externo da Economia Brasileira*, pp. 113–58. Rio de Janeiro: Instituto Brasileiro de Economia of the Fundação Getúlio Vargas.

Lessa, Carlos (1964) "Fifteen years of economic policy in Brazil." *Economic Bulletin for Latin America*, 9 (2), 153–214.

McKinnon, Ronald I. (1973) *Money and Capital in Economic Development*. Washington, DC: Brookings Institution.

Mendonça de Barros, José R., Helenamaria Lobato, Maria Angelica Travolo, and Maria Helena G. P. Zockun (1975) "Sistema fiscal e incentivos às exportações." *Revista Brasileira de Economia*, 29 (4), October–December, 3–24.

Morley, Samuel and Gordon Smith (1970) "On the measurement of import substitution." *American Economic Review*, 60, September, 728–35.

Musalem, Alberto R. (1981) "Política de subsidios e exportações de manufaturados no Brasil." *Revista Brasileira de Economia*, 35 (1), January–March, 17–41.

Pastore, Afonso Celso, José Augusto Arantes Savasini, Joal de Azambuja Rosa, and Honorio Kume (1979) *Promoção Efetiva as Exportações no Brasil*. Rio de Janeiro: Fundação Centro de Estudos do Comércio Exterior.

Pechman, Clarice (1984) *O Dolar Paralelo no Brasil*. Rio de Janeiro: Paz e Terra.

Savasini, José, Helenamaria Lobato, Maria Angelica Travolo, and Maria Helena G. P. Zockun (1974) "O sistema brasileira de promoção as exportações." Mimeo. Instituto de Pesquisas Econômicas, Universidade de São Paulo, São Paulo.

Suplicy, Eduardo (1976) *Os Efeitos das Minidesvalorizações na Economia Brasileira*. Rio de Janeiro: Fundação Getúlio Vargas.

Tavares, Maria da Conceição (1964) "The growth and decline of import substitution in Brazil." *Economic Bulletin for Latin America*, 9(1) 1–59.

Tyler, William G. (1976) *Manufactured Export Expansion and Industrialization in Brazil*. Tübingen: J. C. B. Mohr.

Von Doellinger, Carlos, Leonardo C. Cavalcanti, and Flavio Castelo Branco (1977) *Política e Estrutura das Importações Brasileiras*. Rio de Janeiro: IPEA.

Von Doellinger, Carlos, Hugo Barros de Castro Faria, Raimundo Nonato Mendonça Ramos, and Leonardo Caserta Cavalcanti (1973) *Transformação da Estrutura das Exportações Brasileiras: 1964/70*. Rio de Janeiro: IPEA.

World Bank (1983) *Brasil – Política Industrial e Exportação de Manufaturados do Brasil* (Portuguese version of World Bank Country Study, *Brazil – Industrial Policies and Manufactured Exports*). Rio de Janeiro: Fundaçao Getúlio Vargas.

Part II

Colombia

Jorge García García
Consultant, Colombia
The World Bank, Washington, D.C.

Contents

List of Figures

List of Tables

Acknowledgments

I would like to express my gratitude to Domingo Cavallo, Armeane Choksi, Joaquín Cottani, Michael Michaely, Julio Nogués, and Demetris Papageorgiou for their comments on the drafts presented to the conferences in Buenos Aires, Viña del Mar, and Salvador (Bahía) that formed the basis for the various chapters of this manuscript. The comments made by Joaquín Cottani, Anthony Rayner, and Marcelo Selowsky on the manuscript presented in the final conference in Lisbon were very helpful in improving the content and form and sharpening the focus of the discussion in the manuscript. I would also like to express my gratitude to Franca Casazza de Galante for her invaluable help in this research. Finally, I would like to thank an anonymous reviewer for his comments on a preliminary version of the manuscript.

Mario Blejer started this project and I joined him later, taking over from him when he withdrew in May 1985. Chapter 1, with some modification, is his work. Chapters 4 and 5 reflect collaboration between myself and Javier Fernández, and I thank him for his help.

After the Lisbon conference the manuscript was substantially revised, especially chapters 4 and 5. All the employment figures were checked again and revised when that was necessary, and all the regressions to establish the response of sectors were run again and the costs of liberalization were recalculated. The unemployment cost of liberalization was calculated from 1970 rather than from 1975, as had been done initially. Therefore the estimates in this final version as well as their interpretation are somewhat different from those in previous versions.

Although various people were involved in the preparation of this study, I assume full responsibility for the study.

Introduction

This case study is an analytical history of the factors that contributed to the creation of a more or less open trade regime in Colombia between 1967 and 1982, and the reversal of trade liberalization in 1983–4. Trade liberalization understood as the dismantling of tariff and nontariff barriers to trade did not stand high among policymakers' objectives in Colombia. Trade liberalization understood as the adoption of any policy that results in the reduction of premium associated with the quantitative restrictions (QRs) component of the protective structure did not stand high as an explicit objective of Colombian policymakers.[1] Nevertheless, other policy goals high on the agenda of Colombian policymakers like export promotion and the avoidance of recurrent crises in the balance of payments led to the adoption of trade and macroeconomic policies that finally resulted in trade liberalization understood in both the first and second senses mentioned above.

Although four episodes of trade liberalization are mentioned in chapter 1 (1951–2, 1954–5, 1965–6, and 1967–82), only the last was long enough and sufficiently rich in information to permit a detailed analysis of the impact of liberalization on industrial employment, where most of the negative short-term effects of liberalization would normally be felt. During this period the speed at which tariffs and nontariff barriers to imports were reduced varied, in part because the commitment by the Colombian government to reduce them was not strong enough (chapter 2) and in part because the foreign exchange problems that might have given Colombia a greater incentive to encourage exports and provide protection to import-competing activities via a high real exchange rate (the peso equivalent of foreign prices divided by an index of domestic prices) rather than tariffs and QRs did not persist. In addition, misconceptions about the impact of import liberalization, as well as faulty economic reasoning, inadequate macroeconomic management, and the opposition of vested interests all

---

[1] This is the definition adopted by Anne Krueger in her 1978 summary of the National Bureau of Economic Research project (Krueger, 1978).

helped to reverse much of the liberalization achieved by 1981 (chapters 3 and 6).

Reduction of tariffs and QRs did not encounter much political opposition between 1967 and 1974, chiefly because a high rate of general economic growth (6.4 percent per year) and a much higher rate of growth in the industrial sector (8.9 percent per year) minimized the negative impacts of such reduction. Another important reason was that an increasing real exchange rate at least in part offset the reduction in protection produced by the lowering of tariffs and nontariff barriers. Furthermore, import liberalization did not make deep inroads in the Colombian economy.

From 1975 on, however, reduction of barriers to imports aroused substantial opposition. There seemed to be a real possibility that enlarged inflows of imports would become permanent, since a foreign exchange shortage did not appear likely to occur any time soon due to Colombia's accumulation of substantial reserves to pay for imports. Furthermore, the high rates of economic growth enjoyed by the country prior to 1975 had disappeared. Thus, the advance toward reduction of import barriers slowed down between 1975 and 1978. The trend toward such reduction then accelerated in 1979 as part of a general policy of price stabilization, but the poor economic performance of the country during this period – and, in particular, the poor performance of the industrial sector – brought an end to import liberalization in 1983–4 (chapter 4). The large foreign exchange inflows enjoyed by the country since the mid-1970s reduced the premium associated with the QR component of Colombia's protective structure. The reduction in this premium eased the overall management of QRs but protection for some pockets of the industrial sector was still well entrenched. Thus, although a formal reduction in QRs is not observed in various years, a more relaxed management of QRs did in fact take place after the mid-1970s.

Even though the premium on QRs probably fell considerably in Colombia between 1967 and 1982, by not reducing tariffs and QRs sufficiently the country did not liberalize as much as it could have done. Therefore the story of trade liberalization in Colombia understood as the reduction of tariffs and dismantling of QRs on imports is one of lost opportunities. Policy-induced distortions in the domestic capital market and the use of inadequate instruments of monetary management prevented proper management of foreign exchange inflows. The situation was then exacerbated by inflationary financing of the government's budget deficits. Nor, of course, did the worldwide recession of 1980–2 help matters. Colombia's annual rate of economic growth, which had been declining since 1979, fell to 0.95 percent in 1982, its lowest level since 1950. Industrial production in 1982 decreased by 2.1 percent, the largest decrease since 1950. Given these circumstances, import liberalization became an easy target. It was frequently criticized on grounds that it was primarily responsible for the country's poor economic performance. Attributing the recession in the industrial sector to liberalization was mistaken, however. As shown in chapter 5, import liberalization reduced industrial value added by an average of less than 2 percent in 1980–2.

The development of a huge current account deficit in 1982 (7 percent of gross domestic product (GDP)) and projections that the deficit would be just as large in 1983 were a windfall for industrial capitalists and the better-off industrial workers, who successfully pressed the government to terminate liberalization. Otherwise, they argued, Colombia would suffer a balance-of-payments crisis. Thus, both vested interests and economic ideology played important roles in the policy shift that led to a massive increase in import restrictions between 1983 and April 1984.

Import liberalization was never seen as a primary policy objective in Colombia. Nor was it seen as a way to accelerate the nation's rate of growth or to improve the allocation of economic resources. As a result, its direction and speed were determined mainly by internal macroeconomic policies and international economic conditions. For this reason, in chapter 7, as much emphasis is placed on internal macroeconomic policies as on the economic implications of liberalization itself to explain the sharp reversal of trade policy in 1983–4.

1

An Overview of Colombia's Economy and Commercial Policies

Attributes of the Economy

During the decade of the 1970s, Colombia's primary sector (agriculture and mining) generated 25 percent of total gross output, while industry and services produced 35 percent and 40 percent respectively. In terms of value added, the primary sector contributed, on average, 30 percent of total value added, while the industrial and services sectors contributed 18 percent and 52 percent respectively.

Coffee is Colombia's major legal export commodity, contributing more than 40 percent of exports of goods and services. Industrial exports increased their share in exports of goods and services from 12 percent in the mid-1960s to 30 percent in 1974, and then declined in importance to a 25-percent share of exports in the period 1975–82.

The composition of imports differs widely from that of exports. The bulk of imports of goods and services is composed of manufactured or semi-manufactured goods, which increased their share from 74 to 81 percent between the mid-1960s and early 1970s. Agricultural imports are a low 6 percent of total imports, and the rest of imports comprise services (around 15 percent) and mining (around 4 percent).[1]

Population Trends and the Labor Market

The 1985 Census indicated that the population of Colombia had risen to 28.5 million. (Censuses in 1951, 1964, and 1973 showed the population to be 11.5 million, 17.5 million, and 22.9 million respectively.) The spread of education, migration from rural to urban areas, and an active birth control

---

[1] The figures in this section come from Departamento Administrativo Nacional de Estadística (DANE) (1985) and from unpublished information provided by DANE's Division de Cuentas Nacionales.

campaign, however, have helped to bring about a sharp decrease in the rate of population growth, thereby offsetting falling infant mortality rates and higher life expectancy. The annual rate of population growth accelerated from 2.8 percent in the 1940s to close to 3.4 percent in the 1950s, and then fell to 2.5 percent during the mid-1960s to mid-1970s. In the 1973–83 period, the rate fell even further, to 2.0 percent (see García García, 1988, appendix table 1).

Another important development was a rapid increase in Colombia's urban population. Rural-to-urban migration was the main factor in increasing the urban share of the total population from less than one third in 1938 to almost two third in 1983. The urban population grew by about 4.1 percent per year between 1951 and 1983, well above the national average population growth rate of 2.6 percent (see García García, 1988, appendix table 2).

These demographic features had a strong effect on Colombia's labor market. The rate of growth of the labor force between the mid-1950s and the early 1970s surpassed growth in the rate of increase of demand for labor, and labor market conditions deteriorated. Between 1973 and 1978, however, employment grew by an estimated 6 percent per year, as a result of rapid economic growth and a significant expansion in labor intensive production. The major share of employment growth took place in public utilities (electricity, gas, and water), transportation and communications, trade (commerce, banking, finance, insurance), government services, and personal services. The tertiary (services) sector accounted for about 1.1 million new jobs, or 56 percent of net employment expansion during the period. Manufacturing also contributed strongly to the employment boom of 1973–8, with approximately 445,000 new jobs (22 percent of the total) (see García García, 1988, appendix table 3).

Developments in real wages reflected demographic and labor market trends. The share of labor in value added rose moderately over the second half of the 1960s, declined sharply in the first six years of the 1970s, and then increased in the remainder of the decade. The real wages of the rural and urban poor stagnated until the mid-1970s, and then improved significantly before deteriorating somewhat in the early 1980s. Real agricultural wages were stagnant during the period 1955–64. In the latter year they were equivalent to about 90 percent of the wages of unskilled construction workers and 33 percent of the wages of industrial workers. Except for a small increase in the early 1960s, real wages in agriculture changed little until 1971, after which they increased substantially until 1980 (see García García, 1988, appendix table 4).

The wages of manufacturing workers rose abruptly between 1960 and 1963, accompanied by a smaller increase in the wages of white-collar workers. Wages for both types of workers showed modest gains during the rest of the 1960s, a loss of these gains during the period 1970–6, and then an upturn until the end of the decade. As a whole, the long-term pattern was one of fluctuation around a flat trend. The wage advantage of manufacturing workers over unskilled construction workers, and especially over agricultural workers, narrowed drastically toward the end of the 1970s (see García García, 1988, appendix table 4).

Economic Growth and the Evolution of the Productive Structure

The economy of Colombia expanded at an average rate of 5.7 percent per year during the period 1960–81, a period during which per capita income grew by 3 percent per year (see García García, 1988, appendix table 5). However, there were significant differences over time in the growth rate. Prior to 1967 the economy grew less than 5 percent per year. Diversification and expansion of noncoffee exports, together with greater domestic savings and investment, induced rapid growth during the period 1967–74, when the growth rate reached 6.4 percent per year. In the subsequent period (1974–8) the growth rate fell to 5.4 percent, even though coffee and illegal exports experienced a boom. The pace of growth then tapered off following stabilization measures and the onset of global recession.

Agriculture, manufacturing, and trade have been Colombia's major growth sectors since the 1960s. Agriculture picked up sharply in the late 1960s and continued to grow throughout most of the 1970s as the country benefited from rapid increases in exports of coffee and high coffee prices.[2] Manufacturing growth was most pronounced during the period 1967–74, when the sector responded strongly to export incentives and an expansion in domestic demand. Since then, however, the sector's performance has markedly decelerated. All together, agriculture, manufacturing, and trade accounted for three fifths of the total rise in GDP between 1960 and 1981.

Differential rates of growth caused the relative importance of the various economic sectors to change during this period. Agriculture's share of GDP fell from 33 percent in 1960 to 26 percent in 1981. Manufacturing's share rose from 16.5 to 18 percent during the same period, while trade's share of GDP increased from 16 to 19 percent (see García García, 1988, appendix table 6).

Information on the contribution of the major factors of production to economic growth is provided in table 1.1. It has been estimated that capital growth accounted for roughly 51 percent of the rise in GDP between 1963 and 1980, and that labor accounted for about 25 percent.

A salient feature of the above calculations is the variable importance of changes in the conventional factors of production (capital and labor) in providing a complete explanation of output growth. Residual factors (all

[2] An average 73.6 percent of foreign exchange earnings was derived from coffee exports during that period.

Table 1.1 Sources of growth as a percentage of total gross domestic product growth, 1963–1980

	1963–7	1967–74	1974–8	1978–80	1963–80
Total factor input	76.03	54.09	92.01	96.27	76.45
Labor	22.45	18.48	31.81	32.67	25.23
Capital	53.58	35.61	60.20	63.60	51.22
Residual	23.97	45.91	7.99	3.73	23.55
Total	100.00	100.00	100.00	100.00	100.00

Source: World Bank, 1984, table I.4

those other than capital and labor) were important only during the period of very favorable economic conditions.

Long-term External Developments

Between 1950 and 1967, Colombia carried out a scheme of import substitution; from 1967 on, however, the country gradually opened its doors to imports. During the first period imports fluctuated from a low of US$263 million in 1950 to a high of US$674 million in 1966. Exports fluctuated from a low of US$395 million in 1950 to a high of US$669 million in 1954. Imports plus exports never totaled more than US$1,350 million in any year between 1950 and 1960.

After March 1967, following changes in institutional arrangements for the foreign trade sector and the new strategy of export promotion, foreign trade increased substantially. The sum of imports plus exports increased from US$1,006 million in 1967 to US$8,155 million in 1980. In the period 1967–82, exports as a whole (measured in nominal dollars) grew at an average annual rate of 13.7 percent; nontraditional exports (for example, flowers, textiles) grew at the even higher rate of 16.2 percent. Imports, conditioned on the fluctuating availability of foreign exchange, grew 3.2 percent during the period 1967–9, 8.6 percent during the period 1970–2, 22.5 percent between 1973 and 1975, 24.3 percent in the years 1976–8, 23.2 percent between 1979 and 1981, and 17.2 percent in 1982 (see García García, 1988, appendix table 7).

The real value (in pesos) of exports increased at 4.3 percent per year in 1967–83, while imports grew at 7.2 percent per year. By subperiod, exports increased at 5.3 percent per year between 1967 and 1974 and at 2.9 percent per year in 1975–83. However, real imports grew at 8.7 percent per year in 1967–74 and at 9.9 percent per year in 1975–83. Manufacturing exports other than beverages, food products, tobacco, and petroleum products grew at 15.6 percent per year in 1965–74 but fell to 3.2 percent per year in 1975–83. The rate of growth for imports of this same group of manufactured products was 10 percent for the period 1965–74 and 10.8 percent in 1975–82.

Description of Long-term Commercial Policy Patterns

The use of quantitative controls and price rationing devices (that is, multiple exchange rates and tariffs) to affect the level and composition of imports and to allocate foreign exchange reserves has been a frequent occurrence in Colombia.[3] In 1931, when a fall in world coffee prices caused a drastic reduction in Colombia's foreign exchange earnings, the country established quantitative controls and nontariff barriers, and issued a new tariff schedule. During the 1940s, and particularly during the war period, imports were controlled chiefly through a system of multiple exchange rates. The 1950s began with some relaxation of previous restrictive practices, but strong protectionist policies had been adopted by the middle of the decade. The chief reason for the change was recurrent balance-of-payments crises, but protectionism was also an integral part of the strategy of import substitution.

The first attempt at liberalization occurred in 1951 following a successful devaluation (28 percent) (Currie, 1984). Imports, however, did not grow as much as had been anticipated, which suggests that the real exchange rate was expected to be kept high, that import restrictions were less severe than they seemed, and that devaluation had made imports less desirable. Then, in 1954, a large inflow of foreign exchange because of a coffee boom was accompanied by a substantial liberalization of imports. That period of liberalization was short lived, however. Steps to reverse it started in early 1955 and continued in 1956 and 1957.

The administration which took control of the government in 1957 inherited a serious shortage of foreign exchange. QRs were then adopted to conserve foreign exchange, notwithstanding a devaluation of 114 percent in June 1957. An accumulation of arrears led to intensified restrictions in 1958. Colombia's import-licensing system was officially established in 1957 through the creation of a Superintendencia Nacional de Importaciones (SNI) to administer the system. The government's goal was to promote industrialization and import substitution by giving preference to imports of machinery and raw materials. In addition to administrative control of imports, the system of prior deposits was reinforced, as a means both of controlling imports and of helping to stabilize the economy.

In January 1959, the Colombian Congress issued Law I, which strongly influenced the country's trade policies in subsequent years. The goals of this new law were clearly protectionist. Under this law the government published a new list of prohibited imports, replacing the list published in 1957, and set new priorities in granting import licenses. In addition, the

---

[3] Information for this section is taken from Díaz-Alejandro (1976) and García García (1976, 1989).

new law permitted the replacement of specific duties on imports with *ad valorem* tariffs. By 1960 the new system had cut potential import demand substantially, particularly through the imposition of flat prohibitions on a wide variety of products.

These restrictions were relaxed somewhat in 1961 by reductions in the size of prior deposits and through a shift of some imported goods from the prohibited to the prior-licensing list. This change, however, was largely reversed in 1962 because of balance-of-payments problems created by a reduction in world coffee prices plus expansive fiscal and monetary policies. Virtually all imports became subject to prior licensing. Government policy on imports became even more erratic over the next two years.

The significant problems created by a constantly changing and complicated administrative structure for controlling imports increased the pressure to simplify the structure and to rely less on controls and more on higher effective exchange rates. This pressure led to a third short-lived liberalization attempt. In September 1965 a new foreign exchange system with multiple exchange rates was established. Imports were classified as either preferential (mainly "essential" goods) or intermediate. Preferential imports entered at a lower exchange rate, while items on the intermediate list were only allowed entry at a rate that was 50 percent higher. Commodities could only be transferred from the preferential to the intermediate list, while prior deposits for preferential list commodities were to be reduced each month until they reached zero.

This exchange-rate-based process of liberalization was strengthened by a decision to shift a large number of noncompeting foreign goods from the prior-licensing category to the free list. Competing goods were rarely included on the free list. The original plan, which called for a removal within six months of prior licensing on about half of all imports and then on 65 percent of all imports, went even further. By August 1966, nearly all imports were being paid for at the intermediate market rate, and most commodities were either prohibited or on the free list. At the same time, tariff levels were modified many times, mainly upwards, to compensate for the shift to a less restricted list. By October 1966, 80 percent of all registered imports were on the free list.

This movement toward freer trade was abruptly halted in December 1966. Because of fixed exchange rates, an inflationary environment, and declining world coffee prices, liberalization again led to a balance-of-payments crisis that was met by a reversal in trade policies. Import controls were rigorously enforced, the free list was drastically shortened, and about 40 percent of all import-licensing requests in 1967 were rejected. Furthermore, high prior import deposits were reintroduced.

Over the period 1967–74, however, a large number of liberalization measures were put into place. The period witnessed a slow but firm increase in the use of tariffs (rather than QRs) as the proper tool for government intervention in the foreign trade sector and a gradual move toward exchange rate management (mainly through the introduction of a crawling peg system) as the best policy for reducing excess demand for foreign exchange.

During the period 1971–5 there was a steady decline in the percentage of imports that required licenses as well as in the average tariff. Nonetheless, liberalization was slowed in 1976 and 1977 by the introduction of many administrative obstacles into the procedures for approving imports. As a result, the reduction in formal quantitative controls was not followed by an increase in imports or by greater diversification in imports. The body responsible for foreign trade, the Instituto Colombiano de Comercio Exterior (INCOMEX), used a great deal of discretion in issuing import licenses, even for commodities on the free list.[4]

Formal elimination of restrictions on foreign trade continued in 1978–9, although at a slower pace. The liberalization measures introduced in 1979 included decreases in average tariff levels. In October 1980 an additional 400 items were shifted to the free list (mainly capital goods, inputs, and final goods not produced locally), and in 1981 another 200 were added. More importantly, administrative procedures were streamlined, and a large accumulation of international reserves practically eliminated the rationing of foreign exchange.

However, new balance-of-payments problems and a fall in growth rates in the early 1980s, in combination with worldwide economic recession, brought about a reversal in late 1982 of the trend toward liberalization. A large number of items were transferred from the free to the prior-licensing list during 1983. By April 1984 only 4 percent of the items on the tariff schedule remained on the free list.

A Quantitative Measure: the Apparent Import Tariff

It is possible to construct for the period 1970–83 a measure of the apparent average tariff for the whole economy, using the domestic price index of imports, the international price index of Colombia's importables, and the exchange rate for imports. Thus, if P_j^* and P_j are respectively the international and domestic price indices of commodity j, and E_j is the nominal exchange rate for that commodity, the tariff index for the commodity is defined as

$$1 + t_j = P_j / E_j P_j^* \qquad (1.1)$$

---

[4] For example, if the price for a commodity to be imported under the free-registration regime is considered too low according to INCOMEX standards, the permit will be denied on grounds of "dumping." Moreover, many permits need approval for safety, sanitary, security, and other reasons, which can cause considerable delay.

Since t_j is defined as an index, the apparent tariff $^*t_j$ for each period can be obtained by applying the appropriate index number to the tariff of a base year, that is,

$$^*t_j = \frac{t_j - t_0}{1 + t_0} \tag{1.2}$$

If we adopt a given base year, $^*t_j$ can be obtained for each period. Calculations for $^*t_j$ are presented in figure 1.1. They appear as 12 month

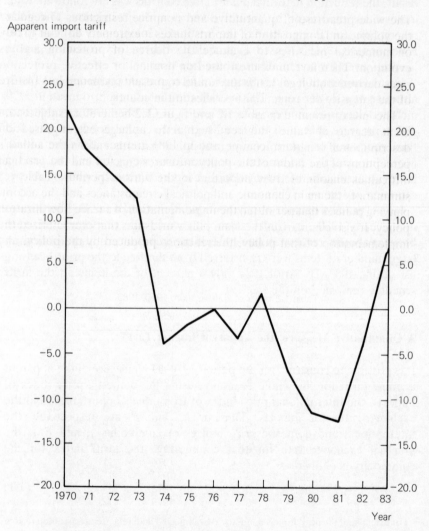

Figure 1.1   Apparent import tariffs, 1970–1983 (base year, 1976)
Source: Author

deviations from the tariff of a base year, in this case 1976. Since the average import tariff paid that year, according to the Customs Bureau, was 16 percent, the apparent average tariff for 1970 was almost 50 percent. The average tariff fell steadily from 1970 to 1974, stabilized until 1978, and then fell again until the reversal of liberalization in 1982.

The Index of Liberalization

The widespread use of quantitative and nonprice restrictions to regulate the volume and composition of imports makes it extremely difficult to rely on numerical measures to evaluate the degree of protection and its evolution. Therefore, measures based on nominal or effective protection rates derived from legal tariffs are bound to present an incomplete picture of the intensity of protectionist policies in the country.

The index presented in table 1.2 and figure 1.2 is therefore subject to a great degree of value judgment and is to a large extent based on descriptions of long-term commercial policy patterns and on the author's perceptions of the intent of the policy measures enacted and the practical difficulties encountered by importers in the various periods. Table 1.3 summarizes the main economic and political circumstances and the accompanying policies that permitted the implementation of a trade liberalization policy. It also summarizes the main policy measures that characterized the implementation of that policy, the reactions produced by the policy, and

Table 1.2 Index of liberalization, 1950–1983

Year	Index	Year	Index
1950	7	1967	6
1951	9	1968	7
1952	9	1969	8
1953	9	1970	8
1954	12	1971	9
1955	9	1972	10
1956	8	1973	10
1957	7	1974	11
1958	6	1975	11
1959	7	1976	11
1960	8	1977	11
1961	9	1978	11
1962	8	1979	12
1963	8	1980	13
1964	9	1981	14
1965	10	1982	13
1966	13	1983	8

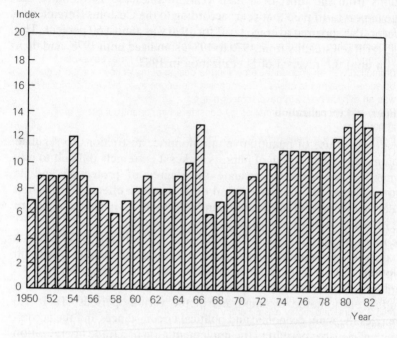

Figure 1.2   Index of liberalization, 1950–1983

Table 1.3 Trade liberalization in Colombia: summary table I

I   Question
   A   Broad nature: initial reduction of QRs, later reduction of tariff levels and
       dispersion and additional reduction of QRs
   B   Size and length of episode: less than full trade liberalization and 15 years'
       duration
   C   Targets and stages: no defined quantitative targets and four stages, that is, (a)
       1967–74 (gradual liberalization, (b) 1975–8 (attempts to liberalize but, actually,
       liberalization was suspended, (c) 1979–81 (liberalization continued), 1982–4
       (suspension of liberalization and build-up of tariff and nontariff barriers to trade)

II   Economic circumstances before introduction of the policy
   A   Balance of payments: deficit and growing negative
   B   Terms of trade: low but stable
   C   Inflation: accelerating
   D   Real GDP growth: falling rate
   E   Degree of openness: increasing due to a short-lived liberalization attempt
   F   External shocks: none
   G   Agricultural output: highly stable growth rate and beginning of an important
       technological change in rice production

III Political circumstances
    A Political structure: stable
    B Implementation: more of a necessity than policy design
    C Ideology: economic model was of the import substitution type, but export promotion was an important element in the design of the policy to avoid recurrent balance-of-payments crises; later, opening the economy to external competition was an explicit policy in development plans
    D Public perception: commercial policy considered important but not of major importance
    E External influence: behind the scenes, the IMF in the late 1960s
    F Government support: major divergences within government agencies when actual implementation had to be done

IV Accompanying policies
    A Exchange rate: crawling peg with variations around trend
    B Export taxes: reduction
    C Export promotion: equal treatment to sectors for almost 7 years and then differential treatment; increasing discretionary treatment to export activities
    D Monetary policy: relatively restrained in the first 5 years of the episode, and then looser and distorting of capital markets, in part due to large increases in international reserves caused by terms-of-trade improvements
    E Fiscal policy: somewhat restrained in the first 7 years, highly restrictive in the next 3 years, and highly expansionary in the last 4 years of the episode
    F Capital controls on inflows: loose in the first half and very restrictive after 1974; on outflows: tight in the first half and loose in the second half of the 1970s
    G Domestic controls: price controls in operation, but changes in controlled prices more or less in accordance with changes in general price level; during the first half nominal minimum wages almost constant, but in second half minimum wages adjusted at or higher than the rate of inflation

V Implementation
    A Transformation of QRs: partial dismantling followed by tariff reductions followed by another reduction in QRs; dismantling of QRs by sector was not uniform, the more protected over the period being textiles and transport equipment
    B Real exchange rate: in 1967–74 reduction of protection was accompanied by an increase in the real exchange rate; in 1975–82 liberalization was accompanied by a substantial decrease in real exchange rate due to improved terms of trade and a large and increasing size of the government sector as well as its deficit
    C Political reactions to liberalization: rather supportive in the 1967–74 period but very vocal and against liberalization in the second half; organized industrial groups, mainly the representatives of the textile and metal sectors, were the main opponents of liberalization; labor organizations were not very active, and labor leaders at the firm level sometimes lobbied against liberalization for specific products

VI Economic performance during and after liberalization
    A Employment: substantial gains in industrial employment in 1967–74, moderate increase until 1978–9, and declining industrial employment afterwards
    B Inflation: relatively low rates until 1972, acceleration in 1973 and 1974, and stabilization at high rates afterwards

C   Growth performance: excellent by historical standards until 1974, and continuous decline in the growth rate, with the exception of 1978, afterwards
D   Real industrial wages: declining until 1977 and rising afterwards
E   Imports: increased throughout the period but shot up in the 1975–82 period
F   Coffee exports: doubled in volume
G   Noncoffee exports: great performance until 1974, and very poor performance afterwards
H   Openness: it took place in the second half of the period
I   Balance-of-payments position: in surplus all but one year of the period
J   External debt: moderate growth until 1978, and more than doubled in 1979–82; most debt growth took place in government debt
K   Capital and investment: high rate of savings and investment until 1977–8
L   Industrial growth: excellent performance until mid-1970s, but very poor thereafter

the economic performance of Colombia during liberalization. Table 1.4 presents a characterization of the main tools of commercial policy and how they were used, and a chronology of the major changes that took place during the period analyzed in this case study.

Table 1.4 Trade liberalization in Colombia: summary table II

I   Commercial policy
A   QRs: widely used throughout the period, but a clear reduction in their use as a tool to achieve balance-of-payments equilibrium or to grant protection; their reduction was gradual and differential by sectors
B   Prior deposits: were used throughout the period, but their purpose changed; thus, in 1967–74 were used for balance-of-payments and import restrictions purposes and were paid prior to obtaining import license, while in 1975–82 were used to discourage private external borrowing, to encourage acceleration of payments abroad and were paid after getting import license but prior to obtaining exchange license (to buy foreign currency to pay for imports)
C   Nominal tariffs: were almost cut in half during the period, and the variance was substantially reduced

II Chronology of major changes

Nov 1966	establishment of general exchange controls
Mar 1967	major legislation on foreign trade issued
Mar 1967	crawling peg system established
Mar 1967	export subsidies established
May 1968	unification of foreign exchange market (except for oil)
1972	indexation for interest payments on the savings and housing system of Colombia was approved
May 1973	prohibited import list abolished; elimination of the foreign exchange budget drawn by the Monetary Board
Jan–Jun 1974	substantial reductions in tariffs

Sep 1974	differential export subsidies introduced on a grand scale
Sep–Nov 1974	enactment of a highly progressive tax reform (at least in the spirit of the law)
Sep–Nov 1974	ceilings on monetary correction on savings in savings and loans institutions introduced
Sep–Nov 1974	upward adjustments in interest rates in general enacted; ceilings, however, remained
1975	severe controls on capital movements for the private sector were imposed
1975–6	increase in the number of items on the free list
1976	substantial drop in rate of crawl of exchange rate
1976–7	reductions in tariffs and in tariff dispersion
Apr 1977	introduction of the exchange certificate system semifloating exchange rate
1979	further reductions in tariffs and in tariff dispersion
1979	substantial drop in rate of crawl
1979	substantial increase in the free-import list and decrease in the prior-licensing list
1979	interest rates on certificates of deposit were set free
1979	true and effective open-market operations were put into operation
1979	beginning of a large fiscal expansion financed with foreign loans and money creation
Late 1981	beginning of the reversal of the liberalization policy started in 1968
Late 1982–mid-1984	full speed backwards in liberalization policy; elimination of free-import list, reestablishment of prohibited import list, and substantial increase in tariffs with a return to the high levels of the 1960s
Apr 1984	massive shift of commodities to prohibited and prior-licensing lists
Aug 1984	reintroduction of the foreign exchange budget by the Monetary Board

2

The Introduction of Liberalization

Broad Nature and Targets of Liberalization

Between 1967 and 1982 there was a gradual process of trade liberalization in Colombia. This liberalization took place through the management of macroeconomic, exchange rate, and export promotion policies which had as their principal objectives to reduce the country's dependence on coffee exports as the principal source of foreign exchange earnings as well as to eliminate the recurrent balance-of-payments crises of the past. Balance-of-payments crises did, in fact, disappear for 15 years at least. Between 1967 and 1974 a real depreciation of the Colombian peso and a cautious management of macroeconomic policies helped to support this liberalization effort. Since 1975 large foreign exchange inflows caused at various times by substantial increases in the external price of coffee, illegal drug exports, and heavy foreign borrowing by the government contributed to eliminate the foreign exchange shortage, thereby reducing the premium on QRs. The reduction of QRs and tariffs took place, however, despite the absence of specific statements by the government about which products would be involved in the liberalization process or the methods that would be used to achieve liberalization. Import liberalization, in short, was not determined by a pre-established plan and in itself was not, in fact, a primary policy objective.

Colombia's various development plans for the period under study did not specify quantitative objectives, nor did they include a timetable for implementing import liberalization. However, their criteria on how commercial and general economic policies could be used to serve the government's objectives did not change. Full trade liberalization was never achieved, and the liberalization episode between 1967 and 1982 analyzed in this case study can only be characterized as having been long and incomplete.

Targets of the Policy

In December 1969 the Lleras Restrepo administration presented to Colombia's Congress a development plan entitled *Planes y Programas de Desarrollo, 1969–1972*. The plan's objective with respect to export policy was " . . . to work for the opening and conquest of new markets" (Departamento Nacional de Planeación, 1969, p. 8). To attain this objective, the government expected to make use of more flexible exchange rates.

The plan had many objectives with respect to imports. One was to provide a reasonable degree of protection for both existing domestic industries and those to be established in the future, and to encourage " . . . the process of import substitution and, at the same time, pave the way to industry, so that it can contribute increasingly to the generation of foreign exchange" (Departamento Nacional de Planeación, 1969, p. V-93). Furthermore, import policy was to be attuned to conditions in the labor market. Lastly, a gradual liberalization of imports was proposed if general economic conditions improved. To attain these objectives the government expected to use both prior licensing and tariffs. To avoid the growth of monopolistic practices, the plan proposed gradual elimination of the list of prohibited imports, but imports were still to be prohibited if speculation was suspected or if prohibiting certain imports would avoid balance-of-payments problems.[1] An effective protection target of 40 percent (to be achieved sometime in the future) was established. However, protection could be higher or lower than that, according to criteria set forth in the plan.[2] Prior import deposits, used chiefly in the past to prevent the entry of speculative imports, were thought likely to become unnecessary for this purpose, since speculation could now be prevented through the use of tariffs and prior licensing.

The Pastrana Borrero administration which entered office in 1970 produced a new development plan called *Las Cuatro Estrategías: 1972–1974*. (The Four Strategies). This plan took a "leading sectors" approach to the development process. That is, it sought to allocate resources among four chief sectors, one of them being the export sector.

---

[1] Thus, the plan stated that "For a long time, governments prohibited imports of any article that could be produced domestically, thereby suppressing competition, for which reason monopolies grew out . . . " (Departamento Nacional de Planeación, 1969, p. V-96).

[2] Protection of more than 40 percent was to be granted whenever a large part of the population depended on the commodity, either for employment or consumption, or temporarily when so required by infant industries. Protection was set below 40 percent whenever there were no possibilities for producing domestically the goods in reference and when for economic or social reasons the domestic price of the commodity was to be kept down (Departamento Nacional de Planeación, 1969, p. V-96).

The plan called for abandoning Colombia's policy of import substitution and for adopting an export promotion strategy as the way to solve the country's unemployment and balance-of-payments problems. To carry out this strategy, various policy instruments were to be used.

1   Tariffs were to evolve toward a relatively uniform level of protection, varying from 20 to 40 percent.[3] Tariffs on imports of essential intermediate and capital goods would be lower than that if domestic production of such goods was not feasible in the short run.

2   The tax saving certificate (CAT) and Plan Vallejo systems were to be modified to stimulate manufactured exports in the short run. CAT was a flat *ad valorem* export subsidy allocated to exports (but excluding coffee, bananas, and other small groups of products) in the form of a tax savings certificate. The Plan Vallejo is a system by which exporters can either import raw materials, intermediate goods, and capital goods used in the production of export commodities on a duty-free basis or receive rebates on import duties paid on such goods.

Control of imports was not seen as a critical issue. It was assumed that Colombia would earn enough foreign exchange to pay for a reasonable volume of imports. Nor did the plan pay much attention to tariffs as a way of controlling imports, since tariff management was seen more as a means of switching to an export promotion strategy. The use of other import control instruments, such as prior licensing and prior deposits, was not mentioned.

Para Cerrar la Brecha, the plan adopted by the López Michelsen administration of 1974–8, established as primary goals a rapid rate of growth in output and employment to benefit the poorest 50 percent of the population. Industry, agriculture, exports, and regional and urban development would be priority sectors for the government.

The government's broad objectives on foreign trade policy were to continue the process of opening up the economy to foreign competition, diversifying exports, and broadening the number of Colombia's trade partners. To achieve these objectives the plan attached the greatest importance to " . . . the design of global policies which, in a coherent and effective manner, will stimulate a greater efficiency and productive capacity in the export sector" (Departamento Nacional de Planeación, 1976, p.

---

[3] This level was considered to be reasonable for the following reasons: (a) the average level of the tariff actually paid on imports at that time was 16 percent, which meant that government revenues would be little affected by the proposed change, and (b) that level was in agreement with the goals set for the common external tariff of the Andean Group and the Asociación Latinoamericana de Libre Comercio (ALALC).

81). On the foreign exchange front, the plan stated that " . . . The main foundation of the foreign trade policy is the maintenance of a realistic exchange rate, which . . . besides being a guarantee for exporters, is an instrument to rationalize the expenditure on imports" (Departamento Nacional de Planeación, 1976, p. 81). Credit was to be one of the principal instruments for promoting exports.

Import policy was deemed to be an integral part of industrial policy, its main objective being the attainment of a better allocation of resources through reductions in tariffs and the elimination of QRs as a permanent instrument of protection.

The *Plan de Integración Nacional* of the Turbay Ayala administration (1978–82) had as its general goal the economic and social development of the country by improving the economic and social infrastructure.

With respect to trade, the plan's goals were to promote growth and diversification in Colombia's exports and to progressively liberalize imports. To achieve these ends the plan emphasized the importance of developing mechanisms to finance nontraditional exports while avoiding retaliation. The CAT (a direct export subsidy) was to be used to maintain the competitiveness of exports only when other steps (such as devaluation) were insufficient. However, the plan also stated that the government should study the possibility of establishing export quotas for important agricultural products. As for import policy, the general objective was to open the economy to foreign competition while also supporting the process of efficient import substitution. To achieve these objectives the plan proposed the creation of a more rational tariff structure that would take the interests of both producers and consumers into account. However, it also stated that import licensing should be used to complement tariffs, especially when necessary to prevent dumping or large fluctuations in the prices of imports.

Intended Sequence of Liberalization

As the summaries above clearly show, the most prominent feature of Colombian trade policy during the years 1967–82 was the goal of promoting exports; import liberalization was always secondary. Only *Las Cuatro Estrategías: 1972–1974* expressly stated the connection between liberalized imports and an increase in exports. *Para Cerrar la Brecha* did not explicitly state the connection because its thrust was both to liberalize imports and to promote exports. Only two of the plans, *Planes y Programas de Desarrollo: 1969–1972* and *Las Cuatro Estrategías: 1972–1974*, set target tariff levels. The former's was effective protection of 40 percent, the latter's a nominal protection rate ranging from 20 to 40 percent. As a matter of policy, however, the governments in power in 1974–8 and 1978–82 wished to maintain an effective protection rate of 60 percent.[4]

The other point that should be stressed is that neither in the development plans nor in policy statements was there a frontal attack on QRs, and no statement about their elimination can be found. They always remained a possibility, either to control dumping or overinvoicing or to prevent speculative imports.

Trade liberalization was implemented in differential stages. When a new trade statute went into effect in March 1967, for example, export promotion policy was implemented almost immediately through the establishment of the CAT, but it took time to implement the credit component of the policy. Policy statements on import liberalization made it clear that such liberalization would be slow. Restrictions on imports of raw materials and intermediate goods would gradually be reduced, while restrictions on imports of consumption goods would come last, especially if some of them were already produced within the country. Luxury consumption goods were hardly mentioned as a target for liberalization.

Implementation of Liberalization

Targets for the amount of liberalization to be achieved during a given period of time were never set. Trade restrictions were to be reduced, but no change in the legal foundations of trade policy was intended. Between 1968 and 1981 there was an attempt to rationalize and reduce QRs, tariffs, and prior import deposits.

Evolution of Quantitative Restrictions and Other Nontariff Barriers

Between 1967 and 1973, liberalization consisted essentially of a gradual reduction of QRs. An important element of the system of restrictions was the establishment by the Monetary Board of a foreign exchange budget which stated the maximum amount of foreign currency that could be spent on imports. (This practice, abolished in 1973, was reestablished in 1984.)

Commodities always required an import license. To administer the system they were classified in one of three lists: free, subject to prior licensing, or prohibited. Commodities not produced in the country were usually classified in the free list, while commodities that competed with domestic production were classified in prior licensing on prohibited import

[4] These assertions are based on the author's participation in policy discussions. Several unpublished government documents discuss this subject, and a 60 percent value of effective protection was the average target value. See, for example, Departamento Nacional de Planeación (1976a).

lists. Although some goods were placed on the free list in 1967, in practice no goods could be imported freely other than certain specified commodities from Ecuador or Paraguay (International Monetary Fund (IMF) 1968, p. 98). Imports of some commodities were formally prohibited, but in 1967 some 15 percent of all approved imports were on the prohibited list; by 1968 the proportion had fallen to 0.3 percent.

QRs and prior deposits on imports were both reduced between 1968 and 1970. Import licensing became more liberal, particularly after 1969, through an increase in the rate of approval and by the gradual transfer of commodities to less restrictive lists. By the end of 1970 the value of free-list imports was 25 percent of the value of reimbursable imports (imports paid for with dollars purchased at the Banco de la República).

Trade restrictions continued to be reduced after 1970. In September 1971, 3 percent of the items on the tariff schedule were on the free list and 16 percent were on the prohibited list. However, 30 percent of the value of licenses issued in 1971 pertained to items on the free list. In August 1973 the list of prohibited imports was abolished, and by June 1974 around 30 percent of all items on the tariff schedule could be freely imported.

By 1976 the need to liberalize became even more pressing, since the monetization of large foreign exchange inflows resulting from a boom in coffee prices jeopardized the government's price stabilization program. Despite enlargement of the free list between 1975 and 1978, however, the actual liberalization that took place during this period was negligible because administration of the licensing system became a barrier to liberalization.[5] Between February 1978 and September 1979 the percentage of items on the free list increased from 53 to 67 percent, but the share of the value of licenses for free-list items stayed relatively constant at 52 percent of total reimbursable licenses. This increased to 62 percent in 1981 and 1982, but declined to 48 percent in 1983. By April 1984 the percentage of items on the free list was only 4 percent of all items. Although the inclusion of goods in the prior-licensing list is not the only determinant of import liberalization, which is also affected by the rate and speed of approval of import applications, the massive move of commodities from the free to the prior-licensing list and from the latter to the prohibited list are clear indications of the intentions of policymakers as well as of the actual evolution of the policy. By resort in 1983 and 1984 to the use of QRs rather than to exchange rate management and macroeconomic policy measures to attack the balance-of-payments disequilibrium the premium on QRs was increased noticeably, thus signaling a clear reversal of the trade liberalization process.

[5] The share of approved commodity imports under the free list declined slightly relative to its 1974 level. It is very likely that between 1976 and 1978 the degree of restrictions on the prior-licensing list increased, but collection of information on the number of import applications had ceased at that time.

The evolution of QRs, both in terms of the number of items on each import list and in terms of the share of the value of licenses for each import regime, is shown in table 2.1.

The liberalization that occurred during the period 1967–82 was not uniform in all sectors, as can be seen in table 2.2. Sectors with the lowest nominal tariff rates (intermediate and nonindustrial goods) in September 1979 also had the largest number of items on the free list, while a high proportion of goods classed as transport equipment or machinery were still on the prior-licensing list. "Low" tariffs on machinery were offset by the high proportion of such items on the prior-licensing list, while high tariffs on transport equipment were strengthened by prior licensing. Although

Table 2.1 Evolution of quantitative restrictions by import regime, 1966–1984 (percent)

	1	2	3	4	5	6
			Value of licenses			
	Number		Total		Reimbursables	
Date	Free	Prior	Free	Prior	Free	Prior
1966	n.a.	n.a.	56.4	42.6	n.a.	n.a.
1967	n.a.	n.a.	3.8	80.7	n.a.	n.a.
1968	n.a.	n.a.	12.0	87.7	18.2	81.6
1969	n.a.	n.a.	17.0	82.9	19.1	80.6
1970	n.a.	n.a.	19.0	80.7	21.0	67.6
Sep 1971	3.0	81.0	27.5	71.7	30.1	69.0
1972	n.a.	n.a.	27.9	71.9	31.0	68.6
1973	n.a.	n.a.	31.2	68.8	34.8	65.2
Jun 1974	29.8	70.2	43.6	56.4	45.8	54.2
1975	n.a.	n.a.	42.8	57.2	51.0	49.0
1976	n.a.	n.a.	39.8	60.2	50.8	49.2
1977	n.a.	n.a.	41.0	59.0	47.5	52.5
Feb 1978	53.0	47.0	43.0	57.0	51.8	48.2
Sep 1979	67.0	33.0	44.0	56.0	48.4	51.6
Sep 1980	n.a.	n.a.	44.0	56.0	50.4	49.6
Dec 1981	71.7	28.3	52.1	47.9	61.8	38.2
Dec 1982	61.7	38.3	54.7	45.3	62.3	37.7
Dec 1983	n.a.	n.a.	41.4	58.6	47.5	52.5
Apr 1984	4.0	79.3	n.a.	n.a.	n.a.	n.a.

n.a., not available.
In 1960–71 and in 1984, totals do not add up to 100 percent because of the existence of the prohibited list. The share based on value is computed on annual value.
Sources: García García, 1976, appendix tables 2, 3, and 4 (columns 3 and 4, 1966–70; columns 5 and 6, 1970); INCOMEX, 1977 (columns 5 and 6, 1968–9, 1971–6); World Bank, 1983 (columns 1–6, 1977–80); INCOMEX, Comercio Exterior, various issues (columns 1–6, 1981–3); Jairo Corredor, División Técnica INCOMEX, personal communication (columns 1 and 2, 1971, 1974, 1984; columns 3 and 4, 1971–6)

Table 2.2 Structure of protection by group of commodities, September 1979 (percent)

	Tariffs				Import regime	
	Nominal		Effective			
Sector	Average	Standard deviation	Average	Standard deviation	Free	Prior
Industrial consumption goods	39.5	22.1	81.2	48.6	68.4	31.6
Transport equipment	33.6	34.1	74.7	91.1	35.7	64.3
Machinery	27.2	16.0	39.1	30.1	58.1	41.9
Intermediate goods	20.0	9.6	29.2	18.2	72.1	27.9
Nonindustrial goods	14.8	7.0	24.1	20.0	71.8	28.2
Total	26.0	17.7	43.8	40.3	67.0	33.0

Source: Giraldo, 1979, table 3

QRs on intermediate and nonindustrial goods were lowered to a greater extent than QRs on machinery and transport equipment, it is possible that a higher rate of approval of applications for imports of commodities in the latter categories, especially at the end of the period, reduced the rate of protection.

Another important indicator of the decrease in restrictions was an increase in the amount of foreign exchange that those traveling abroad could purchase at the Banco de la República, and a reduction in the prior deposit required for such purchases.[6] The reduction of restrictions on travel allowances was gradual until 1976, but then speeded up. The restrictions applicable to special travelers was abolished in 1980, while those for all categories of travelers were abolished in 1981. Restrictions were also reduced by decreasing the red tape involved in legalizing foreign exchange transactions.[7] However, restrictions on travel allowances were restored in 1982. The evolution of restrictions on travel allowances from 1966 to 1984 is shown in table 2.3.

Evolution of Nominal Tariffs

The reduction in QRs between 1968 and 1973 was not accompanied by a reduction in tariffs on imports, which remained fairly constant. In 1974, however, the average tariff fell from 45.5 to 31.9 percent, and the standard

---

[6] The prior deposit was reduced from 100 to 50 percent between 1968 and 1969, and abolished in 1971. It was reinstated in 1974, abolished in 1975, and reinstated again in 1983.
[7] The number of forms that had to be processed by the importer was reduced, and the number of months during which importers could present documentation was increased.

Table 2.3 Legal travel allowances as of December 31, 1966–1984 (US dollars)

	1966	1967	1968	1969	1970	1971	1972	1973	1974	1975	1976[a]	1977[a]	1978	1979	1980	1981	1982	1983	1984
Children under 12																			
Per day	n.a.	n.a.	n.a.	n.a.	n.a.	n.a.	n.a.	n.a.	n.a.	n.a.	30	30	40	n.l.	n.l.	n.l.	n.l.	125	90
Per year	n.a.	n.a.	n.a.	n.a.	n.a.	n.a.	n.a.	n.a.	n.a.	n.a.	1,050	1,050	1,400	3,000	3,000	n.l.	5,000	2,500	1,500
Adults																			
Per day	30	30	30	30	30	30	30	40	40	40	60	60	80	n.l.	n.l.	n.l.	n.l.	250	180
Per year	1,800	1,350	1,350	1,350	1,350	1,050	1,050	1,400	1,400	1,400	2,100	2,100	2,800	6,000	6,000	n.l.	10,000	5,000	3,000
Special travelers[b]																			
Per day	n.a.	50	n.a.	70	70	70	70	70	70	70	200	200	260	n.l.	n.l.	n.l.	n.l.	300	200
Per year	n.a.	4,500	n.a.	6,300	6,300	6,300	6,300	6,300	6,300	6,300	18,000	18,000	23,400	30,000	n.l.	n.l.	30,000	20,000	10,000
Transfers for students																			
Per month	120	120–200	120–200	120–200	120–200	120–200	120–200	200–300	200–300	200–300	200–300	500	500	500	n.l.	n.l.	n.l.	n.l.	500
Special students[c]																			
Per month	n.a.	450	450	450	450	450	450	450	450	450	450	450	450	450	n.l.	n.l.	n.l.	n.l.	500
Family remittances abroad	0	0	0	0	0	0	0	0	0	250	250	250	250[a]	250[a]	n.l.	n.l.	n.l.	n.l.	n.a.
Prior deposits																			
Percentage								0	0	0	0	0	0	0	0	0	0	n.a.	n.a.
Pesos per dollar			100	50	50	50	50	0	10	0	0	0	0	0	0	0	0	15	65
Travel tax[d]	500	500	500	500	500	500	500	500	500	500	500	500	500	500	15	15	15	15	15

n.a. not available. n.l. no limit.
[a] The Exchange Office was empowered to grant larger allocations
[b] Special travelers are those traveling for reasons that are of particular usefulness for the country.
[c] Special students are defined as professional and technical persons undertaking courses abroad
[d] In pesos until 1979 and in US dollars thereafter

Source: Computed by the author from IMF, Annual Report on Exchange Restrictions, several years

deviation and the coefficient of variation fell from 36.8 to 21.74 and from 0.81 to 0.68, respectively.

Imports are subject to surcharges as well as tariffs. These surcharges consist of a 5 percent *ad valorem* tax on the cost, insurance, and freight (c.i.f.) value of imports that accrues to PROEXPO (the Export Promotion Fund) and a 1.5 percent *ad valorem* tax that goes to the national government. Until March 31, 1981, there was also a 1.0 percent consular invoice tax that had to be paid on the free-on-board (f.o.b.) value of imports.[8,9] The total average nominal tariff (tariff plus import surcharges) was fairly constant – around 50 percent – between 1968 and 1973 but it fell to 35.9 percent in 1974; its lowest value, 34.4 percent, was reached in 1980.

Nominal average tariffs by sectors for selected years between 1964 and 1983 are presented in table 2.4. There were sharp reductions in nominal tariffs in 1974 in most sectors except beverages (sector 13), textiles, wearing apparel, and leather (sector 16), wood and wood products (sector 17), chemicals and rubber (sector 19), basic metallurgy (sector 22), machinery and equipment (sector 23), and transport materials (sector 24). Tariffs continued to fall between 1974 and 1980, although usually at a moderate pace. For nonmetallic products (sector 21) and processed tobacco (sector 14) the reductions were strong, but there was virtually no reduction for beverages, textiles, or wood and wood products. Part of the increase in imports of beverages and textile products can be explained by the reduction in QRs in these sectors.

Taxes, Subsidies, and Restrictions on Exports

One common economic objective during this period was export promotion. In 1974, however, direct subsidies (CAT) for nontraditional exports were reduced. That is, the tax credit for certain manufactured exports was limited to their value added rather than their total value. Furthermore, the fairly uniform and stable CAT was reduced in September of that year and differential rates took the place of uniformity. Although differential rates have remained in existence since then, the subsidy for various products has varied considerably, triggered by changes in the external market or the lobbying of interest groups. The direct subsidy was replaced in part by discretionary subsidized credit from PROEXPO, whose main source of

---

8 The *ad valorem* tax on imports accruing to PROEXPO was 1.5 percent until November 11, 1974, 3.5 percent between this date and September 30, 1975, and 5 percent afterwards. The other 1.5 percent *ad valorem* tax on imports accrued to the National Coffee Fund until 1974, when it was transferred to the National Treasury.

9 After March 31, 1981, the consular invoice tax on the f.o.b. value of imports was replaced by a stamp tax, which had to be paid on all imports except newsprint.

Table 2.4 Summary of nominal average tariffs by sectors of national accounts, 1964–1983 (percent)

National accounts	1964	1965	1968	1970	1972	1973	1974	1976	1978	1980	1983
Agriculture production	33.01	34.63	33.34	32.99	34.67	32.54	17.95	17.04	15.84	17.24	19.32
Cereals	20.26	20.81	20.81	20.81	20.81	21.41	15.00	13.81	13.00	13.93	15.70
Sugar cane	22.50	22.50	22.50	22.50	22.50	22.50	20.00	17.50	17.50	17.50	23.00
Raw tobacco	50.00	50.00	50.00	50.00	50.00	37.75	17.75	16.50	17.75	15.25	13.50
Tubers	40.00	40.00	40.00	40.00	40.00	32.33	19.00	15.00	15.00	15.00	20.00
Vegetables and legumes	37.06	37.06	37.06	33.75	37.06	16.75	15.50	13.13	12.81	13.13	16.38
Fruits	30.00	38.40	33.20	33.20	35.60	35.60	24.80	24.80	21.00	24.60	26.88
Oil products	17.47	17.47	18.00	18.00	17.47	13.26	11.16	11.58	12.11	14.74	15.95
Fibers	17.50	17.50	17.50	20.00	20.00	20.00	10.00	10.00	10.00	10.00	13.00
Other agricultural products	47.98	47.98	46.51	46.51	49.68	53.71	20.05	19.02	17.56	18.41	20.44
Animal production	67.58	67.58	67.51	62.78	65.57	51.21	22.12	18.69	17.57	18.31	19.81
Cattle	79.76	79.76	79.76	72.62	79.76	47.81	17.38	18.81	16.90	18.81	18.86
Poultry	86.76	86.76	86.76	86.76	86.76	83.24	34.41	20.29	18.82	20.29	22.18
Other animal production	47.52	47.52	47.34	41.59	42.86	34.90	18.34	17.66	17.31	16.79	19.10
Silviculture	51.11	51.11	51.11	51.11	51.11	61.56	20.19	15.93	15.00	15.19	19.93
Fishing and hunting	80.91	80.91	73.82	59.73	71.36	79.55	23.18	20.00	19.55	19.09	22.09
Mining	19.18	19.18	19.18	19.18	19.18	20.53	11.29	10.41	11.59	10.41	13.59
Mining	21.31	21.31	22.05	22.16	22.55	23.62	12.64	12.19	11.66	11.20	14.70
Processed coffee	182.14	182.14	194.29	194.29	182.14	177.86	35.00	31.43	21.43	22.86	27.14
Meat products	91.80	93.82	91.03	89.84	87.75	87.81	39.72	33.94	30.37	28.91	36.00

Flour products	52.57	53.43	53.20	53.20	53.43	54.00	29.29	24.86	24.14	23.47	26.94
Milk products	89.78	89.78	88.70	62.61	88.70	69.83	30.83	31.52	30.00	30.00	34.70
Sugar	44.00	44.00	39.50	48.50	46.80	48.50	38.00	27.50	23.00	13.13	29.60
Beverages	56.45	56.45	69.68	71.29	69.35	70.32	62.90	58.55	58.87	52.42	69.16
Processed tobacco	124.38	132.50	124.38	124.38	124.38	112.50	50.63	38.13	26.88	26.25	34.88
Other agricultural products	81.06	82.47	77.32	72.39	74.63	78.46	36.87	33.99	31.77	29.88	37.98
Textiles, apparel, and leather	95.85	95.60	95.71	96.20	95.14	81.04	60.78	58.15	57.21	56.19	72.66
Wood and wood products	100.63	100.63	101.44	100.44	100.44	73.03	48.25	42.75	42.75	38.00	49.39
Paper and printing	51.94	51.94	52.46	52.68	52.61	57.63	30.56	31.43	29.63	27.67	35.55
Chemicals and rubber	26.93	26.93	28.05	28.07	28.73	29.59	22.26	22.19	21.16	18.90	23.86
Petroleum refining	22.49	22.49	22.29	22.55	22.82	23.07	14.08	13.67	12.91	12.10	15.68
Nonmetallic products	71.76	71.79	71.28	70.00	64.80	58.24	39.74	38.99	36.01	27.23	35.18
Basic metallurgy	39.71	39.46	42.79	44.40	39.02	43.17	34.38	33.39	32.00	28.91	35.53
Machinery and equipment	29.35	29.39	32.19	31.61	32.50	35.37	31.43	29.10	28.48	25.95	31.59
Transport materials	42.16	40.65	39.17	45.44	41.44	37.63	33.83	33.57	33.99	31.95	41.85
Other manufactures	70.13	69.94	66.70	63.58	57.73	52.96	36.45	32.25	31.82	27.96	33.96
Average	47.12	47.20	47.80	47.42	46.69	45.50	31.88	30.28	29.22	26.87	33.71
PROEXPO	0.00	0.00	1.50	1.50	1.50	1.50	1.50	5.00	5.00	5.00	5.00
Ad valorem tax	0.00	0.00	1.50	1.50	1.50	1.50	1.50	1.50	1.50	1.50	1.50
Consular invoice	0.00	0.00	1.00	1.00	1.00	1.00	1.00	1.00	1.00	1.00	1.00
Total average tariff	47.12	47.20	51.80	51.42	50.69	49.50	35.88	37.78	36.72	34.37	41.21
Maximum tariff	400.00	400.00	400.00	450.00	380.00	350.00	350.00	200.00	200.00	150.00	198.00

–, nil.

Source: Calculations made by the author based on information generated by Ricardo Candelo

funds is a 5 percent tax levied on imports but whose incidence falls almost entirely on exports (see García García, 1981, chapter 4).

Not all Colombian exports are or have been free. Treatment has varied according to economic circumstances. In late 1973, for example, restrictions on exports were imposed after inflation accelerated.[10] In May 1977, when the monthly rate of inflation threatened to result in an annual inflation rate of more than 50 percent per year, a new export regime was accounced.[11]

These two episodes illustrate some elements of Colombian export policy during this period. That is, goods whose prices might have some impact on the cost of living (such as rice and potatoes) became subject to export restrictions. These restrictions were eased only after substantial production surpluses developed. This policy was applied to most agricultural products and to a limited number of industrial products. It is thus evident that the elimination of QRs on exports was not considered to be an important condition for eventual success of the policy of export promotion.

Owing to a large foreign exchange inflow from an increase in coffee prices in 1976 and the problems that sterilization of this inflow posed, severe restrictions on the surrender of invisibles to the Banco de la República were imposed. Receipts in excess of US$500 had to be registered with the Bank, and exchange certificates rather than pesos were issued for foreign exchange surrendered in excess of US$1,000. In addition, commercial banks needed Banco de la República approval to process foreign exchange transactions involving more than US$20,000. The restrictions were strengthened in May 1977, when it was announced that all receipts from invisibles would have to be exchanged for freely negotiable exchange certificates.[12] These restrictions on the sale of foreign exchange pushed many people – especially low income people who received remittances from abroad – into the black market. These restrictions continued to exist until 1983.

[10] INCOMEX's Resolution 26 specified the items that could be exported freely, prohibited exports (including live cattle, sheep and pigs, mutton and pork, poultry, bacon, milk, eggs, certain types of grains, animal and vegetable oils, refined sugar, cocoa, hides and skins, timber, specified iron and steel products, zinc, tin, and lead), and named the exports requiring prior approval (including sugarcane, raw sugar, specified milling products, sulfur, specified chemicals, plastic tubes, and paper products).

[11] Exports continued to be classified in five categories, with the following changes: (a) onions, tomatoes, toothpaste, soap, and several other items were added to the list of exports subject to approval by certain agencies, and all such exports now required prior approval from INCOMEX; (b) tires, notebooks, and glass bottles for soft drinks were added to cement to constitute the list of products that could be exported only by their producers, subject to quotas set by INCOMEX; and (c) the list of suspended exports was extended to include certain basic foodstuffs such as pork, poultry meat, fish, milk, butter, cheese, lentils, pineapples, oranges, lemons, rice, wheat and corn flour, chocolate, and salt.

[12] If sold to the Banco de la República within 90 days of issue, a discount of 10 percent was applied.

Colombia's coffee exports are restricted because of the quota system of the International Coffee Organization, to which Colombia belongs. The trade legislation issued in 1967 abolished the differential exchange rate for coffee and replaced it with a 26 percent *ad valorem* export tax, 4 percent of which goes to the National Coffee Fund. This tax has been steadily reduced and its level in 1984 was 6.5 percent, but 4 percent of it still goes to the National Coffee Fund. Thus coffee seems to have been the only export product that received increasingly favorable treatment during the period. For the evolution of the *ad valorem* tax on coffee exports see García García (1988, appendix table 10).

Prior Import Deposits

Prior import deposits were created by Decree 637 of 1951. The original aim was to restrict imports, but these deposits have also been used as a monetary policy tool. As a result, they have been applied at different stages in the import chain to achieve different objectives.

Prior deposits were reduced gradually after 1968, and this gradual pace accelerated during the first half of the 1970s. All deposits exceeding 10 percent were reduced to 10 percent in February 1973, and in June of the same year the deposits were eliminated. Because this created problems of monetary expansion, the old type of deposits was shortly replaced by another type, the advance deposit or *consignación*. This deposit had to be paid prior to the registration of imports and could be used to obtain exchange licenses for import payments without making the 100 percent advance payment required for exchange licenses.[13] The advance deposit was initially 10 percent but was increased shortly thereafter to 35 percent, and then to 40 percent. The advance deposits for purchasing foreign exchange were eliminated in 1975 but were reestablished in 1976 to accelerate payments abroad. These advance deposits took three forms: (a) deposits prior to customs clearance; (b) deposits on freight payments; and (c) deposits prior to the purchase of an exchange license.

Between 1951 and 1973 the deposits were used to constrain imports. Between 1973 and 1982, however, their purpose was to accelerate payments abroad and thus reduce monetary growth. In both cases there was a monetary impact, and imports became costlier. During the first period the deposits worked in the desired direction, but in the second period their discouragement of imports reduced the contractionary impact that a larger volume of imports might have had. Prior deposits can thus be judged on two counts: their monetary impact, and their effect on the cost of importing.

[13] If unused, the deposit would be repurchased by the Banco de la República at the initial exchange rate.

To assess their impact, the value of import deposits for each year between 1965 and 1982 can be compared with the monetary base and the actual volume of imports for that year. This comparison indicates that the contractionary effect of import deposits was strong in the late 1960s and early 1970s but then became weaker because of the reductions in rates and in the number of items to which they applied. The contractionary effect was strong again in 1977, when the monetary authority could not control the growth of the money supply, but in succeeding years the effect of import deposits was negligible (see García García, 1988, appendix table 11).

Estimates of the opportunity costs of prior deposits for the period 1967–80 indicate that this cost was fairly constant and fairly high between 1966 and 1971, and then declined until 1974. These costs took a sharp upward turn in 1975, fell sharply in 1976, but increased again in 1977 after the establishment of new modalities of deposits (see García García, 1988, appendix table 12). However, many exemptions to prior import deposit requirements were established, especially for imports classified under the nonreimbursable and global license modalities. Since the costs of prior deposits were significant, importers avoided them by registering imports in one of these two classes. The nonreimbursable arrangement was particularly convenient because imports could be paid for with a direct loan from abroad, which could then be repaid with foreign exchange obtained on the black market at a rate lower than the official rate.

3
Trade Liberalization and Macroeconomic Policies

Exchange Rate Policy

Colombia had three different exchange rates in 1966; one for coffee exports, one for crude oil and its derivatives, and one for both noncoffee exports and imports. In 1967 the exchange rate for coffee was eliminated, leaving the crude oil rate and a rate for all other transactions. The exchange rate for coffee exports was unified with that for exports other than oil at 13.5 pesos, while the rate for oil imports was raised from 7.67 to 9 pesos per US dollar. *De facto* unification of the exchange rate for all transactions except those involving oil imports took place in June 1968.

The year 1967 also saw the inauguration of a new era in foreign exchange and export promotion policies. A crawling peg system was established for determining the value of the Colombian peso relative to the US dollar. Because of relatively high inflation rates, the fixed system had produced large variability in the real exchange rate, a variability which had a negative impact on the development of nontraditional exports.[1] However, the new system did not eliminate the uncertainty generated by the previous approach of sporadic and large devaluations. To determine the extent of instability in the real exchange rate in the period 1964–84, an instability index for the quarterly real exchange rate (purchasing power parity *vis-à-vis* the US dollar) was computed following Díaz-Alejandro's methodology. This index, presented in table 3.1, shows that instability was rather high prior to the establishment of the crawling peg system. It decreased

---

[1] An instability index for the real exchange rate computed by Carlos Díaz-Alejandro for the period 1957–72 showed that instability was rather high for the period 1957–67 but fell drastically afterwards. Díaz-Alejandro also did some regression analysis of the factors affecting nontraditional exports and found that the variability of the real exchange rate had a negative effect on the performance of nontraditional exports (see Díaz-Alejandro, 1976, table 4.8).

Table 3.1 Real exchange rate and percentage change by quarter, and annual instability index, 1964–1984 (real pesos per US dollar, end of period)

	Real exchange rate					Percentage change in exchange rate				Instability index
Year	I	II	III	IV	Average	I	II	III	IV	
1964	24.83	23.40	23.36	23.38	23.74	—	− 6.11	− 0.21	0.12	2.14
1965	23.34	22.70	33.01	31.51	27.64	− 0.20	− 2.79	31.23	− 4.76	9.75
1966	30.58	29.06	29.23	28.39	29.31	− 3.03	− 5.25	− 5.25	− 2.97	2.96
1967	28.27	29.59	31.05	31.65	30.14	− 0.40	4.45	4.45	1.89	2.87
1968	32.14	31.81	32.18	33.14	32.32	1.52	− 1.04	− 1.04	2.90	1.65
1969	33.59	33.18	33.35	33.27	33.35	1.35	− 1.23	0.49	− 0.24	0.83
1970	33.79	33.66	34.36	34.88	34.17	1.53	− 0.39	2.06	1.48	1.37
1971	34.48	34.35	34.53	34.08	34.36	− 1.16	− 0.37	0.50	− 1.31	0.83
1972	33.79	33.28	32.44	31.83	32.84	− 0.86	− 1.53	− 2.59	− 1.93	1.73
1973	30.82	29.57	29.07	28.86	29.58	− 3.25	− 4.23	− 1.74	− 0.73	2.49
1974	28.54	29.04	30.56	30.71	29.71	− 1.10	1.72	4.96	0.50	2.07
1975	30.31	31.30	34.12	31.39	31.78	− 1.34	3.18	8.25	− 8.68	5.36
1976	31.09	30.25	29.81	28.88	30.01	− 0.97	− 2.79	− 1.48	− 3.22	2.11
1977	28.10	25.75	26.71	27.06	26.91	− 2.77	− 9.12	3.59	1.30	4.20
1978	26.37	26.00	26.16	26.08	26.15	− 2.64	− 1.42	0.63	− 0.33	1.25
1979	25.41	25.00	24.76	25.29	25.12	− 2.61	− 1.64	− 0.96	2.09	1.82
1980	26.53	26.04	26.23	26.37	26.29	4.66	− 1.86	0.69	0.55	1.94
1981	27.06	26.86	26.97	26.81	26.92	2.53	− 0.74	0.42	− 0.61	1.08
1982	26.30	25.51	25.55	26.05	25.85	− 1.92	− 3.10	0.15	1.91	1.77
1983	26.15	25.63	27.21	28.21	26.80	0.39	− 2.03	5.81	3.55	2.94
1984	28.71	28.98	29.93	30.33	29.49	1.74	0.94	3.15	1.32	1.79

—, not applicable.
The instability index is defined as the average of the absolute values of the quarterly percentage change in real exchange rates. The real exchange rate is defined as the nominal exchange rate (pesos per US dollar) times the US wholesale price index divided by the Colombian wholesale price index (1975 = 100).

Sources: IMF, International Financial Statistics, various issues; IMF, 1981, 1985 for US wholesale price index; Banco de la República Revista, and direct information to author for quarterly wholesale price index since 1970

between 1967 and 1971 but increased subsequently because of an acceleration in domestic inflation and a reduction in the rate of crawl.

The instability index shows that sharp variations occurred in 1975, 1977, 1979, and 1980, when the role of the exchange rate changed from being an export promotion and balance-of-payments mechanism to a price stabilization instrument.[2] The change in the role of the exchange rate was due to

[2] In September 1974 the rate of crawl was increased sharply. The purpose of this acceleration was to promote minor exports, make up for the decline in the real exchange rate that had taken place since 1972, and offset the reduction in the subsidy to minor exports decreed in September 1974. Between 1970 and 1974 the differential between the official and black-market rates fell substantially, and an export subsidy larger than the exchange rate differential led to overinvoicing, faking of exports, and a boom in fictitious nontraditional exports, for which reason the export subsidy was sharply reduced in the second half of 1974.

the difficulty of handling the monetization of large inflows of foreign exchange. These inflows were produced mainly by increases in coffee prices, but another factor was the government's external borrowing in 1979 and 1980.[3] The role of the exchange rate as a price stabilization instrument was very marked in 1977, when the peso was revalued in nominal terms for Colombia's main agricultural exports (coffee, flowers, cotton, beef, bananas), exports of services, foreign exchange revenues for the oil sector, foreign loans, and foreign investment. The increasing role of the exchange rate as an anti-inflationary instrument was enhanced by the fact that the country had abundant reserves of foreign exchange (see Edwards, 1986a). This abundance debilitated the country's export promotion efforts and made import liberalization a more attractive policy. Colombia's industrial sector was then squeezed by reductions in both industrial exports and domestic demand, the latter being induced by increased competition from imports.

Adoption of the crawling peg system did not permanently reduce the instability of the real exchange rate nor prevent its almost continuous fall in the 1970s (tables 3.1 and 3.2).

The coffee boom that started in 1975 and, with some interruptions, lasted until 1979, and the growing size of the government sector and its fiscal deficit were two important factors in Colombia's recent economic history. These two events contributed substantially to the real appreciation of the peso which, in the end, led to a sharp deterioration of the international reserve position of the country (García García and Montes Llamas, 1988). A third important factor was the drug boom, essentially of marijuana and cocaine. According to estimates by Gómez, during the period 1981–5 net income from drug traffic ranged between a low of 2.6 percent of GDP in 1985 and a high of 6.4 percent of GDP in 1982 (Gómez, 1988, tables 7 and 17).

The coffee boom, characterized by a substantial increase in the external price of coffee and in the volume of coffee exports, led to an increase in the real income and expenditure of Colombians. The larger value of coffee exports led to a rapid and strong accumulation of international reserves, to an increase in the rate of monetary expansion, and to the acceleration of inflation. The higher expenditure increased the demand for all commodities (nontraded and traded) and produced a real appreciation of the peso which discouraged production in the noncoffee tradeable sector of the economy. The expansion of the illegal drug trade had a similar impact on the direction of relative price movements and on the allocation of

---

[3] The issue of the Dutch disease in Colombia produced by the coffee boom has been analyzed by several authors. See, among others, Sebastián Edwards (1984, 1986a, b) and Linda Kamas (1986). See also Vinod Thomas et al. (1985), especially chapters 1–4 and Jorge García García and Gabriel Montes Llamas (1988, chapter 3).

Table 3.2 Index of real exchange rates and relative export and import prices, 1965–1981 (1975 = 100)

	1965	1966	1967	1968	1969	1970	1971	1972	1973	1974	1975	1976	1977	1978	1979	1980	1981
Banco de la Republica																	
Noncoffee global	n.a.	n.a.	n.a.	n.a.	n.a.	n.a.	n.a.	n.a.	n.a.	n.a.	100.0	95.3	85.5	85.5	82.6	84.6	81.9
Effective minor exports	n.a.	n.a.	n.a.	n.a.	n.a.	96.9	100.5	103.9	103.2	100.4	100.0	97.6	84.5	86.5	85.2	86.6	n.a.
Morawetz																	
Real exchange rate	n.a.	n.a.	82.3	89.7	91.4	96.5	100.1	99.8	95.5	94.5	100.0	98.2	83.4	80.7	78.4	77.7	74.5
Ruiz																	
Total exports	n.a.	n.a.	n.a.	n.a.	n.a.	n.a.	n.a.	n.a.	n.a.	n.a.	100.0	94.5	86.4	87.5	84.6	85.4	78.5
Effective minor exports	n.a.	n.a.	n.a.	n.a.	n.a.	n.a.	n.a.	n.a.	n.a.	n.a.	100.0	96.9	90.3	92.9	90.1	93.9	93.5
Relative prices of exports[a]																	
Agriculture	103.4	76.5	84.1	77.4	76.0	81.1	85.8	96.3	104.9	107.8	100.0	89.7	85.4	77.4	83.1	79.1	79.7
Processed coffee	65.6	62.9	80.0	87.3	85.7	111.6	92.8	104.6	121.3	102.9	100.0	165.1	235.5	151.7	111.0	111.9	80.2
Broad agriculture[b]	68.3	61.9	77.6	81.3	81.0	100.1	88.0	99.7	114.6	105.6	100.0	140.2	182.9	127.5	101.1	104.0	78.9
Industry	58.7	50.0	48.0	52.2	50.5	56.5	58.3	66.0	77.8	102.7	100.0	96.4	85.7	85.1	88.2	87.5	89.6
Total sectors	74.9	65.4	74.2	75.2	73.4	88.6	81.0	86.3	96.5	102.8	100.0	116.6	125.8	107.5	95.7	101.0	85.6
Relative prices of imports[c]																	
Agriculture	51.0	64.8	65.4	76.3	70.6	62.1	64.1	64.2	89.1	116.2	100.0	81.8	79.3	53.7	65.5	72.8	65.9
Broad agriculture	51.1	64.9	65.7	76.8	71.2	62.9	64.1	64.2	89.1	116.2	100.0	81.8	78.0	47.0	65.5	72.8	65.9
Industry	79.0	87.3	83.3	87.6	83.8	84.0	81.3	79.9	80.2	95.9	100.0	92.4	81.9	79.2	78.2	79.9	77.4
Total sectors	76.9	85.9	83.1	87.4	83.9	83.5	81.1	80.3	81.8	97.0	100.0	92.5	83.3	78.3	79.8	81.1	78.2

n.a. not available.
[a] Implicit price of exports divided by GDP deflator.
[b] Includes processed (washed) coffee and sugar.
[c] Implicit prices of imports divided by GDP deflator.

Sources: Banco de la República, 1984; unpublished information; Morawetz, 1980; Ruiz, 1984; relative prices derived from DANE, *Cuentas Nacionales de Colombia 1970–1983*, and *Matriz Insumo Producto 1970–1983*

resources. The increases in government expenditure, financed initially with foreign borrowing and later, in an increasing proportion, through money creation also led to a real appreciation of the peso. Very likely, the marginal propensity of the Colombian government to spend in nontraded goods is larger than the corresponding marginal propensity of the private sector because the empirical evidence shows that an increase in government expenditure leads to an increase in the price of nontraded goods relative to that of traded commodities (coffee and noncoffee).[4]

While the Colombian economy was subject to these shocks in the second half of the 1970s, none of them was present between 1967 and 1974. Stable coffee prices, moderate fiscal and monetary policies, and the implementation of a crawling peg policy with some trade liberalization worked to produce a real depreciation of the peso that stimulated production of traded commodities and exports. In addition, favorable world economic conditions stimulated overall economic growth, especially in the export sector where new activities and products developed and grew (flowers, for example).

Thus, while in the first half of the period the movements in the real exchange rate were part of a response to overall macroeconomic management which was intended to reduce a foreign exchange shortage, in the second half of the period the real appreciation of the peso was the response of the economy to external shocks and to the conduct of macroeconomic policies by the economic authorities.

As disequilibrium in the foreign exchange markets subsided because of, among other things, the exchange rate management system established in 1967, the differential between exchange rates in the black and official markets became smaller. During some periods the black-market rate was below the official rate, mainly as a result of the implicit tax (the discount on the exchange certificates) on foreign exchange surrendered to the Banco de la República. The differential between the black-market rate and the official exchange rate has generally been negligible since 1975 (see table 3.3). This indicates that there may be substantial inflows and outflows of currency that do not pass through official channels. These flows are probably related to exports of illegal drugs.[5]

---

[4] In 1979 and 1980 the inflationary impact of the reserve accumulation was compounded by an ambitious program of government expenditures financed in part by external loans but, to an increasing degree, by money creation.

[5] For an analysis of the importance of the underground economy, see Junguito and Caballero (1978, pp. 103–39). For a more recent study, see Gómez (1988).

Table 3.3 Ratio of the black-market to the official
exchange rate, 1966–1983 (end of period)

Year	I	II	III	IV
1966	1.98	1.79	1.82	2.19
1966	1.32	1.19	1.21	1.46
1967	1.56	1.31	1.19	1.16
1968	1.14	1.12	1.08	1.07
1969	1.08	1.13	1.14	1.08
1970	1.12	1.17	1.20	1.28
1971	1.24	1.17	1.15	1.11
1972	1.07	1.08	1.11	1.12
1973	1.10	1.11	1.10	1.09
1974	1.11	1.13	1.11	1.05
1975	1.03	1.09	1.08	1.05
1976	1.07	1.06	1.05	1.04
1977	1.05	0.99	1.01	1.01
1978	1.01	1.01	1.01	1.01
1979	1.00	1.01	1.02	1.02
1980	1.01	1.01	1.01	1.01
1981	1.01	1.01	1.01	1.00
1982	1.01	1.03	1.02	1.00
1983	1.02	1.18	1.09	1.20

There were two official exchange rates in 1966.

Sources: Pick's Currency Yearbook, 1974, 1984; IMF,
1985; Banco de la República, Informe del Gerente a la
Junta Directiva, segunda parte, 1968–9, p. 127

Export Promotion Policies

The main instruments used to promote exports since 1967 have been the
exchange rate, fiscal incentives, import–export schemes, and special credit
facilities.[6]

Exchange Rate Policy

Sporadic and large devaluations characterized Colombia's exchange rate
policy until 1967. After that, a fairly stable system of exchange rate
management was established. The system's initial function was to preserve
some degree of competitiveness for minor exports, but large inflows of
foreign exchange and inflationary financing of the deficit overrode the
export competitiveness objective in favor of price stabilization. Given the

[6] The first description of the evolution of the main instrument of export promotion policy
between 1948 and 1973 was prepared by Teigeiro and Elson (1973, pp. 419–70).

institutional setting and the self-imposed constraints in the management of monetary and exchange control policies, minor exports then tended to lose competitiveness.

Fiscal Incentives

An income tax exemption equivalent to 40 percent of the gross value of minor exports was replaced in 1967 by the freely negotiable and tax-exempt tax rebate certificate (CAT) mentioned earlier. Its initial value was 15 percent, and it was redeemable within 12 months. Exports eligible for a CAT were exempted from payment of the 1.5 percent stamp tax. Furthermore, export taxes on cattle on the hoof and meat products were abolished in 1967, and the CAT was extended to include exports of mineral ores, platinum, coke, and coal. The effective value of a CAT could be increased by reducing its redemption period. The CAT was modified quite frequently after 1973, and discrimination became the norm, thereby depriving exporters of clear signals about incentives. In 1983 the CAT was replaced by the Certificado de Reembolso Tributario (CERT), which could be modified more frequently.

Import–Export Schemes

The main provisions of import–export schemes are exempt imported inputs used in the production of exports from the payment of import duties as well as from prior licensing restrictions and prior deposits. Although the original objective was to stimulate the use of excess productive capacity, the schemes also turned out to be an important instrument of export promotion.

Special Credit Facilities

Two systems of special credit facilities have been widely used: the "advance exchange surrender," and credit from PROEXPO. The advance exchange surrender allows an exporter to sell to the Banco de la República foreign currency that has been borrowed abroad and to repay the loan with export proceeds. The foreign currency needed to repay the loan obtained by the exporter is valued at the same rate at which the foreign exchange was purchased by the Banco de la República, resulting in a subsidy that makes up for any devaluation between the time of purchase and the time of resale of the foreign exchange by the Banco de la República. The exchange differential is paid by the government. This system has been alternately used and suspended, depending on the government's views of how much external indebtedness is desirable, on the growth of the money supply, and on the level and rate of increase of international reserves. When allowed to operate freely, the arrangement has provided more than half of the foreign exchange surrendered to the Banco de la República.

Credit from PROEXPO is funded by a tax on imports. Initially set at 1.5 percent, the tax was raised to 5 percent in 1976. Export credits have been granted since 1967, but the subsidy has increased as a result of the increased differential between the interest rate charged by PROEXPO and the market interest rate.

The system of export promotion just described has remained in operation in Colombia with some variations since 1967. Thus, until 1974 the CAT was granted uniformly to all export products eligible to receive it. In the second half of 1974 the CAT was granted on a discriminatory basis, the brunt of the discrimination falling on agriculture and mining. Discrimination against primary commodity exports, mainly agricultural exports, was sharpened in 1977 when a lower differential exchange rate for certain exports – coffee, cattle, cotton, and flowers – was established.

The evolution of the effective exchange rate for minor exports after 1967, and of the relative price of exports after 1970, is presented in table 3.2. There was a close correlation between the real and the real effective exchange rates. Moreover, there was a continuous increase in the real and the real effective exchange rates between 1968 and 1974 which stimulated the growth of minor exports. Thus the initial attempt to improve the profitability of exporting and of increasing the real exchange rate for imports was sustained and improved. This made it possible to liberalize imports, as protection through tariffs and QRs was exchanged for protection via the exchange rate. After 1975, the real effective exchange rate fell. The consequences of this fall indicate that export subsidies had been insufficient to offset the disincentive created by a fall in the real exchange rate.

Another indicator of the profitability of exporting in the period 1967–83 is the ratio of the implicit price of sales in the domestic market to the implicit price of sales in foreign markets. This ratio is shown in table 3.4 (see also García García, 1988, appendix table 13). For manufacturing, in particular, the profitability of exporting increased substantially in 1967–75 and then fell steadily. It should not be surprising, then, that noncoffee exports were stagnant in the second half of the 1970s and early 1980s.

Monetary Policy

Monetary Management

Monetary growth during the period 1966–82 falls into two subperiods: during the period 1966–71 the money supply M1 grew at an annual rate of 16 percent and during the period 1972–82 it grew at a rate of 24 percent per

Table 3.4 Profitability of exporting versus selling in the domestic market, 1965–1983 (1975 = 100)

Year	Broad agriculture	Total industry	Total services	Total sectors
1965	69.6	59.9	61.7	76.1
1966	62.3	50.0	55.8	65.7
1967	77.9	47.4	66.3	73.7
1968	82.2	52.6	69.4	75.4
1969	83.1	51.1	67.1	73.7
1970	103.6	58.5	84.0	90.1
1971	91.9	60.3	86.4	82.1
1972	101.9	68.2	84.8	87.6
1973	110.7	80.1	86.6	98.5
1974	100.8	101.8	98.3	102.7
1975	100.0	100.0	110.0	110.0
1976	139.8	100.8	100.5	119.9
1977	174.4	92.7	96.5	133.2
1978	128.2	90.1	89.2	111.2
1979	108.7	93.0	85.0	98.2
1980	118.8	91.9	89.9	104.3
1981	91.2	91.7	84.2	86.4
1982	89.1	86.5	80.3	81.5
1983	88.2	83.0	82.0	80.3

Source: Derived from DANE, 1985

year. As a result of this increase, the rate of inflation accelerated from 8.9 to 21.5 percent per year, and the velocity of circulation of money increased from 7.1 to 9. Information on the money supply, the monetary base, inflation, and the velocity of money is presented in table 3.5.

One distinguishing feature of monetary growth in Colombia during this period was that the monetary base increased at a higher rate (24.4 percent per year) than the money supply (21 percent per year). Thus the money multiplier decreased at a rate of 3.4 percent per year, falling from 2 to 1.5 between 1966–71 and 1972–82. This decrease in the multiplier was achieved by an increase in the reserve requirements for deposits in commercial banks, which went from 0.18 to 1965 to 0.66 in 1980. Although reserve requirements are normally established on an average basis, the monetary authorities made ample use of the 100 percent marginal reserve requirement in 1972, 1975, and 1977–9. The increasing importance of the reserve requirement was due to an unwillingness to use more efficient instruments of monetary control, such as open-market operations, because the government and the Banco de la República were not willing to pay for the costs of such operations.[7] As the Banco de la República became more

---

[7] In late 1974 and 1975 there was an attempt to implement open-market operations, but opposition from influential groups arguing that these operations increased interest rates and produced a recession led the government to end such operations.

Table 3.5 Money supply, money base, inflation, and money multiplier, 1966–1982 (million pesos)

	1966	1967	1968	1969	1970	1971	1972	1973	1974	1975	1976	1977	1978	1979	1980	1981	1982
Currency in hands of public	4,140	4,781	5,577	6,594	7,913	8,710	10,913	12,851	16,174	21,090	28,943	40,744	53,350	66,706	79,002	100,565	129,094
Demand deposits	6,888	8,669	9,858	11,854	13,714	15,285	18,928	25,721	29,939	37,825	50,440	62,695	81,182	100,524	138,243	158,212	196,605
Savings accounts	1,705	1,990	2,367	2,716	3,426	4,148	5,832	7,974	9,623	12,288	16,917	24,109	33,642	45,970	57,241	72,725	n.a.
Money M1	11,027	13,450	15,435	18,448	21,627	23,995	29,842	38,572	46,113	58,915	79,383	103,439	134,532	167,230	217,245	258,777	325,699
Money M2	12,733	15,440	17,802	21,164	25,053	28,143	35,673	46,546	55,736	71,204	96,300	127,548	168,174	213,200	274,486	331,501	n.a.
Money base	5,542	7,121	8,963	11,254	13,487	14,959	18,404	24,124	28,814	38,063	54,213	74,817	100,906	131,588	170,512	206,232	242,767
Currency/deposits	0.60	0.55	0.57	0.56	0.58	0.57	0.58	0.50	0.54	0.56	0.57	0.54	0.66	0.66	0.57	0.64	0.66
Reserves/deposits	0.20	0.27	0.34	0.39	0.41	0.41	0.40	0.44	0.42	0.45	0.50	0.54	0.59	0.65	0.66	0.67	0.58
M1/money base	1.99	1.89	1.72	1.64	1.60	1.60	1.62	1.60	1.60	1.55	1.46	1.38	1.33	1.27	1.27	1.25	1.34
M2/money base	2.30	2.17	1.99	1.88	1.86	1.88	1.94	1.93	1.93	1.87	1.78	1.70	1.67	1.62	1.61	1.61	n.a.
M1/GDP	13.76	14.31	14.74	14.95	14.84	14.32	13.76	13.56	12.66	12.35	12.17	12.36	12.52	11.90	11.18	13.05	13.04
M2/GDP	15.86	16.50	16.98	17.18	17.09	16.72	16.32	13.84	15.33	15.03	14.82	15.18	15.65	15.16	14.30	16.72	n.a.
Rate of inflation	14.92	8.31	9.36	8.18	12.10	10.81	12.97	20.16	25.38	22.81	25.46	29.15	17.10	24.04	27.62	22.77	24.77
Rate of growth of GDP	5.35	4.20	6.12	6.37	6.74	5.96	7.67	6.72	5.75	2.32	4.73	4.16	8.47	5.38	4.09	2.28	0.95
Velocity of circulation of money[a]	7.27	6.99	6.78	6.69	6.74	6.98	7.27	7.38	7.90	8.10	8.21	8.09	7.99	8.40	8.95	8.96	9.19

n.a. not available.

Money M1 is the currency in circulation plus demand deposits; money M2 is M1 plus savings accounts in banks; money base is the currency in the hands of the public plus actual reserves held by commercial banks; the money multiplier is equal to M1 divided by the money base; the inflation rate is the rate of change of the implicit price deflator of GDP.

[a] Calculated with average M1.

Sources: World Bank, 1984, table 6.1, p. 226; Banco de la República, communications to author.

interested in supplying credit than in acting as a central bank, its monetary policy decisions were subordinated to profit considerations. To offset the increase in the monetary base due to the expansion of directed credit programs, the money multiplier was reduced to assure that monetary expansion would take place at a reasonable rate.[8]

Some actions intended to eliminate forced investments, directed credit programs, and other distortions in the domestic capital market were begun in 1974, but these attempts at reform were short lived, in part because sterilization of the large foreign exchange inflows of 1975 and 1976 was met with traditional and, for that purpose, ineffective instruments of monetary policy (reserve requirements and prior deposits) (see Hanson, n.d.; Jaramillo, 1982, pp. 7–19). Further liberalization of the financial sector was thereby precluded.

Severe, and sometimes incoherent, measures of monetary control were brought into play in 1976–7, and some control was established but probably at the cost of a substantial repression of commercial banks' ability to intermediate resources.[9] Thus, while the money multiplier at the end of 1974 (a "normal" year) was 1.6, at the end of 1977 it was 1.38 (see table 3.5). In addition to the 100 percent marginal reserve requirement established in early 1977, the most important step taken to sterilize the accumulation of international reserves was the establishment of an exchange certificate system in May 1977.[10] The main purpose of this measure was to postpone the monetization of reserves, not to avoid it. As it turned out, exchange certificates only had an impact in 1977. At year end the stock of certificates was equivalent to 21 percent of the monetary base. The certificates were classified by the Banco de la República as an open-market instrument, but they were far from being so despite having a

[8] The increasing role of the Banco de la República as a development bank has been the result of deliberate policy action, which started in the mid-1960s and was later pushed by pressures from interest groups benefiting from such a system. It can be argued that this role has been pushed onto the Banco de la República because authority on monetary policy rests with the Monetary Board, presided over by the Minister of Finance. However, the Banco de la República has considerable clout, and as the implementing agent of monetary policy it can easily block or push certain policy options. The lack of a clear role of the Banco de la República in monetary policy has been one of the most serious problems for the conduct of that policy. For an analysis of this problem, see Currie (1983, chapter 3).

[9] For a defense of the policies implemented between December 1976 and June 1978, see Sarmiento-Palacio (1982, chapter 2).

[10] Under this system, foreign exchange proceeds surrendered to the Banco de la República were paid with freely negotiable foreign exchange certificates, redeemed at par if presented six months from the date of issue or at a 10 percent discount if presented within 30 days from date of issue. This measure, one of several taken by the government, was intended to be temporary. Another measure was the establishment of price controls on housing rentals. Both measures are still in force.

contractionary impact.[11] It is important to note that, as the stock of certificates grew larger over the years, it became more difficult to eliminate them. Their impact on the money supply was feared, but the monetary authorities were reluctant to adopt alternative instruments.[12] The inflationary financing of government expenditures left little room for additional monetary expansion.[13]

The government that entered office in August 1978 expected that a foreign exchange shortage would develop in the medium term and launched a massive program of government investment financed with external resources to earn enough foreign exchange to meet the expected shortfall.[14] The shortage did not materialize, however. Instead, the largest increases in international reserves in the country's history (US$1.6 billion and US$1.3 billion respectively) took place in 1979 and 1980. Fiscal policy, however, continued its pre-established course, inflation accelerated, and nominal and real interest rates increased. In 1979, when growth in the money supply exceeded what could reasonably have been expected, the effectiveness of reserve requirements as instruments of monetary control had reached its limit. The only alternative, other than floating the peso, was to implement open-market operations. To implement open-market operations while avoiding further disintermediation of the financial system, ceilings on term certificates of deposits were lifted in 1980 and the marginal reserve requirement for commercial banks was reduced from 100 to 45 percent. Open-market operations became the principal instrument of monetary control to such an extent that *títulos de participación* represented 16.9 percent of the monetary base at the end of 1980. They were severely criticized by the private sector, however, which blamed such operations for

[11] The uselessness and inefficiency of the instrument were evidenced in 1979 and 1980, when its contribution to sterilization was negligible, and was further exposed in 1983 when (despite a substantial fall in international reserves) the outstanding volume of exchange certificates increased substantially, triggered by expectations of devaluation.

[12] Truly open-market operations were discarded in 1977 because the government did not want to pressure interest rates upwards or lift the ceiling on interest rates, a necessary step for the implementation of open-market operations. It was also argued that, if the expectation of inflation were added, the interest rate to be paid on the open-market titles (*títulos de participación*) would have to be very high. See Jaramillo (1982, p. 15).

[13] The establishment of the exchange certificate was also seen as the introduction in the market of a new financial instrument which would strengthen the development of Colombia's capital market. Moreover, the certificate of exchange was considered an open-market operations instrument which would serve to control the money supply. This was not possible, however, since the monetary authorities had no control over the amounts to be issued or redeemed at any particular moment. For an explanation of the various roles the Banco de la República thought this instrument might have, see Banco de la República, *Informe del Gerente a la Junta Directiva* (1978, pp. 58–60).

[14] The possibility of a foreign exchange shortage after the coffee boom had already been mentioned by Wiesner in March 1978. See Wiesner (1978, p. 195; 1982, pp. 41–2).

the prevailing high interest rates. Open-market operations were abolished in 1982 for the avowed purpose of reducing interest rates, but the causes of high interest rates – a large government deficit and numerous distortions in the financial system – were not attacked.

The lack of a flexible and efficient tool of monetary control marred Colombia's stabilization efforts. Indeed, monetary policy management during the period can only be categorized as clumsy.[15] Monetary policy was used to accommodate all interests, especially those of the Banco de la República and the government.

As tax revenues dropped relative to GDP and government expenditure increased in the late 1970s and early 1980s, new funds from the Banco de la República became an important source of government financing.[16] Inflationary finance in 1982 accounted for 36.7 percent of total tax revenues and was equivalent to 31.6 percent of the monetary base. To avoid further acceleration in the rate of inflation, credit for the private sector was severely restricted.

Restrictions on capital movements were another natural outcome of pursuing a stabilization policy when control of the money supply became more difficult.[17] In general, borrowing abroad was permitted between 1967 and October 30, 1972, when it was prohibited for two months (November and December). It was permitted again during the first six months of 1973, prohibited during the second half of 1973 and all of 1974, permitted during all of 1975 and the first quarter of 1976, and then prohibited again. The prohibitions in 1972, 1973, and 1974 were a response to increases in the money supply caused by external financing of the government deficit and the provision of abundant and cheap Banco de la República credit to certain sectors of the economy. In 1975 the controls were a response to the monetization of the increase in reserves induced by the coffee boom.

---

15 Prior deposits were one instrument widely used during the period, but without much effect. They were used to constrain imports and, as a byproduct, for monetary policy between 1966 and 1974, and to speed and enforce limits on maximum terms of payments abroad and to regulate the use of certificates of exchange between 1975 and 1982. For the operations and use of prior deposits since the mid-1970s, see Clavijo (1982, p. 53).

16 The government's easy access to the Banco de la República was made possible by a facility created in 1967 called "Cuenta Especial de Cambios" (CEC) whose revenues were earmarked for the government. The revenues of the CEC included (a) a tax on coffee exports, (b) a tax on repatriated profits of foreigners, (c) the peso equivalent of interest earned on international reserves, and (d) the accounting profit between the purchase and sale price of foreign exchange by the Banco de la República. See Jaramillo and Montenegro (1982).

17 Permission to borrow abroad for working capital was largely curtailed after 1975, but exceptions to the rule were granted, maximum terms for payments abroad for commodity imports were established, revenue from services was penalized via the discount on a certificate of exchange, and foreign exchange revenue was subject to severe controls to demonstrate its "legitimacy." These measures may have had some value in stabilization policy, but they were evaded by legal or illegal means.

Table 3.6 Domestic interest rates, devaluation rate, parity rate, and Eurodollar rate, 1967–1983 (percent)

Year	Nominal interest rate	Real interest rate	Rate of devaluation	Interest rate differential[a]	Parity rate[b]	Eurodollar rate
1967	13.5	4.7	16.9	− 7.8	23.2	5.4
1968	13.5	3.8	7.1	− 0.3	13.9	6.3
1969	12.8	4.2	5.5	− 2.5	15.7	9.7
1970	13.2	2.7	6.9	− 2.3	16.0	8.5
1971	16.4	5.2	9.5	− 0.2	16.7	6.5
1972	15.5	2.2	9.0	0.5	14.9	5.4
1973	15.7	− 3.6	8.8	− 2.5	18.8	9.2
1974	30.7	4.2	15.5	1.9	28.2	11.0
1975	27.4	3.6	15.1	3.4	23.1	6.9
1976	21.1	− 3.4	10.2	4.1	16.3	5.5
1977	19.8	− 7.1	4.5	8.1	10.7	6.0
1978	20.2	2.6	8.0	2.3	17.4	8.7
1979	30.5	5.1	7.3	8.6	20.1	11.9
1980	34.3	5.2	15.7	1.5	32.3	14.3
1981	37.3	11.8	16.0	1.5	35.1	16.5
1982	38.0	10.7	19.0	2.5	34.6	13.1
1983	33.7	14.1	26.3	− 3.4	38.4	9.6

[a] Interest differential = (1 + nominal rate)/(1 + parity rate) − 1.
[b] Parity rate = (1 + Eurodollar) × (1 + devaluation) − 1.

Sources: Eurodollar figures, IMF, 1984; interest rates 1968–73, Montes and Candelo, 1982; interest rates 1974–83, Correa, 1984

Another boom, mainly in coffee, and a very expansionary fiscal policy resuscitated them in 1979. As inflation heated up and the reserve requirements of commercial banks were increased, domestic interest rates increased, the differential between domestic and external rates widened, foreign loans became more attractive, and restrictions were intensified (see table 3.6). In summary, the many changes in restrictions on capital inflows were triggered by exogenous events and instituted for monetary policy reasons. Their purpose was never to smooth out or to hinder trade liberalization. The restrictions never isolated the domestic capital market from the foreign capital market.[18]

Interest Rates, Devaluation, and Inflation

Interest rates increased continuously between 1967 and 1983 because of rising inflation, an increase in bank reserve requirements, the widespread

[18] A first attempt to study the extent of capital mobility in Colombia is by García García (1978); see also Fernández and Candelo (1983, pp. 49–69). Recent studies showing that capital mobility in Colombia is rather high are those by Edwards and Khan (1985, pp. 377–404) and Edwards (1985a, pp. 59–68).

use of forced investments to enforce selective credit controls, and increases in international interest rates.

The period 1967–77 can be categorized as one of low rates, except for 1973–4, while the period 1978–83 was one of relatively high rates. It is not mere coincidence that Colombia's economic growth slowed down substantially after 1978.

Fiscal Policy

Fiscal policy during most of the 1967–82 period kept the central government's deficit quite manageable. Between 1967 and 1978 the average annual central government deficit was less than 1 percent of GDP. Subsequently, however, a very expansive fiscal policy produced a large and growing deficit each year which had deleterious effects on the real exchange rate, the current account balance, and economic activity in general.

The low deficits of the early 1970s turned into a surplus in 1976–8, partly because of a rise in tax revenues but mainly because of a contraction in public investment carried out as part of stabilization efforts. High deficits then began in 1979. Public revenues fell because of widespread tax evasion induced by high tax rates imposed in 1974 and a poor system of tax administration, and because access to inflationary finance was very easy.[19] Viewed from the perspective of the consolidated public sector, the most dramatic change during the whole period took place between 1978 and 1983, when government expenditures increased from 28.1 to 39.9 percent of GDP while revenues only increased from 27 to 31 percent of GDP. As a result, the consolidated pubic sector deficit increased from 1.2 to 8.6 percent of GDP in 1983 (table 3.7).

These movements in fiscal policy had their counterpart in money creation by the government. Between 1967 and 1975 the deficit contributed to 66.7 percent of the growth of the monetary base. It had a negative impact between 1976 and 1978, but it represented around 92 percent of the growth of the monetary base in 1979–81 (table 3.8).

Wage Policy

Colombia's labor laws cover labor contracts, wages and salaries, fringe benefits, and collective bargaining rights. Wages and fringe benefits are the government's chief preoccupations in designing labor policy.[20]

---

[19] A detailed analysis of the 1974 tax reform is given by Gillis and McLure (1977) and World Bank (1975).
[20] This section draws on Guterman (1984).

Table 3.7 Central government and consolidated public sector operations as a proportion of gross domestic product, 1967–1984 (percent)

| Year | Central government | | | | Consolidated public sector | |
	Tax revenues	Money creation revenue	Total expenditures	Deficit	Expenditures	Deficit
1967	8.8	n.a.	9.80	− 0.28	25.2	3.6
1968	9.2	n.a.	11.40	− 0.59	27.8	5.1
1969	8.5	n.a.	9.30	− 0.84	30.9	7.7
1970	9.2	− 0.27	9.99	− 0.7	30.6	6.9
1971	9.3	− 0.12	10.31	− 0.9	31.6	7.4
1972	8.6	− 0.18	10.42	− 1.7	29.9	6.5
1973	8.3	0.00	9.52	− 1.1	25.2	− 7.1
1974	7.8	0.33	9.00	− 1.1	25.1	0.9
1975	8.7	0.29	9.71	− 0.9	26.0	− 0.9
1976	8.9	0.20	8.33	0.6	28.6	1.9
1977	8.5	0.29	8.04	0.5	27.5	2.7
1978	8.9	0.33	8.60	0.3	28.1	1.2
1979	8.3	1.28	9.15	− 0.7	29.7	4.0
1980	8.3	1.25	10.34	− 1.9	33.5	5.8
1981	7.9	2.43	10.84	− 2.9	35.1	6.8
1982	7.5	2.71	11.66	− 4.1	37.3	8.9
1983	7.1	1.76	11.35	− 4.2	39.8	8.5
1984	7.6	3.66	12.07	− 4.4	n.a.	n.a.

Sources: Dirección General de Presupuesto, 1973, Boletín 64, December, pp. 119–123, for 1967–8; consolidated public sector expenditures for 1967–72, Misión Bird-Wiesner, 1981; Banco de la República, various years, for 1969; Banco de la República, Departamento de Investigaciones Económicas for 1970–84; and/or 1973–82, Departamento Nacional de Planeación, 1984; expenditures and deficit for 1983 are estimated

Minimum Wage

A minimum wage of 2 pesos a day for all rural and urban workers was first established by the government in 1943, and the arrangement remained in force until October 1956, when several categories of minimum wages were established. This system lasted until 1969, when a new arrangement was put into place under which the minimum wage would be determined by sector, but that system was then simplified in 1974, when minimum wages for the primary (agriculture, forestry, fishing, and mining) and nonprimary sectors were established. The minimum wage was then unified again in 1984.

Real minimum wages were very high in the 1950s and 1960s, reaching a peak in 1963 (see García García, 1988, appendix table 15). They then

Table 3.8 Government contribution to change in monetary base, 1967–1981

Year	Change in money base (million pesos)	Government share (million pesos)	(%)	Share as a percentage of GDP
1967	1,290	910	70.5	1.10
1968	2,050	410	20.0	0.40
1969	2,140	1,360	63.6	1.20
1970	2,080	1,040	50.0	0.80
1971	1,370	2,020	147.4	1.30
1972	3,370	2,970	88.1	1.60
1973	5,726	1,142	19.9	0.47
1974	4,539	3,507	77.3	1.07
1975	9,076	5,748	63.3	1.39
1976	15,679	− 3,817	− 24.3	− 0.72
1977	21,439	− 4,330	− 20.2	− 0.60
1978	26,410	− 4,744	− 18.0	− 0.52
1979	30,721	2,368	7.7	0.20
1980	38,126	34,957	91.7	2.20
1981	36,798	64,787	176.1	3.20

Sources: Barro, 1973, table 2; Departamento Nacional de Planeación, 1982

declined steadily until November 1974, when a 33 percent increase in nominal wages was decreed. In 1976 the minimum wage was indexed to approximately the rate of inflation. Indexation in effect produced a floor for adjustment in industrial wages, thereby undermining the industrial sector's ability to adjust to reductions in the real exchange rate and in the demand for industrial products. Moreover, this was compounded by the fact that productivity in the industrial sector declined in the second half of the 1970s; thus the negative impact of import liberalization on the profitability of the industrial sector and on the competitiveness of industrial exports was larger than it would otherwise have been, thereby leading to the strong and, in the end, successful opposition to import liberalization policy pursued in the late 1970s and early 1980s.

Fringe Benefits

Fringe benefits are all payments to employees other than the basic wage. This important element of worker compensation gained increasing importance, rising from 39.7 to 49.4 percent of the wage bill between 1967 and 1980.[21] The increase occurred because of new taxes on wages and changes

[21] For the industrial sector, average benefits as a percentage of wages increased from 26 to 43.7 percent between 1967 and 1982. See García García (1986, table B.6.3).

in the way severance payments were calculated. Increases in wages increased the value of severance payments (see García García, 1988, appendix table 15).[22]

Other Interventions

Government intervention also occurs in other spheres of the labor market. The government has substantial influence on collective bargaining and serves as a mediator in many employee–employer disputes. In addition, labor courts are part of the Ministry of Labor and are not in the judiciary system.

Layoffs and firings require, in many instances, prior consent of the Ministry of Labor, and it is difficult to fire workers with ten or more years of service. As a result, one-year contracts have become more common, especially for unskilled workers. Although highly skilled workers continue to work year after year, many are dismissed at the end of the ten-year period. The consequence of this legislation, whose purpose was to guarantee stability to workers, has been an increase in the turnover rate, thereby depriving both companies and workers of the benefits of long association. The inflexibility of labor legislation leads to rigidities in the labor market that affect large enterprises more than small ones, because large companies are more visible, are unionized, and thus are more likely to come under scrutiny.

---

[22] Severance pay is the most important fringe benefit. See Isaza (1981) and Ocampo and Villar (1982).

4

Economic Performance during Liberalization

Economic Circumstances and Developments in 1966–1970

Colombia's economic situation in August 1966 was not good. Net international reserves were negative, the differential between official and free-market exchange rates was 50 percent, the GDP deflator was increasing at an annual rate of 19.7 percent, consumer prices were rising at an annual rate of 14.6 percent, and the central government deficit was 1.7 percent of GDP. Unemployment had increased from 8.9 percent the previous year to 10.1 percent.

Management of economic policy had been inconsistent for several years, and as a result the life span of government policies was perceived to be short.[1] Therefore, when imports were liberalized between September 1965 and August 1966, the private sector intensified its demand for imports.

The signs that this liberalization was unsustainable were clear. Total commodity exports had been declining since 1964, while the value of merchandise imports (which had declined 23 percent between 1964 and 1965) increased 48 percent in 1966. Terms of trade, which had been fairly stable in 1965, dropped 21 percent in 1966, and the deficit in the current account increased from 0.6 percent to 5.9 percent of GDP. These events took place in the context of an annual rate of inflation of 20 percent and in the presence of a pegged exchange rate. Businessmen knew that liberalization would have to be reversed or a major devaluation would have to take place.

The new administration that took office in 1966 continued the liberalization policy, but it refused to devalue the currency when pressed by the IMF

---

[1] For a description of the events that took place between November 1962 and November 1966, the conduct of economic policy during that period, and the implications of such events for the establishment of a full exchange control system in late 1966, see Díaz-Alejandro (1976, chapter 7) and García García (1976, chapters 1–3).

to do so. The government opted for a strict exchange control regime, and Colombia's most ambitious liberalization attempt up to that time ended in November 1966.

To achieve balance-of-payments equilibrium, severe trade restrictions and exchange controls were established. A strong effort was made to increase tax revenues by establishing a system of tax withholding, reducing tax exemptions, and by attacking tax evasion and fraud. Government expenditures increased substantially, and priority was given to investment expenditures. External financing of the government deficit permitted alleviation of the restrictions on imports. The rate of growth of the money supply was maintained at 14–15 percent per year, and efforts were made to control the money supply more effectively. The legal reserve requirement was raised, and the percentage of those reserves which could be invested by banks was reduced substantially, thereby increasing the effective average reserve requirement. The rediscount quota for commercial banks at the Banco de la República was kept low, and an effort was made to increase interest rates above the rate of inflation.[2]

Trade restrictions, handled through QRs, were severe, and import volume fell from an index of 83.1 in 1966 to 59.3 in 1967. At the same time, the terms-of-trade index improved from a low of 67.6 in 1966 to 79.3 in 1967, a surplus in the balance of trade was achieved, and the deficit in current account dropped sharply, to 0.9 percent of GDP in 1967. Between 1966 and 1967 the rate of GDP growth fell from 5.4 to 4.2 percent, and the unemployment rate increased from 10.1 to 12.2 percent. The external environment also became more favorable, with annual rates of growth of Colombia's main trading partners reaching slighly more than 4 percent. A full picture of Colombia's economic circumstances between 1964 and 1967 is presented in table 4.1.

It can be said that the basis for liberalization was established in 1967 when various economic reforms were effected, the most important, perhaps, being the adoption of the crawling peg system. This prevented a substantial decline in the real exchange rate that would have been generated by the pegging of the nominal exchange rate under inflation and reduced the instability of price signals to the export sector until the mid-1970s. The export sector was probably the sector most affected by the policy of fixed exchange rates (see Díaz-Alejandro, 1976, pp. 51–7).

The Structure of Protection

A detailed study by Hutcheson and Schydlowsky on the structure of effective protection in Colombia in 1969 shows that the protection mainly

[2] An official description of the various measures taken during the Lleras Restrepo administration is given by Espinosa Valderrama (1970).

Table 4.1 Economic circumstances at introduction of liberalization, 1964–1967

Economic variable	1964	1965	1966	1967
Trade balance (million US$)	41	151	− 113	88
Current account balance (million US$)	− 142	− 21	− 288	− 73
Capital account other than reserves (million US$)	291	− 40	290	− 12
Balance of payments (million US$)	17	6	− 25	− 34
Total change in reserves (million US$)	− 30	− 16	17	28
Exports (million US$)	548.1	539.1	507.6	509.9
Coffee exports (million US$)	394.2	343.9	339.2	322.4
Noncoffee exports (million US$)	153.9	195.2	168.4	187.5
Imports c.i.f. (million US$)	586.3	453.5	674.2	496.9
Export volume index (1975 = 100)	77.2	81.4	94.5	78.1
Import volume index (1975 = 100)	67.5	57.1	83.1	59.3
Export unit value (US$ 1975 = 100)	48.5	45.2	36.7	44.5
Import unit value (US$ 1975 = 100)	58.1	53.1	54.3	56.1
Terms-of-trade index	83.4	85.0	67.5	79.5
Export unit value (percentage change)	19.5	− 6.8	− 18.9	21.5
Import unit value (percentage change)	− 1.2	− 8.5	2.2	3.2
Terms-of-trade index (percentage change)	20.9	1.9	− 20.6	17.7
Exports/GDP (%)	9.72	10.1	12.38	12.0
Imports/GDP (%)	10.9	9.24	15.44	11.4
GDP deflator (percentage change)	17.1	8.5	14.6	8.3
Consumer price index (percentage change)	17.7	3.4	19.7	8.2
Industrial countries, GDP index (1980 = 100)	55.4	58.5	61.7	63.8
Venezuela's GDP index (1980 = 100)	49.9	52.9	54.3	56.3
Per capita food output (kg)	673.6	667.4	703.6	725.1
Unemployment rate in Bogota	7.1	8.9	10.1	12.1
Real GDP (percentage change)	6.2	3.6	5.4	4.2

Sources: Trade balance, current account, capital account, balance of payments, total change in reserves, exports, coffee exports, imports, industrial countries' GDP index, and Venezuela's GDP index, IMF, 1984; export and import volume and value, IFS Supplement Series nos. 2 and 4, Banco de la República, Informe del Gerente a la Junta Directiva, 1971

benefited the manufacturing sector, while the primary sector was heavily discriminated against. Net incentives for all exports were negative, but discrimination against exports of manufactured products was rather small (see García García, 1988, appendix table 16).

This structure of protection discouraged employment because there was a positive correlation between effective protection and capital investment intensity by sectors. Similar results were found by Thoumi for 1973 (see Thoumi, 1981, pp. 135–79).

The geographic incidence of protection seems to have been quite varied. Since the primary sector (mining and agriculture), which is the export sector, was penalized by protection, producers of agricultural, livestock, and forestry products in the lowlands and along both the Caribbean and Pacific coasts got lower prices. Industrial production, the main recipient of the benefits of protection, was concentrated in the country's three largest cities (Bogotá, Medellín, and Cali). Producers of milk, wheat, and maize, who are concentrated in the temperate regions where industrial production is concentrated, also received some benefits from protection.

Favorable treatment for industrial production, especially production by large firms, was also evident in the differing treatment of import applications by officials of INCOMEX. In 1970, Díaz-Alejandro analyzed the pattern of approval of import applications by size of the workforce for firms located in Bogotá, Medellín, and elsewhere. He found that large firms – those with more than 200 employees – in Bogotá and Medellín were better treated than firms located elsewhere. Díaz-Alejandro's conclusions were that "sharp differences in approval percentages between Bogotá or Medellín and the rest of Colombia emerge clearly only for the three largest employment categories and the two largest categories of minor exporters. . . . firms from Bogotá or Medellín with at least $50,000 in minor exports in 1970 have the largest percentage of approvals, while . . . the largest employers in Bogotá and Medellín have the most successful performance of those shown" (Díaz-Alejandro, 1976, p. 171). Moreover, "When partial rejections are omitted from the sample, the combined approval rate for firms that imported less than $2 million in 1970 or were located outside Bogotá and Medellín was 68.4 percent; the corresponding rate for the big firms in Medellín or Bogotá was 83.7 percent. The null hypothesis, that is, that there is no relation between chance of approval and the circumstances of being a big firm located in Bogotá or Medellín, must be rejected at the 1 percent level of significance" (Díaz-Alejandro, 1976, p. 172).

The Colombian Economy in the Liberalization Period

The liberalization that took place in Colombia between 1968 and 1982 was the result of a general policy aimed at gradually opening up the economy, promoting exports, and rationalizing instruments of foreign trade. Liberalization intensified during the late 1970s when it was used to reduce inflationary pressures brought about by a foreign exchange surplus and a growing fiscal deficit. Our analysis here concentrates on the identification of differences in the pattern of liberalization in various sectors.

Performance of Major Economic Variables

Information on the major economic variables for the period 1967–83 is presented in tables 4.2 and 4.3. These data are analyzed in the following sections.

1   Real domestic production and real aggregate demand grew fairly rapidly throughout most of the period. Production grew at 6.4 percent per year during the period 1967–74 and at 5.4 percent between 1975 and 1980. The corresponding rates for real aggregate demand were 6.9 and 6.3 percent.

2   The urban unemployment rate rose until 1975 and then declined in a moderate and irregular manner until 1981, when it rose again, climbing from 8.2 percent in 1981 to 11.7 percent in 1983. Employment in the industrial sector grew continuously but at an irregular rate until 1979, and then dropped.

3   The net foreign reserve position of the country improved continuously from 1967 until 1981. Reserve growth accelerated in 1975, and by the end of 1981 Colombia's international reserves had reached a high of US$5.6 billion. After 1981, however, the country's net international reserves declined rather rapidly. That decline undoubtedly contributed to the abandonment of liberalization. Colombia's external debt position was very favorable until 1980, when it began to deteriorate sharply.

4   Inflation began to accelerate in 1972, and after 1973 it fluctuated between 17.1 and 29.1 percent per year when measured by the GDP deflator, and between 17.8 and 33.1 percent per year when measured by the consumer price index.

5   Nominal industrial wages grew during the period 1967–75 at an average of 15.1 percent per year. This was only slightly higher than the 13.8 percent annual increase in the consumer price index during the period. In the second half of the 1970s, however, and even during the 1980–2 recession industrial wages grew much faster than the general price level. The index of the real unit cost of labor in manufacturing (nominal wages deflated by prices in the sector) grew at 47 percent between 1975 and 1982.

6   The real rate of interest behaved in an irregular manner until 1977, after which an upward trend began which can be attributed to the effect of world interest rates and to Colombia's growing fiscal deficit. The effect of rising interest rates on aggregate demand and output seems to have been strongly negative.

7   The trade sector played a decisive role in the pace of economic activity and the level of employment:

    (a)   Terms of trade improved during most of the 1967–82 period, and substantially so between 1975 and 1977. The 1975–7 improvement contributed to an increase in real income and consumer expenditures. The terms of trade then deteriorated, but that change was largely compensated for by an increase in the volume of exports, mostly coffee, during the

Table 4.2 Performance of major economic variables before and during the liberalization episode, 1967–

Variable	1967	1968	1969	1970	1971	1972	1973	1974
GDP index at 1975 prices	61.5	61.3	69.5	75.9	80.4	86.6	92.4	93.
Index of real aggregate demand	62.6	67.8	72.2	78.2	84.5	88.1	93.6	99.
Rate of urban unemployment	n.a.	n.a.	n.a.	7.5	8.5	8.6	n.a.	10.
Index of total employment in manufacturing	64.3	66.2	71.5	76.0	77.4	84.0	92.6	98.
Index of business failures	166.7	105.4	120.5	122.1	110.3	n.a.	76.0	71.
Trade balance (million US$)	88.0	− 10.0	24.0	− 14.0	− 148.0	130.0	280.0	− 16.
Current account balance (million US$)	− 73.0	− 164.0	− 175.0	− 293.0	− 454.0	− 190.0	− 55.0	− 350.
Foreign exchange net reserves (million US$)	− 36.2	35.2	96.5	152.0	170.0	345.0	516.0	429.
Debt service ratio					21.4	21.4	20.2	21.
GDP deflator	33.1	36.2	39.2	43.2	47.8	54.0	64.9	81.
Consumer price index	35.5	37.6	41.4	44.2	47.9	54.3	65.5	81.
Implicit price deflator of exports	23.5	27.3	30.6	38.3	38.8	46.7	62.7	83.
Implicit price deflator of imports	25.9	29.9	32.6	36.1	38.8	43.4	53.1	79.
Index of nominal wages in manufacturing	32.2	34.8	39.3	46.1	51.9	59.1	66.1	81.
Index of real unit cost of labor in manufacturing	97.4	99.6	105.1	109.7	112.9	115.1	107.0	99.
Real interest rate	4.8	3.8	4.2	2.8	5.3	2.3	− 3.7	4.
Exports f.o.b./(volume index)	63.2	67.4	73.2	71.8	75.1	84.1	90.4	87.
Coffee				76.9	79.0	79.7	81.5	84.
Noncoffee				68.9	73.1	87.7	96.0	89.
Imports c.i.f. (volume index)	56.5	73.9	77.5	94.4	113.4	98.5	102.1	112.
Competive imports (volume index)	n.a.	n.a.	n.a.	89.8	105.6	96.7	113.2	123.
Index of unit price of export	44.5	45.5	45.7	56.3	53.6	59.9	75.5	101.
Index of unit price of import	56.0	55.4	56.3	56.9	57.8	61.5	72.9	93.
Terms of trade	79.4	82.1	81.1	99.0	92.7	97.3	103.6	108.
Exports f.o.b./gross value of output (%)	10.2	10.2	10.4	9.7	9.5	10.0	10.1	9.
Imports c.i.f./gross value of output (%)	8.2	10.1	9.9	11.3	12.7	10.4	10.1	10.
Competitive imports/gross value of output (%)	n.a.	n.a.	n.a.	18.0	19.2	16.0	18.1	17.
Index of real effective exchange rate								
For imports	79.8	81.3	82.1	79.2	78.4	82.3	87.8	99.
For minor exports	88.4	88.2	90.3	88.4	93.7	96.0	98.5	102.
For coffee exports	85.3	92.2	91.9	119.6	100.2	104.3	125.7	113.

n.a., not available.

Source: Prepared by the author

'75	1976	1977	1978	1979	1980	1981	1982	1983
00.0	104.7	109.1	118.3	124.7	129.8	132.7	134.0	135.3
00.0	105.7	110.8	122.1	127.8	135.7	139.4	142.3	141.2
10.6	10.2	9.4	7.6	8.9	9.7	8.2	9.1	11.7
00.0	102.8	106.7	109.6	113.1	113.0	109.8	107.1	n.a.
00.0	67.1	73.3	39.1	44.7	21.8	20.4	29.9	38.2
293.0	578.0	734.0	642.0	510.0	− 238.0	− 1,544.0	− 2,189.0	− 1,494.0
109.0	207.0	440.0	322.0	491.0	− 159.0	− 1,895.0	− 2,895.0	− 2,745.0
547.0	1,166.0	1,830.0	2,482.0	4,106.0	5,416.0	5,630.0	4,891.0	3,078.0
13.9	12.6	11.2	11.7	14.9	10.2	21.8	21.7	29.6
100.0	125.5	162.0	189.7	235.4	300.3	368.7	460.0	559.6
100.0	120.4	160.2	188.7	235.2	297.6	379.0	472.6	566.1
100.0	146.3	203.9	203.9	225.1	303.3	315.6	371.8	442.2
100.0	116.0	135.1	148.6	187.7	243.6	288.3	330.4	388.2
100.0	126.5	160.7	218.9	273.5	354.4	465.9	624.3	n.a.
100.0	106.0	110.1	124.6	124.7	128.0	135.0	147.0	n.a.
3.7	− 3.4	− 0.7	2.7	5.2	5.3	11.8	10.8	14.2
100.0	96.8	92.5	115.7	125.4	131.8	116.2	114,2	113.0
100.0	86.5	67.4	116.3	143.9	147.1	122.8	120.3	124.0
100.0	103.1	105.4	114.2	112.9	123.3	113.2	110.2	106.0
100.0	112.3	123.3	148.8	150.0	178.1	186.8	202.4	182.0
100.0	111.3	152.4	187.0	184.7	214.2	231.2	268.9	335.0
100.0	146.4	215.2	179.8	177.3	197.6	176.9	175.5	175.9
100.0	104.3	110.5	123.8	136.5	149.7	158.8	162.3	158.8
100.0	140.3	194.8	145.3	129.8	132.0	111.4	108.1	110.7
10.3	9.5	8.8	10.1	10.3	10.4	9.0	8.8	8.7
9.1	9.8	10.3	11.5	10.9	12.4	12.8	13.8	12.4
14.4	15.6	17.9	20.4	19.3	23.1	24.8	26.1	29.1
100.0	93.3	81.9	81.2	77.6	71.8	70.0	67.2	65.7
100.0	94.7	83.5	90.0	90.0	89.2	87.3	81.6	83.5
100.0	169.3	257.7	178.2	128.8	135.1	97.6	111.1	n.a.

Table 4.3 Percentage change in major economic variables before and during the liberalization episode, 1968–1983

Sector	1968	1969	1970	1971	1972	1973	1974	1975	1976	1977	1978	1979	1980	1981	1982	1983
GDP index at 1975 prices	-0.39	13.30	9.30	5.97	7.65	6.73	1.42	6.69	4.73	4.16	8.46	5.37	4.11	2.27	0.95	0.96
Index of real aggregate demand	8.33	6.55	8.25	8.06	4.24	6.30	6.32	0.47	5.66	4.89	10.14	4.69	6.20	2.70	2.10	-0.82
Index of total employment in manufacturing	2.89	8.10	6.22	1.84	8.57	10.21	5.89	1.99	2.84	3.71	2.74	3.21	-0.08	-2.82	-2.52	n.a.
Index of business failures	-36.77	14.33	1.33	-9.66	-100.00	-6.32	40.45	-32.90	9.24	-46.66	14.32	-51.23	-6.42	46.57	27.76	n.a.
Foreign exchange net reserves	-197.24	174.15	57.51	11.84	102.94	49.57	-16.86	27.51	113.16	56.95	35.63	65.43	31.90	3.95	-13.13	-37.07
GDP deflator	9.37	8.29	10.20	10.65	12.97	20.19	25.42	22.85	25.50	29.08	17.10	24.09	27.57	22.78	24.76	21.65
Consumer price index	5.92	10.11	6.76	8.37	13.36	20.63	24.27	22.85	20.40	33.06	17.79	24.64	26.53	27.35	24.70	19.78
Implicit price deflator of imports	16.10	11.96	25.07	1.25	20.44	34.24	33.63	19.45	46.26	39.38	0.03	10.41	34.70	4.07	17.80	18.95
Implicit price deflator of exports	15.38	9.02	10.54	7.54	11.91	22.37	48.74	26.57	15.99	16.43	10.00	28.38	29.76	18.32	14.63	17.49
Index of nominal wages in manufacturing	8.07	12.93	17.20	12.61	13.90	11.86	22.59	23.44	26.49	27.05	36.19	24.95	29.59	31.45	34.00	n.a.
Index of real unit cost of labor in manufacturing	2.27	5.50	4.34	2.93	1.98	-7.09	-7.38	0.93	5.98	3.88	13.17	0.07	2.65	5.45	8.90	n.a.
Exports f.o.b. (volume index)	6.96	8.56	-1.87	4.57	11.89	7.56	-3.34	14.44	-3.19	-4.50	25.17	8.36	5.10	-11.83	-1.76	-1.02
Coffee	n.a.	n.a.	n.a.	2.75	0.98	2.22	3.52	18.53	-13.51	-22.07	72.55	23.73	2.24	-16.50	-2.08	-3.08
Noncoffee	n.a.	n.a.	n.a.	6.08	20.06	9.38	-6.95	11.98	3.14	2.22	8.33	-1.11	9.20	-8.18	-2.68	-3.81
Imports c.i.f. (volume index)	30.71	4.85	21.83	20.14	13.14	3.71	9.99	-10.98	12.33	9.75	20.73	0.78	18.75	4.90	8.31	-10.06
Competitive imports (volume index)	n.a.	n.a.	n.a.	17.65	-8.42	17.07	8.73	-18.78	11.28	36.91	22.72	-1.19	15.93	7.98	16.27	24.60
Index of unit price of export	2.23	0.44	23.37	-4.90	11.80	26.07	34.04	-1.18	46.44	46.97	-16.44	-1.43	11.49	-10.50	-0.78	0.23
Index of unit price of import	-1.07	1.59	1.10	1.56	6.49	18.48	26.55	6.71	4.34	5.88	12.06	10.28	9.65	6.10	2.17	-2.12
Terms of trade	3.33	-1.13	22.03	-6.37	4.99	6.41	4.28	-7.39	40.35	38.80	-25.43	-10.62	1.68	-15.65	-2.88	2.40
Index of real official exchange rate																
For imports	1.88	0.98	-3.53	-1.01	4.97	6.68	13.21	0.60	-6.70	-12.22	-0.85	-4.43	-7.47	-2.51	-4.00	-2.23
For minor exports	-0.23	2.38	-2.10	6.00	2.45	2.60	3.96	-2.34	-5.30	-11.83	7.78	0.00	-0.89	-2.13	-6.53	2.33
For coffee exports	8.09	-0.33	30.14	-16.22	4.09	20.52	-9.55	-12.05	69.30	52.22	-30.85	-27.72	4.89	-27.76	13.83	n.a.

n.a. not available

1978–80 period. Between 1980 and 1982, though, a fall in the terms of trade was accompanied by a decline in the volume of coffee exports, as well as other exports, because of the international economic recession and a prolonged decline in the real rate of exchange.

(b)   The real effective exchange rates for imports and noncoffee exports rose steadily from 1967 until 1974. From 1975 to 1982, Colombia's foreign exchange surplus created both by the coffee boom and by heavy foreign borrowing by the government led to a reduction of 25 percent in the real rate of exchange for exports and of 30 percent for imports.

(c)   A reduction in nontariff barriers, along with the fall in the real rate of exchange, allowed imports to rise after 1975. During the 1979–82 period, the growth of imports was encouraged by the execution of a development plan based on massive investment in the energy sector (coal, oil, electricity) and in infrastructure for transportation and communication. Thus, import volume grew 10.5 percent per year between 1975 and 1982. Moreover, the volume of competitive imports grew even more rapidly, its volume in 1983 being 3.4 times its 1975 level. The ratio of imports to production, which fluctuated between 9.1 and 10.4 percent during the period 1972–6, rose to 13.8 percent in 1982. The increase in the ratio of competitive imports to domestic production was even greater, expanding from 14.4 to 29.1 percent between 1975 and 1983.

General Characteristics of the Liberalization Process

A detailed study of policy instruments and their effects on the ratio of imports to domestic production reveals two different stages in the liberalization process between 1967 and 1982.

The 1967–75 period was characterized by an increase in the real effective exchange rate for exports and imports, an intensive effort to promote exports, a decline in the use of nontariff barriers to imports, and elimination of "water" in tariffs without incurring significant import growth. In fact, the import-to-output ratio remained virtually stable during this period and even declined for some competitive imports (for example cars). The period from 1976 to 1981–2, however, was characterized by a drop in the real effective exchange rate for imports that produced a sizeable increase in the import-to-output ratio.

There were noticeable differences between sectors with respect to the instruments used to control imports prior to and during the liberalization process, and it is difficult to detect a pattern of liberalization by looking

Table 4.4 Liberalization indices by sector, 1975–1982

Sector	1	2	3	4	5	6	7	8	9	10
	Average nominal paid tariff		Column 1 – column 2	Percentage of imports in free-import regime		Column 5 – column 4	Imports c.i.f./ gross value of output (%)		Column 8 – column 7	Column 8 divided by column 7
	1975	1982		1977	1982		1975	1982		
Beverages	42.9	52.4	– 9.5	99.8	97.5	– 2.3	3.7	4.4	0.7	1.19
Tobacco	0.5	19.2	– 18.7	0.0	44.9	44.9	10.5	21.1	10.6	2.01
Other manufactured agriculture	9.3	26.7	– 17.4	75.0	90.0	15.0	9.1	40.6	31.5	4.46
Textile, apparel, and leather	16.6	22.4	– 5.8	45.1	80.6	35.5	3.1	9.3	6.2	3.00
Wood and wood products	23.3	28.2	– 4.9	21.6	73.9	52.3	1.1	6.7	5.6	6.09
Paper and printing	17.1	14.5	2.6	54.8	82.8	28.0	18.8	24.7	5.9	1.31
Chemicals and rubber	16.8	20.2	– 3.4	78.1	81.1	3.0	32.8	38.7	5.9	1.18
Petroleum refining	4.5	6.8	– 2.3	27.1	49.8	22.7	14.7	35.0	20.3	2.38
Nonmetallic products	23.8	28.6	– 4.8	57.3	68.1	10.8	7.3	9.8	2.5	1.34
Basic metallurgy	15.9	15.5	0.4	78.3	63.9	– 14.4	47.2	95.9	48.7	2.03
Machinery and equipment	21.4	16.0	5.4	73.5	56.1	– 17.4	108.7	205.7	97.0	1.89
Transport materials	19.9	45.4	– 25.5	38.8	18.3	– 20.5	93.4	163.0	69.6	1.75
Other manufactures	22.7	26.8	– 4.1	86.5	41.4	– 45.1	42.3	77.0	34.7	1.82

Source: Fernandez and Garcia Garcia, 1986, part III

only at the way these instruments were handled. This point is illustrated in table 4.4, which presents three different indices of liberalization for each industrial branch. Two were derived from the handling of instruments of protection (changes in tariffs and percentage of imports classified under the free-licensing regime), while the third is based directly on changes in the ratio of imports to production.

The average tariffs paid in most sectors actually increased between 1975 and 1982, although they did decline marginally for paper and printing, basic metallurgy, and machinery and equipment. Ranking the sectors according to absolute or relative changes in the average tariff paid would produce a different ranking from that which would result from choosing changes in the percentage of imports under the free-licensing regime. Yet we cannot say that the government increased tariffs because it was willing to eliminate nontariff barriers. Although that appears to have been true for certain sectors, such as textiles, it was not true of others, such as machinery and equipment, where effective tariffs declined (primarily owing to the implementation of preferential schemes to promote investment). In an attempt to prevent fraud in custom invoices, nontariff controls were increased.

There are no official data on the distribution of imports between prior- and free-licensing lists by manufacturing sector or by chapters of the tariff schedule for the years prior to 1979. However, by using information from the study by Marin et al. (1980), it was possible to arrive at an estimate of the distribution of imports between the prior- and the free-licensing lists by sectors for 1977 and to construct a second liberalization indicator defined as the change in the percentage of imports under the free-licensing regime between 1977 and 1982. On the basis of that indicator a majority of the sectors underwent substantial liberalization during the last part of the 1970s. However, in sectors 22–5 (basic metallurgy, machinery and equipment, transport materials, and other manufactured products) the percentage of imports on the free-licensing list actually declined, even though the import-to-output ratio of these sectors increased substantially.

The last fact suggests that during this period the percentage of imports in each sector on the free list may not have accurately reflected the real degree of liberalization because a number of imports were afforded "prior-free" treatment. That is, although these imports were on the prior-licensing list, import licenses for the goods were granted more or less automatically. Many imports remained on the prior-licensing list as a way of controlling under- or overinvoicing, or for other reasons not related to efforts to restrict imports. A change in the import-to-output ratio is the clearest indication of the extent of liberalization in a sector. In the statistical analysis this variable has a significant effect on production.

Liberalization within Individual Sectors

Table 4.4 suggests that the sectors where liberalization was slow included 18 (paper and printing), 19 (chemicals), and 21 (nonmetallic products). The import-to-output ratio (MOR) for these sectors grew moderately during liberalization, and reductions in tariff and nontariff barriers on imports were significantly less than those in other sectors. It is relevant to point out that at the beginning of the 1970s these three sectors, together with 22 (basic metallurgy), 23 (machinery and equipment), and 24 (transport materials), were chosen for "industrial programming" within the Andean Group. This scheme called for a majority of the products in these sectors to be withdrawn from the intraregional process of liberalization and reserved for a process of complementary integration whereby production of different goods would be allocated to member countries. The object was to expressly eliminate regional competition while establishing common tariffs that applied to the rest of the world and that were generally quite high.

It is important to highlight certain special characteristics of the imports in sectors 13 (beverages), 14 (tobacco), 20 (petroleum refining), and 23 (machinery and equipment). There is a broad subsector in beverages comprising nonalcoholic beverages whose transportation costs make competition from external sources more difficult, and a subsector of alcoholic beverages where high tariffs make smuggling highly profitable. Given the prevalence of these contraband goods, imports of alcoholic beverages might be said to have always been liberalized. Much the same is true of tobacco imports. Registered tobacco imports are but a fraction of actual imports, since a goodly portion of the market is supplied by contraband goods. Thus, rather than having an effect on the ratio of total imports to production, liberalization may have affected the ratio of registered imports to contraband goods. Sector 20 (petroleum refining) is represented essentially by Ecopetrol, a state-owned firm whose prices have always been kept lower than international prices. Imports of gasoline and crude oil rose rapidly during the second half of the 1970s. This was the result not of liberalization but rather of a decline in domestic supply due to a decrease in exploration and in proven oil reserves.

Imports in sector 23 (machinery and equipment) generally have no domestic competition, and the rapid growth of imports in this category during the late 1970s and early 1980s was due primarily to public sector purchases made for development projects in mining (coal and nickel), oil, electricity, and transportation. However, there was also an effective liberalization process for the private sector, implemented through reductions in tariffs and approval of import licenses. A majority of these imports remained on the prior-licensing list simply as a means of controlling overinvoicing.

Sectors demonstrating more effective liberalization included 15 (manu-factured agricultural products), 16 (textiles, apparel, and leather), 17 (wood and wood products), 22 (basic metallurgy), and 25 (other manufac-tured products). The decision to liberalize imports in these sectors, either by transferring goods from the prior to the free list or through virtually automatic granting of import licenses, was influenced by the need to stabilize domestic prices during the last of the 1970s and the early 1980s.

Time Pattern of Sector Responses

What follows is a summary of sectoral behavior during the 1967–82 period for each of the sectors analyzed. The pattern of sector responses is shown in figures that depict the evolution of production, employment, imports, exports, relative prices, import-to-output and export-to-output ratios, value added per worker, and capital intensity (energy consumption per worker) in each sector.

Figures 4.1–4.12, and the statistical analysis in chapter 5, allow the following conclusions.

1   Real industrial output is explained well by aggregate demand, import-to-output and export-to-output ratios, and relative prices. Employment is explained by sector output and unit cost of labor. Imports and exports seem to have had rather high price elasticities. The decrease in import prices relative to the prices of domestic products explains fairly well the increase in the import-to-output ratio in most sectors during liberalization.

2   For most manufacturing sectors the elasticity of output with respect to aggregate demand seemed to be near unity. These results tend to show that the weakness of aggregate demand during the period 1980–2 had an important negative effect on manufacturing output.

3   Since the import-to-output ratio showed large increases between 1975 and 1982, it appears that the negative short-run effect of liberalization on domestic production reinforced the effects of the domestic and world economic recession.

4   The increase in the unit costs of labor made it more difficult for producers to adjust domestic prices to the falling real exchange rate, thus giving rise to an increase in the ratio of imports to production that was larger than would have been expected if the labor market had been more flexible.

5   An export promotion policy prior to liberalization could have reduced the short-run unemployment costs arising from the adjust-ment process.

6   The behavior of import prices accounted for a significant part of the increase in unemployment between 1975 and 1982.

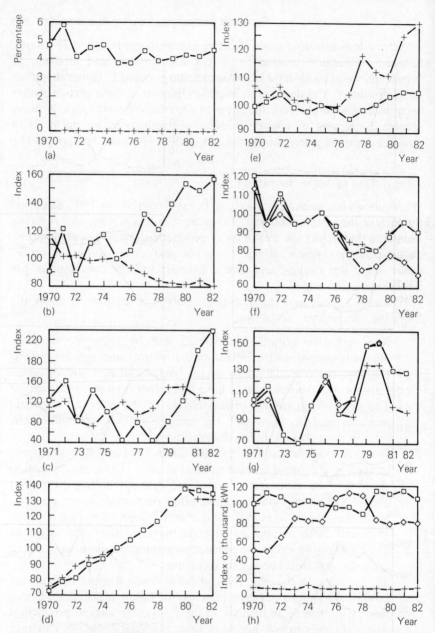

Figure 4.1 Beverages: (a) ratio of imports to product (□) and ratio of exports to product (+); (b) real imports (□) and ratio of the price of import plus tariff to the index of gross output of each sector (+); (c) real exports (□) and the ratio of the price of exports to the gross domestic product deflator (+); (d) real production (□) and employment (+); (e) price of product (□) and real cost of labor (+); (f) price of imports (including tariffs) divided by the gross domestic product deflator (□), the nontraded goods deflator (+), and the unit cost of labor (◇); (g) price of exports divided by the gross domestic product deflator (□), the nontraded goods deflator (+), and the unit cost of labor (◇); (h) value added per worker (□), consumption of energy in kilowatt hours per worker (+), and total white-collar employment divided by total blue-collar employment (percent) (◇)

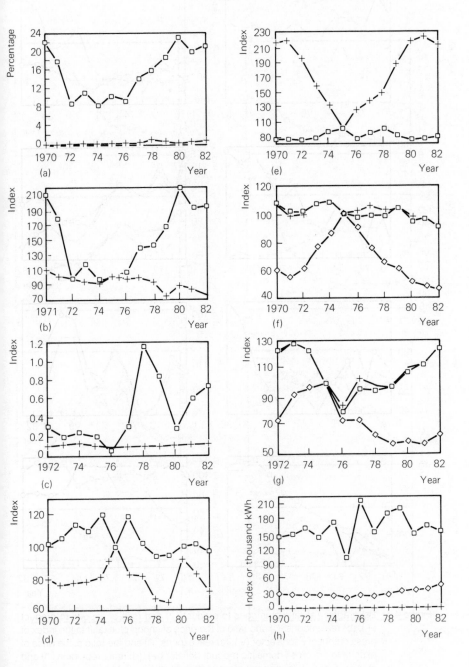

Figure 4.2   Tobacco: for key, see figure 4.1

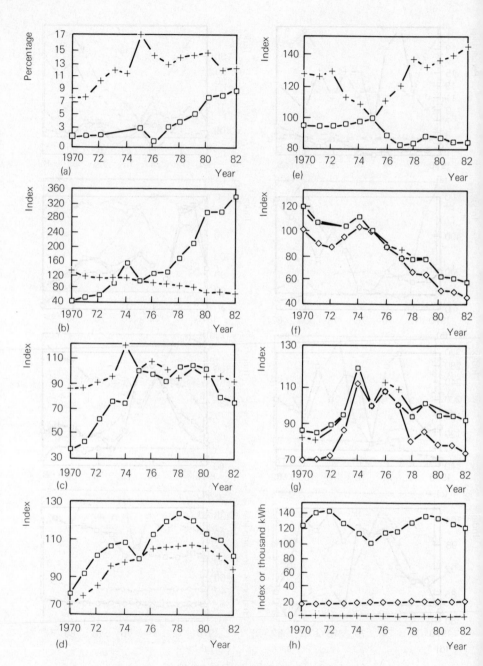

Figure 4.3 Textiles, apparel, and leather: for key, see figure 4.1

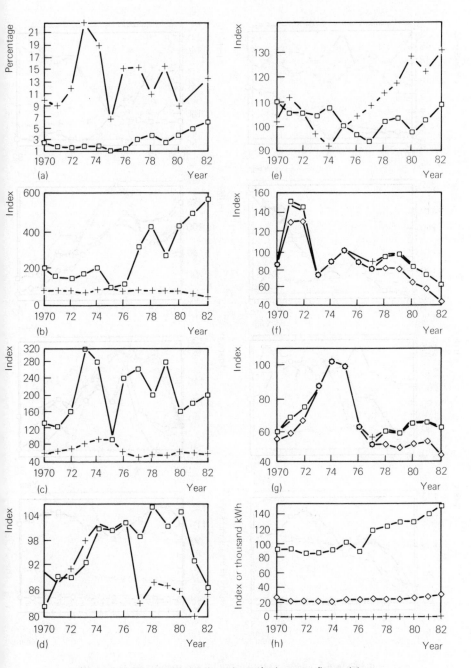

Figure 4.4   Wood and wood products: for key, see figure 4.1

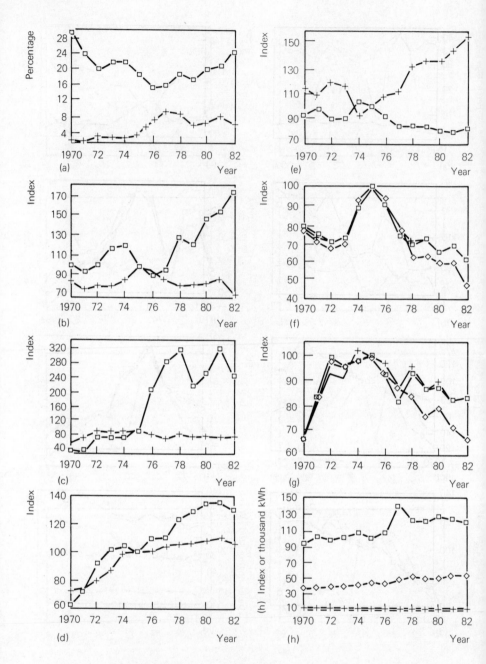

Figure 4.5 Paper and printing: for key, see figure 4.1

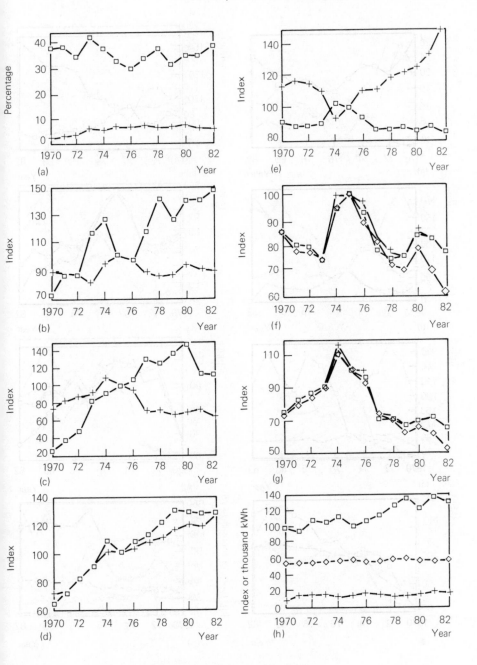

Figure 4.6 Chemicals and rubber: for key, see figure 4.1

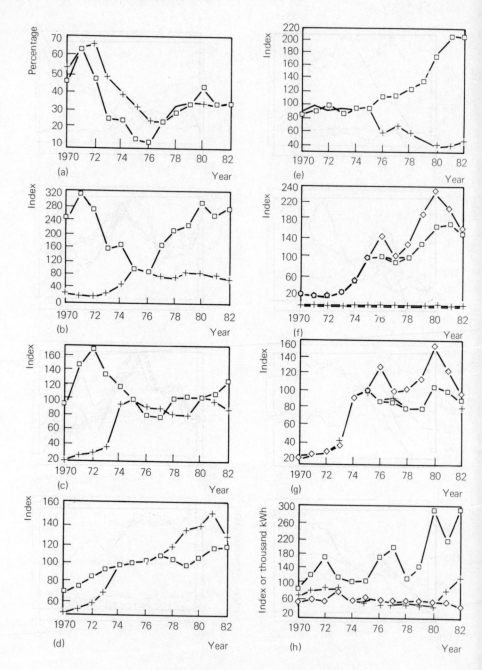

Figure 4.7 Petroleum refining: for key, see figure 4.1

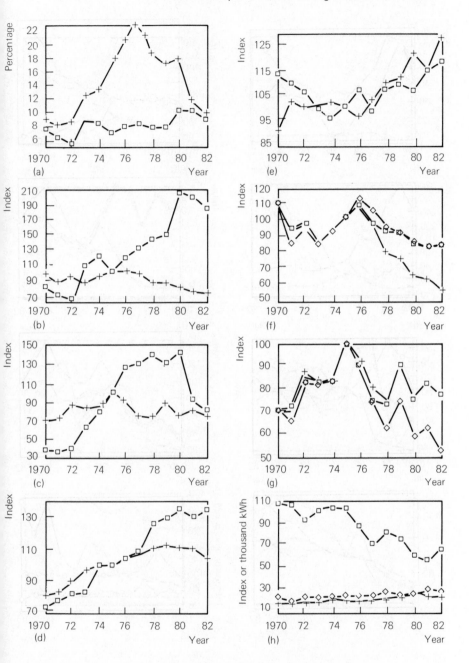

Figure 4.8 Nonmetallic products: for key, see figure 4.1

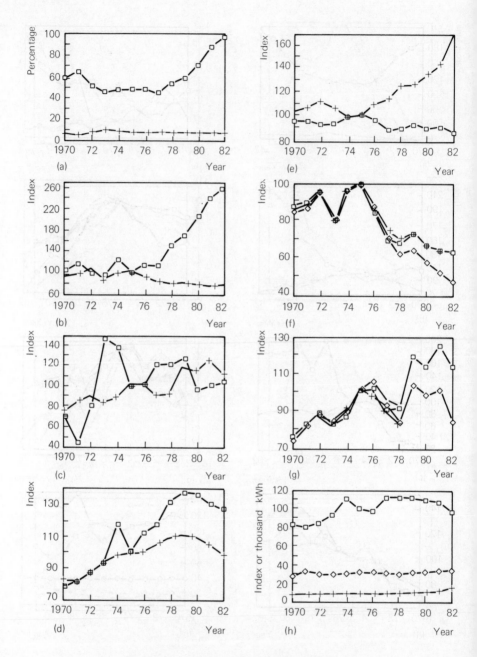

Figure 4.9 Basic metallurgy: for key, see figure 4.1

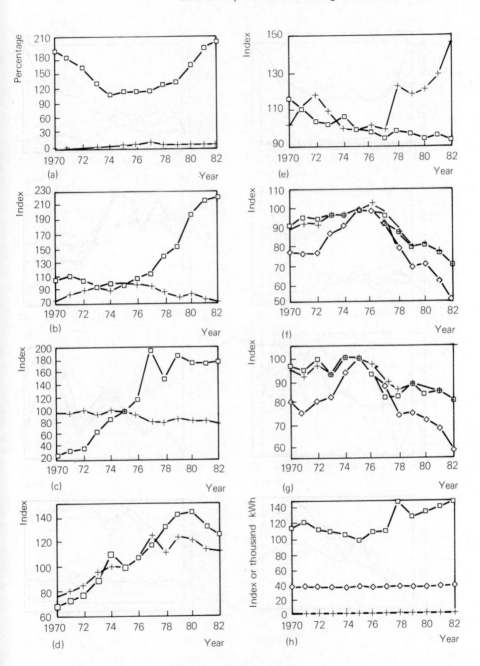

Figure 4.10 Machinery and equipment: for key, see figure 4.1

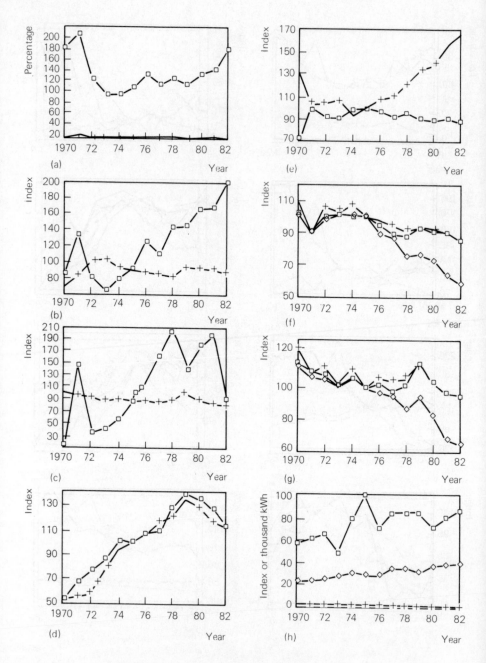

Figure 4.11 Transport materials: for key, see figure 4.1

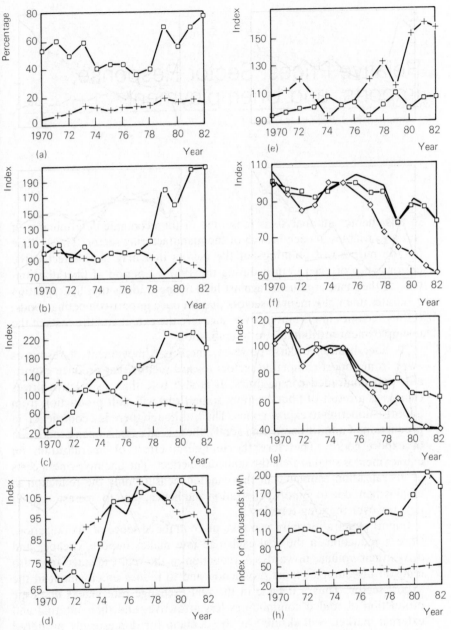

Figure 4.12 Other manufactures: for key, see figure 4.1

5

Relative Prices, Sector Response, Imports, and Unemployment

In this chapter an analysis is presented of the economic determinants of certain variables in each branch of the manufacturing sector. This is done for the purpose of pointing out the factors that may have affected the performance of each branch during the 1967–82 period of liberalization. One of the main arguments against liberalizing trade is that liberalization generates unemployment in sectors that produce import-competing goods. It thus becomes important to try to measure the extent and the costs of the unemployment attributable to liberalization.

As liberalization occurs, however, there is a movement of resources away from import-competing sectors toward sectors that produce exportable and nontraded commodities. It is also true that, as relative prices change as a result of liberalization, some firms will shift production from import-competing to export goods. Thus, although there is a contraction in production of import-competing goods, there is an expansion in production of export goods. Therefore the long-term effect of liberalization on employment is smaller than the immediate effect. The unemployment costs of liberalization estimated in this chapter measure only the reduction in employment due to import penetration and hence, tend to overestimate its net cost over the long term.

Import penetration may also take place in the absence of liberalization, since a reduction in the real exchange rate makes imports cheaper and drives their volume upwards. A reduction in the real exchange rate also tends to discourage export production and to reduce employment in the export sector. Thus a decline in the real exchange rate makes domestic production of traded commodities less attractive, and their internal and external markets will shrink. As the demand for domestically produced tradeable goods falls, domestic economic activity in tradeable sectors and the corresponding demand for labor will tend to decline. When this occurs, popular pressure to impose further restrictions on imports may be difficult to resist. One of the main features of the second half of the liberalization process in Colombia was a substantial fall in the real exchange rate, which explains part of the penetration of imports and the stagnation of manufactured exports, with a consequent negative impact on employment.

In this analysis of unemployment due to liberalization, no attempt was made to separate the effect of reduction in trade barriers from the effect of a fall in the real exchange rate. Therefore the estimated costs of unemployment attributable to liberalization tend to overstate the true costs.

Response of the Various Sectors

In this section an empirical analysis of the response of the various manufacturing branches to changes in relative prices, aggregate demand, and external demand is presented. This analysis was done for the purpose of measuring the cost of unemployment due to liberalization. Our basic assumption is that demand for labor in each sector responds to changes in the real wages and output of that sector. Each sector's output, in turn, is affected by changes in real aggregate demand, competition from imported commodities, and external demand as reflected in the volume of exports of the sector. Demand for imports in any sector is a function of the price of imports relative to some level of internal prices and of the general level of aggregate demand. Demand for exports, in contrast, depends on relative prices and conditions in world markets. Although exports are not taken into consideration in measuring the costs of unemployment, it is important to establish whether exports are responsive to changes in prices and external conditions. Some empirical evidence showing that exports do respond to changes in prices serves to support our contention that the cost of unemployment is overestimated when the employment-creating effects of trade liberalization are ignored.

In order to explore the responses of output, employment, imports, and exports to the relevant variables, least squares regressions were run for each variable of each industrial branch, for the aggregate of some branches, and for the entire manufacturing sector. When regressions for a sector are not reported, this means that the statistical results were not satisfactory. Several efforts have been made to estimate labor demand, import demand, and export supply functions in Colombia, but these estimates were not used because for our purposes it was necessary to have a set of estimates fully compatible with the classification adopted to estimate the level of unemployment due to liberalization in each sector.[1]

[1] For import demand functions, see Gómez, (1982, pp. 89–149) and Villar (1985, pp. 61–101), and the references cited therein. For export supply functions, see Teigeiro and Elson (1973); Cardona (1977); Echavarría (1982); Carrizosa (1981); and Edwards (1985b, appendix B). For labor demand functions for the whole of the industrial sector, see Kugler and Reyes (1984) and Bourguignon (1986). For labor demand functions by industrial branches, see Guterman (1984, chapter 7).

Several regressions were run to estimate the impact of liberalization on employment. The paragraphs below describe the regressions and the use given to them in the analysis. When necessary, the regressions were corrected for autocorrelation.

Regressions were run for an index of real output on an index of aggregate demand (GDP plus imports minus exports), the ratios of real imports-to-real output, the ratios of real exports-to-real output, and relative prices. The relative prices of the output of each manufacturing branch were measured as the implicit price deflator of output in that branch divided by the GDP deflator or by the implicit price deflator of gross output in the nontraded goods sector. The results are presented in table 5.1.

The purpose of this set of regressions was to try to establish empirically the main determinants of output in each industrial branch. One obvious influence on output is the state of aggregate demand in the economy. Other things being constant, it would be expected that the higher the aggregate demand is, the higher is the demand for that sector's production. Another obvious influence on output is its relative price. In this case it would be expected that producers in each industrial branch increase output when its price increases relative to prices in the rest of the economy. The effects of import penetration or export expansion in each industrial branch are measured by the import-to-output and export-to-output ratios. The import-to-output ratio measures the strength of the competition of imports to domestic production; thus the coefficient of the import-to-output ratio measures the impact of liberalization on the performance of each sector. It is expected that the impact of import liberalization will be negative because it reduces the demand for the sector's output. Therefore the expected sign of the estimated coefficient for the import-to-output ratio is negative. Finally, the expected sign for the export-to-output coefficient is positive because an increase in exports increases the demand for the sector's output. Results are reported only for those sectors where a negative effect of imports on output was found.

The results show that import penetration negatively affects the output of textiles, wood and wood products, petroleum refining, basic metallurgy, machinery and equipment, transport materials, and other manufactured goods. In the case of petroleum refining the sign of the coefficient is correct, but the reason why the import-to-output ratio increased was the decline in production induced by fixing the price of crude oil well below the international price. The taxation of oil discouraged exploration and production and the balance between consumption and production had to be supplied by imports as consumption increased and production declined. The effect of exports on output, however, was significant only for wood and wood products and transport materials. Exports did not appear to have had a significant effect on output in the remaining sectors.

Table 5.1 Least squares regressions of real output on aggregate demand, import-to-output ratio, export-to-output ratio, and relative price of output

Sector	Period	Constant	Aggregate demand	MOR		XOR		Relative price		R^2	Durbin–Watson coefficient	Auto correlation coefficient
				t	$t-1$	t	$t-1$	RPON	RPOG			
Textiles	1971–82	40.541 (4.222)	0.799 (7.390)		−4.890 (−5.995)					0.827	2.425	
Wood and wood products	1971–82	55.747 (5.547)	0.417 (3.724)	−4.252 (−3.605)			0.598 (2.313)			0.629	2.330	
Petroleum refining	1970–82	84.937 (21.255)		−0.518 (−7.253)				0.232 (10.464)		0.932	1.384	
Basic metallurgy	1971–82	4.295 (0.341)	1.201 (9.063)	−0.353 (−1.939)						0.894	2.879	−0.366 (−1.119)
Machinery and equipment	1970–82	−180.928 (−2.991)	1.722 (10.687)	−0.250 (−5.341)					1.147 (2.970)	0.968	1.661	
	1971–82	−163.247 (−2.239)	1.587 (10.190)	−0.185 (−2.251)				1.271 (2.111)		0.959	1.547	0.348 (0.786)
Transport materials	1970–82	−23.208 (−0.707)	1.169 (9.632)	−0.311 (−4.251)		3.913 (2.653)			0.270 (1.043)	0.939	2.003	
	1971–82	6.690 (0.484)	1.125 (10.231)	−0.311 (−3.686)		4.054 (2.279)				0.911	1.978	
	1970–82	8.082 (0.606)	1.098 (10.864)	−0.271 (−4.322)		3.205 (2.435)				0.938	1.607	
	1971–82	6.312 (0.407)	1.128 (8.969)	−0.305 (−3.216)		3.862 (1.874)				0.899	1.991	0.058 (0.143)

MOR, ratio of real imports to real output XOR, ratio of real exports to real output; RPOG, implicit price of gross output for each sector divided by the GDP deflator; RPON, implicit price of gross output each sector divided by the implicit price deflator of gross output in the nontraded goods sector; t-statistics are given in parentheses.

The measurement of the effect of imports on sector's output presented in table 5.1 is only the first step in measuring the impact of import liberalization on employment. To determine this effect the hypothetical employment that would have been observed in the absence of liberalization needs to be calculated. To measure the effect on sectoral employment of a change in output the demand for labor in each sector is estimated. The idea behind this exercise is that an increase in the import-to-output ratio reduces output and this leads to a reduction in the demand for labor which produces an equivalent reduction in employment. To estimate the demand for labor, a regression of an index of employment on an index of real output and real unit cost of labor was run for each sector. The real unit cost of labor for each branch is defined as the index of wages and salaries in the branch divided by the implicit price deflator of output of the branch. The expected signs of the coefficients are positive for output and negative for the unit cost of labor. The results of the regressions are presented in table 5.2 (regression results using logarithmic values are given by García García, 1988, appendix table 25). The estimated coefficients reported in table 5.2 have the expected sign and most of them are highly significant.

For those sectors where no direct response of output to the import-to-output ratio was obtained or where it was not possible to estimate a demand for labor, a different approach was followed. In this case, sectoral employment was estimated directly as a function of several variables. More specifically, regressions were run for an index of employment on total aggregate demand or sector output, the import-to-output ratio, the export-to-output ratio, relative prices, and the real unit cost of labor. The relative price for each branch is the implicit price of gross output in that branch divided by the GDP deflator, or by the implicit price of gross output of nontraded goods, or by an index of wages and salaries for the branch. The regressions selected to calculate the impact of liberalization on wood and wood products, paper and printing, and nonmetallic products are presented in table 5.3. Additional regressions for these sectors and results for other sectors are reported by García García (1988, appendix table 26). The regressions presented were selected on the basis of criteria of overall fitness, the significance of the import-to-output ratio variable and the size of this coefficient. In general those regressions which produced a higher (absolute) value for the coefficient of the import-to-output ratio were selected. This procedure was followed because it led to higher estimates of the impact of and hence an upper bound for the cost of liberalization on employment.

The ground on which import liberalization is usually opposed is the expected negative short-term effect on labor employment. However, trade liberalization also has positive effects. One effect of liberalization is to lead to a better allocation of economic resources, and whether this better allocation takes place is determined by the response of sectors to changes

Table 5.2 Least squares regressions of employment on real output and real unit cost of labor

Sector	Period	Constant	Output		Real unit cost of labor	R^2	Durbin–Watson coefficient	Autocorrelation coefficient
			T	t − 1				
Textiles	1971–82	18.736 (1.103)	0.921 (6.252)		− 0.166 (− 1.521)	0.774	1.274	0.003 (1.212)
Wood and wood products	1970–82	121.843 (5.911)	0.251 (1.421)		− 0.501 (− 4.319)	0.600	2.210	
Paper and printing	1971–82	52.015 (6.429)	0.792 (9.737)		− 0.347 (− 3.611)	0.917	1.576	0.003 (1.330)
Petroleum refining	1970–82	− 5.646 (− 0.140)	1.431 (4.570)		− 0.485 (− 3.003)	0.901	1.866	
Nonmetallic products	1971–82	87.369 (5.869)	0.570 (7.884)		− 0.435 (− 2.258)	0.907	1.858	− 0.002 (− 1.153)
Basic metallurgy	1971–82	54.420 (6.601)	0.465 (6.690)		− 0.057 (− 0.566)	0.876	2.817	− 0.002 (− 0.727)
Machinery and equipment	1970–82	59.994 (4.574)	0.647 (9.351)		− 0.230 (− 1.798)	0.886	2.191	
	1971–82	89.513 (4.772)		0.562 (5.574)	− 0.376 (− 1.985)	0.733	1.951	
Transport materials	1971–82	32.638 (2.421)		1.168 (7.753)	− 0.418 (− 2.392)	0.893	1.491	
Other manufactures	1971–82	79.546 (5.033)		0.560 (2.773)	− 0.313 (− 1.866)	0.341	1.583	

t-statistics are given in parentheses.

Table 5.3 Least squares regressions of employment on aggregate demand, import-to-output ratio, export-to-output ratio, real unit cost of labor, and relative prices

Sector	Period	Constant	Aggregate demand for period t	MOR for period t	t − 1	t − 2	XOR for period t − 2	RPOG	R²	Durbin–Watson coefficient
Wood and wood products	1972–82	−18.741 (−0.504)			−5.402 (−4.343)		0.774 (2.545)	1.111 (2.997)	0.662	2.171
Paper and printing	1970–82	56.957 (4.679)	0.576 (8.515)	−1.034 (−2.904)					0.904	1.280
Nonmetallic products	1972–82	79.827 (11.374)	0.197 (2.141)			−1.623 (−2.452)	0.980 (3.275)		0.884	1.405

MOR, ratio of real imports to real output; XOR, ratio of real exports to real output; RPOG, implicit price of gross output for each sector divided by the GDP deflator.
t-statistics are given in parentheses.

in relative prices. The results presented in tables 5.1–5.3 indicate that most branches of the manufacturing sector do respond to relative price changes. By moving resources from import-competing activities to activities that produce exportable commodities, employment expands in the latter while it contracts in the former. Therefore the negative impact of import liberalization on employment is overestimated when only the effect of import penetration on employment in import-competing activities is considered. It is not intended to remedy this problem in the empirical analysis of the following sections and thus the estimated cost of unemployment due to liberalization is overstated if there is some response of exports to changes in relative prices. Moreover, since trade liberalization corrects the distortions in relative prices introduced by QRs and tariffs, to show empirically that imports and exports respond to changes in relative prices serves to stress the point that by looking at the short-run impact of liberalization on employment the costs of trade liberalization are being overstated.

The set of regressions presented below measures the response of industrial imports and exports by manufacturing branch and main aggregates of the manufacturing sector to changes in relative prices and conditions of domestic and world demand.

To measure the response of imports in each manufacturing branch regressions were run of an index of real imports on an index of aggregate demand and relative prices. Relative prices are defined as the implicit price of imports of each branch divided by the GDP deflator, or by the implicit price of nontraded goods, or by an index of wages and salaries for the branch. The results are presented in table 5.4.[2] Similar regressions to estimate the demand for the aggregate of industrial imports were also run. The results are presented in table 5.5.

To measure the response of exports in each manufacturing branch regressions of an index of real exports on an index of foreign demand and the relative price of exports for that branch were run. Relative prices for each branch are defined as the implicit price of exports for that branch divided by the GDP deflator, or by the implicit price of nontraded goods, or by the index of wages and salaries for the branch. The results are presented in table 5.6.[3] To estimate the supply of broad aggregates of industrial exports regressions were run for an index of real industrial exports or the ratio of real exports-to-output on an index of foreign

[2] Regressions of the ratio of real imports to real output on an index of aggregate demand and relative price of imports for each branch were also run. These results are reported in García García (1988, appendix table 27).
[3] Regressions of the ratio of real exports to real output on an index of foreign demand and the relative price of imports for that branch were also run. The results are reported in García García (1988, appendix table 28).

Table 5.4 Least squares regressions of imports on aggregate demand and relative prices of imports

Sector	Period	Constant	Aggregate demand			RPMTN			RPMTG		RPMTW			R^2	Durbin–Watson coefficient	Autocorrelation coefficient
			t	$t-1$	$t-2$	t	$t-1$	$t-2$	t	$t-1$	t	$t-1$	$t-2$			
Tobacco	1972–82	3.596 (3.251)		0.876 (5.568)							−0.655 (−5.998)			0.927	1.609	−0.424 (−2.097)
Textiles	1972–82	−2.528 (−0.728)	2.467 (5.322)											0.937	2.050	−0.914 (−2.714)
	1972–82	0.920 (0.142)	2.111 (2.747)	−1.281										0.917	2.219	
Paper and printing	1971–82	5.065 (4.945)	0.773 (6.140)				0.900 (5.508)							0.887	2.171	
	1971–82	4.605 (4.089)	0.657 (4.312)											0.853	2.294	−0.678 (−4.600)
	1971–82	5.609 (4.338)	0.684 (4.608)											0.856	1.835	
Chemicals and rubber	1971–82	3.339 (2.367)		0.859 (5.618)			−0.578 (−2.093)							0.754	2.015	
	1971–82	4.102 (2.886)		0.806 (5.688)							−0.932 (−4.666)			0.793	2.028	
	1971–82	3.411 (2.234)		0.749 (4.516)							−0.696 (−2.624)			0.743	1.948	
Nonmetallic products	1972–82	2.056 (0.653)			1.586 (5.884)				−0.994 (−1.919)					0.864	1.566	−0.483 (−1.953)
Basic metallurgy	1971–82	6.977 (3.293)		0.869 (3.727)			−1.386 (−5.016)							0.921	1.690	
Machinery and equipment	1970–82	8.939 (4.998)	0.744 (4.543)			−1.674 (−6.209)								0.926	2.118	
	1970–82	12.252 (5.134)	0.457 (2.259)						−2.118 (−5.976)					0.921	2.143	
Transport materials	1971–82	16.591 (3.689)	0.803 (2.652)			−3.414 (−4.400)								0.870	1.972	0.177 (0.483)
Other manufactures	1971–82	8.410 (2.786)	0.982 (3.161)			−1.812 (−4.266)								0.901	2.414	−0.123 (−0.430)

RPMTN, implicit price of imports of each sector divided by the implicit price of gross output in the nontraded sector; RPMTG, implicit price of imports of each sector divided by the GDP deflator; RPMTW, implicit price of imports of each sector divided by the implicit price of wages and salaries. t-statistics are given in parentheses.

Table 5.5 Least squares regressions of industrial imports on aggregate demand and relative prices (logarithms)

Period	Sectors[a]	Constant	Aggregate demand	Relative prices (imports/deflator)			R^2	Durbin–Watson coefficient	Autocorrelation coefficient
				GDP	Nontraded	Wage			
Levels of imports									
1970–83	09–11,13–19,21–25	5.185 (2.440)	0.897 (4.643)	−1.018 (−3.317)			0.909	1.796	
1970–83	09–11,13–19,21–25	4.505 (2.821)	0.962 (6.271)		−0.932 (−4.042)		0.927	2.114	
1970–83	16–19,21–25	5.477 (2.422)	0.837 (4.112)	−1.025 (3.153)			0.903	1.761	
1970–83	16–19,21–25	4.180 (2.902)	0.917 (5.934)		−0.957 (−3.953)		0.923	2.093	
Import-to-output ratio									
1971–83	09–11,13–19,21–25	8.324 (6.356)		−1.159 (−3.894)			0.722	1.887	0.328 (1.170)
1970–83	09–11,13–19,21–25	8.475 (10.763)			−1.188 (−6.673)		0.770	1.673	
1971–82	09–11,13–19,21–25	6.433 (10.684)				−0.747 (−5.357)	0.784	2.010	0.227 (0.769)
1970–83	16–19,21–25	8.579 (5.168)		−1.121 (−2.971)			0.704	1.763	0.473 (1.905)
1971–83	16–19,21–25	9.184 (7.410)			−1.254 (−4.475)		0.758	1.436	0.304 (1.124)
1971–82	16–19,21–25	6.877 (8.686)				−0.754 (−4.101)	0.753	1.889	0.409 (1.568)

[a] Sectors correspond to National Accounts classifications.
t-statistics are given in parentheses.

Table 5.6 Least squares regressions of exports on foreign demand and relative prices of exports

Sector	Period	Constant	Foreign demand	RPXN t	RPXN $t-1$	RPXG	RPXW	R^2	Durbin–Watson coefficient	Autocorrelation coefficient
Textiles	1970–82	− 8.026 (− 3.692)	1.469 (3.960)	1.207 (2.491)				0.741	2.074	
	1970–82	− 7.376 (− 4.250)	1.660 (5.320)				0.896 (3.119)	0.787	2.055	
Paper and printing	1970–82	− 17.632 (− 8.940)	4.854 (11.451)					0.915	1.727	
Chemicals and rubber	1970–82	− 21.746 (− 8.683)	4.375 (12.419)	1.332 (4.573)				0.927	2.240	
	1970–82	− 22.447 (− 7.599)	4.514 (11.147)			1.347 (4.018)		0.914	2.076	
	1970–82	− 21.462 (− 11.449)	4.509 (16.497)				1.142 (6.969)	0.938	2.333	
Nonmetallic products	1970–82	− 16.637 (− 5.541)	3.574 (8.033)				1.036 (3.016)	0.839	1.791	
Machinery and equipment	1971–82	− 22.461 (− 20.060)	4.897 (34.699)				0.979 (6.472)	0.975	2.197	− 0.639 (− 1.943)
	1971–82	− 30.185 (− 7.865)	5.282 (18.078)	2.264 (3.755)				0.952	2.022	− 0.469 (− 1.467)
Transport materials	1971–82	− 32.177 (− 2.459)	2.943 (3.148)		4.969 (2.028)			0.471	1.804	
Other manufactures	1970–82	− 32.401 (− 4.413)	6.378 (6.912)	1.686 (2.337)				0.923	1.305	

RPXN, implicit price of exports of each sector divided by the implicit price of gross output in the nontraded sector; RPXG, implicit price of exports of each sector divided by the GDP deflator; RPXW, implicit price of exports of each sector divided by the index of wages and salaries. t-statistics are given in parentheses.

Table 5.7 Least squares regressions of industrial exports on world demand and relative prices (logarithms)

Period	Sectors[a]	Constant	World demand	Relative prices (exports/deflator)			R^2	Durbin–Watson coefficient	Autocorrelation coefficient
				GDP	Nontraded	Wage			
Levels of exports									
1970–83	09–11,13–19,21–25	−5.561 (−3.714)	1.350 (4.830)	0.833 (2.966)			0.771	1.938	
1970–83	09–11,13–19,21–25	−4.943 (−3.469)	1.318 (4.610)		0.725 (2.831)		0.762	1.866	
1971–82	09–11,13–19,21–25	−5.507 (−4.056)	1.788 (8.395)			0.379 (2.455)	0.82	2.256	−0.153 (−0.408)
1970–83	16–19,21–25	−14.451 (−6.514)	2.282 (8.645)		1.848 (4.525)		0.876	1.519	
1971–82	16–19,21–25	−13.855 (−10.500)	2.380 (16.680)			1.023 (6.785)	0.944	2.041	−0.215 (−0.533)
Export-to-output ratio									
1970–83	09–11,13–19,21–25	−1.531 (−1.437)		0.740 (3.102)			0.398	2.095	
1970–83	09–11,13–19,21–25	−1.144 (−1.217)			0.652 (3.103)		0.399	2.084	
1971–82	09–11,13–19,21–25	−2.666 (−3.053)	0.611 (4.2400)			0.370 (3.486)	0.420	2.403	−0.411 (−1.238)
1970–83	16–19,21–25	−9.510 (−3.574)	1.180 (4.226)	1.359 (2.869)			0.615	1.501	
1970–83	16–19,21–25	−9.181 (−4.537)	1.062 (4.411)		1.406 (3.775)		0.707	1.852	
1971–82	16–19,21–25	−9.520 (−9.602)	1.684 (12.534)			0.868 (7.232)	0.848	2.064	−0.456 (−1.450)

[a] Sectors correspond to National Accounts classifications.
t-statistics are given in parentheses.

demand and the relative price of exports for the industrial sector (table 5.7). Relative prices are defined as for each branch but taking the aggregate of the sector.

The results reported in tables 5.4–5.7 indicate that there is a strong response of imports and exports to changes in relative prices and to domestic and foreign demand conditions. It should be noted that the elasticities of demand and supply of imports reported in these tables are short- to medium-term elasticities and not long-run elasticities. Thus, we are not measuring the impact of changes in relative prices on capital accumulation, technical change, and improvements in the quality of the labor force. This response indicates that there are substantial gains to be obtained from trade liberalization as resources move to activities where their contribution to production are the highest. Thus the estimated cost of liberalization by looking only at the effect on unemployment due to the competition from imports is overestimated.

Moreover, the cost of liberalization is also overestimated for the following reason. Changes in relative price can occur because protection for a particular activity changed or because the real exchange rate changed. During part of the period analyzed there was a substantial real appreciation of the Colombian peso. Although this large inflow served to eliminate the premium associated with QRs, tariffs were not reduced as much as they could have been. In any case a substantial reduction in the relative price of imports because of reductions in trade barriers and a real appreciation of the peso, is observed since 1975, and as a result, imports increased.

By not distinguishing between the effects of reduction in protection and the real appreciation, the cost of liberalization is overestimated when the entire increase in imports is considered as resulting from trade liberalization. This is the procedure followed in this case study. Summarizing, the employment cost of trade liberalization in Colombia will be overestimated for two reasons: it does not consider the positive effect of liberalization on export expansion and it attributes all the increase in imports to trade-liberalizing measures. Tables 5.4–5.7 serve to support these assertions, because they show empirically that imports respond negatively to changes in relative prices while exports do respond positively. Keeping these points in mind, we proceed now to estimate the cost of unemployment attributable to liberalization.

Liberalization and Employment

Definition of Sector Unemployment

There are no statistics in Colombia on unemployment rates by sector or industrial branch. Any estimate of unemployment by branch must be based on assumptions about labor supply and thus will be conjectural.

If labor were perfectly mobile among sectors, fluctuations in employment in each sector would not result in unemployment. Workers laid off in one sector would offer their services to other sectors, presumably at lower wages, and be hired in those sectors. If labor is not perfectly mobile, however, fluctuations in employment in the sectors can lead to unemployment. Of course, labor mobility is not an absolute concept but is related to the velocity of adjustment in the labor market. The following assumptions about labor supply were made in order to try to capture the speed of response of the labor supply in each sector to changes in employment in the sector:

$$S_1(t) = \max[E(t), E(t-1)] \tag{5.1}$$
$$S_2(t) = \max[E(t), E(t-1), E(t-2)] \tag{5.2}$$

where $S_1(t)$ and $S_2(t)$ are the labor supply for the sector in year t and $E(t)$ is the actual sector employment in year t. The equations apply for each sector, but subscripts have been omitted for simplicity.

The first specification assumes that the supply of labor for year t is equal to the highest level of actual employment registered for year t or year $t - 1$. that is, when employment in year t decreases, the supply of labor in year t is equal to actual employment in year $t - 1$.

The second definition assumes that the supply of labor for year t is equal to the highest level of actual employment observed in years t, $t - 1$, or $t - 2$. Thus, when employment in year t falls, the supply of labor remains at the highest level registered during years $t - 1$ or $t - 2$. This definition implies a lower mobility of labor than the first definition.

With these definitions of labor supply, and assuming that actual employment equals the quantity of labor demanded at the prevailing real wage rate, total unemployment can be defined as

$$D_j(t) = S_j(t) - E(t) \qquad j = 1, 2 \tag{5.3}$$

Because of the definitions adopted for labor supply, there is never an excess demand for labor.[4] By these same definitions, measured unemployment by sector will always be zero when employment is growing and an excess supply of labor will never arise. This is not entirely correct, since it is possible that a sector which pays high wages relative to other sectors and where employment is growing quickly may be faced with an excess supply of labor and be obliged to reject potential employees. With the information at our disposal, however, it is not possible to capture this effect.

---

[4] To facilitate comparisons between the results of the two specifications of labor supply given above, the rate of unemployment can be defined as the ratio of excess supply to actual employment (rather than to the level of labor supply):

$$U_j(t) = S_j(t)/E(t) - 1 \qquad j = 1, 2$$

Information on unemployment rates for each industrial branch for the two measures of unemployment (U_1 and U_2 are given by García García (1988, appendix tables 17 and 18).

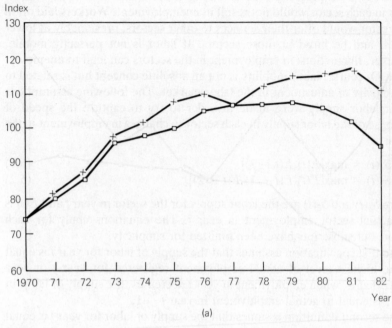

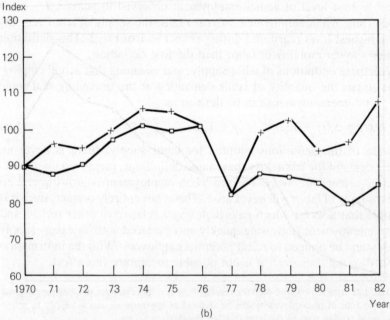

Figure 5.1 Actual and estimated employment according to the import-to-output ratio for (a) textiles, apparel, and leather; (b) wood and wood products; (c) paper and printing; (d) petroleum refining; (e) nonmetallic products; (f) basic metallurgy; (g) machinery and equipment; (h) transport materials; (i) other manufactures: □, paid employment; +, estimated employment

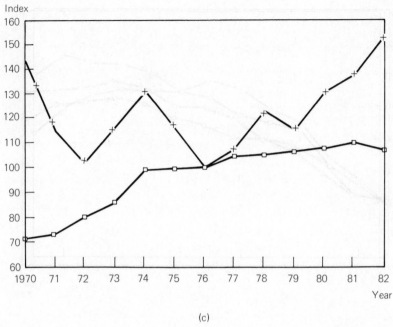

(c)

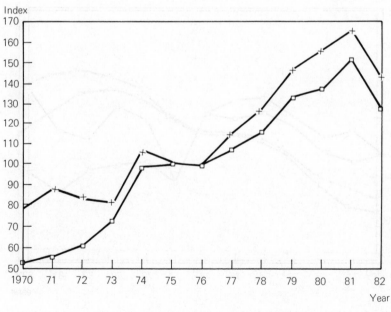

(d)

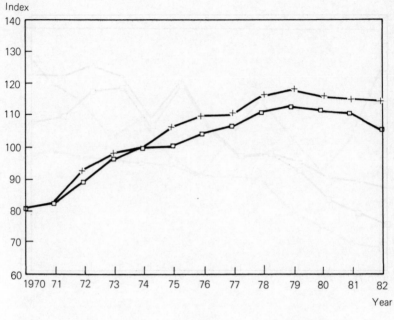

(e)

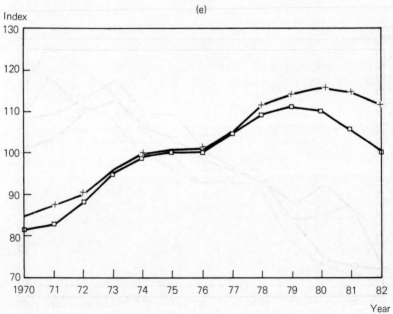

(f)

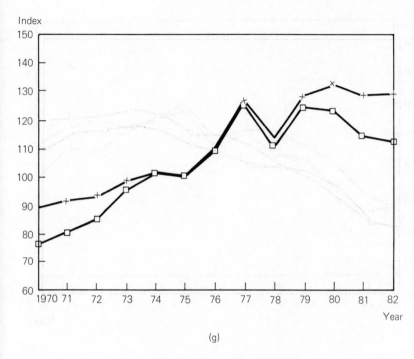

(g)

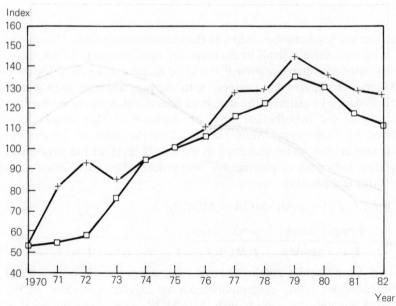

(h)

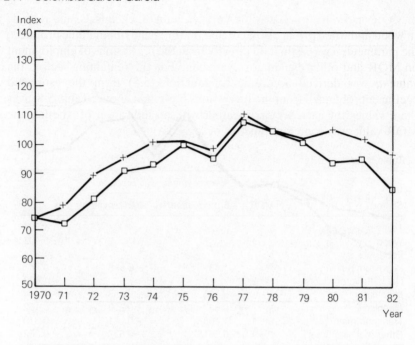

(i)

The method used above to estimate the unemployment cost of liberaliza-tion is inexact, since it tends to attribute any unemployment to liberaliza-tion. A more reasonable approach would be to link employment losses to the volume of imports that compete with the production of each sector. That was done. To estimate the impact of liberalization on employment in each sector, the hypothetical level of employment that should have occurred in each year, *ceteris paribus*, had the ratio of imports to production in each sector remained at the lowest level for the period was calculated. Estimated employment E^* was generated for each sector using the following equations:

$$E^*(t) = E(t) + a[\text{MINMOR} - \text{MOR}(t)] \tag{5.4}$$

$$a = \frac{\delta(\text{employment})}{\delta(\text{production})} \frac{\delta(\text{production})}{\delta(\text{MOR})} \tag{5.5}$$

where E is the actual employment in each sector, MOR is the actual import-to-output ratio, contemporaneous or lagged, according to the estimated equation for each branch, MINMOR is the minimum level of MOR during the period, and δ is a small increment.

Tables 5.1 and 5.2 show that no significant statistical relation between employment and MOR – either directly, or indirectly through the effects of MOR on production – was found for beverages, chemicals, and rubber. In wood and wood products, paper and printing, and nonmetallic products, the parameter a was estimated directly from the regressions of employment on MOR and other explanatory variables. For the remaining sectors the value a was derived according to equation (5.5) from the estimated coefficients obtained from the regressions presented above. Table 5.8 gives the a values for each sector, together with an indication of whether the MOR value was contemporaneous or lagged.

Table 5.8 Values of a for each sector

Sector	MOR	$\dfrac{\delta(employment)}{\delta(production)}$	$\dfrac{\delta(production)}{\delta(employment)}$	a
Textiles	$t-1$	0.921	– 4.89	– 4.504
Wood	$t-1$			– 5.402
Paper	t			– 1.034
Petroleum refining	t	1.431	– 0.518	– 0.741
Nonmetallic products	$t-2$			– 1.623
Metallurgy	t	0.465	– 0.353	– 0.164
Machinery	t	0.647	– 0.250	– 0.162
Transport materials	$t-1$	1.168	– 0.271	– 0.319
Other manufactures	$t-1$	0.561	– 0.627	– 0.352

This method tends to overestimate unemployment, since the import-to-output ratio tends to increase with liberalization and the difference between the actual and the minimum MOR will increase, thereby making the measured cost of unemployment appear to be larger than it really is. Moreover, even if $E^*(t)$ is accepted as representing a fair estimate of the level of employment in the absence of liberalization, it is not reasonable to assume that the supply of labor going to each sector that is being liberalized would have continued growing even when the rate of growth of employment was falling or negative in that sector. Therefore the presentation of this exercise is not intended to suggest that the difference between $E(t)$ and $E^*(t)$ accurately measures the effect of liberalization on employment, but to shed light on the effect of changes in MOR on the level of employment in each sector, thus permitting us to appreciate certain differences between sectors that are relevant in evaluating the impact of liberalization.[5]

The series of actual (E) and estimated (E^*) employment figures for each sector are presented in figure 5.1. The vertical difference between the

[5] The corresponding level of unemployment and the rate of unemployment for the employment series E^* are defined as

$$D_3(t) = E^*(t) - E(t)$$

$$U_3(t) = E^*(t)/E(t) - 1$$

Information for the unemployment rate U_3 for each industrial branch is given by García García (1988, appendix table 19).

curves in each graph, all of which are drawn on the same scale, measures the hypothetical effect of liberalization on employment.

Figure 5.1, together with the statistical results presented in tables 5.1 and 5.2, offers evidence leading to the following conclusions.

1   Sectors where employment appeared to be very responsive to changes in MOR were textiles, apparel, and leather; wood and wood products; paper and printing; and nonmetallic products. Sectors where the response of employment to MOR appeared to be small were basic metallurgy, machinery and equipment, transport materials, and other manufactured products.

2   In textiles and wood and wood products, the high rate of response of employment to changes in MOR, in combination with a large increase in MOR at the end of the period, produced an important effect on employment. Moreover, in machinery and equipment, transport materials, and other manufactures, sizeable increases in MOR at the end of the period generated significant effects on the employment level.

An Estimate of Transitory Losses

The level of unemployment calculated or estimated for each sector can be used as a proxy to measure the unemployment costs of trade liberalization, although the results will most likely be an overestimation because it is not reasonable to impute every change in employment to liberalization.[6] Other policies also have a substantial bearing on employment.

Therefore, to say that all the excess supply of labor in each sector was the result of liberalization is not correct, for reasons already discussed. What should be attributed to liberalization is the *increase* in unemployment

---

[6] If all unemployment derived according to our three definitions is attributed entirely to liberalization, the total unemployment cost of liberalization (COL$_j$) measured as a proportion of total industrial value added will be given by

$$COL_j = D_j\{rw \text{ or } rvaw\}/RVAI \qquad j = 1, 2, 3$$

where D is total unemployment, rw is the average real manufacturing wage in each sector, rvaw is the real value added per worker in each sector, and RVAI is the total real value added in the manufacturing sector (sections 311–90 of the International Standard Industrial Classification). Estimates of this cost are presented by García García (1988, appendix tables 20–2).

due to liberalization, and what should then be compared is "actual" unemployment, as measured by definitions D_1 and D_2, with the unemployment generated by the new labor demand and supply conditions induced by liberalization. Therefore, in order to obtain more realistic estimates of the cost of unemployment due to liberalization, the following procedure was followed.

1   It was assumed that, without liberalization, employment would have been given by E^*.

2   Using this hypothetical employment series (E^*) and definitions 1 and 2 of labor supply (equations (5.1) and (5.2)), new labor supply series S^*_1 and S^*_2 were generated for each sector and for the whole period.

3   Based on the information on E^* and S^*_1 and S^*_2, new series D^*_1 and D^*_2 of total unemployment and series U^*_1 and U^*_2 of rates of unemployment were calculated for the period:

$$S^*_1(t) = \max[E^*(t), E^*(t-1)] \tag{5.6}$$
$$S^*_2(t) = \max[E^*(t), E^*(t-1), E^*(t-2)] \tag{5.7}$$
$$D^*_j(t) = S^*_j(t) - E^*(t) \qquad j = 1, 2 \tag{5.8}$$
$$U^*_j(t) = S^*_j(t)/E^*(t) - 1 \qquad j = 1, 2 \tag{5.9}$$

For the definition of unemployment given by equation (5.8) the cost of that unemployment can be calculated as

$$\text{COL}^*_j = D^*_j\{\text{rw or rvaw}\}/\text{RVAI} \qquad j = 1, 2 \tag{5.10}$$

where COL^*_j measures the cost of liberalization corresponding to unemployment levels D^*_j, rw is the average real manufacturing wage in each sector, rvaw is the real value added per worker in each sector and RVAI is the total real value added in the manufacturing sector (sections 311–90 of the International Standard Industrial Classification). This measure has the problem that it overestimates the employment cost attributable to liberalization, probably by a large margin.[7]

To measure the cost of liberalization correctly, the unemployment that should be imputed to liberalization is the *increase* in the excess supply of labor in each sector induced by liberalization. In other words, the unemployment cost of liberalization is the difference between the unemployment level in the presence of liberalization and that in the absence of liberalization. Unemployment in the presence of liberalization is given by D_j ($j = 1,2$), while unemployment in the absence of liberaliza-

---

[7] The unemployment cost of liberalization as determined by these definitions of unemployment, not shown here, is presented by García García (1988, appendix tables 23 and 24).

Table 5.9 Costs DAL_1 attributable to liberalization under labor supply definitions S_1 and S'_1 (percent of manufacturing value added)

	1970	1971	1972	1973	1974	1975	1976	1977	1978	1979	1980	1981	1982
Total costs													
Textiles, apparel, and leather	0.00	0.04	0.00	0.00	0.00	0.00	0.00	-0.74	0.00	0.00	0.26	0.61	0.09
Wood and wood products	0.00	0.04	-0.02	0.00	0.00	0.02	-0.05	0.01	0.00	0.01	-0.12	0.08	0.00
Paper and printing	0.00	-2.14	-0.98	0.00	0.00	-0.90	-0.94	0.00	0.00	-0.48	0.00	0.00	0.22
Petroleum refining	0.18	0.00	-0.38	-0.14	0.00	-0.27	-0.07	0.00	0.00	0.00	0.00	0.00	0.01
Nonmetallic products	0.14	0.00	0.00	0.00	0.00	0.00	0.00	0.00	0.00	0.00	-0.14	0.00	0.23
Basic metallurgy	0.00	0.00	0.00	0.00	0.00	0.03	0.00	0.00	0.08	0.00	0.08	0.28	0.18
Machinery and equipment	0.00	0.00	0.00	0.00	0.00	0.00	0.00	0.00	0.00	0.00	0.07	0.21	0.07
Transport materials	1.27	0.00	0.00	-0.31	0.00	0.00	0.00	0.00	0.00	0.00	-0.09	0.17	0.09
Other manufactures	0.58	0.03	0.00	0.00	0.00	0.00	0.01	0.00	-0.03	0.01	0.09	-0.05	0.07
Total	2.17	-2.11	-1.38	-0.45	0.05	-1.12	-0.99	-0.74	0.05	-0.47	0.15	1.29	0.97
Cost to workers													
Textiles, apparel, and leather	0.00	0.00	0.00	0.00	0.00	0.00	0.00	-0.24	0.00	0.00	0.10	0.25	0.04
Wood and wood products	0.00	0.02	0.01	0.00	0.00	0.01	-0.02	0.00	0.00	0.00	-0.05	0.03	0.00
Paper and printing	0.00	-0.91	-0.38	0.00	0.00	-0.36	-0.33	0.00	0.00	-0.14	0.00	0.00	0.07
Petroleum refining	0.05	0.00	0.07	-0.03	0.00	-0.06	-0.01	0.00	0.00	0.00	0.00	0.00	0.00
Nonmetallic products	0.07	0.00	0.00	0.00	0.00	0.00	0.00	0.00	0.00	0.00	-0.02	0.00	0.10
Basic metallurgy	0.00	0.00	0.00	0.00	0.00	0.00	0.00	0.00	0.03	0.00	0.03	0.11	0.08
Machinery and equipment	0.00	0.00	0.00	0.00	0.00	0.01	0.00	0.00	0.00	0.00	0.03	0.08	0.03
Transport materials	0.54	0.00	0.00	-0.14	0.00	0.00	0.00	0.00	0.00	0.00	-0.04	0.07	0.04
Other manufactures	0.22	0.01	0.00	0.00	0.00	0.00	0.01	0.00	-0.01	0.01	0.04	-0.02	0.03
Total	0.88	-0.88	-0.46	-0.17	0.00	-0.41	-0.36	-0.23	0.02	-0.13	0.09	0.52	0.39

Source: Garcia Garcia (1986).

Table 5.10 Costs DAL_2 attributable to liberalization under labor supply definitions S_2 and S'_2 (percent of manufacturing value added)

	1970	1971	1972	1973	1974	1975	1976	1977	1978	1979	1980	1981	1982
Total costs													
Textiles, apparel, and leather	0.00	0.00	0.00	0.00	0.00	0.00	0.00	− 0.74	0.00	0.00	0.26	0.85	0.70
Wood and wood products	0.00	0.04	− 0.02	0.00	0.00	0.02	− 0.06	− 0.05	0.16	0.01	− 0.11	0.00	0.01
Paper and printing	0.00	− 2.14	− 3.20	0.00	0.00	− 0.90	− 1.94	− 0.67	0.00	− 0.48	0.00	0.00	0.22
Petroleum refining	0.18	0.04	− 0.38	− 0.44	0.00	− 0.27	− 0.39	0.00	0.00	0.00	0.00	0.00	0.01
Nonmetallic products	0.14	0.03	0.00	0.00	0.00	0.00	0.00	0.00	0.00	0.00	− 0.04	− 0.04	0.23
Basic metallurgy	0.00	0.00	0.00	0.00	0.00	0.00	0.00	0.00	0.00	0.00	0.08	0.36	0.47
Machinery and equipment	0.00	0.00	0.00	0.00	0.00	0.03	0.00	0.00	0.05	0.02	0.07	0.28	0.29
Transport materials	1.27	1.30	0.00	− 0.31	0.00	0.00	0.00	0.00	0.00	0.00	− 0.09	0.07	0.27
Other manufactures	0.58	0.58	0.00	0.00	0.00	0.00	0.01	0.00	− 0.03	− 0.01	0.14	0.03	0.02
Total	2.17	− 0.15	− 3.60	− 0.76	0.00	− 1.12	− 2.37	− 1.46	0.21	− 0.45	0.32	1.55	2.22
Cost to workers													
Textiles, apparel, and leather	0.00	0.00	0.00	0.00	0.00	0.00	0.00	− 0.24	0.00	0.00	0.10	0.35	0.31
Wood and wood products	0.00	0.02	− 0.01	0.00	0.00	0.01	− 0.03	− 0.02	0.07	0.00	− 0.04	0.00	0.00
Paper and printing	0.00	− 0.91	− 1.23	0.00	0.00	− 0.36	− 0.69	− 0.16	0.00	− 0.14	0.00	0.00	0.07
Petroleum refining	0.05	0.01	− 0.07	− 0.09	0.00	− 0.06	− 0.05	0.00	0.00	0.00	0.00	0.00	0.00
Nonmetallic products	0.07	0.01	0.00	0.00	0.00	0.00	0.00	0.00	0.00	0.00	− 0.02	− 0.02	0.10
Basic metallurgy	0.00	0.00	0.00	0.00	0.00	0.01	0.00	0.00	0.00	0.01	0.03	0.14	0.20
Machinery and equipment	0.00	0.00	0.00	0.00	0.00	0.00	0.00	0.00	0.03	0.01	0.03	0.11	0.13
Transport materials	0.54	0.49	0.00	− 0.14	0.00	0.00	0.00	0.00	0.00	0.00	− 0.04	0.03	0.12
Other manufactures	0.22	0.22	0.00	0.00	0.00	0.00	0.01	0.00	− 0.01	0.00	0.06	0.01	0.01
Total	0.88	− 0.16	− 1.31	− 0.24	0.00	− 0.41	− 0.77	− 0.42	0.09	− 0.13	0.12	0.62	0.95

Values for 1970 correspond to those of Garcia Garcia (1988, appendix table 20) because there is no estimated unemployment for 1970.

tion is given by D^*_j ($j = 1, 2$). Therefore the unemployment attributable to liberalization (DAL_j) is given by

$$\text{DAL}_j = D_j - D^*_j = (S_j - E) - (S^*_j - E^*) \qquad j = 1, 2 \qquad (5.11)$$
$$\text{DAL}_j = (S_j - S^*_j) - (E - E^*) \qquad\qquad\qquad j = 1, 2 \qquad (5.12)$$

Equation (5.11) can be interpreted as saying that the unemployment due to liberalization can be measured as the difference between unemployment levels in the presence and in the absence of liberalization, while equation (5.12) can be interpreted as saying that unemployment due to liberalization is equal to the difference between the change in the supply and the change in the demand for labor induced by liberalization. Therefore, for liberalization to have a cost in terms of lost employment, it is necessary that the excess supply of labor should increase as a result of liberalization (equation (5.11)), or that the change in the supply of labor should be larger than the change in the demand for labor (equation (5.12)).[8] There will thus be a cost attributable to liberalization if $D_j > D^*_j$ ($j = 1,2$), that is, when the excess supply of labor (unemployment) in the presence of liberalization is greater than the excess supply of labor (unemployment) in the absence of liberalization. If $D_j < D^*_j$, liberalization may generate a benefit rather than a cost.

The cost of unemployment attributable to liberalization (CDAL_j) ($j = 1,2$) is then given by

$$\text{CDAL}_j = \text{DAL}_j\{\text{rw or rvaw}\}/\text{RVAI} \qquad j = 1, 2 \qquad (5.13)$$

The estimates of the unemployment cost attributable to trade liberalization that result from applying this procedure are shown in tables 5.9 and 5.10.

If labor supply definitions S_1 and S^*_1 are used, the overall unemployment cost of liberalization would have reached its maximum value in 1981, and would have been equivalent to 2.20 percent of total manufacturing value added. The direct cost to workers would have been equivalent to 0.69 percent of total manufacturing value added. The year with the second highest unemployment cost would have been 1970, with 2.17 percent of manufacturing value added, and with the cost to workers equivalent to 0.88 percent of manufacturing value added.

During the period 1980–2 the sectors with the greatest unemployment cost attributable to liberalization for definitions S_1 and S^*_1 were textiles, apparel, and leather, basic metallurgy, and machinery and equipment (see table 5.9). The cost of liberalization for these sectors represented more than 50 percent of the total cost of liberalization for the manufacturing sector as a whole. These sectors contributed 30 percent of manufacturing value added.

---

[8] The word "change" should be understood as referring to the algebraic rather than the absolute value.

If definitions S_2 and S^*_2 of labor supply are used, the overall cost would have reached a maximum in 1982 – equivalent to 2.22 percent of total manufacturing value added, with the direct cost to workers being equivalent to 0.95 percent of total manufacturing value added. The year with the second highest unemployment cost would, again, have been 1970. It is worth noting that between 1971 and 1977 there were no costs attributable to liberalization except in 1974. Only in the last three years of the period that is, 1980–2 did liberalization produce systematic costs.

During the period 1980–2 the sector with the greatest unemployment cost for definitions S_2 and S^*_2 of labor supply was the textiles sector, whose cost represented close to 45 percent of the total cost of liberalization for the entire manufacturing sector. Second in importance was the basic metallurgy sector, where the unemployment cost was equivalent to 22 percent of the overall cost. These sectors, along with machinery and equipment, accounted for 83 percent of the maximum yearly cost of unemployment attributable to liberalization for the period. They contributed 23 percent of manufacturing value added.

6

The Political Economy of Trade Policy in Colombia

Protection Instruments and Institutional Mechanisms

The main instruments of protection in Colombia have been QRs, *ad valorem* tariffs, and prior import deposits.[1] Tariffs have been used mainly to generate government revenue, but after 1972 their role also included that of protecting domestic economic activities. QRs, the predominant instrument of protection until the late 1960s, lost importance in the 1970s but regained their preeminence after 1982. Prior import deposits, initially used for protection, reached such large amounts that they turned out to be an important tool of monetary policy.

Quantitative Restrictions

The Ministry of Economic Development (MED) has the dual and contradictory task of both promoting exports and protecting import-competing industries. MED's export promotion agency is PROEXPO, whose main instrument is subsidized export credits. PROEXPO sometimes gives direct export subsidies or price supports to commodities facing difficult external markets. Protection through QRs is implemented by INCOMEX, which classifies imports under one of three categories: free, prior licensing, and prohibited. Final decisions on classification are made by the Consejo Directivo de Comercio Exterior (CDCE), which is chaired by the Minister of Economic Development.[2] These decisions are based on studies and

---

[1] This section draws in part on García García (1989).

[2] The members of the Council are the Minister of Economic Development (Chairman), the Ministers of Foreign Affairs, Finance, and Agriculture, the chief of the National Planning Office, and general managers of the Banco de la República, PROEXPO, the Industrial Promotion Institute (IFI), the National Federation of Coffee Growers, and INCOMEX. Three members of this Council (PROEXPO, IFI, and INCOMEX) head organizations which are dependencies of the MED.

recommendations by the Imports Management Section of INCOMEX. A committee of five decides on requests for imports of goods on the prior-licensing list.[3]

MED's authority and power stem mainly from its management of foreign trade. In addition, INCOMEX makes recommendations as to whether commodities will be admitted freely or placed under restrictions. As a result, the institutional organization of foreign trade has an inherent bias toward prior licensing. Moreover, a powerful director of INCOMEX using administrative procedures, can thwart attempts to liberalize imports – for example, by subjecting items on the free list to considerable red tape.[4]

In short, protection via QRs is largely discretionary. Moreover, members of the INCOMEX Board of Imports may be subjected to severe criticism and intellectual blackmail by injured or potentially injurable parties. For example, they may be blamed for the bankruptcy of a firm and the unemployment of its workers if they give authorization to imports of commodities which compete with domestic products. Given this institutional setting, it is no wonder that members of the Board of Imports tend to develop a protectionist bias. Thus, even in periods during which liberalization was an important goal, the Minister of Economic Development and INCOMEX were important allies of groups which were opposed to trade liberalization.

Ad Valorem Tariffs

Tariff policy is administered by the National Council of Tariff Policy (CTP), which is under the direction of the Ministry of Finance. The Council has seven members, two of which represent agencies of the Ministry of Finance and three of which represent agencies of the MED.[5] The CTP usually convenes with deputies of the head members of the Council. CDCE sessions, in contrast, are attended by the heads of its member organizations. Thus QRs are more important than tariffs in the policymaking process.

[3] This committee, known as Junta de Importaciones (Board of Imports), has five members: the Director of INCOMEX, the Director of the Imports Management Section of INCOMEX, and three advisers appointed by the MED in consultation with the CDCE.
[4] A noteworthy example was the Director of INCOMEX between 1976 and 1978, a protectionist, who made a mockery of the government's liberalization policy. This could not have been done, of course, without the consent and acquiescence of, among others, the Minister of Economic Development.
[5] The members of the CTP are the Minister of Finance (Chairman), the Ministers of Agriculture and Economic Development, the head of the National Planning Office, the Director of INCOMEX, the General Manager of IFI, and the Director of the General Customs Department (Ministry of Finance).

Notwithstanding their control of QRs, the CTP representatives of the MED and its associated agencies can be a serious obstacle to tariff reduction or rationalization, since such steps mean accepting some degree of liberalization. An important potential enemy of the reduction and rationalization of tariffs is the General Customs Department, since the opportunities of department officials to make private gains from deliberate distortions in the tariff structure are decreased.

The Why of Liberalization Attempts

Trade liberalization during the 1967–82 period was a gradual process that depended very much on external events and on the implementation of policies which either did or did not favor the process.

The process of liberalization between 1967 and 1974 was in part the result of deliberate changes in government policies, but its acceleration in 1973–4 was triggered by increases in the international prices of imported raw materials and intermediate goods and by the acceleration of domestic inflation. The government then sought to counteract these trends by expanding imports.

The liberalization did not have many enemies at first, in part because the process meant reducing the red tape created when restrictions were increased massively in 1967, and also because restrictions were reduced on industrial intermediate inputs and raw materials not produced in the country. Moreover, since the increase in restrictions had been announced as a temporary measure to be phased out following an improvement in the balance of payments, and the policies being applied were achieving that improvement, it was reasonable to think of the reduction in restrictions as a natural outcome of the normalization process.

Liberalization was not perceived by the public as being of major importance. It was simply seen as a pragmatic move. Moreover, liberalization was not applied to all goods.

Liberalization efforts continued in 1975, but were short lived. This is hard to understand, since Colombia experienced a coffee boom between 1975 and 1977. The government had originally expected the coffee boom to be a short-term phenomenon and concluded that the best thing to do would be to accumulate international reserves to enhance the reserve position of the country. The length of the boom took the monetary authorities by surprise, and the sterilization of international reserves flowing into the country was managed with instruments of limited usefulness. More effective instruments, such as open-market operations were avoided because of their feared impact on interest rates. Higher rates, it was thought, would further harm the industrial sector, which went through a recession in 1975–6. In the meantime, the increase in domestic prices due to reserve accumulation had caused the real exchange rate to appreciate. It was thought that trade liberalization under the lowest real exchange rate during that period would be an additional blow to the industrial sector, which strongly opposed any further liberalization. This view was held by some high ranking government officials, the Minister of Economic Development among others. By January 1977 a new economic team which opposed liberalization was in charge of trade policy.[6] In other words, certain economic developments helped those who opposed liberalization take over the direction of policy, and no further steps were taken at that time to liberalize trade despite the large accumulation of international reserves.[7]

Liberalization gained impetus again in 1979, however, mainly because of the need to sterilize huge gains in reserves resulting from an increase in coffee exports and prices and a large inflow of official capital. The increase in government expenditures and increases in private expenditures induced by real income gains due to higher coffee prices further contributed to revaluation of the peso. Later, the worldwide economic recession of the early 1980s and the application of a monetary policy aimed at keeping inflation fairly stable while financing the government deficit through money creation crowded the private sector out of the credit markets and produced a general economic recession. That was an unfortunate climate for liberalization of imports.

Thus, the establishment of new trade restrictions in late 1982 and its accumulation in 1983 was done more for political and ideological reasons than for economic reasons, while the main cause of economic problems (inflation, low growth, and balance-of-payments deficits) – the government's fiscal deficit – were not attacked. One important actor was the Minister of Finance, a native of Medellín, who had been the head of the National Planning Department when the Lleras Restrepo administration imposed massive trade restrictions in 1966. Medellín, Colombia's second largest industrial city, was hard hit by the recession in 1982. Some of its largest, oldest, and most protected industries had lost competitiveness and had serious cash flow problems caused by the fall in the real exchange rate and the increase in real interest rates. As in 1966, however, the govern-

---

6 The main actors in 1975 and 1976 were the Ministers of Finance and Economic Development, the Chief of the National Planning Department, and the Director of INCOMEX. Of these four officials, the Ministers of Finance and the Chief of the National Planning Department were in favor of liberalizing while the Director of INCOMEX was neutral on the issue, since his direct boss was the Minister of Economic Development. The Minister of Economic Development thought that his Ministry was a sort of "industrial red cross," and was not very keen on liberalizing. At the beginning of 1977, with the exception of the National Planning Department, all the posts were held by people who were in favor of protectionism. The Minister of Finance was the same person who launched the successful economic policies in 1967–70.

7 An analysis of the opposition to liberalization in 1975–7 can be found in Urrutia (1983).

ment opted for a massive increase in QRs instead of allowing price mechanisms to determine the fate of these industries.[8]

Although the Minister of Economic Development was a native of Barranquilla, located on the Atlantic Coast, a region whose poverty could be traced in part to protectionism, that was insufficient to stem the protectionist tide. The negative effect of protectionism on the real income of the rural inhabitants of the Atlantic Coast is still not well understood, in part because these effects are not visible in terms of increased unemployment and closures of industrial plants.

Political Reactions to Liberalization

We now give a very tentative analysis of political reactions to liberalization.

Income Groups Who May Have Gained or Lost

Trade liberalization probably did have some favorable impact on the distribution of income in the country (see Urrutia and Berry, 1975, p. 32). Among those who very likely gained were rural laborers. Improvements in the rural real wage occurred when the sector's terms of trade improved (see García García and Montes Llamas, 1988, chapter 5). Since most (73 percent) of Colombia's agricultural output is tradeable and around 80 percent of it can be classified as exportable, import liberalization increased the relative price of exports, the demand for rural labor, and real wages in agriculture.

Also likely to have gained were workers in the export manufacturing sector and the unprotected import-competing sectors. The import-competing and noncompeting industries paid the highest wages in the manufacturing sector in 1980.[9] Blue- and white-collar workers in 13 out of the 28 manufacturing sectors (as classified under the International Standard Industrial Classification system) received salaries and wages higher than the national average. Of those 13, only two (tobacco, and glass and glass products) are classified as exportables, while nine are import competing and two are noncompeting. Production in the high-wage industries was

---

[8] One reason why devaluation was discarded may have been that some of the most important industrial companies had, on top of their cash flow problems, a relatively large external debt. A devaluation without any government assistance would have led them into bankruptcy and caused more serious unemployment problems.

[9] This classification follows Thoumi's which is aggregated at the three-digit level. Two sectors (pulp and paper products, and rubber products), classified as importables, had importable and exportable subsectors. The classification used by Thoumi was the International Standard Industrial Classification while we have used DANE's national accounts system.

concentrated in a few large enterprises with relatively strong unions. Under a free-trade regime, however, these industries take a risk in raising wages, since this may lead to collapse of the firms unless they are able to improve their productivity at the same time. Thoumi found that wages in 1973 for blue-collar workers in import-competing, export, and noncompeting industries were very similar. However, he also found that wages for white-collar workers were lowest in the export sector, followed by the import-competing and noncompeting sectors (Thoumi, 1981, table 4.9). For management, the lowest wages were paid in the export sector and the highest in the import-competing sector. Assuming that this structure of remuneration remained unchanged in the late 1970s and early 1980s, liberalization would have caused the wages of managers in import-competing and noncompeting activities to fall relative to the wages of managers in export activities. Owners of capital in protected industrial activities may have been harmed by liberalization, while owners of capital in unprotected activities may have benefited.

Landowners, in contrast, may have gained from liberalization, since the price of land tends to increase when agricultural prices rise. Landowners can be an important pressure group, but their geographical dispersion and diversity of interests make it difficult for them to present a strong and united front on behalf of trade liberalization. Consumers also are among the potential beneficiaries of trade liberalization, but their large numbers preclude effective mass action.

Government bureaucracies may be one of the largest losers in trade liberalization, since the job of enforcing trade restrictions may become superfluous and the elimination of QRs may result in the loss of large rents for some groups in the bureaucracy. Tariff reductions may also cause losses to bureaucrats in charge of enforcing tariff regulations, since the possibility for profitable bargains ("deals") with private importers diminishes.

Supporters and Opponents of Liberalization

The liberalization process in Colombia faced serious obstacles: ideology was one obstacle, interest group pressures another.

The main opponents were large urban capitalists, organized labor, and, probably, urban rent seekers and the government bureaucracy. Production in some of the most protected sectors of Colombian industry is concentrated in a few firms with strong unions. The threat of unemployment arising from the threatened closure of large plants was therefore one argument for halting liberalization. The owners of capital in large and highly protected import-competing firms probably lost part of their monopolistic rents and also hoped for an end to liberalization, as did those bureaucrats in charge of enforcing restrictions. Rent seekers, who can wield substantial political power, tended to collude with bureaucrats and urban capitalists to oppose liberalization.

The supporters of liberalization were chiefly exporters, agricultural producers, the owners of production factors used in unprotected import-competing activities, landowners, and the agricultural labor force. Coffee growers, Colombia's most important group of agricultural producers, are chiefly interested in the internal price of coffee, which is not necessarily linked in the short run to trade liberalization.[10] Agricultural labor, the other group which would have gained from further trade liberalization, is not organized politically, is difficult to organize, and has very little political power. Capital and labor in unprotected import-competing activities, supporters of liberalization, are usually found in small companies, which can put very little pressure on the government.

Thus protectionism has triumphed over liberalization in Colombia, at least for the time being. This is nothing new. As Marco Palacio has remarked, "The old quarrel between protectionism and free trade was politically settled in the mid-fifties [that is, the 1850s], and it never was a cause of serious discrepancy among political parties" (Palacio, 1983, p. 39). The benefits of liberalization are not clearly understood even by those who might gain from liberalization, while the benefits that might arise from liberalization are not fully appreciated even by those favoring more employment and less income inequality. Rather often, in fact, they are the ones most in favor of protectionism.

Why Was Liberalization Slow?

The liberalization of 1954 involved the elimination of QRs on imports for nine months. The free flow of imports was triggered by a large increase in coffee prices, which did not last long. The end of the boom brought about an end to liberalization in the first half of 1955. Another attempt to eliminate QRs began in September 1965, and by Ocrtober 1966 around 90 percent of all imports were on the free list. This attempt at liberalization, however, was accompanied by inconsistent macroeconomic policies that led to a substantial increase in speculative imports. Later events proved that speculation made economic sense. These two episodes show that a hasty attempt to achieve liberalization will not be believed to be a lasting policy shift if it is not accompanied by the introduction of consistent macroeconomic policies.

Given Colombia's institutional setting and a clear national preference for consensus, a gradual process of liberalization would have been more likely to gain wide political support.[11] The best organized groups in

[10] On the influence of coffee growers on exchange rate policy, see Urrutia (1981, pp. 209–10).
[11] For this preference for consensus among Colombian politicians, see Solaún (1980).

Table 6.1 Index of real wages and real unit cost of labor, 1970–1982 (1975 = 100)

	1970	1971	1972	1973	1974	1975	1976	1977	1978	1979	1980	1981	1982
Beverages													
Real unit cost	106.9	102.4	106.5	101.3	101.6	100.0	98.1	103.5	117.7	111.3	109.8	124.0	129.2
Real wages	107.4	103.9	109.4	99.5	99.1	100.0	101.2	99.6	116.4	112.1	115.2	128.0	132.9
Tobacco													
Real unit cost	216.1	218.5	198.2	160.8	133.9	100.0	126.6	139.1	151.1	190.3	222.5	230.3	217.6
Real wages	185.5	188.8	167.6	138.9	128.3	100.0	114.5	132.4	151.7	171.8	188.7	196.5	189.9
Textiles, apparel, and leather													
Real unit cost	127.1	125.6	129.1	113.1	108.9	100.0	112.0	119.7	137.2	132.1	136.7	139.9	146.5
Real wages	122.6	120.7	123.0	108.4	106.8	100.0	104.6	100.7	117.2	117.8	121.9	116.5	121.6
Wood and wood products													
Real unit cost	101.2	112.5	106.7	97.0	91.6	100.0	104.2	107.8	113.0	117.5	128.7	121.9	130.3
Real wages	113.0	119.8	113.5	100.6	98.6	100.0	105.1	102.1	116.2	121.9	126.9	122.0	138.8
Paper and printing													
Real unit cost	113.8	108.9	119.8	116.4	91.6	100.0	108.8	111.1	131.7	135.8	136.5	144.8	155.4
Real wages	107.2	106.6	107.1	104.0	95.3	100.0	104.2	94.7	112.3	114.1	112.1	113.4	125.9
Chemicals and rubber													
Real unit cost	112.9	116.9	115.9	110.0	91.9	100.0	110.7	110.9	118.8	122.4	125.0	134.3	149.8
Real wages	102.8	103.7	102.2	98.3	94.3	100.0	108.9	97.7	104.1	108.3	108.3	116.9	124.9
Petroleum and refining													
Real unit cost	94.0	103.1	97.1	99.6	95.4	100.0	57.6	73.4	57.9	46.7	36.9	38.1	44.6
Real wages	82.6	98.0	101.7	88.7	95.2	100.0	71.5	90.1	78.6	69.3	71.3	81.1	93.6
Nonmetallic products													
Real unit cost	89.0	102.8	100.0	101.1	102.4	100.0	95.7	103.0	109.7	111.2	121.8	115.2	125.2
Real wages	102.3	112.5	106.6	99.8	97.9	100.0	106.6	102.0	117.7	121.3	131.1	128.3	144.9
Basic metallurgy													
Real unit cost	102.4	105.5	110.7	105.5	98.0	100.0	108.8	113.4	124.3	125.2	132.3	139.7	164.5
Real wages	100.1	100.3	101.5	96.9	96.3	100.0	108.3	98.5	110.1	114.5	117.5	121.4	134.6
Machinery and equipment													
Real unit cost	101.8	112.8	119.1	108.7	100.1	100.0	102.1	99.6	123.1	118.8	121.2	128.4	146.7
Real wages	119.9	125.9	123.6	111.1	107.3	100.0	105.5	96.0	122.8	117.2	117.3	122.0	136.3
Transport materials													
Real unit cost	70.8	102.9	103.9	107.6	94.8	100.0	109.1	110.9	121.9	133.9	138.8	115.3	166.3
Real wages	94.6	103.2	95.7	97.4	93.8	100.0	110.6	104.3	117.9	122.4	126.2	138.1	144.2
Other manufactures													
Real unit cost	105.4	108.0	114.7	104.5	90.7	100.0	103.5	114.9	127.5	110.7	143.2	150.1	147.1
Real wages	99.4	104.3	112.0	102.4	95.4	100.0	110.1	108.6	128.8	118.8	142.6	153.7	151.3

Real wages, nominal wages deflated by the consumer price index; real unit cost of labor, nominal wages deflated by the index of sector prices of gross output.

Table 6.2 Relative prices of domestic production and imports, 1970–1982 (1975 = 100)

	1970	1971	1972	1973	1974	1975	1976	1977	1978	1979	1980	1981	1982
Beverages													
rpon	97.8	98.0	101.1	99.9	98.9	100.0	102.7	101.8	101.3	100.4	105.2	104.0	103.3
rpmn	114.6	98.5	102.9	97.5	98.4	100.0	95.4	89.9	84.7	82.3	85.6	87.9	82.9
rpom	85.3	99.5	98.2	102.5	100.6	100.0	107.7	113.3	119.5	121.9	123.0	118.2	124.6
Tobacco													
rpon	83.2	82.9	82.3	87.5	97.0	100.0	90.0	101.2	102.9	90.1	85.3	86.3	87.9
rpmn	99.4	94.9	98.2	84.4	109.4	100.0	100.4	102.2	96.4	85.1	80.3	79.6	75.6
rpom	83.7	87.3	83.8	103.7	88.7	100.0	89.6	98.9	106.8	105.8	106.1	108.4	116.2
Textiles, apparel, and leather													
rpon	93.1	92.0	92.2	96.8	99.3	100.0	92.9	89.5	87.6	89.1	90.0	84.9	84.3
rpmn	105.7	100.5	101.6	101.0	108.2	100.0	88.3	80.6	74.3	67.4	60.4	58.5	55.9
rpom	88.1	91.5	90.8	95.9	91.7	100.0	105.3	111.1	117.9	132.1	149.1	145.1	150.8
Wood and wood products													
rpon	107.6	101.9	102.9	104.8	108.9	100.0	100.3	100.9	105.4	103.7	99.6	102.0	108.1
rpmn	85.3	84.6	81.5	74.3	90.2	100.0	86.3	84.5	89.9	88.2	83.4	71.6	59.8
rpom	126.1	120.4	126.3	141.0	120.7	100.0	116.3	119.5	117.3	117.6	119.5	142.5	180.7
Paper and printing													
rpon	91.7	94.5	87.3	90.6	105.5	100.0	95.3	90.4	87.3	83.8	82.6	79.3	81.9
rpmn	78.6	73.8	71.1	73.1	92.8	100.0	92.2	78.8	71.3	69.9	69.1	70.3	61.9
rpom	116.5	128.1	122.8	123.9	113.7	100.0	103.3	114.7	122.5	119.9	119.5	112.8	132.3
Chemicals and rubber													
rpon	89.3	86.1	86.5	91.0	104.1	100.0	97.9	93.2	89.7	88.1	86.8	87.7	83.7
rpmn	80.6	75.8	75.2	73.7	99.0	100.0	94.6	82.1	76.2	76.2	82.0	79.0	74.1
rpom	110.8	113.6	115.1	123.5	105.2	100.0	103.6	113.5	117.7	115.6	105.9	110.9	113.0

Petroleum refining													
rpon	85.7	91.6	102.1	90.7	101.1	100.0	123.7	130.2	139.1	147.9	193.8	213.9	210.4
rpmn	18.2	15.9	14.8	22.8	49.8	100.0	105.4	94.4	99.6	122.2	166.7	167.4	148.8
rpom	469.6	576.3	688.7	397.4	202.9	100.0	117.3	138.0	139.7	121.0	116.2	127.8	141.4
Nonmetallic products													
rpon	111.0	105.8	103.3	99.7	96.8	100.0	110.9	105.4	110.0	109.0	108.6	113.3	117.2
rpmn	104.2	85.3	86.3	84.4	93.2	100.0	108.8	102.6	92.0	86.7	85.2	80.3	79.4
rpom	106.5	124.1	119.6	118.2	103.8	100.0	101.9	102.8	119.6	125.7	127.5	141.0	147.7
Basic metallurgy													
rpon	94.2	91.6	89.1	93.0	99.5	100.0	99.1	92.3	90.7	91.3	89.4	88.3	82.7
rpmn	78.0	76.8	73.8	79.1	98.3	100.0	83.6	71.5	65.5	65.2	65.9	60.1	56.0
rpom	120.8	119.3	120.7	117.6	101.3	100.0	118.5	129.0	138.5	139.9	135.8	146.6	147.6
Machinery and equipment													
rpon	114.9	107.8	101.4	103.7	108.6	100.0	102.8	102.3	102.2	98.4	97.4	96.2	93.8
rpmn	94.7	95.3	95.0	97.6	100.8	100.0	104.5	100.1	91.3	83.0	86.0	79.5	73.5
rpom	121.3	113.1	106.8	106.2	107.8	100.0	98.4	102.1	112.0	118.5	113.2	121.1	127.7
Transport materials													
rpon	129.3	96.1	89.5	91.6	100.2	100.0	100.9	99.8	99.2	91.2	91.6	90.1	87.5
rpmn	101.7	94.8	102.0	100.2	100.3	100.0	100.7	92.2	87.3	81.6	76.1	72.9	69.8
rpom	127.1	101.4	87.7	91.4	99.8	100.0	100.2	108.2	113.6	111.8	120.3	123.6	125.5
Other manufactures													
rpon	91.3	92.7	94.9	99.3	106.5	100.0	106.0	100.3	103.6	107.1	100.1	103.4	103.7
rpmn	101.4	94.7	91.6	91.0	97.8	100.0	100.8	97.7	94.0	76.6	86.9	84.1	75.7
rpom	90.0	97.9	103.7	109.2	108.8	100.0	105.1	102.6	110.2	139.8	115.2	123.0	137.0

rpon, price of domestic production relative to the price of nontraded goods; rpmn, price of imports relative to the price of nontraded goods; rpom, price of domestic production relative to the price of imports.

Colombia are those who work in import-competing sectors, namely capitalists and unionized industrial workers. Consumers are not organized and are not an effective pressure group, while noncoffee exporters are organized but are relatively few. This means that political support for liberalization, if it is to become strong enough to overcome opposition, must be built up gradually. On the other hand, a gradual process of building support may fail because of opposition from groups which pay lip service to the idea of liberalization but drag their feet when actual decisions must be made. Real wages in the industrial sector continued to rise between 1979 and 1982 despite reductions in both employment and output (table 6.1), and the domestic prices of import-competing goods did not fall toward the international prices of such goods (table 6.2). Domestic prices of these goods, as well as real wages, did not fall because industrial producers and workers expected the shift toward liberalization to collapse, as in fact it did.

7

Conclusion

The preceding chapters of this case study have described the slow and hesitant progress of trade liberalization in Colombia between 1967 and 1982, the reversal of the move toward liberalization in late 1982, and the substantial increase in QRs and tariffs in 1983 and 1984. Colombia thus lost a good opportunity to fully liberalize its trade during a 15-year period when the economic circumstances favorable to such a shift were present. The disappearance of these favorable circumstances in the early 1980s then led to a reversal in policy.

There are several reasons why complete liberalization was never achieved in Colombia. One was that a substantial reduction or elimination of tariffs and the total removal of QRs was never high on the agenda of various administrations, while another was that it was opposed by powerful economic groups represented mainly by the Associación Nacional de Industriales (National Association of Industrialists, ANDI). Thirdly, there was fear of its possible bad effects on industrial employment. A fourth reason was the substantial appreciation of the peso (in real terms) induced by the coffee and drug booms and by government borrowing abroad. Liberalization could therefore only be achieved slowly if it was to be achieved at all and inevitably depended upon extremely favorable economic circumstances. The advent of economic recession in the early 1980s was skillfully used by those opposing liberalization to bring it to a stop and then to reverse it.

Colombia's economic situation in 1982 was quite poor. The rate of economic growth reached its lowest point since 1950. Real industrial output fell for the second year in a row. Industrial employment had been falling since 1980, and the 1982 deficit in Colombia's current account was 7.4 percent of GDP, up from 4.7 percent in 1981 and a surplus of 0.3 percent in 1980. The unemployment rate in urban areas was rising – from 8.1 percent in September 1981 to 9.2 percent in September 1982 – and the central and consolidated public sector deficits stood at 4.6 percent and 8.6

percent of GDP respectively. Reserves of foreign exchange, although still high, had started to decline, and further substantial losses were expected in 1983 and 1984. Industrial exports were stagnant, and agricultural exports other than coffee had been falling for several years. However, real imports of manufactured goods and agricultural commodities between 1979 and 1982 had been rising at rates of 16 percent and 10.2 percent per year respectively.

This dismal economic climate was exceptionally favorable to the arguments of those opposed to trade liberalization, whether for ideological or economic reasons. Moreover, the renewed impetus toward import liberalization in 1979–81 had come more from a need to sterilize large inflows of foreign exchange than from a belief that liberalization in itself was a worthy policy objective. Thus, by late 1982, during 1983, and until April 1984 the erection of barriers to imports was viewed as a means to revive (*reactivar*) Colombia's industrial sector, which was the main source of opposition to liberalization. In addition, the bureaucracies at INCOMEX and the Customs Department, under the disguise of economic arguments, saw the weak economic situation as a vehicle for returning to them the power and benefits that they had lost during the slow shift toward liberalization.

Measures to reverse trade liberalization were taken in late 1982 after a new government came into office. Both the new President and the new Minister of Finance were natives of the state of Antioquia, whose capital Medellín was the main center of opposition to liberalization. Criminal violence, mainly related to the cocaine trade, was rampant in Medellín, but this criminality also stemmed in part from the decline of employment opportunities in legal activities. These circumstances "closed the circle," and the shift toward liberalization ended completely in 1983.[1]

Unemployment costs that can be attributed to liberalization, as shown in chapter 5, occurred only in 1970 and in the period 1980–2. The measured unemployment costs in 1980–2 were relatively small – less than 2 percent of industrial value added – and were not very different from the measured cost of unemployment for 1970, which was 2.2 percent of industrial value added. Furthermore, the rate of growth of industrial imports in the late 1960s and early 1970s (1965–1974) was 9.0 percent, which was not very different from the 10 percent rate of growth of industrial imports in 1979–82.

Nonetheless, there was little opposition to liberalization in 1970 and fierce opposition in 1980–2. This may seem surprising given that the costs of liberalization during both periods were very similar.

---

[1] It should be noted that the liberalization experiment in Chile was having difficulties at the same time, and many compared the extent of liberalization in Colombia with that in Chile. In Colombia, as in Chile, although at a much less sophisticated level of economic discussion, import liberalization was blamed for the poor performance of the economy.

The economic circumstances of the two periods, however, differed greatly. In 1970, real industrial output grew 9.2 percent. Although real industrial exports fell that same year, they had grown during the previous five years at an annual rate of 14 percent. However, during the period 1980–2, both industrial output and exports declined. Furthermore, Colombia's main trading partners were growing at 3.3 percent in the late 1960s and early 1970s, but had entered into deep recession (no growth at all) in 1980–2. Real interest rates were low in the early 1970s, but they were high in 1980–2. The Colombian peso depreciated in real terms in 1967–71, providing real exchange rate protection to industrial import-competing and export activities in 1970, thus limiting the spread of opposition to trade liberalization. Substantial appreciation of the peso after 1977, however, removed that source of protection for domestic industrial products in 1980–2.

Thus, general economic conditions (rather than trade liberalization) had the greatest bearing on the performance of the industrial sector in both periods. The small difference in unemployment costs due to liberalization during the two periods – less than 0.5 percent – hardly accounts for the substantial differences in the rates of growth of industrial output and employment in these two periods.

The disappointing performance of the industrial sector in 1980–2 was caused mainly by domestic economic policies, especially wage and fiscal policies, and also by external events (world economic recession and rising real interest rates). In 1979 Colombia's industrial sector accepted an increase in the minimum wage which was far above what could be justified by increases in productivity and the expected rate of inflation.

The industrial sector does not have much influence on overall macroeconomic policies, but it is able to influence trade policy, and in many instances the shift of a commodity from the prior-licensing list to the free list was cleared beforehand by INCOMEX officials with the directors and principal economic advisors of ANDI. Thus the losses inflicted by liberalization on the textile producers of Medellín, who comprise the most influential group among the nation's industrialists, meant that the industry's major lobbying efforts were directed against import liberalization.

Despite opposition, however, some liberalization did take place in 1979–82 to counteract the monetization of the substantial increase in international reserves. When this gain in reserves ended, however, the inclination to liberalize subsided and the views of those opposed to liberalization gained strength.

Moreover, the slow pace of liberalization during the period 1979–82 also contributed to its downfall. In earlier years, when both the economy and the industrial sector had grown quickly, opposition to liberalization had remained dormant. Thus the excellent economic performance of 1967–74 could have been used as a reason to proceed toward liberalization at a faster pace. This did not happen though, because ideas about the importance of import substitution were still entrenched, and its supporters remained influential. Moreover, certain industries believed to be in need of protection (for example cars and autoparts) were just getting under way.

Another major point that worked against liberalization was the poor performance of industrial exports after 1975. Export promotion had been a major policy objective since 1967, and this policy appeared to be blessed by success until 1974. The policy worked until 1974 because of sharp increases in the real exchange rate for industrial exports, which were induced mainly by good macroeconomic management. After 1975, however, no efforts to promote exports achieved much success. In part, this was because of inconsistency in these efforts, but the main reason was that the coffee boom which started in 1975 and lasted until 1977 produced a substantial appreciation in the real exchange rate for noncoffee exports which more than offset direct export incentives. This highlights another point, which is that direct export incentives or subsidies are not necessary to promote exports. Real exchange rate protection is more effective in achieving this aim.

As export expansion came to a halt, Colombia's industrialists saw expansion of the internal market as the only source of increase in demand for their products. However, import liberalization seriously threatened to reduce internal demand for domestic products, and opposition to liberalization began as early as 1976. In addition to opposition outside the government, opposition also came from officials within the government who favored import substitution.

In summary, the saga of import liberalization efforts in Colombia had an unhappy ending because liberalization was not an important policy objective in itself, implementation was too slow, and the most serious effort at implementation was accompanied by the unfavorable economic circumstances of 1980–2. The larger negative impact of liberalization on Colombia's most powerful industrial sectors in that period of deep economic recession was a bonus for those who strongly opposed liberalization on economic or political grounds. A decline in industrial exports and the increased competition of imports ultimately undermined the trade liberalization process which Colombia had sought to strengthen at the wrong time – a time when the peso was rising in value and recession had stymied economic growth in Colombia and throughout the world.

References and Bibliography

Banco de la República (1984) "Indice de la tasa de cambio real del peso colombiano." In *Ensayos sobre Política Económica*. Bogotá: Banco de la República.

Banco de la República, *Informe del Gerente a la Junta Directiva*, Statistical Appendices, various years. Bogotá: Banco de la República.

Barro, Robert J. (1973) "El dinero y la base monetaria en Colombia: 1967–72." *Revista de Planeación y Desarrollo*, 5 (2) April–June, 68–87.

Bourguignon, François (1986) "The labor market in Colombia: an overview of its evolution over the past three decades." Washington, DC: World Bank, Discussion Paper no. DRD 157.

Cardona, Marta Helena (1977) "El crecimiento de las exportaciones menores y el sistema de fomento a las exportaciones en Colombia." *Revista de Planeación y Desarrollo*, 9 (2), September, 49–78.

Carrizosa, Mauricio (1981) "El futuro de la balanza comercial." In *La Economía Colombiana en la Década de los Ochenta*. Bogotá: FEDESARROLLO.

Clavijo, Sergio (1982) "Los depósitos previos de importación su operatividad y comportamiento reciente." In *Ensayos sobre Política Económica*. Bogotá: Banco de la República.

Correa, Patricia (1984) "Determinantes de la cuenta de servicios de la balanza cambiaria." In *Ensayos sobre Política Económica*. Bogotá: Banco de la República.

Currie, Lauchlin (1983) *Moneda en Colombia: Comportamiento y Control*. Bogotá: Fondo Cultural Cafetero.

Currie, Lauchlin (1984) *Evaluación de la Asesoría Económica a los Países en Desarrollo: El Caso Colombiano*. Bogotá: Fondo Editorial CEREC.

DANE (Departamento Administrativo Nacional de Estadística) (1984) *Matriz Insumo Producto 1970–1983*. Bogotá.

DANE (1985) *Cuentas Nacionales de Colombia 1970–84*. Bogotá.

DANE, *Anuarios de Comercio Exterior*, various years. Bogotá

DANE, *Encuesta Manufacturera*, various years, Bogotá.

DANE, *National Account Statistics Worksheets*. Bogotá.

Departamento Nacional de Planeación (1969) *Planes y Programas de Desarrollo: 1969–1972*. Bogotá.

Departamento Nacional de Planeación (1972) *Las Cuatro Estrategías: 1972–1974*. Bogotá.

Departamento Nacional de Planeación (1976) *Para Cerrar la Brecha*. Bogotá.

Departamento Nacional de Planeación (1976a) *Análisis de la Propuesta de Arancel Externo Común de la Junta del Acuerdo de Cartagena*. Bogotá: Departamento Nacional de Planeación, Documento DNP-1352–UEI–DIE, March.

Departamento Nacional de Planeación (1982) *La Situación Fiscal de Colombia: 1970–1981*. Bogotá.

Departamento Nacional de Planeación (1984) *Consolidación Financiera del Sector Público Colombiano: 1973–82*. Bogotá.

Díaz-Alejandro, Carlos F. (1976) *Foreign Trade Regimes and Economic Development: Colombia*. New York: Columbia University Press for the National Bureau of Economic Research.

Dirección General de Presupuesto (1973) *Boletín 64*.

Echavarría, Juan J. (1982) "La evolucíon de las exportaciones colombianas y sus determinantes: un análisis empírico." In *Ensayos sobre Política Económica*, September. Bogotá: Banco de la República.

Edwards, Sebastián (1984) "Coffee, money and inflation in Colombia." *World Development*, November–December, 1107–17.

Edwards, Sebastián (1985a) "Money, the rate of devaluation and nominal interest rates in a semi-open economy: Colombia, 1968–82." *Journal of Money, Credit and Banking*, February.

Edwards, Sebastián (1985b) "The exchange rate and non-coffee exports." In Vinod Thomas et al., eds, *Linking Macroeconomic and Agricultural Policies for Adjustment with Growth: The Colombian Experience*. Baltimore, MD: Johns Hopkins University Press.

Edwards, Sebastián (1986a) "Commodity export prices and the real exchange rate in developing countries: coffee in Colombia." In Sebastián Edwards and Liaquat Ahamed, eds, *Economic Adjustment and Exchange Rates in Developing Countries*, pp. 235–60. Chicago, IL: University of Chicago Press.

Edwards, Sebastián (1986b) "A commodity export boom and the real exchange rate: the money inflation link." In J. Peter Neary and Sweder van Wijnbergen, eds, *Natural Resources and the Macroeconomy* pp. 229–51. Cambridge, MA: MIT Press.

Edwards, Sebastián and Mohsin Khan (1985) "Interest rate determination in developing countries: a conceptual framework." *IMF Staff Papers*, 33.

Espinosa Valderrama, Abdón (1970) *Memoria de Hacienda: 1966–1970*. Bogotá: Talleres Gráficos del Banco de la República.

Fernández, Javier and Ricardo Candelo (1983) "Política monetaria y movilidad de capitales en Colombia." In *Ensayos sobre Política Económica*. Bogotá: Banco de la República.

Fernández, Javier and Jorge García García (1986) "The timing and sequencing of a trade liberalization policy: the case of Colombia," Part III: "Inferences for the sequencing of liberalization policies." Mimeo. Bogotá, February.

García García, Jorge (1976) "A history of economic policies in Colombia." Ph.D. dissertation, University of Chicago.

García García, Jorge (1978) "Movilidad de capitales: algunos aspectos conceptuales y sus determinantes en Colombia." In Eduardo Wiesner, ed., *Política Económica Externa de Colombia 1978*. Bogotá: Asociación Bancaria de Colombia.

García García, Jorge (1981a) *The Effects of Exchange Rates and Commercial Policy on Agricultural Incentives in Colombia: 1953–1978*. Washington, DC: International Food Policy Research Institute, Research Report no. 24, June.

García García, Jorge (1981b) "El modelo de desarrollo colombiano y su impacto sobre la economía de la costa atlántica." In *Primer Foro de la Costa Atlántica*. Mimeo. Santa Marta, March.

García García, Jorge (1986) "The timing and sequencing of trade liberalization: Colombia." Unpublished background papers. Washington, DC: World Bank.

García García, Jorge (1988) "The timing and sequencing of trade liberalization policies: Colombia, statistical appendices." Available from the Brazil Department, World Bank, Washington, DC.

García García, Jorge and Gabriel Montes Llamas (1988) *Coffee Boom, Government Expenditure and Relative Prices in Agriculture: The Colombian Experience*. Washington, DC: International Food Policy Research Institute, Research Report no. 68, September.

García García, Jorge (1989) "Impediments to trade liberalization in Colombia." In Martin Wolf and Larry Sjaastad, eds, *Impediments to Trade Liberalization in Latin America*. London: Gower for the Trade Policy Research Center.

Gillis, Malcolm and Charles E. McLure, Jr (1977) *La Reforma Tributaria Colombiana de 1974*. Bogotá: Talleres Gráficos del Banco Popular.

Giraldo, Gonzalo (1979) "Estructura de la protección arancelaria y para arancelaria en Colombia después de las reformas." *Revista de Planeación y Desarrollo*, 11 (2), May–August, 7–47.

Gómez, Hernando J. (1982) "La demanda colombiana de importaciones." In *Ensayos sobre Política Económica*, March. Bogotá: Banco de la República.

Gómez, Hernando J. (1988) "The Colombian illegal economy: size, evolution, characteristics and economic impact." In Bruce Bagley, Francisco Thoumi, and Juan Tokatlian, eds, *State and Society in Contemporary Colombia: Beyond the National Front*. Boulder, CO: Westview Press.

Guterman, Lía (1984) "La política laboral y sus efectos sobre la remuneración y el empleo en la industria manufacturera: 1950–1980." In *Política Económica y Desarrollo Industrial en Colombia: 1945–1982*, vol. 5. Bogotá: Corporación Centro Regional de Población.

Hanson, James A. (n.d.) *Liberalizing the Financial Sector in Colombia*. Mimeo. Washington, DC: World Bank.

IMF (International Monetary Fund), *Report on Exchange Restrictions*, various years. Washington, DC: IMF.

IMF (1981) *Supplement on Price Statistics*, vol. 2. Washington, DC: IMF.

IMF (1982) *Supplement on Trade Statistics*, vol. 4. Washington, DC: IMF.

IMF (1984) *International Financial Statistics Yearbook*. Washington, DC: IMF.

IMF (1985) *Supplement on Exchange Rates*, vol. 9. Washington, DC: IMF.

IMF, *Annual Report on Exchange Restrictions*, various years. Washington, DC: IMF.

IMF, *International Financial Statistics*, various years. Washington, DC: IMF.

INCOMEX (1977) *Comercio Exterior: 1968–1976*. Bogotá: Italgraf.

INCOMEX, *Comercio Exterior de Colombia*, various years, Bogotá.

Isaza, José F. (1981) "Efecto de la retroactividad de las cesantías en los porcentajes de incremento salarial." *Coyuntura Económica*, 11 (3), October, 146–51.

Jaramillo, Juan Carlos (1982) "La liberación del mercado financiero." In *Ensayos sobre Política Económica*. Bogotá: Banco de la República.

Jaramillo, Juan Carlos and Armando Montenegro (1982) "Cuenta especial de cambios: descripción y análisis de su evolución reciente." In *Ensayos sobre Política Económica*. Bogotá: Banco de la República.

Junguito, Roberto and Carlos Caballero (1978) "La otra economía." *Coyuntura Económica*, 8 (4) December, 101–39.

Junguito, Roberto and Carlos Caballero (1982) "Illegal transactions and the underground economy in Colombia." In Vito Tanzi, ed., *The Underground Economy in the United States and Abroad*. New York: Lexington.

Kamas, Linda (1986) "Dutch disease economics and the Colombian export boom." *World Development*, 9, September, 1177–98.

Krueger, Anne (1978) *Foreign Trade Regimes and Economic Development: Liberalization Attempts and Consequences*. Cambridge, MA: Ballinger for the National Bureau of Economic Research.

Kugler, Bernardo and Alvaro Reyes (1984) "Demanda por trabajo en el sector industrial Colombiano." Mimeo. Paper presented to the Fifth Latin American Meeting of the Econometric Society, Bogotá, July.

Marin, Wilson et al. (1980) *Análisis General de las Importaciones del Régimen de Licencia Previa*. Bogotá: INCOMEX.

Maullin, Richard (1967) *An Interpretation of the Colombian–IMF Disagreement and its Place in Colombian Politics*. Santa Monica, CA: Rand Corporation.

Misión Bird-Wiesner (1981) *Finanzas Intergubernamentales en Colombia*, Table II–I for 1967–1972. Bogotá: Departamento Nacional de Planeación.

Montes, Gabriel and Ricardo Candelo (1982) "El enfoque monetario de la balanza de pagos: el caso de Colombia, 1968–1980." *Revista de Planeación y Desarrollo*, 14 (2), May–August, 11–40.

Morawetz, David (1980) "Why the emperor's new clothes are not made in Colombia." Washington, DC: World Bank, Staff Working Paper no. 368.

Musalem, Alberto R. (1971) *Dinero, Inflación y Balanza de Pagos: La Experiencia de Colombia en la Post-Guerra*. Bogotá: Talleres Gráficos del Banco de la República.

Nelson, Richard, T. Paul Shultz, and Robert L. Slighton (1971) *Structural Change in a Developing Economy: Colombia's Problems and Prospects*. Princeton, NJ: Princeton University Press.

Ocampo, José Antonio and Leonardo Villar (1982) "Evolución del régimen de cesantías del sector privado." *Desarrollo y Sociedad: Cuaderno*, 5, November.

Palacio, Marco (1983) *El Café en Colombia 1850–1970: Una Historia Económica, Social y Política*. Bogotá: Siglo XXI/El Ancora Editores.

Pick Publishing Corporation (1974, 1984) *Pick's Currency Yearbook*. London.

Ruiz, Alvaro (1984) "La competitividad de las exportaciones menores en el período 1975–1983 y el déficit en la balanza de pagos registrado entre 1980–1983." *Revista de Planeación y Desarrollo*, 16 (2–3), April–September, 57–98.

Sanín Angel, Héctor (1981) "El salario real en la industria manufacturera colombiana: 1970–1980." *Boletín Mensual de Estadística*, no. 360, July, 35–73.

Sarmiento-Palacio, Eduardo (1982) *Inflación, Producción y Comercio Internacional*. Bogotá: PROCULTURA-FEDESARROLLO.

Solaún, Mauricio (1980) "Colombian politics: historical characteristics and problems." In R. Albert Berry, Roland Hellman, and Mauricio Solaún, eds, *Politics of Compromise: Coalition Government in Colombia*. New Brunswick, NJ: Transaction Books.

Teigeiro, José D. and R. Anthony Elson (1973) "The export promotion system and the growth of minor exports in Colombia." *IMF Staff Papers*, July, 414–70.

Thomas, Vinod et al., eds (1985) *Linking Macroeconomic and Agricultural Policies for Adjustment and Growth*. Baltimore, MD: Johns Hopkins University Press.

Thoumi, Francisco E. (1981) "International trade strategies, employment, and income distribution in Colombia." In Anne Krueger et al., eds, *Trade and Employment in Developing Countries: Individual Studies*. Chicago, IL: University of Chicago Press.

Urrutia, Miguel (1981) "Experience with the crawling peg in Colombia." In John Williamson, ed., *Exchange Rate Rules*. New York: St Martin's Press.

Urrutia, Miguel (1983) *Gremios, Política Económica y Democracia*. Bogotá: FEDESARROLLO.

Urrutia, Miguel and Albert Berry (1975) *La Distribución del Ingreso en Colombia*. Medellín: Editorial La Carreta.

Villar, Leonardo (1985) "Determinantes de las importaciones en Colombia: un análisis econométrico." In *Ensayos sobre Política Económica*, December. Bogotá: Banco de la República.

Wiesner, Eduardo (1978) "Devaluación y Mecamismo de Ajuste en Colombia." In Eduardo Wiesner, ed., *Política Económica Externa de Colombia 1978*. Bogotá: ASOBANCARIA.

Wiesner, Eduardo (1982) *Memoria del Departamento Nacional de Planeación*, pp. 41–2. Bogotá: Ediciones del Banco de la República.

World Bank (1975) *Economic Position and Prospects of Colombia*, vol. 3, *Colombian Tax Reform of 1974/1975*. Washington, DC: World Bank.

World Bank (1983) "Colombia: manufacturing sector development and changes in foreign trade and financial policies." Washington, DC: World Bank, report no. 4093–CO.

World Bank (1984) *Colombia: Economic Development and Policy under Changing Conditions*. Washington, DC: World Bank.

Part III

Perú

Julio J. Nogués
The World Bank, Washington, D.C.
with the collaboration of Patrick Saint Pol and
Jorge Vega Castro

Contents

List of Figures

List of Tables

Acknowledgments

Patrick Saint Pol and Jorge Vega Castro helped complete this study. They assembled part of the data, drafted different parts of the preliminary report and commented on the analysis and conclusions.

During the year when this project was initially drafted (September 1984 to September 1985), we received outstanding support from the resources of the Banco Central de la Reserva del Perú, which at that time was headed by Richard Webb. We also received extensive statistical support from the Gerencia de Estudios Económicos of the Banco Central de la Reserva del Perú headed by José Valderrama, as well as from the Ministries of Labor and Industry.

Colleagues who have made useful comments on various parts of this study include Donald Coes, Armeane Choksi, Vittorio Corbo, Jaime de Melo, Arnold Harberger, Anne O. Krueger, Paul Meo, Demetris Papageorgiou, Guy Pfeffermann, and Pablo Spiller.

In Perú, Carlos Paredes provided efficient research assistance, and Denise Brooking, Jackson Magargee, and Nellie Artis furnished excellent typing services.

A final word of appreciation to my wife Sylvina and children, who often waited patiently while I was trying to understand the nature of Perú's institutions.

I remain extremely grateful to all of these people. I alone am responsible for any remaining errors.

1

Trade, Employment, and Growth in Perú after World War II

In geographic size, Perú with approximately 1,290,000 km² is the third largest country in South America, bordering on Ecuador and Colombia in the north, Brazil and Bolivia in the east, Chile in the south, and the Pacific Ocean in the west.

One of the poorest countries in this region, Perú's annual per capita income in 1981 was US$1,170, higher only than that of Guyana and Bolivia. This relatively low level of income is the result of a significant slowdown of Perú's economic growth, combined with relatively rapid population growth. Per capita income growth rates, which rose from 2.9 percent in the 1950s to 3.2 percent in the last half of the 1960s, dropped to an average of 0.5 percent between 1970 and 1981 (World Bank, 1983a). In South America, only Chile had a lower per capita growth rate during the 1970s. A central argument of this chapter is that the astonishing slowdown of the Peruvian growth process is closely related to economic policies which, particularly in respect of trade, severely distorted the allocation of resources.

The discussion of economic growth and employment trends in Perú begins with a history of Peruvian economic policies in general and of import policies in particular since the late 1940s. The consequences of these economic policies for Perú's economic performance and growth are then discussed, and comparisons are made with the growth characteristics of other countries, particularly some of Perú's Latin American neighbors. The structure and growth of gross domestic product (GDP) is analyzed in the third section, while Perú's long-run foreign trade characteristics are examined in the fourth. In the fifth section, on population and employment, the long-run urbanization trend and the allocation of labor among economic sectors are reviewed. Finally some concluding comments are given.

Nature of Peruvian Trade and Exchange Rate Policies: 1945–1985

In the 1950s, Peruvian economic policies were relatively liberal.[1] Since then, they have become increasingly protectionist and inward looking, markedly so during the 1970s when, in addition to import substitution policies, severe distortions were introduced into factor and foreign exchange markets and state economic intervention increased. The trend was interrupted in 1979 with the reintroduction of more liberal and market-oriented policies, but it resumed and by 1985 policy-induced distortions were much the same as those that had prevailed in 1979. This story is illustrated in figure 1.1, which presents an ordinal and subjective index of trade policies for the period 1950–84.[2] In this chart, 1 stands for the most closed trade regime and 20 would represent free-trade policies.[3]

1945–1959

After World War II, Perú's balance-of-payments behavior was affected by several domestic policies, including the use of generalized quantitative restrictions (QRs) and unrealistic exchange rate policies. In addition, increasing government expenditures, unsupported by the taxation needed to finance them, had induced fiscal deficits and a strong inflationary trend by 1946–7.

Between 1945 and September 1948, a fixed official exchange rate was maintained in spite of domestic inflation well above international levels: the result was significant overvaluation of the sol. An increasingly sophisticated and discriminatory system of export and import licenses was used to control foreign exchange flows. However, as the overvaluation of the sol increased, the import regime became more restrictionist and the percentage of license applications that were denied increased, reaching 44 percent in 1946. In an attempt to make the import regime less obscure and discretional, the government introduced lists of goods classified in order of priority for importing. At one end of the scale (list A) were goods whose import faced minor restrictions. The list included foodstuffs, capital goods, and other essential intermediate inputs. At the other end, list D included goods whose import was prohibited.

---

[1] Many comments in this section draw on Bolóña (1981).
[2] The framework for the discussion of figure 1.1 follows the methodological guidelines of the country studies prepared for the research project of which this is a part (see the preface to the volume). Starting in 1950, the numbers on the vertical axis are the following: 16, 16, 16, 16, 16, 16, 15, 15, 15, 14, 13, 11, 10, 10, 9, 8, 7, 6, 4, 1, 1, 1, 1, 1, 1, 1, 1, 1, 1, 7, 13, 12, 11, 10, 7.
[3] In order to support the index presented in figure 1.1, the discussion that follows will use the available evidence on real exchange rates and the trade regime. In later sections of this chapter trade and output performance which also support this index, are discussed.

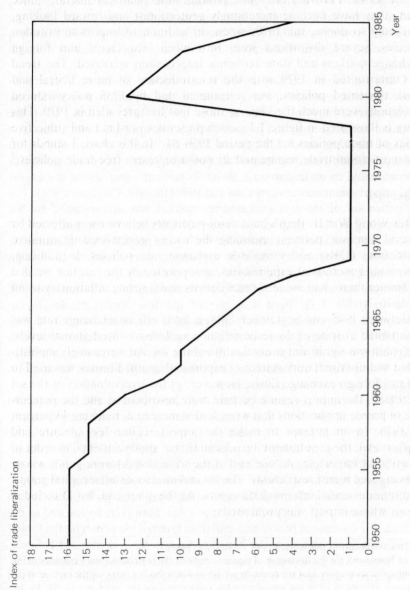

Figure 1.1   Indicator of trade liberalization for Perú, 1950–1985

In mid-1948, despite the licensing system, foreign exchange reserves were virtually nonexistent. Clearly, there was no longer room for maneuver within the existing policy mix: in September of 1947 imports of many goods in lists B and C (mainly noncompeting intermediate imports) had to be suspended. Under these conditions there was no way that the Peruvian economy could function smoothly. In October of 1948, President Bustamante y Rivera was deposed by a military coup headed by General Odría.

Odría's economic cabinet aimed to reintroduce liberal economic policies; the first essential policy change in this direction was to let the exchange rate move to its intervention-free level. By October 1950, the nominal exchange rate had jumped to 14.9 soles per US dollar, that is, a nominal devaluation of 129 percent from the fixed exchange rate of 6.5 soles per US dollar of the immediate post-war years. This devaluation was accompanied by an important – about 30 percent – increase in the export and import quantum between 1948 and 1950 (Bolóña, 1981, table 4.1). The liberalization of the foreign exchange market was accompanied by the dismantling of the complicated system of QRs and of the price control system that had also been reinforced during the presidency of Bustamante y Rivera. Furthermore, the new legislation gave freedom to foreign investment to flow into the traditional export sector.

Because the structure of tariffs that remained in place was quite low and uniform (table 1.1), Perú was one of the few important developing economies that remained closely integrated in the world economy during the 1950s. This was true in particular in relation to its Latin American neighbors, most of which did not dismantle their state control apparatus after World War II and which, at that time, intensified import substitution strategies for economic development.

While the trade regime kept Perú well integrated in the international trading system, the 1950s also witnessed increasing activity from domestic pressure groups in favor of protection. In the early years of the decade the major exporting industries, represented by the National Agricultural Society (SNA, Sociedad Nacional Agraria), and the National Society for Mining and Petroleum (SNMP, Sociedad Nacional de Minería y Petróleo) had considerable political influence, which they used in the cause of an open economy and a high real exchange rate.[4] However, by the end of the decade the balance of power had shifted in favor of the protectionist lobby, principally represented by the National Society for Industry (SNI, Sociedad Nacional de Industrias). To some extent, this process was facilitated by policy errors that led to increased macroeconomic disequilibria. A fixed

---

[4] For example, in May of 1953, and because of pressure from the SNA and SNMP, the government annulled a decree that it had legislated a few months earlier which imposed an *ad valorem* duty of 50 percent on many goods (see Bolóña, 1981).

Table 1.1 Nominal official tariff by Brussels Trade Nomenclature sections, selected years[a] (percent)

BTN sections	1955–60	1967	1973	1979	1980
Animals	3	36	50	35	32
Vegetable products	7	56	65	46	35
Fats and oils	1	45	51	32	31
Foods, beverages, tobacco	17	109	120	78	53
Mineral products	3	46	55	20	18
Chemical products	5	43	49	25	24
Resins, plastics, rubber	4	60	69	39	38
Hides and leather	11	128	128	71	31
Wood, cork, etc.	3	73	84	39	36
Paper	8	70	72	46	41
Textiles	22	133	138	76	52
Footwear, headgear, etc.	16	158	168	93	60
Articles of stone, cement, etc.	18	73	80	47	42
Precious stones and metals	11	101	104	65	42
Basic metals	4	61	70	36	35
Machinery	2	37	50	33	33
Transport equipment	3	41	49	39	34
Instruments	9	62	73	40	38
Arms	9	77	77	41	40
Miscellaneous	9	102	113	37	51
Works of art	0	20	32	10	10
No. of tariff lines	4,234	4,571	n.a.	n.a.	5,104

n.a., not available; BTN, Brussels Trade Nomenclature.
These figures correspond to the *ad valorem* equivalent of the specific duties. In addition, during the 1950s, there existed an *ad valorem* import duty of 7 percent on the majority of imports.
[a] Simple average legal tariff rates.
Sources: 1955–1973, Bolóña, 1981, table 3.3; 1979–80, BCRP (Banco Central de la Reserva del Perú), *Annual Reports*, various issues

exchange rate was maintained between 1953 and 1957 and in the same period accumulated domestic inflation of 33 percent was well above international inflation (table 1.2). The result was a payments problem, tackled during 1955–7 by several protectionist measures. These included an increase in specific tariffs which implied *ad valorem* rates ranging from 25 percent to 100 percent depending on the type of goods. Also, in these years "the authorities suspended the import of private cars, and imposed several additional *ad valorem* duties" (Bolóña, 1981, p. 156). Eventually, the fiscal deficit was reduced and an important real devaluation was implemented during the late 1950s.

By now SNA and SNMP had lost much of their leverage. In particular, they were unable to prevent the government from implementing in 1959

Table 1.2 Real exchange rate, 1950–1983

		Consumer price index		
Year	Nominal exchange rate	United States	Perú	Real exchange rate
1950	14.9	29.2	1.4	314.9
1951	15.3	31.5	1.5	315.4
1952	15.6	32.2	1.6	307.9
1953	19.9	32.5	1.8	361.4
1954	19.0	32.6	1.9	329.7
1955	19.0	32.5	2.0	313.9
1956	19.0	33.0	2.1	302.4
1957	19.2	34.2	2.2	293.7
1958	24.1	35.1	2.4	353.4
1959	27.9	35.4	2.7	364.5
1960	27.4	35.9	2.9	335.0
1961	26.8	36.3	3.1	311.7
1962	26.8	36.7	3.3	295.7
1963	26.8	37.2	3.5	282.8
1964	26.8	37.6	3.9	260.7
1965	26.8	38.2	4.5	228.2
1966	26.8	39.4	4.9	215.4
1967	30.7	40.5	5.4	231.2
1968	38.7	42.2	6.4	254.8
1969	38.7	44.5	6.8	252.7
1970	38.7	47.1	7.2	255.0
1971	38.7	49.1	7.6	248.9
1972	38.7	50.8	8.2	240.0
1973	38.7	53.9	9.0	232.8
1974	38.7	59.8	10.5	221.0
1975	40.8	65.3	13.0	205.7
1976	57.4	69.1	17.3	229.4
1977	83.8	73.6	23.9	258.3
1978	156.3	79.2	37.7	328.5
1979	224.5	88.1	62.8	315.0
1980	288.7	100.0	100.0	288.7
1981	422.9	110.4	175.4	266.1
1982	697.6	117.1	288.4	283.3
1983	1,625.1	120.9	609.0	322.7

The real exchange rate is defined at the nominal exchange rate times the ratio of the US consumer price.

Source: computed with statistics published in IMF, International Finance Statistics, various years

the Industrial Promotion Law, which ushered in a new protectionist era that would affect the development of Perú for the next 20 years.

Bolóña (1981, p. 158) has concluded that the "tariff level of 1949–1959 was similar to that of 1910–1922, and both can be considered as liberal ones in Peruvian tariff history." Between 1950 and 1955, the index allots 16 points to the Peruvian trade and exchange rate policies. From here on, the trade policy indicator declines, reaching a mark of 14 in 1959 (figure 1.1).

1959–1968

In its 1959 report, the Economic Commission for Latin America (ECLA) concluded that, unlike many of its Latin American neighbors, Perú had a tariff structure that was not conducive to industrialization. By Latin American standards, the ECLA report showed that Perú had relatively low tariffs on consumer goods that it could produce domestically and relatively high tariffs on intermediate and capital goods that it could not develop in the near future (ECLA, 1959, pp. 157–8).

Peruvian policymakers responded to ECLA's recommendations by introducing a protectionist and escalated tariff structure. In a few years, Perú's structure of incentives changed drastically. As we shall see, the cost to Perú of this and other distortions has been heavy.

The Industrial Promotion Law of 1959 (Law 13270) was crucial in opening the way for manipulation of incentives. From an analysis of trade policies introduced by this and other promotional laws, Thorp (1977, p. 128) concluded that "basic industries received the largest benefits such as complete exemption from tariff duties, but the coverage of the term 'basic' was continually increased in subsequent legislation. The law was almost entirely extended to all consumer goods." At around the same time "Perú's traditionally low level of tariffs was increased in several steps. Higher duties on final goods, combined with exemptions on inputs and capital goods, now created the familiar ISI [import substitution industrialization] situation of extraordinarily high effective protection." Table 1.1 shows how much the tariff structure had changed by 1967.

Boloña (1981, table 3.3) shows that this tariff structure did not differ significantly from the 1964 tariff structure (introduced by Law 14816) which, according to Boloña, had the following objectives: (a) to reduce import duties on capital goods; (b) to increase import duties on consumer goods in accordance with the possibilities of domestic production; and (c) to bring the tariff level closer to those of other Latin American Free Trade Association (LAFTA) countries.

These protectionist measures were implemented during the first government of Fernando Belaúnde Terry who was elected President in 1963; trade liberalization measures were implemented during his second presidency nearly 20 years later.

Once again, between 1964 and 1968, protectionist commercial policies were accompanied by increasing fiscal deficits and inappropriate exchange rate policies that finally led the country into a new balance-of-payments crisis.[5]

Between 1959 and 1967, the exchange rate remained fixed at a value of around 27 soles per US dollar, while accumulated domestic inflation during this period was on the order of 100 percent (table 1.2). The initial measures to cope with the balance-of-payments problem included a timid devaluation in 1967 and, most importantly, an increase in tariffs and nontariff barriers including a tax surcharge on imports and suspension of imports of many goods.

In 1968 the nominal exchange rate increased to 38.7 soles per US dollar, implying a real devaluation of about 10 percent in relation to 1967. Other policies to reduce the fiscal imbalance included macrostabilization measures, increased import protection and real devaluation. However, unfortunately for the future development of Perú, Belaúnde's political clout had vanished, and in mid-1968 his government was deposed by a military coup.

In concluding the policy overview of the 1959–68 period, two points should be stressed. The first is that protectionist policies were accompanied in the long run by a declining real exchange rate (see table 1.2): the average real exchange rate during the relatively open trade regime of 1950–5 is 22 percent higher than the closed economy real exchange rate of the 1960s.

The second point refers to how changing commercial policies affected Perú's role in international forums. During the era of commitment to open trade policies after 1948, Perú profited from its relatively active participation in the initial post-World War II rounds of trade negotiations. Unlike many other developing countries, Perú was offering concessions as early as the Torquay Round of trade negotiations. As trade policies became more protectionist, however, Perú had to request waivers in the General Agreement on Tariffs and Trade (GATT) and, by the Kennedy Round, was neither participating actively in the negotiations nor granting concessions. Thus, as Perú abandoned liberal trade policies, it also isolated itself from multilateral trade negotiations. The concessions from other countries that were lost as a result represent an additional cost to the Peruvian economy of following import substitution policies.

The above history is reflected in the trend in our trade policy indicator (figure 1.1): the numbers decline from 14 points in 1959 to 6 in 1968.

1968–1978

The military coup on October 3, 1968, replaced Fernando Belaúnde Terry with General Juan Velasco Alvarado. Twelve years later, the military

---

[5] To a great extent, these deficits arose from attempts to satisfy the demands of urban groups whose power was growing rapidly in step with impressive rural-to-urban migration.

handed back the political power to the civilians, and on July 28, 1980, Belaúnde Terry was once again sworn in as President of Perú.

The extreme nationalism characteristic of the military regime, particularly during the presidency of General Velasco Alvarado (1968–75),[6] was the consequence of the military government's perception of the causes of Peruvian underdevelopment. The underdevelopment was thought to be closely linked to the penetration of foreign capital, and the inability of past Peruvian leaders to negotiate good terms under which such capital should enter the country. Underdevelopment and poverty were also associated with the high concentration of landownership. These characteristics were thought to be central in explaining the Peruvian pattern of income distribution, one of the most unequal among Latin American countries (see Altimir, 1982).

Structural Reforms Introduced by Velasco
The Velasco government's solutions to these problems were radical, and by 1970 Perú began suffering the effects of the most dramatic policy shock of its history. Agrarian reform, nationalization of foreign enterprises and the banking system, price controls, nationalization of foreign trade, increased intervention that distorted factor markets, and prohibitive protection were among the major structural policy reforms that, according to the Velasco government, would help to build a more just society.[7]

Many scholars have concluded that these, as well as other economic policies, were a failure in achieving the intended goals of redistribution as well as in relation to economic performance following the changes in the pattern of property ownership. For example, the land reform did not reach the majority of landless poor peasants and although " . . . the large estates disappeared, there was no lasting qualitative change in the rural power structure" (Schydlowsky and Wicht, 1983, p. 104). More generally, income appears to have been redistributed between the rich and middle income groups without much advantage to the poor (Webb, 1977).

Price controls instituted earlier were reinforced during the military government. These controls significantly affected the cost of food. It was Velasco's view that subsidizing urban consumption via controlled food prices was in the nature of a just social order. He rejected advice to increase food prices on the grounds that " . . . the peasants now had the land and should not get more advantages" (Schydlowsky and Wicht, 1983,

---

[6] In mid-1975, General Morales Bermúdez replaced General Velasco Alvarado as President of Perú. Many authors have associated this change with Perú's chaotic economic situation in that year. See, for example, Cline (1981) and Schydlowsky and Wicht (1983).

[7] Some important literature analyzes this experience. Interested readers should consult, among others, papers in McClintock and Lowenthal (1983) and Preeg (1981). The intention here is to provide a brief summary of the policy interventions.

p. 104). As we shall see, land reform and agricultural pricing policies led to an important slowdown of Perú's agricultural sector.

However, nationalization of key foreign enterprises was, in the government's view, essential for the Peruvian government to gain control of the profits that were perceived, under the existing structure of property ownership, as not being used in the national interest.

The significant extent of nationalization is reflected in table 1.3, which shows the pattern of enterprise ownership in the formal sector as measured by the share in value added of different groups of owners.[8] The figures show that the share in value added by state enterprises jumped from 15 percent, while the share of foreign enterprises decreased by 13 percent.

The economic role of the government also expanded quite significantly, not only through nationalization but also by the creation of new enterprises. State enterprises such as steel mills, basic metal industries, and paper products industries were created, and because foodstuffs were imported, new state trading enterprises distributed and sold foodstuffs at subsidized prices. In line with food subsidies, the degree of participation of the government in foreign trade increased significantly. "During 1971–76 government imports were on average 30 percent of total imports, increasing from 21 percent to 35 percent between the beginning and the end of this period. If we adjust our figures by an estimate of imports for national defense purposes, the average value increases to about 51 percent (in 1976)" (Bolóña, 1981, p. 181).

Policy-induced distortions in factor markets were also severe. Interest rate controls below expected inflation rates, overvalued exchange rates,

Table 1.3 Pattern of enterprise ownership in the modern sector (value added as a percentage of gross national product)

Ownership	Pre-reform	Post-reform
State	11	26
Domestic private capital	30	22
Foreign capital	21	8
Cooperative	–	6
Total modern sector	62	62

–, negligible.

Source: Fitzgerald, 1976, as quoted in Thorp, 1977

[8] The formal sector includes the public sector and that part of the private sector that receives the benefits and costs of the legal structure of incentives and taxes directly. For example, the formal manufacturing sector includes the enterprises that are covered by the Survey of Manufactures that is collected annually by the Ministry of Industry, Commerce, Tourism, and Integration (MICTI) and excludes those small firms and family processing shops that operate in the underground economy.

and tax incentives for investment purposes reduced the price of capital well below its opportunity cost. Moreover, a labor management and profit-sharing scheme along Yugoslavian lines was implemented, which involved the eventual takeover of firms by labor. Entrepreneurs' initial reactions, not surprisingly, were to dismiss workers as fast as they could, but the government responded by introducing a labor stability law restricting such dismissals. All these distortions increased wage-to-rental ratios faced by private entrepreneurs while significantly reducing factor mobility. (See Nogués, 1986, for a more detailed discussion of the role of factor market distortions.) As shown, these policies considerably impaired the capacity of the formal economy to generate productive employment opportunities.

The drastic transformation in the structure of enterprise ownership was accompanied by an expanding role of the state: government current expenditures as a percentage of GNP jumped from 14 percent in the early 1960s to 18 percent during 1974–6. Nevertheless, as the restructuring proceeded, the state seemed less and less able to raise the taxes necessary to finance it. As a consequence, government borrowing grew and fiscal deficits increased steadily, reaching 7.7 percent of GDP in 1977. This trend was accompanied by increasing inflation, which rose from an average annual rate of 10 percent between 1960 and 1968 to 26 percent between 1968 and 1970.

Trade and Exchange Rate Policies
The fixed exchange rate policy followed since 1968, together with inflation well above the international level, once again brought overvaluation of the sol. The current account deficit went to record levels in the mid-1970s (tables 1.2 and 1.4). The devaluation attempts of 1975 and 1976 were not

Table 1.4 Long-run balance-of-payments position, 1970–1983 (million US dollars)

Year	Merchandise exports	Trade imports	Net service	Current account	Net direct investment	Long-term capital[a]	Other capital[b]	Change in reserves
1970	1,034	700	− 149	185	− 79	103	48	257
1975	1,330	2,427	− 438	− 1,535	316	819	− 177	− 577
1976	1,341	2,016	− 397	− 1,072	171	471	− 438	− 868
1977	1,726	2,148	− 361	− 783	54	674	− 294	− 349
1978	1,972	1,668	− 468	− 164	25	419	− 204	76
1979	3,676	3,090	− 927	− 101	27	435	361	1,579
1980	3,916	3,090	− 927	− 101	27	435	361	722
1981	3,249	3,802	− 1,175	− 1,728	125	523	576	− 504
1982	3,293	3,721	− 1,181	− 1,609	48	1,152	533	124
1983	2,970	2,670	− 1,182	− 882	15	1,244	− 402	− 40

[a] Long-term capital of public sector plus loans to private sector.
[b] Short-term capital and errors and omissions.

Source: BCRP, *Annual Reports*, various years

accompanied by a coherent fiscal–monetary policy and therefore did not result in a sufficient increase in the real exchange rate. It was not until the end of 1977, when the exchange rate was floated, that a real devaluation began to take place. More appropriate exchange rate policies were accompanied during 1978 and 1979 by more coherent monetary and fiscal policies.

Because domestic savings were insufficient to finance increasing public sector expenditure programs, Perú resorted to foreign borrowing. Between 1970 and 1979, total external debt increased from US$3.7 billion to US$9.3 billion. During the same period, the public sector debt increased from US$450.9 million to US$5.8 billion. Even during the crisis years of 1974–6, the international financial community continued lending to a government that, at the time, was introducing severe distortions and macroeconomic imbalances into the economy.

The protectionist trend observed during the first government of Belaúnde was strongly reinforced by the military government. The industrial law (Ley General de Industrias, Decree law 18350 of 1970) provides an extreme example of irrational industrialization policies: "This law and its regulations gave them [businessmen] more tax exemptions, and higher protection, including a total ban on the importation of any good that was produced domestically, than any of the traditional government programs" (Schydlowsky and Wicht, 1983, p. 104).

By 1975 the value-added weighted average rate of protection for manufacturing was 198.3 percent (World Bank, 1983d)[9] and the discrimination against the exportables sector was significant. A comparison with other Latin American countries during periods when import substitution policies predominated reveals similar levels of protection for manufacturing (table 1.5).[10]

Initially, import prohibitions granted by the Industrial Promotion Law were included in the National Register of Manufactures (Registro Nacional de Manufacturas, RNM). Goods similar to those produced domestically were automatically prohibited, and other import prohibitions were imposed over time to cope with the balance-of-payments difficulties. In addition, the allocation of foreign exchange was made firm specific.

The tariff structure was modified in 1973 but its allocative role was preempted by the system of import prohibitions. Also, and because the Industrial Promotion Law granted tariff exemptions in a discriminatory way – according to industry and region – an additional administrative procedure had to be created for distributing these exemptions, the fiscal

---

[9] In the World Bank study (1983c), implicit nominal rates of protection are derived from price comparisons.

[10] Until the late 1970s, export taxes in Perú were not important. However, export promotion incentives for nontraditional exports have been discriminatory.

Table 1.5 Average rate of effective protection for manufacturing industries in Latin American countries during the periods of import substitution policies[a]

Country	Year	Average EPR for manufacturing (%)	Range of EPR (%)
Argentina	1969	111	– 30/308
Brazil	1963	184	60/687
Chile	1967	175	– 23/1190
Perú	1975	198	3/694
Uruguay	1965	384	17/1014

[a] EPRs are estimated for sales in the domestic market.

Sources: Argentina, Nogués, 1983; Perú, World Bank, 1983c; other countries, Krueger, 1983, table 3.1

costs of which were far from negligible. In 1975, these exemptions were equivalent to 56 percent of import duties collected (Abusada-Salah, 1977, p. 30).

Between 1969 and 1978, I have given the trade policy indicator a value of 1. The reason should be clear. In a country where everything that is domestically produced is protected from foreign competition by import prohibitions, and where such prohibitions are granted irrespective of long-run efficiency considerations, we are sure to be confronting one of the most restrictive trade regimes that can be envisaged. I therefore see no reason why the trade policies during these years should be ranked any higher.

1978–1985

A change of president in 1975 gradually brought a change of direction and, in early 1979, trade liberalization policies began to be implemented in Perú. The discussion that follows summarizes the major characteristics of this liberalization, which are spelled out in detail in chapter 2.

Peruvian liberalization policies were carried out in two phases: in 1979 the majority of nontariff barriers were phased out, and in late 1980 ad valorem tariff rates were reduced.

The first step in reducing import barriers was the abolition of the RNM in March 1979. Initially, many of the goods in the RNM were included in a list of "temporary" import prohibitions, but by December 1979 import of only nine items of the trade nomenclature remained prohibited (table 1.6). Nontariff barriers continued to be lifted during 1980, and by December of this year only 2.4 percent of the items of the trade nomenclature were

Table 1.6 Number of tariff lines affected by nontariff import barriers, 1978–1984

Type of restrictions	Dec 1978	Mar 1979	Dec 1979	Dec 1980	Dec 1981	Dec 1982	Dec 1984
Free	1,753	1,753	3,745	4,980	5,089	5,075	4,996
Restricted	1,038	1,038	1,258	117	111	144	126
Prohibited	1,852	1,313	9	7	7	7	7
Temporarily prohibited	0	539	0	0	0	0	172
Total	4,643	4,643	5,012	5,104	5,207	5,226	5,301

Source: BCRP, 1983, table 1

affected by some form of nontariff barrier. Products that remained on the prohibited list included unprocessed cotton, fireworks, and arms.

Tariff reductions were also implemented during 1979 and 1980. In September 1979 a new tariff schedule was published which consolidated the previous specific and *ad valorem* rates in an *ad valorem* tariff structure, reduced the maximum *ad valorem* rate from 355 percent to 155 percent, and simplified and reduced import duty exemptions (BCRP, 1983).

Import barriers were rationalized still further by a new tariff structure introduced in September 1980, which reduced the maximum legal rate from 155 percent to 60 percent. As a consequence, the last quarter of 1980 and the early months of 1981 saw the most liberal import regime that Perú had had since the early 1960s.

From then on, there was a slow but gradual reversal. During 1981, some tariffs on intermediate and capital goods were reduced. Since the majority of the goods affected by those tariff reforms were not produced domestically, this measure provided a higher effective protection rate to domestic producers. A 15 percent tariff surcharge on all imports was imposed in 1981. In 1982 this surcharge was increased first to 10 percent-age points and in 1983 to 15 percentage points. During 1984, the degree of escalation of the tariff structure was reinforced, as the level of new tariff increases was positively correlated with the level of existing tariffs.

Meanwhile, nontariff barriers, which were at their minimum by the end of 1980, became more restrictive. During 1982 and 1983, some items began to be added to the list of goods whose imports had to be approved by some government office, and during 1984 and 1985 numerous tariff lines were added.

From the brief discussion above, it is clear that trade policies imple-mented during 1979 and 1980 resulted in a trade regime considerably more open than the regime of the 1960s and 1970s. Nevertheless, even at the peak of liberalization at the end of 1980, the trade regime of Perú was not as liberal as in the 1950s, when tariff rates were systematically lower (see table 1.1). For 1980, we have given a value of 13 to the trade policy indicator. Thereafter, the indicator shows a declining trend.

The drastic increase in protection after the 1950s combined with the major policy distortions of the 1970s had predictably profound effects on the structure and performance of the Peruvian economy. In this context, in the next sections the Peruvian growth process since the 1950s is examined, beginning with the growth and structure of the economy.

Growth and Structure of the Gross Domestic Product

The preceding discussion has described the progress of the Peruvian economy from one in which a relatively open trade regime gave the main signals for resource allocation in an economic system where factor mobility was relatively high, to one of substantial government intervention as well as major fiscal imbalances. In theory, such a change in the policy environment is likely to affect the growth and structure of GDP in two principal ways. First, as the degree of government intervention and protectionist measures increases, competitive pressures decline and re-source allocation worsens. *Ceteris paribus*, this is expected to result in a decline in the rate of economic growth. Second, inward-looking policies are expected to increase the share of the protected sector in GDP.

Table 1.7 shows annual growth rates of GDP for 1951–84. First note that, with the exception of 1983, significant slowdowns in economic growth coincide with each of the years in which there were major foreign exchange problems and an important real devaluation (1958, 1968, 1977, and 1978).

Table 1.7 Annual real growth rates of gross domestic product, 1951–1984 (percent; base year, 1970)

1951	7.7	1962	8.2	1973	4.3
1952	5.5	1963	4.1	1974	7.5
1953	5.3	1964	7.3	1975	4.5
1954	6.0	1965	5.2	1976	2.0
1955	4.2	1966	6.4	1977	− 0.1
1956	3.8	1967	3.4	1978	− 0.5
1957	6.5	1968	− 0.3	1979	4.1
1958	0.3	1969	3.9	1980	3.8
1959	4.7	1970	5.4	1981	3.9
1960	11.3	1971	5.0	1982	0.4
1961	7.0	1972	1.7	1983	− 11.8
1951–9	4.9	1970–8	3.3	1984	4.7
1960–9	5.7	1979–82	3.1		

Source: derived from Instituto Nacional de Estadística (INE), 1983, p. 42, table 2

(The 1983 decline in GDP should be attributed primarily to natural disasters.) Clearly, in the long run, there has been an inverse relation between the height of trade barriers and the growth performance. In the medium term, however, other factors have also played an important role in determining growth performance. For example, by the early 1960s the fishing industry was becoming important and its rapid growth during these years boosted overall growth. Further, during the early 1960s, expansionary fiscal policies encouraged rapid growth of construction and government activities. These developments to some extent counteracted the effects on growth of increasing resource misallocation, arising from protectionist and other distortionary policies: apparently, expansionary elements predominated, and the average rate of the 1960s was consequently higher than that of the 1950s.

A similar argument is applicable to the early 1970s, when a booming construction sector partly attributable to expansionary government policies helped to sustain growth rates in spite of the huge distortions introduced during those years. However, it is also clear that the adjustment policies in the middle and late 1970s were a consequence of the inflation of earlier years. Therefore, although high growth rates were maintained for some time during the early 1970s, a more realistic view of the growth performance of the military period is given by the growth rates over the whole decade, which averaged around 3 percent, a figure much lower than that of the preceding two decades.

Another interesting observation (table 1.8) is that the performance of the manufacturing sector, assumed to have benefited the most from the incentive system put in place in the 1960s and 1970s, in fact worsened in relation to the 1950s. A long-run slowdown in manufacturing growth and overall economic growth following the adoption of import substitution policies has also been observed in other Latin American countries, in sharp contrast with the spectacular progress in industrialization and economic performance of other developing countries that followed relatively open trade policies after the 1960s. In sum, it appears that distortionary policies in general, and protectionist policies in particular, sooner or later turn out to obstruct industrialization and, more generally, to impede economic growth.

The years of trade liberalization – from 1979 to 1984 – were accompanied by low average rates. In chapter 4 it is argued that this relatively poor formance should be attributed to a great extent to other accompanying policies and also, particularly, to external shocks, including declining terms of trade and adverse climatic conditions.

Table 1.9 shows the structure of GDP for selected years since 1950. It is seen that, using the 1970 structure of relative prices, agriculture, fishing, and mining – the major exportable industries of Perú – accounted for 28 percent and 30 percent of economic activity in 1950 and 1960 respec-

Table 1.8 Annual real growth rates of gross domestic product and its components for selected periods, 1950–1984 (percent)

GDP components	1950–5	1955–60	1960–5	1965–70	1970–5	1975–8	1978–82	1978–83	1984
GDP	6.0	4.4	6.7	4.4	5.3	0.4	2.7	– 0.3	4.5
Supply									
Agriculture	5.0	1.3	2.7	4.0	1.5	– 0.1	3.5	1.1	8.0
Fishing	15.8	22.1	15.2	10.4	– 16.8	14.2	– 2.8	– 11.7	8.9
Mining	8.6	20.3	2.4	3.8	– 1.7	17.8	1.9	0.0	6.0
Manufacturing	7.8	10.9	8.9	5.8	7.1	– 2.0	1.6	– 2.5	2.5
Construction	10.0	0.0	7.7	– 0.3	13.2	– 9.0	8.8	1.9	1.5
Government	4.1	4.2	7.7	3.6	4.5	1.4	1.3	1.5	0.0
Others[a]	5.4	0.8	7.6	4.1	6.9	– 0.1	3.1	0.0	3.7
Demand									
Private consumption	6.3	1.4	8.4	5.4	6.3	– 1.4	1.4	– 1.3	3.1
Public consumption	5.5	3.2	9.2	7.9	7.4	– 1.4	3.5	1.0	– 14.0
Gross domestic investment	9.2	– 1.6	6.3	– 1.3	16.0	– 15.5	15.6	5.8	2.9
Exports	7.8	11.9	5.3	2.5	– 4.3	8.7	6.3	2.2	5.7
(Imports)	12.3	– 7.3	13.6	3.5	11.6	– 18.6	15.4	5.9	– 19.8

[a] Includes mainly commerce, banking, housing, electricity, and transport.

Source: BCRP, Annual Reports, various issues

Table 1.9 Structure of gross domestic product, 1950–1983 (1970 prices)

GDP component	1950	1955	1960	1965	1970	1975[a]	1978[a]	1979[a]	1980[a]	1982[a]	1983[a]
GDP (million 1970 soles)	84,813	113,448	140,638	194,407	240,666	311,131	314,969	328,527	337,749	351,059	309,691
Supply											
Agriculture	22.6	21.5	18.5	15.3	15.1	12.6	12.4	12.2	11.4	12.7	13.3
Fishing	0.4	0.6	1.4	2.1	2.7	0.8	1.3	1.3	1.2	1.0	0.7
Mining	4.5	5.1	10.4	8.5	8.2	5.9	9.5	10.0	9.3	9.2	9.7
Manufacturing	13.6	14.8	20.0	22.2	23.8	25.9	24.0	23.9	24.5	22.9	21.5
Construction	5.1	6.2	5.0	5.2	4.2	6.0	4.4	4.4	5.1	5.6	5.0
Government	8.8	8.0	7.9	8.3	8.0	7.7	8.0	7.6	7.5	7.6	8.7
Others[b]	45.0	43.8	36.8	38.4	38.0	41.1	40.4	40.6	41.0	41.0	41.1
Demand[c]											
Consumption	81.0	81.8	71.4	77.6	83.0	87.8	83.1	67.9	81.5	80.0	80.6
Investment	20.2	23.5	17.4	17.1	12.9	21.0	12.5	13.4	17.0	19.9	16.8
Trade ratios											
Export/GDP	15.0	16.4	23.1	21.6	19.7	12.2	15.5	19.2	17.3	17.8	17.7
Import/GDP	16.2	21.6	11.9	16.3	15.7	21.0	11.1	11.2	15.9	17.8	15.1

[a] Approximate figures.
[b] Includes mainly commerce, banking, housing, electricity, and transport.
[c] Includes private and public components.

Source: BCRP, Annual Reports, various issues

tively. By 1975, a year of clear inward-oriented policies and overvalued domestic currency, the GDP share of these industries had dropped to 19.3 percent. (This picture does not change when we exclude the fishing sector, which is quite vulnerable to climatic conditions.)

Foreign Trade: Structure, Performance, and Partners

In the previous section some of the characteristics of the aggregate patterns of Peruvian economic growth since the early 1950s were indicated. In this section we concentrate on the part played by foreign trade in this growth process and on how changing trade policies affected the structure of trade and Perú's relationship with its trading partners. We begin with a brief comment on trends in trade-to-output ratios and then discuss in greater detail changes in exports, imports, and finally trading partners.

One important caveat should be mentioned. Our analysis is based on trade flows reported in Perú. In all likelihood, these statistics understate the value of trade. First, since the late 1970s, output and exports of drugs have been flourishing, but unfortunately there are no reliable estimates of the amount or the trend of these exports; an unofficial estimate of around US$400 million per year is sometimes mentioned as an approximation of illegal drug exports. Secondly, on the import side, the replacement of import prohibitions and nontariff barriers with tariff protection is believed to have facilitated smuggling. Unfortunately, once again there are no recent estimates of the importance of these activities.

Trade-to-output Ratio

Trade-to-output ratios are usually used as a measure of the importance of trade, and also for assessing the effects of different trade policies on individual countries over time. In this connection, it is usually assumed that protectionist policies and declining real exchange rates reduce trade-to-output ratios. Changing trade-to-output ratios over time might also be affected, however, by changes in tastes and in the structure of factor endowments.

These influences should be borne in mind when evaluating table 1.9's depiction of the trade-to-output ratio for selected years since 1950. At current prices the highest figure (38.0 percent) is observed for 1955 when the Peruvian economy was quite integrated in the world trading system. Nevertheless, the figure for 1965 is similar: this is mainly due to the fishing boom of the early 1960s. From that date, and as expected from the closing of the economy in the late 1960s and 1970s, the estimates show a declining trend to a value of 26.6 percent in 1978, and an increase thereafter.

Table 1.10 Structure and current value of exports for selected years, 1950–1984[a] (percent)

Sector and goods	1950	1960	1970	1973	1975	1978	1980	1983	1984
Minerals	21.1	43.0	45.0	55.4	44.3	46.6	44.8	50.0	41.3
Copper	(24.4)	(49.7)	(54.2)	(54.0)	(31.1)	(46.2)	(42.8)	(29.4)	(34.0)
Iron	(0.0)	(17.3)	(15.5)	(10.7)	(8.8)	(8.1)	(5.4)	(5.0)	(4.4)
Silver	(19.5)	(6.3)	(6.3)	(6.2)	(15.6)	(13.0)	(17.9)	(25.9)	(17.4)
Lead	(31.7)	(17.8)	(13.5)	(13.0)	(16.8)	(17.8)	(21.8)	(19.4)	(17.9)
Zinc	(24.4)	(8.9)	(10.5)	(16.1)	(27.7)	(14.9)	(12.0)	(20.3)	(26.2)
Fishing	3.1[b]	8.8	29.3	12.4	12.6	9.9	5.0	2.6	4.3
Agriculture	51.0	32.7	15.2	18.4	27.9	12.8	5.8	6.5	6.3
Cotton	(68.7)	(50.3)	(33.1)	(30.7)	(14.3)	(15.0)	(31.9)	(22.4)	(11.6)
Sugar	(30.3)	(32.4)	(38.9)	(38.1)	(72.5)	(18.6)	(5.7)	(17.9)	(24.7)
Coffee	(1.0)	(17.2)	(28.0)	(31.2)	(13.2)	(66.4)	(62.4)	(59.7)	(63.7)
Petroleum	12.9[c]	4.1	0.7	1.4	3.1	9.4	20.2	18.1	19.6
Other products[d]	11.9	11.4	9.8	12.4	12.1	21.3	24.2	22.8	28.5
Total	100.0	100.0	100.0	100.0	100.0	100.0	100.0	100.0	100.0
Value of merchandise exports (thousand US$)	194	444	1,034	1,112	1,330	1,972	3,916	3,015	3,147

[a] Figures in parentheses indicate export composition within sectors.
[b] Includes fish derivatives.
[c] Includes derivatives.
[d] Includes relatively unimportant metals and nontraditional exports.

Source: BCRP, Annual Reports, various issues

Exports: Structure and Performance

Until the mid-1970s 90 percent of Perú's exports consisted mainly of natural-resource-based goods (table 1.10). The table also shows a high but changing export concentration in a few primary products. In the early 1950s, cotton and sugar provided the bulk of foreign exchange earnings. In the early 1960s copper replaced cotton as the principal export good, and in the early 1970s was in turn replaced by fishmeal. During the rest of the 1970s fishmeal declined in importance but still provided, together with petroleum, copper, and silver, the bulk of foreign exchange earnings.

Within the narrow set of primary goods, the pattern of comparative advantage of Perú thus shifted quite dramatically over time. The evidence suggests that Perú took advantage of the new opportunities that arose and that, until the late 1950s, exports were the engine of growth.

The declining growth of exports that followed can be attributed, with some confidence, to the import substitution policies and declining real exchange rate discussed above. Import substitution policies pulled resources out of the exportables and nontradeables sectors into the new protected industries. The accompanying reduction in the real exchange rate, plus additional discriminatory pricing policies against primary goods, particularly agricultural products (in the interests of subsidizing urban consumption), shifted the components of aggregate demand from exports to domestic consumption. This shift is reflected in table 1.8 which shows that between 1965 and 1970 aggregate growth resulted from relatively high growth rates of domestic consumption. The eventual outcome, in the early 1970s, was a negative export growth rate (though part of this decline should be attributed to reductions in the fish catch, which reduced fish exports from US$300 million in 1970 to around US$173 million in 1975). Table 1.8 also shows relatively rapid growth of private and public consumption during these years, indicating that after the mid-1960s Peruvian growth was oriented toward the domestic market.

Table 1.11 shows Perú's export performance in a cross-country perspective. This table shows the ratio of average 1979–80 to average 1969–70 trade figures in current US dollars for a group of Latin American and southeast Asian countries. Two conclusions emerge quite clearly. First, the increase in the total value of exports of southeast Asian nations during the 1970s was twice that of Latin American countries. These two groups of countries had similar aggregate value of exports in the base period – around US$10 billion. Second, among the Latin American countries and except for the Dominican Republic, Perú was the poorest performer. All this confirms the point made earlier – that increasing and ill-conceived government interference was closely related to the declining economic performance of the Peruvian economy.

Table 1.11 Country-specific trade performance during the 1970s (current US dollars)

Country	Exports			Imports		
	1969–70 (million US$)	1979–80 (million US$)	Ratio 1979–80 over 1969–70	1969–70 (million US$)	1979–80 (million US$)	Ratio 1979–80 over 1969–70
Latin America						
Argentina	1,692.6	7,914.6	4.7	1,629.6	8,615.8	5.3
Brazil	2,524.8	17,688.2	7.0	2,555.8	22,340.1	8.7
Colombia	665.3	3,622.8	5.4	764.1	3,947.9	5.2
Costa Rica	210.4	982.9	4.7	280.9	1,521.3	5.4
Dominican Republic	198.7	726.2	3.7	247.6	1,240.5	5.0
Guatemala	272.8	1,323.5	4.9	267.2	1,460.4	5.5
Perú	955.0	3,322.6	3.5	610.9	2,024.4	3.3
Uruguay	216.4	923.1	4.3	214.9	1,412.5	6.6
Venezuela	3,154.6	16,780.0	5.3	1,568.7	10,133.8	6.5
Total	9,890.6	53,283.9	5.4	8,139.7	52,696.7	6.5
Southeast Asia						
Hong Kong	1,816.3	12,415.6	6.6	2,681.2	19,582.1	7.3
Indonesia	927.4	18,749.5	20.2	781.7	9,008.9	11.5
The Philippines	941.4	5,161.5	5.5	1,233.3	7,453.8	6.0
Singapore	1,551.1	16,804.4	10.8	2,250.3	20,820.3	9.3
Korea	723.3	16,198.8	22.4	1,903.1	21,262.1	11.2
Taiwan	1,239.0	17,864.4	14.4	1,371.9	17,314.6	12.6
Malaysia	1,668.4	12,007.2	7.2	1,285.2	9,284.8	7.2
Thailand	681.3	5,788.1	8.5	1,289.8	8,291.0	6.4
Total	9,618.2	104,989.5	10.9	12,796.5	113,017.7	8.8

Source: author's elaboration, based on the World Bank Trade Data Files

Imports: Structure and Performance

A stylized observation of import substitution policies in developing countries is that, typically, they follow normal time patterns which are a consequence of the changes in the domestic structure of production resulting from these policies.

The policies usually start by fostering the production of consumer goods which, because of capital requirements or technological constraints are relatively easier to produce domestically. Once these possibilities begin to be exhausted, further substitution policies encourage the production of intermediate and capital goods. This natural dynamic predicates that, in the initial stage, the participation of consumer goods in the structure of imports will decline.

Table 1.12 shows this sequence of events in operation for the Peruvian economy: the share of consumer goods in total imports declined steadily during the import substitution years, most steeply during the first stage, between 1960 and 1975.

Thus import substitution policies, often advocated as a stimulus to economic independence, frequently have the opposite effect. Perú may be an extreme example. Protectionist policies resulted in a volume and composition of imports that, since the government had to import basic foodstuffs, to a great extent determined living standards in the short run. Further, potential manufacturing output levels hinged on imports of intermediate goods not produced domestically.

The significant slowdown in growth of Perú's agricultural output has already been stressed. It is closely linked to pricing policies (discussed in more detail in chapter 2) that discriminated heavily against this sector, in some cases resulting in trade reversals (that is, goods that would have been exportables became importables and vice versa). Rice is a case in point: traditionally, Perú had been a rice exporter, but during the 1970s the policy of subsidizing domestic consumption brought price controls that put domestic prices well below international prices. On average between 1970 and 1979, at prevailing exchange rates, the ratio of domestic producer prices to border prices was 0.84. In addition, price discrimination was compounded by the overvaluation of the sol prevalent during most of the 1970s. For example, using the 1978 real exchange rate as an approximation to the "equilibrium" exchange rate, the ratio is reduced to 0.72 (Orden et al., 1982).

The effect of this discrimination on output was significant. Rice production stagnated during the 1970s and imports jumped from nil to 150,000 metric tons in 1979, an increase of approximately US$50 million.

More generally, the value of crop imports increased from US$41 million to US$231 million between 1970 and 1979. This suggests that protectionism and price controls worked together against agricultural exportables.

Table 1.12 Structure of current value of merchandise imports for selected years, 1950–1984 (percent)

Type of goods	1950	1960	1970	1973	1975	1978	1979	1980	1981	1982[a]	1983[a]	1984[a]
Consumption	24.0	19.7	10.7	13.9	8.9	5.6	7.9	13.2	15.9	12.5	12.8	14.2
Nondurable	15.4	11.2	7.0	8.7	5.9	3.4	6.1	9.8	8.7	6.9	7.1	11.5
Durable	8.6	8.5	3.7	5.2	3.0	2.2	1.8	3.4	7.2	5.6	5.7	2.7
Raw materials and intermediate inputs	40.0	38.2	36.7	37.5	48.3	44.7	46.3	37.2	36.2	35.5	37.7	51.0
Fuels	2.3	4.2	3.1	6.2	10.8	4.5	2.8	1.3	2.1	2.1	2.2	3.4
For agriculture	1.1	2.3	1.4	1.6	4.1	3.1	2.9	2.2	3.0	2.9	3.1	3.0
For industry	36.6	31.7	32.2	29.7	33.4	37.1	40.6	33.7	31.1	30.5	32.4	44.6
Capital goods	35.4	32.9	26.7	30.8	32.8	27.0	32.0	35.2	38.2	37.9	33.1	34.6
For construction	4.0	3.5	1.6	1.7	4.3	2.2	1.6	1.3	3.7	3.6	3.1	2.4
For agriculture	4.0	2.6	1.0	1.6	0.8	0.9	1.3	1.6	1.0	1.1	1.0	1.0
For industry	16.0	17.4	16.1	22.4	21.0	10.6	20.9	22.2	21.9	21.7	19.0	21.6
Transport equipment	11.4	9.4	8.0	5.1	6.7	5.3	8.2	10.1	11.6	11.5	10.0	9.6
Adjustments	0.6	9.2	25.9	17.8	10.0	22.7	13.8	14.4	9.7	14.1	16.4	0.2
Total	100.0	100.0	100.0	100.0	100.0	100.0	100.0	100.0	100.0	100.0	100.0	100.0
FDB value of imports (million US dollars)	175	341	700	1,033	2,427	1,668	1,954	3,090	3,802	3,721	2,722	2,140

[a] The structure within each type of good is similar to 1981.

Source: BCRP, *Annual Reports*, various years

Not only were living standards tied to import capacity, but also the manufacturing sector became heavily dependent on the use of imported intermediate inputs and capital goods. Table 1.12 shows that imports of capital goods and intermediate inputs for industry represented a growing proportion of the import bill. The component of imported intermediate inputs in the value of production of the manufacturing sector was 19 percent in 1973. The import dependence of some import substitute industries such as chemicals, plastics, and rubber was quite high. This dependence is particularly harmful at times of foreign exchange problems. Because everything that is imported is essential, import cutbacks must necessarily affect the production possibilities of industries dependent on imports. Predictably, therefore, in each of the post-World War II balance-of-payments crises, the economic swings of the manufacturing sector have been higher than those of other sectors.

Finally, the timing of the changes in import share of consumer goods supports our view that Perú adopted import substitution policies later than the other larger Latin American countries. In Argentina, for example, the share of consumer goods in total imports was 5 percent during 1955–9, while the corresponding figure for Uruguay is 11.8 percent for the period 1952–6 and it did not decline thereafter.

Trading Partners

Table 1.13 shows that the United States is the most important market for Perú's exports. While the importance of Peruvian trade with the United States has remained relatively stable, the importance of other partners has been changing. The most visible changes have been with the European and Latin American countries, the share of Peruvian exports to the former declining during the 1970s and the share to the latter increasing quite significantly.

The growing importance of Latin American countries for Peruvian exports must to some extent be attributed to integration efforts. Table 1.14 presents a classification of trading partners that illustrates their changing importance during the 1970s. The table has been constructed for broad Standard International Trade Classification (SITC) commodity groups. The trading partners include Latin America, capital surplus countries, centrally planned economies, industrial market economies, and other developing economies.

Several conclusions about exports can be drawn from this table.

1   As remarked earlier, Perú's overall export growth was lower than that of other Latin American countries. This performance was particularly noticeable in exports of nonfuel materials where Perú has traditionally had a comparative advantage. During the same

Table 1.13 Structure of exports by destination, 1970–1983 (percent; current US dollars)

Country	1970	1971	1972	1973	1974	1975	1976	1977	1978	1979	1980	1981	1982	1983
USA	32.9	28.4	33.0	34.9	35.7	24.0	25.7	29.9	37.4	30.3	33.0	30.3	36.3	41.5
Germany	15.0	15.4	13.9	17.0	13.8	11.5	13.6	12.0	12.9	9.9	9.0	15.6	14.8	12.8
Japan	13.5	12.3	11.2	7.6	7.8	9.7	7.1	5.3	4.6	3.7	7.0	5.3	4.7	4.2
Holland	9.6	7.4	6.8	3.9	3.3	6.7	6.1	4.3	4.2	3.6	4.3	4.5	4.3	3.8
Belgium and Luxembourg	4.6	4.0	3.5	2.9	3.1	6.3	4.8	3.8	3.5	3.4	4.0	3.0	3.2	3.0
UK	2.5	2.9	2.6	2.8	3.1	3.4	4.6	3.8	3.1	3.1	3.1	2.8	3.2	2.5
Italy	2.4	2.6	2.5	2.6	2.9	3.3	4.3	2.5	2.9	2.4	2.9	2.7	3.1	2.4
Spain	2.3	2.4	2.0	2.1	2.8	2.9	3.8	2.3	2.7	1.9	2.8	2.6	3.0	2.3
Yugoslavia	2.0	2.0	1.6	1.9	2.7	2.8	2.2	2.2	2.5	1.8	2.6	2.5	2.2	2.2
Poland	1.9	1.7	1.6	1.9	2.6	2.7	2.0	2.2	2.3	1.6	2.5	2.5	2.2	2.0
Subtotal	86.7	79.1	78.7	77.6	77.8	73.3	74.2	68.3	76.1	61.7	71.2	71.8	77.0	76.7
Others[a]	13.3	20.9	21.3	22.4 (9.0)	22.2	26.7	25.8	31.7	23.9 (14.1)	38.3	28.8	28.2	23.0	23.3
Total	100.0	100.0	100.0	100.0	100.0	100.0	100.0	100.0	100.0	100.0	100.0	100.0	100.0	100.0

[a] Figures in parentheses are the share of exports going to other Latin American countries.

Source: prepared by Banco Central de la Reserva del Perú staff

Table 1.14 Value of trade: trading partners of Latin America and Perú by broad commodity categories during the 1970s (thousand US dollars)

Destination, export category, and origin	Latin America (a)	(b)	Southeast Asia (a)	(b)	Capital surplus (a)	(b)	Centrally planned economies (a)	(b)	Industrial market economies (a)	(b)	Other developing economies (a)	(b)	Total value 1969–70 (a)	1979–80 (b)	1979–80 over 1969–79
Exports															
Total exports															
Latin America	20.41	25.29	0.97	1.16	0.04	0.57	2.87	6.65	71.37	57.03	4.34	9.30	9,890.7	53,283.8	5.39
Perú	6.58	24.37	0.73	3.79	0.03	−0.01	2.98	5.10	87.31	56.65	2.37	9.61	955.0	3,322.6	3.48
Nonfuel merchandise															
Latin America	14.11	21.57	1.31	1.62	0.06	0.84	4.11	9.49	76.39	55.74	4.02	10.65	6,899.6	36,298.1	5.26
Perú	6.35	30.55	0.73	5.02	0.03	−0.01	3.00	6.28	87.59	47.63	2.29	10.53	948.1	4,725.4	4.98
Fuel															
Latin America	34.94	32.90	0.19	0.21	0.00	0.00	0.02	0.69	59.78	59.73	5.07	6.46	2,991.0	16,595.8	5.65
Perú	38.78	7.76	0.00	0.06	0.00	0.00	0.00	1.53	48.25	83.83	12.97	6.82	6.9	597.2	86.60
Nonfuel materials															
Latin America	9.06	11.00	1.31	1.78	0.06	0.08	4.46	13.18	81.20	63.25	3.91	9.91	6,065.3	24,856.3	5.00
Perú	5.68	23.09	0.70	6.96	0.03	−0.02	0.61	1.17	41.43	34.62	3.61	14.72	13.0	522.9	86.60
Manufactures															
Latin America	51.58	41.49	1.37	1.35	0.02	0.79	1.60	3.02	40.81	43.13	4.61	10.23	799.8	1,130.9	13.90
Perú	51.04	49.23	3.31	0.24	0.00	0.02	0.61	1.17	41.45	34.62	3.61	14.72	13.0	522.9	40.22
Imports															
Total imports															
Latin America	14.78	16.80	0.72	11.66	31.40	17.10	1.71	1.35	78.32	59.36	3.08	13.53	8,137.8	52,696.7	6.48
Perú	18.13	13.88	0.90	2.88	0.00	0.01	1.14	2.11	78.58	78.55	1.26	2.57	610.9	2,024.4	3.31
Nonfuel merchandise															
Latin America	13.69	16.40	0.76	2.12	0.15	0.03	1.71	1.22	81.98	77.40	1.70	2.89	7,615.0	40,746.3	5.35
Perú	16.74	13.18	0.76	2.94	0.00	0.01	1.17	2.17	80.11	79.05	1.22	2.66	593.3	1,969.3	3.13
Fuel															
Latin America	30.60	17.97	0.20	0.34	19.50	27.75	1.63	2.48	24.93	7.06	23.15	44.40	522.8	11,950.4	22.89
Perú	64.98	39.93	5.51	0.67	0.00	0.00	0.00	0.08	26.90	60.21	2.55	−0.88	17.6	55.1	3.13
Nonfuel materials															
Latin America	34.71	36.32	2.12	3.28	0.02	0.01	1.84	0.04	52.82	55.64	3.50	4.70	1,600.5	8,900.0	5.56
Perú	47.14	14.39	1.73	7.40	0.00	0.00	3.18	−1.33	46.75	74.67	1.19	4.87	158.3	506.1	3.20
Manufactures															
Latin America	6.74	10.79	0.40	1.80	0.19	0.04	1.68	1.57	89.77	83.51	1.22	2.38	5,975.2	31,718.3	5.31
Perú	5.67	12.78	0.41	1.43	0.00	0.02	0.44	3.36	92.25	80.50	1.23	1.92	435.0	1,460.5	5.36

Column (a) shows the share in total trade in the base period, while column (b) shows the share in the increment of trade during the 1970s. The figures correspond to simple averages of the values (current US dollars) of trade for 1969–70 and 1979–80. When the table was prepared, trade data of reporting countries for these years were available for Argentina, Brazil, Colombia, Costa Rica, Dominican Republic, Guatemala, Perú, Uruguay, and Venezuela. The trade categories include the following SITC chapters: manufactures 5 + 6 − 68 + 7 + 8; nonfuel materials, 0 + 1 + 2 + 3 + 4 + 68, fuel, 3; nonfuel merchandise, all except 3.

Source: based on UN trade statistics

period, in contrast, exports of fuels and manufactures performed well above the average observed for other Latin American countries.

2   The figures endorse the contention that the most important destination of Peruvian exports is industrial market economies.

3   During the 1970s, the group of countries included in centrally planned economies and other developing economies represented growing markets for Latin American and Peruvian exports. In particular, the other developing countries took an increasing share of Peruvian exports of nonfuel materials and manufactures.

4   In the early 1970s, the share of Perú's exports to Latin America was a much smaller fraction that that recorded for other Latin American countries. Because Perú had a smaller manufacturing sector than other Latin American countries whose integration efforts had started in the early 1960s and were well under way in the 1970s, it had relatively few manufactured products for which to request preferential tariff margins in exchange for trade preferences that it could offer to other partners.[11] As Peruvian industrialization continued during the 1970s, Perú was able – so the hypothesis goes – to request and obtain additional trade preferences, and thereby to sell more of its protected products to other Latin American countries.

It is important to note that Latin American integration efforts have been aimed at fostering trade in protected goods. This casts considerable doubt on the social profitability of Latin American trade in manufactured goods (see Nogués, 1983, and Corbo and Meller, 1981, for discussion of this topic in relation to Argentina and Chile). If import-competing industries tend to export relatively more to markets that are protected by integration arrangements, while efficient exportables industries export to open economies, there is *prima facie* evidence to hypothesize that trade with Latin America is driven more by policy than by competitive forces. Consequently, these exports are socially less profitable than those made by exportables industries.

Ideally, assessment of the social profitability of trade flows should be informed by detailed knowledge of the structure of the policy incentives that accompany these flows. Because such detailed data are not readily available, and also because the issue is not central to this study, an indirect method of assessment has been adopted.

The pattern of comparative advantage across manufacturing industries can be determined in different ways, not all of which give the same results. Thus this exercise always involves some degree of arbitrariness. In this analysis, I have classified two-digit manufacturing industries in exportable

---

[11] Perú is a member of the Andean Group and of the Latin American Integration Association.

and import-substituting industries according to their revealed comparative advantage as determined by their trade balance (table 1.15).[12]

According to this classification,[13] Peruvian exportables manufacturing industries include food and tobacco (31), textiles and clothing (which also enjoy a protected domestic market) (32), wood and wood products (33), basic metals (37), and other industries(39). These industries are based on natural resources, and we shall see later that they are also relatively labor intensive. Therefore, with the exception of basic metals, these industries accord with *a priori* expectations about the Peruvian pattern of comparative advantage in manufacturing industries.

Table 1.15, column 4, shows export ratios (that is, the value of exports as a proportion of the value of production) and it can be seen that the industries classified as exportables have on average a higher export ratio. The three most important exportables industries (food and tobacco, textiles and clothing, and basic metals) exported on average 26 percent of their output in 1980 compared with 11 percent for the import-substituting industries.

Table 1.15, column 5, shows that the bulk of exports made by exportables industries goes to industrial markets. In contrast, exports by import-substituting industries are directed mainly to other Latin American countries.

Finally, the textiles and clothing industries sell most of their exports to industrial countries. This can be taken as evidence of the international competitiveness of these industries. Nevertheless, what is striking, as we shall see, is that these industries have traditionally enjoyed high levels of domestic protection. Our suspicion is that their relative export performance plus the fact that they are among the most unskilled labor intensive industries imply good prospects for growth of their export capacity.

Population Growth, Urbanization, and Employment

Perú's population is the fourth largest in South America, estimated at 17 million inhabitants in mid-1981. During the 1970s, Perú's rate of population growth was high by international standards, and among the larger South American nations only Ecuador and Venezuela had higher rates of population growth (table 1.16). As in other developing nations, the natural death rate has been declining faster than the natural birth rate, but in a

---

[12] Exportables (import substitution) industries are those having a positive (negative) trade balance. Table 1.15, column 3, presents trade balances for 1980.
[13] Other studies using this and closely related indicators for classifying manufacturing industries by their trade orientation include those in Krueger (1983).

Table 1.15 Trade indicators for two-digit manufacturing industries, 1980

	1	2	3	4	5	6	7	8
					Destination of exports			
Industry	Exports[a]	Imports[a]	Trade balance[a]	Export ratio[b]	Industrial economies[c]	Latin America[c]	Other developing economies[c]	Other[a]
31 Food and tobacco	455.5	276.8	178.7	18.7	60.4	5.8	26.3	7.5
32 Textiles and clothing	244.4	26.3	218.1	22.1	68.3	9.5	21.8	0.4
33 Wood and wood products	14.4	9.1	5.3	6.3	61.5	14.4	23.6	0.5
34 Paper and printing	6.1	73.0	−66.9	1.5	8.3	84.1	7.6	0.0
35 Chemicals and plastics	297.8	545.0	−247.2	15.7	21.7	33.0	25.8	19.5
36 Nonmetallic minerals	40.5	28.3	12.2	14.5	5.8	88.0	6.2	0.0
37 Basic metals	806.3	183.3	623.0	34.7	64.7	6.6	27.7	1.0
38 Machinery and equipment	70.3	1,137.8	−1,067.5	6.3	23.1	56.9	20.0	0.0
39 Other	26.5	18.4	8.1	5.0	27.6	52.1	20.3	0.0
Total	1,961.6	2,298.0	−336.2	16.1	54.2	12.4	28.2	5.2

a In million US dollars.
b 1980 exports as a proportion of 1977 estimates of gross value of production in current US dollars.
c Percentage composition.

Source: based on figures presented by World Bank, 1983b

Table 1.16 Social indicators in a sample of South American countries, 1960 and 1979

Country	Population 0–14 years (%)		Crude birth rate (%)		Crude death rate (%)		Life expectancy (years)		Population per physician 1970–80	Infant mortality (%) 1978	Adult literacy rate (%) 1978	1978
	1960	1979	1960	1979	1960	1979	1960	1979				
Argentina	30.8	28.2	23.6	20.9	8.6	8.7	65.4	69.9	1.6	420[a]	46.8	93.0
Bolivia	42.0	43.9	46.4	43.6	22.1	16.7	42.7	49.6	2.6	1,940[b]	144.8[b]	63.2[c]
Brazil	43.6	41.5	42.7	31.4	12.9	8.6	54.7	62.6	2.1	1,510[b]	81.4	76.1
Chile	39.1	33.1	36.6	25.2	12.3	7.8	56.9	66.5	1.7	2,040	45.7	89.0[d]
Colombia	46.8	38.0	46.7	30.2	15.8	8.2	53.1	62.4	1.9	1,710[a]	58.8	80.8
Ecuador	44.4	44.5	46.6	41.3	16.6	10.2	50.7	60.2	3.4	1,620	85.1	76.6
Perú	43.6	42.8	45.5	36.7	18.3	11.7	47.5	57.5	2.6	1,440[e]	92.3	79.7
Uruguay	28.5	27.4	21.9	70.4	9.8	67.6	67.8	73.3	0.4	540[e]	41.3	94.0
Venezuela	46.1	42.3	46.1	36.0	11.3	5.9	57.3	66.9	3.4	950	44.2	82.0

a 1977.
b 1975.
c 1976.
d 1970.
e 1979.

Source: World Bank, 1983c.

cross-country comparison life expectancy in Perú is still relatively low.[14]

Urbanization has made rapid progress in Perú. To a great extent this process was fueled by policies which changed goods and factor markets, such as minimum wage and labor laws, and by the increasing discrimination, through pricing policies, against the agricultural and mining sectors. More recently, political violence in the countryside has been pushing people out of the affected rural regions to the cities. The impressive response to these signals is seen in the increase in urban population from 33 percent of the total population in 1940 to 59.6 percent by 1972 and 65 percent by 1981.

This urbanization has affected all Peruvian departments except Amazonas, but has been particularly substantial in two of the major coastal departments, Lima and Callao; indeed, 41 percent of Perú's urban population was living in Lima in the early 1970s. A principal cause of the concentration has been that industrialization, accelerated by import substitution policies, has gravitated toward a few cities because the others lacked the necessary infrastructure: in 1971, 69 percent of manufacturing output was processed in Lima and Callao. By 1977, despite huge incentives for decentralization offered by various laws, the proportion declined by only 1 percent.

Perú's labor force since the early 1970s has been around 31 percent of its population. Because of its demographic characteristics (approximately 62 percent of this labor force is between 16 and 34 years old) its growth rate has been increasing: from 2.1 percent during the 1960s to 3.0 percent a year during the 1970s.

As a result of urbanization, the labor force has grown much more quickly in the cities, where it reached a rate of 4.5 percent a year between 1970 and 1979. During the same period, the agricultural labor force grew at an annual rate of 0.9 percent (table 1.17).

The statistics show a diminishing capacity for the nonagricultural economy to provide jobs for the growing urban workforce. This imbalance should again be attributed to policies which, while fueling the rural-to-urban migration process, also increased the urban wage-to-rental ratio above levels that would have been observed otherwise and, by so doing, increased the capital-to-employment ratio of the economy in general and of the urban sector in particular.

The increasing damage done by the lack of employment opportunities is reflected in the steadily rising open unemployment rates of the 1970s, which in 1979 had reached a value of 7.1 percent of the labor force. The

---

[14] These average figures hide important regional differences in social indicators. In Perú the highest living standards are found in some departments of the Costa region including Lima, Callao, and Tacna. The poorest regions are found in the southern part of the country, and also in the frontier areas with Bolivia and Ecuador. Living standards in these regions are extremely low (Webb, 1977).

Table 1.17 Employment, unemployment, and underemployment, 1970–1984

Variable	1970	1971	1972	1973	1974	1975	1976	1977	1978	1979	1980	1981	1982ᵃ	1983ᵃ	1984
Population (thousands)ᵇ	12,791.0	13,160.0	13,538.0	13,886.0	14,242.0	14,607.0	14,982.0	15,367.0	15,761.0	16,165.0	16,580.0	17,005.0	17,442.0	17,889.0	18,348.0
Labor force (thousands)	4,167.3	4,281.0	4,401.7	4,534.3	4,672.9	4,817.5	4,968.0	5,124.7	5,283.4	5,441.9	5,665.2	5,779.0	5,958.0	6,136.7	6,320.8
Agriculture	1,879.5	1,900.8	1,919.1	1,936.1	1,948.6	1,955.9	1,977.3	2,003.8	2,026.0	2,042.0	2,052.2	2,072.7	2,097.2	2,118.2	2,133.3
Nonagriculture	2,287.8	2,380.2	2,482.6	2,598.2	2,724.3	2,861.6	2,990.7	3,120.9	3,257.4	3,399.9	3,553.0	3,706.3	3,860.8	4,018.5	4,176.8
Unemployed															
Total (%)	4.7	4.4	4.2	4.2	4.0	4.9	5.2	5.8	6.5	7.1	7.0	6.8	7.0	9.2	10.9
Agriculture (%)	0.3	0.3	0.3	0.3	0.3	0.3	0.3	0.3	0.3	0.3	0.3	0.3	0.3	0.3	n.a.
Nonagriculture (%)	8.3	7.7	7.3	7.1	6.6	8.1	8.4	9.4	10.4	11.2	10.9	10.4	10.6	13.9	16.4
Underemployed															
Total (%)	45.9	44.4	44.2	41.3	41.8	42.4	44.3	48.2	52.0	51.4	51.2	47.9	49.9	53.9	n.a.
Agriculture (%)	64.3	63.6	67.0	65.4	65.4	68.2	68.8	62.1	65.4	63.5	68.2	61.5	60.9	68.2	n.a.
Nonagriculture (%)	30.9	29.0	26.6	23.3	25.0	24.8	32.7	39.2	43.7	44.1	41.4	40.3	43.9	46.3	n.a.

ᵃ Approximate.
ᵇ Between 1961, 1972, and 1981 from National Census. Between 1961 and 1972 figures assume annual growth rate of 2.88 percent, while between 1972 and 1984 the rate is 2.566 percent.

Source: Ministry of Labor

incidence of unemployment has been particularly acute in nonagricultural activities, where the open unemployment rate was estimated to be 11.2 percent in 1979 (table 1.17).

The number of underemployed workers[15] – always a significant proportion of the labor force – has also been increasing in recent years; in 1979 underemployment was estimated to affect 52 percent of the labor force. While overall the problem remains more severe for agricultural workers, the situation in that sector has remained relatively stable, whereas for the nonagricultural labor force the rate has been increasing quite dramatically.

Where are the underemployed working, and at what types of jobs? These questions until recently have received little research attention. Table 1.18 shows that in Lima most of the informal labor force work in the commercial sector, but some of the output of other economic sectors can also be attributed to informal activities.

Table 1.18 Structure of Lima's informal employment by economic sector, 1982

Sector	Percentage share
Commerce	47
Industry	27
Services	13
Construction	8
Transport	5

Source: Vega Castro, 1984, table 2

The evidence so far presented shows considerable factor mobility between the urban and rural sectors. However, Perú's informal sector has cushioned the incapacity of the formal economy to generate sufficient employment opportunities. This could also be an indication of the adaptability of Perú's labor force to changing economic circumstances. The evidence is that such rigidities in labor mobility as exist in Perú arise not so much from specificity of factors or unionization – though these might in some cases be important – as from formidable barriers to labor mobility resulting from interventionist policies.

Structure of Employment and Trends in Employment-to-output Ratios

At the beginning of the 1970s the agriculture and fishing sector was the largest employer in Perú, followed by manufacturing, commerce, and the public sector (including both communal and government services). By

---

[15] An underemployed person is defined here as someone who works less than 35 hours a week, or whose salary is below the 1962 minimum salary adjusted for inflation.

1982, though agriculture and fishing remained at the top of the league, its share had declined, while the commercial and government sectors had outstripped manufacturing to vie for second place (table 1.19). Between 1970 and 1978 employment in the public sector increased by 38 percent – an annual growth rate of 4.1 percent (table 1.20).

Schydlowsky and Wicht (1983) have estimated trends in labor productivity measured by output per worker for different urban sectors, as well as for the rural sector. Some of their figures are reproduced in table 1.21. The urban sectors included are (a) traditional informal production units with less than five workers, as well as self-employed workers, (b) traditional formal production units including public administration, construction, commerce, and professional services, and (c) the modern sector, including manufacturing, mining, transport, energy, and fishing. The rural sector excludes sugar but includes commercial activities taking place in small rural towns.

The picture that emerges tends to confirm our previous analysis. Urbanization has been accompanied by an increasingly negative growth rate of labor productivity in the traditional informal urban sector. Migrants who could not find jobs in the modern sector became unemployed or underemployed; eventually this excess urban labor supply led to the adoption of more labor intensive production techniques in the informal sector. Without this adaptation, the open urban unemployment rate would have grown faster than it did.

Labor productivity in the modern urban sector, however, has grown relatively quickly even during the 1950s. It is in this segment of the urban economy that the process of capitalization appears to have been particularly intense. Within the modern urban economy, manufacturing industries have played and will continue to play an increasing role.

Final Remarks

After the liberal decade of the 1950s, government policies led to major structural shifts in the economy. A principal goal of the Peruvian political leadership of the 1960s and 1970s had been the achievement of a less skewed distribution of income. For these policymakers, the lesson drawn from Peruvian economic history was that liberal policies had apparently failed to improve the widespread incidence of poverty. This perception has been attributed to the enclave nature of the dynamic sectors: agriculture and fishing activities were concentrated in the coastal region and mining activities created few employment opportunities. In any case, Peruvian policymakers concluded that one natural way to achieve their distribution goals was by enlarging the direct and indirect role of the state in economic affairs.

Table 1.19 Employment by sector, 1970–1982[a] (thousands)

Sector	1970		1975		1978		1979		1980		1981		1982	
Agriculture and fishing	2,011.9	(48.0)	2,119.7	(44.1)	2,197.3	(41.7)	2,222.4	(40.8)	2,248.0	(40.1)	2,272.3	(39.2)	2,296.1	(38.4)
Mining	63.8	(1.5)	65.3	(1.4)	66.5	(1.3)	66.9	(1.2)	67.3	(1.2)	67.7	(1.2)	68.2	(1.2)
Manufacturing	522.4	(12.5)	612.9	(12.7)	675.0	(12.8)	697.6	(12.8)	717.3	(12.8)	736.2	(12.7)	753.9	(12.6)
Electricity, gas, and water	7.5	(0.2)	9.9	(0.2)	11.4	(0.2)	11.8	(0.2)	12.2	(0.2)	12.5	(0.2)	12.9	(0.2)
Construction	175.4	(4.2)	214.9	(4.5)	232.7	(4.4)	236.8	(4.5)	243.2	(4.3)	247.2	(4.3)	250.7	(4.2)
Commerce, restaurants,	474.5	(11.3)	603.1	(12.5)	745.4	(14.1)	809.1	(14.9)	865.1	(15.4)	929.0	(16.0)	993.1	(16.6)
Transport, storage, and communications	167.5	(4.0)	211.5	(4.4)	240.6	(4.6)	250.5	(4.6)	260.7	(4.6)	271.3	(4.7)	282.0	(4.7)
Finance	55.8	(1.3)	72.3	(1.5)	85.0	(1.6)	89.6	(1.7)	94.5	(1.7)	99.6	(1.7)	104.9	(1.8)
Communal services	274.5	(6.6)	363.4	(7.6)	432.4	(8.2)	467.8	(8.6)	501.0	(8.9)	529.4	(9.2)	570.8	(9.5)
Government services	281.0	(6.7)	367.2	(7.6)	407.1	(7.7)	404.0	(7.4)	416.1	(7.4)	434.8	(7.5)	447.4	(7.5)
Other	154.3	(3.7)	168.8	(3.5)	180.2	(3.4)	184.1	(3.4)	188.1	(3.4)	192.5	(3.3)	197.7	(3.3)
Total	4,188.6		4,809.0		5,273.6		5,440.6		5,613.5		5,792.5		5,977.6	

[a] Figures in parentheses are sectoral participation in percentages. The estimates include informal workers.

Source: INE, 1983

Table 1.20 Central government employees by
sector, 1970 and 1978

Sector	1970	1978
Armed services	4,416	14,224
General services	49,046	64,699
Social services	140,309	173,189
Economic services	14,965	23,113
Other	184	12,483
Total	208,920	287,708

Source: data provided by Instituto Nacional de
Planificación, 1983

Table 1.21 Labor productivity growth rates by sector[a] for
selected periods, 1950–1978

		Urban			
Period	Rural	Traditional informal	Traditional formal	Modern	Total
1950–60	2.7	1.1	1.1	2.9	3.1
1960–8	0.8	− 0.2	0.4	1.0	2.0
1968–75	1.1	− 2.3	1.0	2.3	1.7
1975–8	0.0	− 6.0	− 2.8	− 0.3	− 2.1

[a] See text for definition of sectors.
Source: Schydlowsky and Wicht, 1983; original source is Instituto
Nacional de Planificación

The adoption of import substitution policies was accompanied by the
introduction of severe policy-induced distortions in factor markets and by
an impressive growth of government economic activities. However, the
shift of attention away from resource allocation and towards distributive
objectives exacted a high price in terms of GDP and employment growth,
while the statistical indicators do not show a change in income distribution
significant enough to reduce existing tensions between Peruvian social
groups.

A summary of aggregate indicators shows the magnitude of the economic collapse. Average annual growth rates declined from around 6 percent in
the 1950s and early 1960s to around 3 percent in the 1970s. At the same
time, average annual real export growth rates declined from more than 6
percent to negative values. Strenuous efforts to industrialize behind high
import barriers also led to disappointing results. During the 1950s the
average real annual growth rate of the manufacturing sector was 9.4 percent. Since then, the growth performance of this sector has been declining

systematically. Clearly the only feasible option for further industrialization is for Perú to stabilize and liberalize trade and to become an efficient exporter of labor intensive manufactures.

Stop–go cycles are another long-run macroeconomic characteristic of Perú. In each of the decades that we have reviewed since the 1940s there have been important devaluation episodes. The magnitude of nominal devaluation episodes increased between the 1940s and the 1970s. This is not surprising. The importance of fiscal deficits increased as government expenditures rose. For example, government expenditures as a proportion of GDP rose from around 14 percent in the 1950s to 40 percent in the 1970s. In each decade the exchange rate remained fixed for several years, but, as the pressure of inflation increased over time, the magnitude of nominal devaluation necessary to restore approximate equilibrium in the balance of payments also increased.

Finally, the extremely poor performance of the economy in generating productive employment opportunities has been noted. This, again, has been attributed to trade and factor market distortions. One indication of the serious consequences of these distortions for Perú is the magnitude of the informal labor market, estimated by some researchers to represent, in recent years, around 50 percent of the urban labor force.

2

Introduction of a Trade Liberalization Policy

Political Circumstances

In 1975, General Morales Bermúdez replaced General Velasco Alvarado as President of Perú. His slogan was "Consolidate the Achievements of the Revolution" (*Consolidar los Logros de la Revolución*), but in practice he began, slowly but surely, to reverse many of the socialist planning policies that had been introduced by his predecessor.

In 1977 the objective of achieving a labor-managed economy was renounced, and since then workers can no longer (compulsorily) become owners of the firms in which they work. At the same time, the interval between the moment the worker starts working in any given occupation and the moment that the entrepreneur is obliged to give him tenure (*Estabilidad Laboral*) was increased from three months to three years. In 1976, Morales announced that the agrarian reform process introduced by Velasco Alvarado had come to an end, and in 1979 the RNM was eliminated. Meanwhile, the macroeconomic disequilibrium as measured by fiscal deficits was being tackled by stabilization policies introduced by Javier Silva Ruete, who became Economic Minister in 1978.

On the political side, Morales had announced from the beginning that his goal was to return the country to a democratic system. The regime's objectives were embodied in a new constitution formulated and approved by the various political parties in 1979. This constitution, and in particular its economic philosophy, was strongly influenced by the Partido Popular Cristiano (PPC). Free trade was included among the constitutional economic objectives. (Less successful in influencing the constitution was the more interventionist party Alianza para la Revolución Americana (APRA), which was to win the presidential election of 1985.)

Nevertheless, the regime's economic goals were quite far from anything resembling a competitive market economy. The economic policies of

Morales' government were much more pragmatic – dissociating themselves from the failures of Velasco's – than ideological.

The rationalization of the import regime was one of these pragmatic policies. Because, as we shall argue below, this rationalization did not hurt import substitution interests, it was not rejected by industrialists. In addition, because of the way trade policies were introduced (see the next section), they did not confront opposition within the government. In fact, the Ministry of Industry, Commerce, Tourism, and Integration (MICTI), which had managed the RNM in the past, was now responsible for introducing the import liberalization measures.

That Morales Bermúdez should find it politically expedient, as well as relatively easy, to introduce a degree of liberalization into the economy is not very surprising, given the perceived failures of his predecessor's interventionist policies. More unexpected was the continuation of these policies by Morales' successor, Fernando Belaúnde Terry. Belaúnde, the presidential candidate of Acción Popular, was elected president, with 45 percent of the popular vote, in July 1980, 12 years after he had been deposed by the military. As the initiator, during his first presidency, of the protectionist policies that followed the liberal decade of the 1950s, he was far from being personally committed to the elimination of interventionism, and few would have guessed that his second government would implement a significant reduction of trade barriers. However, one of the first actions of the new regime was the important tariff reduction of September 1980.

The reasons for this unexpected *volte face* are intimately associated with the role played by key personalities in the economic cabinet, including Dr. Manuel Ulloa, the new Minister of Economy, Finance, and Commerce, and particularly his vice Minister of Commerce, Dr. Roberto Abusada-Salah. All of them agreed on the importance of introducing trade liberalization measures; Abusada, as a consultant to MICTI, had been among the advisers who had recommended that rationalization of the import regime in 1979, during the last months of Morales' presidency, and was given the responsibility for implementing these policies.

To ensure that import liberalization policies would in fact be implemented, Belaúnde shifted the vice Minister of Commerce from the Ministry of Industry to the Ministry of Economy. This institutional change was made because the new Minister of Industry was a member of the PPC, appointed as a *quid pro quo* for the PPC's agreement to cooperate with the new government of Acción Popular. (APRA, who had come second, refused to do so.) This effectively meant that the new Minister of Economy and Finance could not necessarily count on the permanent support of the Minister of Industry for more open trade policies. The management of trade policy instruments was consequently transferred from the Ministry of Industry and assigned to the vice Minister of Commerce, under the Ministry of Economy.

In summary, the tariff reform implemented in September of 1980 was essentially a question of the critical influence of individuals within the government. The design of the reform was not preceded by any major debate within the government nor between the government and the private sector. We shall argue that, unlike the rationalization of the import regime introduced in 1979, the tariff reform of 1980 led to increased import competition.

The Introduction of Liberalization

Nature and Targets of the Policy

As the preceding account indicates, the reform of Peruvian import policies was completed in two steps and under two different political regimes: the first was the replacement of the QR import regime with an *ad valorem* tariff structure in 1979; the second was the reduction of the maximum legal tariff rate from 155 percent to 60 percent in 1980. (Table 2.1 gives a chronology of import policy between 1979 and 1985.)

The First Step: the 1979 Reforms

In December of 1978 – before the QR regime was dismantled – Perú's Brussels Trade Nomenclature (BTN) had 4,643 tariff lines; the import of 1,038 of these was prohibited outright (table 1.6). The goods included in the other tariff lines could in principle be imported (Lista de Productos Suceptibles de Importación, LPSI), but only under license. For 1,753 tariff lines of the LPSI, import licenses were given quite automatically provided that the importer was included in the Register of Importers (Registro de Importadores). In general, goods included in the so-called free list were those considered "essential for the socioeconomic development" of the country – intermediate imports and capital goods not produced domestically, some foodstuffs, and medicines. The public sector had monopoly rights to import many of these goods, including some agricultural goods (soybean, maize, rice, fruits, milk, etc.),[1] some manufacturing imports (caustic soda, polyester, and copper wire), and beverages, minerals, and fuels. The rest of the tariff lines in the LPSI were included in a restricted list known as observed items (*items observados*), for which import licenses were rarely granted.

The bulk of tariff lines protected by outright import prohibitions were also included in the RNM. (Domestic producers of manufactured goods had to request the Minister of Industry for their products to be included in the RNM. After acceptance, imports of these goods were prohibited.) In

[1] See chapter 3 on agricultural pricing policies.

Table 2.1 Chronology of principal import policy measures between 1979 and 1984

Date	Tariff policy	Quantitative restrictions
1979		Elimination of the Registro Nacional de Manufacturas in Mar 1979. From here several decrees shifted a majority of items from the QR list to the free-import list. By Dec 1980, 98% of the tariff lines were included in the free-import list
Dec 1979	Maximum tariff rate was reduced from 355% to 155%. Also, specific duties were eliminated and rules for import duty exonerations were tightened	
Sep 1980	Maximum tariff rate was reduced from 155% to 60%	
Feb 1981	Reduction of tariff rates on agricultural products	
Mar 1981	Reduction of tariff rates on intermediate products and capital goods for manufacturing	
Apr 1981	Reduction of tariff rates on intermediate products and capital goods for agriculture	
Dec 1981	Reduction of tariff rates on machinery and equipment for printing industry	
Jan 1982	Introduction of a 15% tariff surcharge	
1982	Increase in tariff rates of some products produced by the steel and paper industries	Several steel products were included under the license regime
Mar 1983	The tariff surcharge was raised to 10 percentage points	
Apr 1984	The tariff surcharge was raised to 15 percentage points	
July 1984	The escalation of the tariff was changed and the new tariff structure was significantly more protectionist than the previous one	
Dec 1984		Import prohibitions were reintroduced on various domestically produced goods such as clothing, tobacco, and footwear
Aug 1985		Additional import prohibitions and across the board import-licensing procedures were implemented

early 1979, approximately 14,000 domestically produced products were on the register.

Products included in the RNM could only be imported if domestic supply and/or quality were shown to be "inadequate." When someone requested authorization to import some of these goods, or requested the elimination of a product from the RNM, government officials would often leave the decision to the domestic producer who could potentially be "hurt" by an affirmative decision. Thus the domestic producers who benefited from the RNM effectively administered import prohibitions.

This was the situation when the new economic team, under Javier Silva Ruete as Minister of Economy, came to power in May 1978. They recognized the high costs imposed by this trade regime and set to work to introduce substantial modifications. Dissatisfaction with Velasco Alvarado's policies in general, and trade policies in particular, was a primary stimulus, but other pressures were also influential.

An important exogenous force was the aim of the Andean Group to implement a common external tariff (CET). The Junta del Acuerdo de Cartagena (Junta) had proposed that the CET would be based on *ad valorem* tariffs and that import duty exonerations and import-licensing measures would be eliminated. MICTI had consequently created the Comisión de Política Arancelaria (CODEPA) in 1976 to study the Peruvian import regime and to consider ways to rationalize it along the lines suggested by the Junta. CODEPA studied such matters as the impact of eliminating the specific tariff component of Perú's tariff structure and also the elimination of import duty exemptions. (The analysis brought to light irrationalities such as the case of an imported item for which the records showed that 21 different tariff rates had been paid. The rate depended on who had been the importer and where he was located.)

December 1979 was the target date that Andean Group countries had set for approving the CET; countries would then have until 1983 to implement its provisions. In the meantime, intra-regional tariffs were to be phased out and prohibitions were to be lifted on imports from other Andean Group member countries. In the event the CET was never defined, and a common market among Andean Group countries has not yet been achieved.

Two other circumstances were pushing Perú to rationalize its import regime. First, a Program Loan from the World Bank provided MICTI (CODEPA) with technical assistance for reforming trade policies. The Program Loan itself was built on trade policy reform. Second, the Chilean experience at that time, which generated considerable public debate, furnished a persuasive example of successful rationalization of the trade regime.

In response to these pressures, the first move in dismantling the QR regime was to design a tentative *ad valorem* tariff structure. At that time, the tariff structure in place was the one that had been introduced in 1973.

This was a mixed tariff structure where each BTN line had a specific and an *ad valorem* tariff set in soles. By 1979, domestic inflation had eroded much of their protective effect. This tariff regime had to be replaced by an *ad valorem* tariff structure and import prohibitions had to be dismantled.

Once a tentative tariff structure had been completed (around June 1979), Jorge Du Bois (the Minister of Industry, Commerce, Tourism, and Integration) requested from entrepreneurs their opinions on the appropriateness of the revised tariff structure. MICTI was prepared to introduce upward adjustments in specific cases, though technical advisers suggested that this maximum tariff rate should not exceed 100 percent. The consultation process showed that the ceiling would be too low for many entrepreneurs, and their political power was sufficient to persuade Du Bois to raise the maximum tariff rate to 121 percent. Finally, the new tariff structure was approved and published in August 1979, when Du Bois announced in a national television broadcast the government's intentions to reform trade policy. In his speech (see *El Peruano*, August 12, 1979, for a complete transcript) Du Bois announced the transformation of the import regime and explained why it was necessary. The effect of protection through import prohibitions, he said, had been to create "a high-cost industry that has shown little ability to react toward foreign markets when domestic demand declines . . . ." Meanwhile, neglect or instability of quality standards "had discredited . . . all potential exporters . . . ." The Minister went on to specify objectives for the reform, such as simplification of administrative procedures, benefits to the consumer, the treasury, and the importer, reduced uncertainty, favorable effects on small firms, and a more solid base for making industrial policy.

By December 1979 the majority of nontariff barriers had been replaced by an *ad valorem* tariff structure. The range was 0 percent to 155 percent, compared with 0 percent to 355 percent in the previous *ad valorem* structure. Only automobiles were included in the maximum rate. The standard deviation was 24 percent.

The Second Step: the 1980 Tariff Reduction
The second phase leading to the reform of the Peruvian import regime was undertaken in significantly different political circumstances, but it was linked to the first phase by the participation of key technocrats. The second major step in the trade liberalization process of Perú – the reduction in September 1980 of the maximum *ad valorem* tariff rate from 155 percent to 60 percent – was originally intended to open the way for further more radical reductions. Shortly after its implementation in November 1980, the Vice Minister of Commerce, under the Ministry of Economy, announced in a public address to the Conferencia Anual de Empresarios (CADE, the major annual meeting of Peruvian industrial entrepreneurs) the economic cabinet's intention to introduce a target tariff structure with a simple

average *ad valorem* tariff rate of 25 percent and a standard deviation of 5 percent. The changes necessary to attain these objectives, however, were never achieved: in fact, trade policy measures introduced after the reduction of the maximum tariff rate began to reverse the trade liberalization of Perú.

Finally, contrary to what occurred during 1979, industries were not consulted on what was good or bad for them. Those that used to be protected with tariff rates higher than 60 percent were particularly affected by the tariff reduction. They included, among others, producers of textiles, clothing, footwear, and automobiles. With this change, Perú, which used to be the most protected member of the Andean Group, became the most open.[2]

Changes in the Structure of Protection

How did the structure of protection change as a consequence of this rationalization of the trade regime? The most useful way to answer this question would be by comparing how differentials between domestic factory prices and cost, insurance, and freight (c.i.f.) prices changed as a consequence of the reform. Unfortunately, since the data necessary to analyze the question in this way are not available, we must settle for a tentative answer to the more limited question: how did the legal structure of tariff protection change as a consequence of the rationalization measures?

Estimates of simple average tariff rates by sections of the BTN for selected periods between 1973 and 1984 show that the 1979 rationalization policies resulted in a significant and generalized reduction in average tariff rates from their 1973 levels (table 2.2). At the same time, the escalation of the tariff structure did not change dramatically: industries such as footwear, textiles, hides, and leather that had enjoyed the highest levels of tariff protection during the early 1970s continued to do so after the 1979 rationalization.

As stated, the 1979 tariff structure was very much a product of consultation between the government and private industry: it could reasonably be assumed, therefore, that the new tariff rates were sufficiently high to maintain the level of protection that firms had previously

2 Its new maximum tariff was in many cases lower than the minimum external tariff of the Andean Group. This triggered several complaints from other member countries. For example, the new tariff rate of 60 percent on refrigerators was lower than the Andean Group's minimum external tariff of 110 percent. At that time Perú used to import refrigerators, at zero tariffs, from Andean Group countries. Peruvian officials still remember how insistent some top officials of member countries were in defending the 110 percent minimum external tariff rate.

Table 2.2 Simple average legal tariff rates by Brussels Trade Nomenclature sections, 1973 and 1979–1984

BTN sections		1973	Dec 1979	Jul 1980	Dec 1980	Dec 1981	Dec 1982[a]	Dec 1983[b]	Dec 1984[c]
I	Animals	50	35	35	32	30	35	40	46
II	Vegetable products	65	46	37	35	28	31	36	45
III	Fats and oils	51	32	32	31	26	29	35	50
IV	Foods, beverages, tobacco	120	78	63	53	51	59	61	79
V	Mineral products	55	20	20	18	16	18	26	34
VI	Chemical products	49	25	25	24	21	25	32	47
VII	Resins, plastics, rubber	69	39	41	38	34	39	44	61
VIII	Hides and leather	128	71	71	51	51	58	60	79
IX	Wood, cork, etc.	84	39	39	36	36	41	45	62
X	Paper	77	46	47	41	36	41	46	63
XI	Textiles	138	76	70	52	51	59	61	80
XII	Footwear, headgear, etc.	168	93	94	60	60	69	70	91
XIII	Articles of stone, cement, etc.	80	47	47	42	37	43	47	65
XIV	Precious stones and metals	104	65	65	42	42	48	52	70
XV	Basic metals	70	36	38	35	32	37	42	59
XVI	Machinery	50	33	35	33	31	35	41	57
XVII	Transport equipment	49	39	38	34	29	34	39	54
XVIII	Instruments	73	40	40	38	34	38	43	60
XIX	Arms	77	41	41	40	40	46	50	68
XX	Miscellaneous	113	57	58	51	50	58	60	80
XXI	Works of art	32	10	11	10	7	8	17	27
	Total	n.a.	40	39	34	32	36	41	57

n.a., not available.
[a] Includes 15 percent temporary tariff surcharge.
[b] Includes 10 percent temporary tariff rate on c.i.f. value.
[c] Includes 15 percent temporary tariff rate on c.i.f. value.
Source: 1973, Bolóña, 1981, table 3.3; other years, BCRP, Annual Reports, various years

enjoyed. If this is so it is likely that the tariff structure of the early 1970s was more than sufficient to isolate domestic industry from foreign competition – that is, the situation was one of "generalized water in the tariff."

Table 2.3 shows that, as a consequence of the subsequent reduction of the maximum tariff rate to 60 percent in 1980, the new frequency distribution resulted in a bunching of tariff lines at the 21–30 percent and 51–60 percent tariff rate levels. Other characteristics of the tariff structure including the minimum 0 percent rate and the number of lines in the different tariff ranges remained virtually unchanged.

Table 2.3 Frequency distribution of the tariff structure, 1980–1982

Tariff range (%)	Jul 1980	Dec 1980	Dec 1981	Dec 1982
0	30	31	37	64
1– 10	390	388	594	582
11– 20	773	755	1,297	1,314
21– 30	1,535	1,577	1,223	1,217
31– 40	773	768	647	641
41– 50	440	436	380	377
51– 60	455	1,149	1,029	1,031
61– 70	209	0	0	0
71– 80	175	0	0	0
81– 90	135	0	0	0
91–100	106	0	0	0
101– 10	11	0	0	0
111– 20	60	0	0	0
121– 55	6	0	0	0
Total	5,097	5,104	5,207	5,226

Source: BCRP, 1983, table 3

The 1980 reform reduced the dispersion of the tariff structure quite significantly. Both the range and standard deviation of the tariff structure indicate a generalized reduction in the dispersion of the tariff rates between December 1979 and December 1982 (table 2.4).

A comparison of the July 1980 (table 2.3) and December 1979 (table 2.4) tariff structures reveals that the subsequent reforms implemented in September 1980 resulted in a generalized reduction in average tariff rates. These reductions were more significant in the BTN sections where a great number of tariff lines had been protected by tariff rates above 60 percent – hides and leather, textiles, and footwear. Despite the higher-than-average reductions, these industries continued to enjoy the highest level of legal tariff protection.

Finally, table 2.5 presents estimates of effective rates of protection (EPRs) by International Standard Industrial Classification (ISIC) for 1978 and 1981. These estimates have shortcomings because they are based on simple average legal tariff rates and on the Andean Group input–output matrix. Nevertheless, the fact that the methodology used was the same for both years provides a common basis for analyzing some of the changes that were taking place.

The figures show a significant decline in the weighted average EPR for the manufacturing sector from 122 percent to 74 percent. The reduction of the EPR of the primary sector is also important, but the new level is still below the corresponding figure for the manufacturing sector.

Table 2.4 Dispersion of the tariff structure by Brussels Trade Nomenclature sections, 1979 and 1982

BTN sections		December 1979			December 1982		
		Minimum	Maximum	Standard deviation	Minimum	Maximum	Standard deviation
I	Animals	5	86	21.4	0	60	18.0
II	Vegetable products	10	96	23.1	0	60	14.8
III	Fats and oils	15	51	9.7	10	40	9.5
IV	Foods, beverages, tobacco	11	121	27.4	10	60	16.0
V	Mineral products	0	41	8.9	0	40	7.4
VI	Chemical products	0	101	11.5	0	60	10.0
VII	Resins, plastics, rubber	10	91	15.8	5	60	15.8
VIII	Hides and leather	16	121	30.6	5	60	17.0
IX	Wood, cork, etc.	11	81	19.6	10	60	16.9
X	Paper	0	101	26.0	0	60	19.9
XI	Textiles	21	141	35.0	10	60	13.6
XII	Footwear, headgear, etc.	51	101	12.1	50	60	1.7
XIII	Articles of stone, cement, etc.	10	101	21.8	5	60	16.9
XIV	Precious stones and metals	0	151	48.3	0	60	19.6
XV	Basic metals	5	90	17.4	5	60	17.1
XVI	Machinery	5	110	17.5	5	60	16.6
XVII	Transport equipment	0	155	32.2	0	60	18.1
XVIII	Instruments	10	91	19.7	5	60	15.8
XIX	Arms	0	71	19.8	0	60	18.3
XX	Miscellaneous	25	101	19.3	5	60	13.2
XXI	Works of art	10	10	0	0	15	4.7
	Total	0	155	26.5	0	60	17.7

Source: BCRP, 1983, annex 7

Within the manufacturing sector, the reform affected the structure of EPRs. Among the 21 industries, the EPRs of three (furniture, petrochemicals, and basic metals) increased, while the most important proportional reductions in EPR (excluding miscellaneous manufactures) were in tobacco, foodstuffs, beverages, and footwear.

Departures from Pre-announced Schemes

The goal of Belaúnde's economic cabinet, announced by the vice Minister of Commerce in his address to the CADE, was an eventual uniform legal tariff structure of 25 percent. This objective was never achieved.

Table 2.5 Effective protection rates by sector[a], 1978 and 1981

Sectors	1978	1981
Primary production	58.9	18.3
Manufacturing (weighted average by value added)	121.9	74.3
Processed foods	216	94
Beverages	140	88
Tobacco	281	55
Textiles	132	121
Clothing	85	87
Footwear	177	89
Wood	71	52
Furniture	69	97
Paper	78	56
Printing	68	32
Leather	124	106
Rubber	64	44
Chemicals	47	27
Petrochemicals	58	75
Nonmetallic minerals	85	50
Basic metals	113	40
Metals products	41	66
Nonelectrical machinery	41	31
Electrical machinery	75	50
Transport equipment	44	27
Miscellaneous manufactures	147	57

[a] Based on Andean Group input–output, using simple average nominal tariffs by subgroup and assuming zero nominal protection for nontradeables.
Source: estimates from World Bank, 1983c

Departures from the new tariff structure began soon after it had been introduced. The departures, which increased protection to domestic producers not only through changes in tariff rates but also through some QRs, were introduced relatively slowly during 1981 and 1982 but accelerated quite drastically during 1983 and 1984.

The revisions of the tariff structure were both general and sectoral. Until 1984 the more generalized policy reversals were largely implemented for reasons related more to fiscal needs than protectionist goals. The many sector-specific changes, however, can more plausibly be attributed to the pressures exerted by politically powerful groups affected by the new trade policies.

The generalized measures implemented for fiscal or balance-of-payments reasons, but also incidentally leading to overall increased protection, included the introduction in January 1982 of a 15 percent "temporary" tariff surcharge. In March 1983 this surcharge was replaced by a "temporary" 10 percent increase in tariffs, and in April 1984 the new "temporary" tariff was increased to 15 percentage points. Announced as temporary, these tariffs have in fact been permanent but with unstable rates. The instability has naturally contributed to uncertainty in the private sector.

Unfortunately, by 1984 political pressures and economic hardships persuaded policymakers to tackle the economic problems by reversing trade policies and returning to a protected economy. This time, protection was not intensified with across-the-board uniform policy measures but by introducing increased escalation to the tariff structure. This is shown clearly in the July 1984 tariff changes. Decreto Supremo 325–84 from the Ministry of Economy, Finance, and Commerce changed the tariff structure according to the following schedule:

Previous tariff rates (%)	Increase in tariff rates (percentage points)
5–9	5
10–15	8
16–40	12
More than 40	16

By 1984 the highest level tariff rate was 91 percent (15 percentage points from the temporary import tariff, plus 16 percentage points from the 1984 tariff changes added to the original 60 percent of the 1980 tariff structure). This policy change benefited the industries that traditionally had been more protected. Compared with 1981, the year with the lowest level of tariffs, the simple average had increased from 32 percent to 57 percent (table 2.2).

Sectoral tariff reforms have also been quite frequent since the trade liberalization measures were introduced in 1980. These reforms have usually consisted of reducing tariffs on intermediate imports and capital goods for both the primary and the manufacturing sectors. The changes began to be introduced as early as March 1981, only six months after the tariff liberalization had been implemented. While in general they do not appear to have changed the tariff structure significantly, they showed that, with some political pressure, policymakers could be persuaded to introduce some tailor-made changes.

QRs were also used to provide increased protection to certain domestic import-competing industries. From December 1980 to December 1982, only seven out of more than 5,000 tariff lines were affected by import prohibitions (table 1.6). These goods were in the cotton and arms sectors. During 1984, 172 new items were "temporarily" added to that list, including clothing, tobacco, and footwear.

In 1981 the minimum number of tariff lines for which imports had to be discretionally approved by some government office was 111; goods in this category included some agricultural products, paper, fertilizers, petroleum derivatives, and ships. By December 1982 the number of tariff lines affected by some type of import-licensing procedure had increased to 144. The additions included goods associated with the nuclear power industry and 26 tariff lines corresponding to goods produced domestically by the basic steel industry. The latter change, as we shall see, represented a clear protectionist measure. By 1983, however, the number of goods affected by QRs decreased to 118, mainly as a result of the elimination of 28 tariff lines corresponding to noncompeting imports of intermediate goods, including fertilizers for the agricultural industry.

Finally, as mentioned, several tariff lines were included in the so-called list of temporary prohibitions. This trend continued during 1985. By 1986 the reversal of the trade liberalization policies implemented in 1979 and 1980 was complete.

Final Remarks

The first stage of the reform of the import regime, implemented by the military government of Morales, should be viewed as one of several policies which had the objective of reversing the impact of some of the major policy distortions brought in during the previous socialist government of General Velasco Alvarado. While these reforms implied the substitution of *ad valorem* tariff rates for QRs, there is no evidence to suggest that this resulted in an important change in the structure of protection. The reason for this lies basically in the nature of the process by which the 1979 trade policy reforms were designed. All along the way, the private sector and also public sector enterprises were consulted on the extent to which the reforms could hurt them.

In contrast, the tariff reform implemented in September 1980 was rushed through by individual personalities within the government. Unlike the 1979 rationalization measures, the 1980 reform was not preceded by any major debate within the government nor between the government and the private sector.

By 1985, these trade liberalization policies had been reversed. What follows is an attempt to explain why this happened and what lessons can be derived for the future. To do so, it is important to study the nature of policy-induced distortions that accompanied the trade liberalization policies, in order to assess the extent to which the accompanying policies sustained or damaged the shift toward more open trade policies. In the next chapter we begin this analysis by looking at the changes in export subsidies and taxes.

3

Structure and Consequences of Export Subsidies and Taxes

As mentioned in chapter 1, Perú's patterns of trade have been distorted not only by import barriers but also by trade policies that directly affect export activities. These policies have included subsidization of exports of nontraditional goods, the use of export taxes levied on traditional exportable goods with clear comparative advantage, and discriminatory pricing policies against primary activities.

Incentives for Nontraditional Exports

In Perú, export incentives are escalated, discriminatory, and unstable. On the one hand, efficient exports produced mainly by the primary sector are taxed as a general rule. On the other hand, nontraditional exports, made by protected manufacturing industries, are the products that benefit most from export incentives. Therefore export subsidies do not compensate for the discrimination against efficient exports brought by import barriers. On the contrary, to the extent that these subsidies attract resources into inefficient industries, and also to the extent that they help to maintain a real exchange rate lower than would otherwise have been the case, they tend to worsen the allocation of resources. In addition these subsidies have elicited extensive counter measures from the United States.

Those that favor export subsidies for nontraditional exports in general argue their case on one or more of the following grounds: the existence of some type of externality and infant industry considerations; an inappropriate exchange rate (currency overvaluation); the need for export diversification. As a general rule, the "scientific" (externality) argument has not been the moving force behind export subsidies in Perú;[1] these subsidies have been more closely associated with the objective of export diversification under an import substitution industrialization strategy.

Even if it could be argued that export subsidies are justified on grounds of externalities or the need to foster infant industries, there is good reason to doubt whether the results will enhance the national interest in the long term. Real life observations in policymaking repeatedly prove that once discriminatory export subsidies are introduced, for whatever reasons, it is in the interest of those receiving them to maintain and, if possible, to increase them. If as a corollary the official exchange rate can be kept low, so much the better, simply because the protected enterprises in question are major buyers of unprocessed exportables and imported intermediate and capital goods. The low exchange rate, in turn, discourages efficient exports in general. While this situation could be ameliorated by devaluation, the political realities in Perú (that is, the pressures of the interest groups spawned by the policies) have instead often elicited the policy response of increasing export subsidies still further, either by augmenting the export subsidy rate with the instruments in place, or by creating new export incentives, or both.

The most important policies in terms of average amount of subsidies have been the Certificado de Abono Tributario (CERTEX) and the Fondo de Exportaciones no Tradicionales (FENT). The CERTEX is a tax certificate issued to exporters by the government in an amount equal to a percentage of the free-on-board (f.o.b.) value of export shipments. The FENT was established by the government to grant financial support to nontraditional export activities. A review of US countervailing duties (CVDs) against imports from Perú further shows that Perú's exporters of nontraditional goods have received subsidies other than those provided by the CERTEX and FENT. Finally, the Law for the Promotion of Nontraditional Exports (Law 22307) provides an important number of subsidies to this type of export. Note also the clear discriminatory title of this export law.

Certificado de Abono Tributario

The CERTEX[2] was first introduced in 1969, at a single rate of 15 percent. In 1976, a major reform of the CERTEX incentive was undertaken in

[1] There has been some attempt to justify subsidies on infant (export) industry considerations (Westphal, 1982). Unfortunately, little research effort has been devoted to testing the existence and quantitative importance of infant industries. The available estimates show little support for this argument (Krueger, 1983). For a strong defense of export subsidies in Perú, see Schydlowsky et al. (1983).

[2] Background information on CERTEX comes from Schydlowsky, Hunt, and Mezzera (1983, chapter VIII).

which the CERTEX rate, which had been fairly uniform, became escalated. Table 3.1 shows that the average CERTEX rate increased from 14 percent in 1975 to 27 percent in 1977–8. Also, as part of the drive to decentralize economic activity, the 1976 reform increased the CERTEX by 10 percent for nontraditional exports produced outside the Lima–Callao region.[3]

The 1976 structure of the CERTEX remained quite stable until early 1981 when an important reform was introduced (Decreto Legislativo 26, January 1981). Two major changes characterized the 1981 reform: (a) the number of products eligible for CERTEX was reduced, and (b) the rate was also reduced. Schydlowsky, Hunt, and Mezzera (1983) have estimated that under the new legislation only 76.4 percent of the total value of 1979 nontraditional exports, or 16 percent of total exports, continued to be eligible for CERTEX. The changes in tax rates initially proposed by the government included only two categories, 10 percent and 15 percent, but the government was not able to resist domestic pressures[4] and the resulting new CERTEX had three rates: 15 percent, 20 percent, and 22 percent.

While these were the major changes introduced to the CERTEX incentive in 1981, other modifications are worth mentioning. First, not only was the number of products eligible for CERTEX reduced, but also several industries were excluded from the additional 10 percent CERTEX for nontraditional exports manufactured outside the Lima–Callao area. Second, the CERTEX which used to be firm specific (its level being determined according to pre-established points given to variables such as employment, technology, value added, etc. for each) was transformed into a product-specific (BTN tariff line) incentive. This change eliminated much of the potential or *de facto* interfirm discrimination that existed in the previous regime. It must also have simplified and reduced administrative costs.

Finally, other relatively minor changes were introduced in the CERTEX. (a) In the previous regime, 2 percent of the CERTEX was earmarked for the Fomento de Exportaciones (FOPEX) (an organization whose funds are used for providing information and marketing services for nontraditional exports). While this remained unchanged, an additional

[3] Note that the political economy response to the balance-of-payments problems of those years (chapter 1) was to delay the necessary devaluation. One way of doing this was to increase the export subsidy rates.

[4] According to Schydlowsky, Hunt, and Mezzera (1983, p. 187) "The incentive rate in the original project of those products that continued to be promoted was either 10 percent or 15 percent. Given that the rates implied a drastic reduction in relation to existing rates, the original project caused alarm to affected industries which mobilized in order to reestablish previous rates . . . ." Political pressures were organized by the Asociacíon de Exportadores (ADEX). This is a powerful group, one of whose major functions is to lobby for export subsidies for nontraditional exports.

Table 3.1 Average Certificado de Abono Tributario rates of free-on-board exports, 1970–1981

Sector	1970	1971	1972	1973	1974	1975	1976	1977	1978	1979	1980	1981
Agriculture	6.7	6.7	6.7	10.8	10.8	10.8	15.3	19.8	20.0	19.7	19.7	10.7
Fishing	15.0	15.0	15.0	15.0	15.0	15.0	24.1	33.1	33.1	32.4	32.4	12.9
Textiles	15.0	15.0	15.0	15.0	15.0	15.0	21.7	28.3	28.2	27.0	26.4	17.3
Metal machines	15.0	15.0	15.0	15.0	15.0	15.0	20.6	26.2	26.2	25.7	25.7	19.9
Chemical	15.0	15.0	15.0	15.0	15.0	15.0	18.8	22.5	22.5	22.0	22.0	15.8
Nonmineral metals	11.3	11.3	11.3	11.3	11.3	11.3	17.4	23.4	22.4	22.9	22.9	15.5
Iron and steel	14.6	14.6	14.6	14.6	14.6	9.6	15.5	23.4	22.9	20.0	18.8	9.0
Wood	15.0	15.0	15.0	15.0	15.0	15.0	22.0	28.9	28.9	20.3	28.3	19.2
Leather	15.0	15.0	15.0	15.0	15.0	15.0	19.6	24.8	24.2	23.7	23.7	15.0
Artisan	0.0	0.0	12.4	24.9	24.9	24.9	27.4	29.8	29.8	29.2	29.2	26.5
Various	6.9	6.9	6.9	6.9	6.9	6.9	12.7	22.1	31.4	22.8	22.8	9.6
Total	12.9	12.9	13.5	14.3	14.3	13.8	21.0	26.6	27.2	26.3	25.4	15.2

Source: Schydlowsky et al., 1983, tables II–14

10 percent of the CERTEX rate received by the exporter now became earmarked for the municipalities in which production took place. Therefore, under the new legislation, exporters only received 88 percent of the corresponding CERTEX. (b) Under the old legislation, the exporter was entitled to receive the incentive on a c.i.f. basis when exports were shipped under national flag. In the new CERTEX, the exporter always received the amount of the incentive calculated by applying the CERTEX rate to the f.o.b. value. The new CERTEX legislation also eliminated additional incentives of 2 percent granted on the f.o.b. value of new nontraditional exports and of 10 percent granted in "special" cases. Finally, at a later date – July 1983 – the exchange rate for estimating the sol value of exports on which the CERTEX incentive was calculated was changed from that prevailing on the day of the shipment to that prevailing on the date on which the CERTEX certificate was issued (Decreto Supremo 178-83-EFC). Because of the inflationary trend of the Peruvian economy, this effectively increased the subsidy received by exporters – by about 1–1.5 percentage points according to some estimates made by officials in the Vice Ministry of Commerce. Also, from 1983 exporters were exempted from paying income tax on the CERTEX.

Table 3.1 summarizes the effects of the modification of the CERTEX regime on the average incentive rates received by major economic sectors. The figures show that, indeed, the reduction in the rates of the CERTEX incentive, some of which used to be as high as 40 percent of the f.o.b. export value, was substantial. On average, and excluding the decentralized CERTEX, Schydlowsky, Hunt, and Mezzera (1983) have estimated that the weighted average basic CERTEX rates for products that continued to be eligible for CERTEX were reduced from 25.4 percent in 1980 to 15.2 percent in 1981. (Weights are given by the 1979 value of exports.) Finally, we must recall that the 1981 modifications to the CERTEX remained unchanged until mid-1984 with the one exception of textile exports, for which incentives were eliminated following US CVD actions.[5]

We have asserted that, in the main, export subsidies have favored industries whose sales in the domestic market are heavily protected. There are some exportables industries, however, such as fishing and artisanal products, that have also benefited from export subsidies (table 3.1). Further, in spite of enjoying protection in the domestic market, the textile industry has exported significant amounts. In these cases there is a presumption that export subsidies have pulled resources in the right direction.

Finally, the products that became ineligible for CERTEX in the 1981 legislation were primary commodities and natural-resources-based manu-

[5] Further changes introduced in August 1984 have increased the average CERTEX rate by approximately 20 percent.

factured goods with low value added. The discriminatory aspects of the CERTEX were thus increased, with the objective of promoting exports of goods with high value added. In fact the 1981 budget law says that " . . . the fiscal budget assigns 40,000 million soles to be disbursed as fiscal reimbursement to nontraditional exporters and delegates to the Executive the task of administering the CERTEX so that it is granted in line with value added,"[6] but the goods whose domestic value added is increased because of the protective regime are precisely those enjoying relatively high EPRs.

Financing of Nontraditional Exports

Financing of nontraditional exports is provided by the FENT, administerd by the Banco Industrial. Resources for FENT credits come from (a) direct transfers from the treasury, (b) allocation in the monetary program of the Banco Central de la Reserva del Perú, (c) 90 percent of the income generated for this and other purposes by a 1 percent tariff on importts, and (d) credits that the Banco Industrial could obtain for this purpose. FENT credit is given for pre-shipment operations for up to 90 percent of the f.o.b. export value. Until 1981, only domestic currency was used in FENT credit lines. Since 1982, exporters have had access to credit in soles and US dollars.

FENT credit has been granted at prefential rates – between 1979 and 1983 the interest rate charged was below the commercial controlled rate (table 3.2). Assuming that this is the alternative rate that the nontradi-

Table 3.2 Interest rate subsidies for nontraditional exports

| Year | Annual interest rates (%) | | | Potential interest rate subsidy (% per sol exported) |
	FENT	Commercial credit	Inflation rate (WPI)	
1979	26.9	43.3	67.8	5.1
1980	27.0	43.4	53.9	5.1
1981	49.0	71.0	68.1	6.3
1982	46.5	69.6	56.3	6.5
1983	49.5	69.6	121.3	5.7
1983[a]	62.0	96.1	121.3	9.1

WPI, wholesale price index.
[a] The interest rate subsidy is $k(r - p)$ where k is the legal maximum proportion financed per sol exported, r is the six-month commercial interest rate, and p is the six-month FENT preferential interest rate.
Source: based on interest rate information provided by the Banco Central de la Reserva del Perú

[6] Author's translation. Quote taken from Schydlowsky, Hunt, and Mezzera (1983, p. 204).

tional exporter faces for financing his exports, then the table shows that the interest rate subsidy per sol exported for credit in soles has been increasing in recent years and in 1983 was close to 9 percent. (The potential subsidy rates presented in table 3.2 underestimate the implicit subsidy of FENT credits *vis-à-vis* the shadow interest rate that clears the financial market. Also, since 1983 up to 90 percent of the f.o.b. export value could be financed by FENT, that is, $K = 90$ percent.)

Nevertheless, because the average proportion of exports financed by FENT is less than the legal maximum, the importance of interest rate subsidies is not appropriately represented by the potential maximum. Table 3.3 shows the ratio of FENT financing to the value of nontraditional exports since 1976. The figures show a drastic decline of FENT financing until 1979, and a slow upward trend since then.

While the average FENT financing ratio is low, it should be noted that the bulk of the funds is quite concentrated by industry. In particular, since 1978 the bulk of FENT resources has financed exports of processed foods and textiles. For example, during 1980 35 percent of FENT funds were used for financing of textiles. This figure is quite similar to the share of these exports in total nontraditional exports.

Table 3.3 Fondo de Exportaciones no Tradicionales financing and value of nontraditional exports, 1976–1984 (million US dollars)

Category	1976	1977	1978	1979	1980	1981	1982	1983[a]	1984[a]
FENT disbursement	80.0	88.3	77.0	107.3	124.1	123.7	215.3	117.9	204.8
Nontraditional exports	136.9	223.8	353.4	809.5	845.1	693.1	762.0	555.0	726.0
Ratio of first row to second row	58.4	39.4	21.8	13.3	14.7	17.8	28.3	21.2	28.2

[a] Preliminary estimates.

Source: prepared by staff of Banco Central de la Reserva del Perú

United States Countervailing Duties against Perú

Countervailing and antidumping subsidies are two of the discriminatory trade instruments accepted by the GATT. The nominal intention of these policies is to make international trade "fair." International rules on CVDs were extended during the Tokyo Round and are presented in the "Agreement on Interpretation of Articles VI, XVI, and XXIII of the GATT" (GATT, 1986). This document is better known as the Subsidy Code.

The code – like the GATT – opposes export subsidies, but an exception is made for developing country signatories provided that "export subsidies shall not be used in a manner which causes serious prejudice to the trade or production of another signatory . . . " (Article XIV). Industrial countries have consequently reserved the right to impose CVDs on subsidized exports from developing countries whenever these subsidies are causing "serious prejudice." Since "serious prejudice" is nowhere specified, the only clear policy scenario where exports will not produce "prejudice" is when subsidies are simply not used. Because of this, in the United States a distinction is made between countries that have committed themselves not to use export subsidies and those that have not. The first group of countries are the signatories to the Subsidy Code and benefit from the "injury test."[7]

Since Perú is a signatory to the GATT but not to the Subsidy Code, the United States does not have to prove material injury as a condition for the imposition of CVDs against imports coming from Perú but only that the imports into the United States have received some form of subsidy. Perú's export promotion policies are so visible that it has been easy to prove the existence of subsidies, among them CERTEX, FENT, and several incentives included in the Law for the Promotion of Nontraditional Exports (Law 22307). As a consequence, CVD investigations have resulted in positive findings.

The CVDs imposed against Perú have been extremely high by US standards. Among the most important were CVDs of 30.0 percent and 38.0 percent imposed in November 1982 against import of Peruvian cotton yarn and cotton sheeting and sateen. The 1984 administrative review of these cases reduced the CVDs on cotton yarn and cotton sheeting to 20.7 percent and 19.7 percent respectively; because Perú continued implementing export promotion policies, however, additional CVDs against the country have been imposed recently. Later in 1984 the United States imposed a 44 percent CVD against imports of cotton towels and in late March 1985 CVDs of 22.3 percent and 19.9 percent against certain textile mill products and apparel coming from Peru. The policies that were countervailed included CERTEX, FENT, and several fiscal incentives included in the Law for Promotion of Nontraditional Exports.[8]

---

[7] According to the GATT, " . . . the term material injury means harm which is not inconsequential, immaterial or unimportant." In the United States the factors which the International Trade Commission (ITC) considers in determining material injury include (a) the volume of imports of the merchandise in question, (b) the effect of imports of the merchandise on prices in the United States for like products, and (c) the impact of imports of such merchandise on domestic producers of like products (Trade Agreement Act of 1979, Title I, Subtitle D). As can be seen, the determination of the existence of material injury is not straightforward, but it seems reasonable to expect that the ITC will come up with a positive finding whenever low levels of profitability are accompanied by a relatively high volume of imports.

[8] In this law, Articles 8 and 9 allow exporters to upgrade the tax priority status of their enterprises; Article 12 allows exporters faster depreciation allowances; Article 14 allows enterprises that increase the number of permanent jobs in relation to those existing in the previous year to " . . . deduct as an expense of the fiscal year the amount of remuneration paid out as a result of the new jobs created, receiving income tax credits ranging from 30 to 60 percent . . . ." Finally, " . . . Article 16 of the Export Law has been determined to provide a benefit, in that an enterprise which imports machinery is relieved of the liability for the payment of import duties on machinery if certain export targets are subsequently met . . . " (US Federal Register).

In 1983 the value of US imports from Perú affected by CVDs was US$35.8 million, 3 percent of the total value (US$1,157.8 million) of US imports from Perú that year. Since Perú's export subsidies are given quite exclusively to manufactures, the more significant comparison is with the total value (US$82 million) of manufactured products imported by the United States from Perú. CVDs against this category were 43 percent.

Clearly, Perú's current export promotion strategies run high risks of provoking countervailing action from the United States, making that country an uncertain market for Perú. In addition, Perú is paying high legal fees to defend its exports in the US markets, while the CVDs themselves could be regarded as a simple transfer of resources from Perú to the US Treasury.

In 1982, the United States offered a bilateral agreement according to which Perú would dismantle its export promotion policies and in exchange, while the dismantling was taking place over a three-year period, the United States would apply the injury test before imposing further CVDs. This course of action was strongly resisted by the Asociación de Exportadores (ADEX), one of whose principal functions has been to lobby in favor of export subsidies for nontraditional exports (Schydlowsky, Hunt, and Mezzera, 1983). The US bilateral agreement was ultimately rejected, and the decision not to sign the Subsidy Code remained unchanged, despite requests from producers whose exports were being countervailed that the government discontinue the subsidies. Therefore, and except for textiles producers who relinquished their rights to use export subsidies, the threat of CVDs remains high for nontraditional exports.

A Note on the Performance of Nontraditional Exports before Import Liberalization

The share of nontraditional exports has increased (table 1.10) from 10 percent in 1970 to 21 percent and 29 percent in 1978 and 1984 respectively. A large part of the increase took place between 1975 and 1978, before the trade liberalization policies were introduced.

This proportional increase is not simply a function of the decline in traditional exports but is also attributable to the fact that higher shares of output are being exported by manufacturing industries. For a sample of manufacturing industries Schydlowsky, Hunt, and Mezzera (1983, table II-2) have estimated that, as a proportion of output, nontraditional exports increased from 4 percent in 1975 to 10 percent and 13 percent during 1978 and 1979 respectively. Most of this change is explained by increased textile exports. In this industry the proportion of gross value of production that was exported increased from 1.2 percent to 18.3 percent between 1975 and 1979.

Thus the relatively long-run stagnation of nontraditional exports ends in the mid-1970s. A likely impetus for this improved performance is the significant improvement in the real effective exchange rate for nontraditional exports, arising mainly from the real devaluation of 1978 (table 1.2) plus the significant increase in the CERTEX incentive in 1977 and 1978 (table 3.1). Moreover, the substantial decline in domestic demand following the stabilization program of the late 1970s provided another incentive for producers of nontraditional exports to look into export markets.

Pricing Policies Affecting Efficient Exportables Industries

Since the early 1960s, but particularly during the military government of Velasco, economic policies have discriminated heavily against the primary sector. As well as protectionist policies and overvalued exchange rates, direct discriminatory policies have been applied with various objectives, principal among them being income redistribution through subsidizing the consumption of the urban poor, protecting specific import substitute industries, and raising treasury income.

Nature of State Interventions in Primary Commodity Markets

For many years Perú has been subsidizing the consumption of food in cities. Many of the food programs affect the prices of goods that are produced in Perú, for instance rice. The effect of these discriminatory pricing policies has been exacerbated by the unstable system of land tenure arising from the state expropriations of Velasco's agrarian reform program. Despite subsequent reversion of some agrarian reform lands into private holdings, purchase and lease of land remains restricted. (Although mining companies were also expropriated in the early 1970s, property rights in this industry have been much more stable in recent years.)

Admittedly some state interventions have subsidized the use of agricultural inputs (fertilizers) and to this extent have partially compensated for the discriminatory policies against final primary goods. The cost of credit and the price of fertilizers have been among the major subsidized agricultural inputs. Orden et al. (1982, table 7.2) show that the average subsidy rate per sol of fertilizer was 34 percent in 1976. However, from October 1979 the price of fertilizer was no longer subsidized. Also, in January 1983 the monopoly power given to Empresa Nacional de Comercialización de Insumos (ENCI) was terminated. On average, therefore, the discrimination against the agriculture sector has been quite severe.

In any case, both the discriminatory pricing policies and the counteracting subsidies have spawned numerous and powerful government agencies.

The inevitable outcome of increased uncertainty together with expanded opportunities for rent seeking could only lead to direct waste of resources.

The nature of state interventions in rice and wheat (see Orden et al., 1982) illustrates the point quite clearly. The producer and consumer prices of rice, one of the basic foods for Perú, were set until 1980 by Empresa Comercializadora de Arroz Sociedad Anónima (ECASA), a state-owned enterprise. ECASA also holds monopoly rights on imports of rice and controls its distribution. Decree 22056 of 1980 has given ECASA continuing rights to perform these duties except that of fixing prices. The latter exercise is currently performed by the Dirección General de Agroindustria y Comercialización of the Ministry of Agriculture.

The price of wheat for bread or noodles is also controlled, but only a small proportion of domestic output of wheat goes into the flour-milling industry. The manufacturing of bread and noodles is dependent on imports of wheat, which are controlled by a quota system allocated among flour mills by ENCI and the Ministry of Agriculture. In 1980, wheat flour prices for bread and noodles were around 50 percent below the price paid by flour mills for other uses (Orden et al., 1982, table 5.2).

State controls on primary products have also been used to subsidize the price of some intermediate imports for manufacturing. Of major importance have been the subsidies received by textile producers on the price they paid for cotton. In the past, the government of Perú has set cotton prices well below international prices and has also controlled the distribution of output.

ENCI controls the purchase of all cotton from farmers and the distribution of fiber and seed to domestic and foreign markets. According to Orden et al. (1982, p.42) the administrative procedure followed by ENCI is the following:

> Prior to each production season, ENCI announces base prices which will be paid to farmers upon delivery of raw cotton containing fiber and seed to the ginning mills. This initial payment is based on a weighted average of the expected unit value of domestic and foreign sales of fiber (less processing and marketing costs, and export taxes) and on the expected sales values of cotton seed. Upon delivery the raw cotton is weighted and graded. ENCI then sells the entire season's production, calculates its profit on total sales, and issues a second payment to farmers based on total net earnings and the quality and quantity of each producer's share of output. Thus, the final price received by a farmer depend on the quality of his cotton, the pricing decisions of the Ministry of Agriculture regarding sales of cotton seed and fiber to domestic mills, the level of world prices, and ENCI's success as an international marketing agent.

The foregoing brief comments illustrate the way in which state controls have been applied to primary products. We now turn to a description of the long-term effects of these controls on producer prices and trade.

Long-run Consequences of Government Pricing Policies

Table 3.4 shows estimates of the ratio of domestic producer prices to c.i.f. prices for the period 1970–82 for wheat, rice, and cotton. Three points are worth mentioning. First, on average during this period state interventions have resulted in domestic prices below those that producers would have received in an open economy, although in recent years domestic prices, particularly for wheat and rice, have tended to move closer to international prices. Second, the degree of discrimination has been unstable, contributing to uncertainty about the returns from agricultural activities.

Table 3.4 Ratio of domestic producer to international cost, insurance, and freight prices in a sample of agricultural products, 1970–1982

Year	Wheat	Rice	Cotton[a]	Exchange rate deviations[b]
1970	1.29	1.14	0.81	0.78
1971	1.27	1.37	0.79	0.76
1972	1.12	1.21	0.82	0.73
1973	0.89	0.53	0.80	0.71
1974	0.60	0.39	0.66	0.67
1975	0.82	0.80	1.06	0.63
1976	0.96	0.92	0.66	0.70
1977	1.10	0.75	0.57	0.79
1978	0.97	0.68	0.58	1.00
1979	0.91	0.77	0.75	0.96
1980	0.73	0.79	0.96	0.88
1981	0.92	0.79	0.89	0.81
1982	0.75	1.21	n.a.	0.86

n.a., not available.
[a] Prices paid by the mills.
[b] Ratio of observed to 1978 real exchange rate estimated from table 1.2.
Source: abridged from tables in Orden et al., 1982, appendix B

The situation has been aggravated by the additional discrimination and uncertainties associated with unstable exchange rate policies. The final column in table 3.4 presents the ratio of the observed real exchange rate for each year to the real exchange rate for 1978, during which year the nominal exchange rate was closer to equilibrium. A comparison with table 1.4, which indicates that the current account was closer to equilibrium, reveals significant exchange rate fluctuations which, in 1975, had more impact than the direct price discrimination on all three of the products shown in table 3.4.

In recent years, export taxes have increased quite dramatically. These taxes have also discriminated against the primary sector. Until 1976, export taxes had not been used extensively to raise revenues (a 10 percent export tax had been introduced on traditional exports in 1974 but could be used as a credit against income tax liabilities). In 1976, a 15 percent export tax was applied on exports of traditional goods, and in May 1978 the rate was increased to 17.5 percent (Decreto Legislativo 21,528, 21,529, and 22,166). This was an important component of the stabilization attempt of that year (chapter 1). After 1980, however, the government was committed to reducing the level of export taxation, and by 1983 tax rates had been reduced significantly (table 3.5). Unfortunately, the fiscal problems of 1983 put an end to the program of reduction, and export taxes on traditional exports have been reintroduced since 1984. The rate varies between 0 and 10 percent according to pre-set levels of international prices. Given currently depressed prices, export tax collections have not been important, representing in 1984 only 0.9 percent of the value of traditional exports compared with a much higher incidence in previous years (table 3.5). Moreover, exports produced by state enterprises such as Hierro Perú and Minero Perú were exempted from payment of export taxes.

Earlier in this chapter we have argued that pricing policies and other government interventions have quite drastically affected the growth performance of the primary sector, particularly the agricultural sector. We have documented in chapter 1 the slowdown of the primary sector over the long term, and its accompanying trade reversals. For example, the agricultural sector which used to be a net exporter during the 1950s became a net importer during the 1970s. Rice is a dramatic example. Orden et al. (1982) have estimated that, on average, between 1970 and 1979 the ratio of

Table 3.5 Reduction in export tax rates, 1980–1983 (percentage of the free-on-board price)

Year	Coffee[a]	Fish products[b]	Wool and alpaca[c]	Mining[d]				Export tax incidence[e]
				A	B	C	D	
1980	17.5	17.5	17.5	17.5	17.5	17.5	17.5	13.9
1981	12.5	14.0	6.0	12.0–11.0	10.0–8.0	7.0–5.0	3.5	10.8
1982	8.0	12.0–9.0	6.0–1.0	10.0–7.0	7.0–6.0	3.5	3.5	6.7
1983	4.0	7.0–5.0	1.0	6.0–5.0	3.0–2.0	3.5	3.5	2.4

[a] Decreto Legislativo 2 (Ley de Promoción y Desarrollo Agrario).
[b] Decreto Legislativo 167 of 1981. In 1982 and 1983 there were different rates.
[c] Decreto Supremo 049, Ministry of Economy, Finance, and Commerce.
[d] Decreto Legislativo 160 of 1981: A, big mining (Gran Minería), essentially petroleum and derivatives; B, medium mining (Mediana Minería), essentially silver; C, small mining (Pequeña Minería) (mainly other mineral products) and also ongoing investment projects promoted by the government; D, other small firms.
[e] Export tax collections as a proportion of the value of nontraditional exports.

prices received by Perú's producers of rice to international c.i.f. prices was 0.72. During this same period rice production stagnated and imports went from nil to 150,000 metric tons in 1979.

Final Remarks

In this chapter we have reviewed the policies that affect export activities directly and have examined how trade liberalization policies changed their importance. In considering these policies and their effects, a leitmotif has been the different treatment accorded to nontraditional exports, the bulk of which are made by the protected manufacturing sector, and traditional exports made by the primary sector, which in Perú has a natural comparative advantage.

Our contention is that Perú's subsidization of nontraditional exports has been misguided when it has supported protected industries at the expense of efficient primary sector exports. Furthermore, CVDs imposed on major nontraditional exports have diverted Peruvian resources into US coffers while unsettling the foreign market access of Perú's subsidized exports. Finally, we have noted the role played by powerful lobbies in favor of these subsidies and have hypothesized that in some instances they could have been used as a substitute for devaluation with obvious negative consequences for traditional exports and resource allocation.

We have also emphasized that, in the late 1970s, there was an important improvement in the performance of nontraditional exports, attributable to a significant increase in the effective exchange rates received by nontraditional exports and the consequent decline in domestic demand after the stabilization program of the late 1970s had been implemented.

With respect to traditional exports, nationalization of the mining industry and land reform policies were two of the major nonprice interventions that affected the trade output performance of primary activities during the 1970s (chapter 1). In addition, the policy discrimination against primary activities arising from protectionist policies and an overvalued currency was increased by direct export taxes.

The government of Belaúnde Terry attempted to reduce direct intervention by decreasing export subsidies for nontraditional goods and export taxes on traditional exports while at the same time curtailing direct price interventions. Unfortunately, these changes in export policies were reversed along with the closing-up of the economy that started in 1984.

4

Reasons for the Collapse of Trade Liberalization Policies

The exploration in this chapter of the reasons why Perú's trade liberalization policies failed begins with a discussion of macroeconomic and export performance following the liberalization, as a background to the political economy interpretation in the subsequent section. The interpretation is based on an analysis of exchange rate policies and of the economic and political consequences of maintaining severe factor market distortions, and also examines the behavior of the government sector in general and of some public sector enterprises in particular. In the final section we discuss the impact of the trade liberalization policies on the government budget and briefly consider some transitory losses and gains.

Macroeconomic Indicators and Growth Performance

Between 1979 (the year when trade liberalization measures began to be introduced) and 1984 (when several of the trade liberalization measures had been reversed) the government followed expansionary policies. The ratio of government expenditures to GDP increased from 44 percent in 1979 to values that in some years considerably exceeded 50 percent (table 4.1). The figures show that, although during this period government revenues were increasing, expenditure was growing faster, with the result that the fiscal deficit also increased to an average figure of 7.7 percent of GDP between 1980 and 1984.

Expansionary government policies and high and increasing fiscal deficits had several consequences. First, the annual inflation rate (consumer price index, CPI) which had increased rapidly during the late 1970s, reaching 38 percent in 1977, had climbed to 125 percent and 112 percent during 1983 and 1984 respectively. These inflationary pressures complicated the management of exchange rate policy, bringing with them an overvalued currency and increasing current account deficits.

Table 4.1 Macroeconomic indicators, 1978–1984

Variable	1978	1979	1980	1981	1982	1983	1984
A Real growth rate (%)							
Gross domestic product	- 0.5	4.1	3.8[a]	3.9[a]	0.9[a]	- 10.9[a]	4.8[a]
Agriculture	- 1.5	3.9	- 5.8[a]	12.0[a]	2.9[a]	- 9.6[a]	12.5[a]
Manufacture	- 3.9	4.2	5.7[a]	- 0.2[a]	- 2.5[a]	- 16.0[a]	3.9[a]
B Unemployment (%)							
Open	6.5	7.1	7.0	6.8	7.0	9.2	10.9[a]
Under-employment[b]	52.0	51.4	51.2	47.9	49.9	57.1	57.4[a]
C Fiscal deficit/GDP (%)							
Revenue	37.8	42.8	48.8	44.1	47.1	49.7[a]	43.7[a]
Expenditure	- 43.3	43.8	53.0	51.5	55.7	60.8[a]	50.6[a]
Deficit	- 5.5	- 1.0	- 4.2	- 7.4	- 8.6	- 11.1[a]	- 6.9[a]
D CPI inflation (%)	57.9	66.7	60.8	72.7	72.9	125.1	111.5
E Nominal lending interest rate	n.a.	52.9	53.0	71.2	69.6	77.9	103.3
F Real wages (index, 1980 = 100)	84.2	88.6	100.0	95.0	95.0	74.6	70.0
G Real exchange rate[c]	322.9	313.5	288.9	262.8	269.3	301.3	312.5
H Balance of payments							
(million US$)	1,972	3,676	3,916	3,249	3,293	3,015	3,147
Imports	1,620	1,954	3,090	3,802	3,721	2,722	2,429
Current account balance	- 164	953	- 100	- 1,728	- 1,609	- 872	- 252
Net international reserves	- 1,025	544	1,276	722	896	856	1,104
I Debt							
Total outstanding (million US$)	9,324	9,339	9,594	9,638	11,340	12,443	13,303
Proportion (%) of GDP	86.9	67.2	55.8	47.9	56.0	76.5	78.6[a]
J Terms of trade (1980 = 100)	67.4	91.9	100.0	82.9	69.3	73.1	64.5

n.a., not available.

[a] Preliminary.

[b] A person is underemployed whenever he works less than 35 hours per week and/or his salary is below the 1962 minimum salary adjusted for inflation.

[c] Nominal exchange rate inflated by the US wholesale price index and deflated by Perú's CPI (1980, 288.9 soles per dollar).

Source: GDP, National Statistical Institute; unemployment and real wages, Ministry of Labor; CPI inflation estimated from CPI elaborated by the National Statistical Institute; remaining data for the variable provided by the Banco Central de la Reserva del Perú

Second, the capital inflows required to finance public sector deficits as well as ambitious government projects, particularly in the energy sector, were the principal culprits in the enormous increase in Perú's total outstanding debt, from US$9.6 billion in 1980 to US$13.3 billion in 1984. High inflation also complicated the management of the interest rate, which remained controlled by the Banco Central de la Reserva del Perú. Measured against the CPI, the real lending interest rate was negative during all these years.

In fact, during and after the implementation of the trade liberalization policies of 1979 and 1980, instability is evident in all major macroeconomic variables, including the real interest rates and the real exchange rate.

Finally, growth was poor and erratic. Some growth was recorded until 1982, but the natural disasters of 1983 led to a significant slowdown. In any case, the aggregate economic performance was not sufficient to halt rising rates of aggregate unemployment and underemployment which are esti-mated to have been at around 11 percent and 57 percent respectively during 1984.

In short, between 1978 and 1984 government policies were excessively expansionary, and the macroeconomic performance of the economy was consequently inappropriate for sustaining a policy shift to a more open trade regime. Before analyzing this assertion in more detail, it is of interest to examine the trade performance that followed the reduction in trade barriers.

Trade Performance

Tables 4.2, 4.3, and 4.4 show the values (in current US dollars) of exports and imports for the period 1978–84. A first observation is that during 1979 there was an export surge. The growth of exports can be attributed to three factors. First, during 1979 the international prices of copper and lead increased significantly. Second, in the same year the value of petroleum exports also increased. As a consequence, export revenues from these three products were US$953 million higher than in 1978. Finally, nontradi-tional exports also increased, but this cannot plausibly be attributed to the trade liberalization policies implemented during 1979 since these policies were introduced only toward the end of the year. Moreover, the elimina-tion of nontariff barriers – including import licensing – during 1979 is not expected to have led to increased import competition and therefore to improved export performance (see chapter 2); indeed imports during 1979 increased much less rapidly than exports. The increase in exports of nontraditional products should rather be ascribed primarily to the major devaluations of 1978 and 1979, which put the real exchange rate at a level unequalled since 1960 (chapter 1).

Table 4.2 Value of traditional exports, 1978–1984 (million US dollars)

Item	1978	1979	1980	1981	1982	1983	1984
Fishmeal							
Value (million $)	196.0	256.0	195.0	141.0	202.0	79.0	137.3
Volume (thousand tons)	483.0	657.0	416.4	315.0	616.0	205.0	401.0
Coffee							
Value (million $)	168.0	245.0	141.0	106.0	113.0	117.0	126.0
Volume (thousand tons)	54.0	69.0	44.0	46.0	44.0	56.0	51.4
Copper							
Value (million $)	425.0	693.0	752.0	529.0	460.0	443.0	441.9
Volume (thousand tons)	349.0	377.0	350.0	324.0	335.0	292.0	337.2
Lead							
Value (million $)	164.0	330.0	383.0	219.0	216.0	293.0	233.1
Volume (thousand tons)	165.0	156.0	152.0	146.0	177.0	191.0	180.2
Zinc							
Value (million $)	137.0	174.0	210.0	267.0	268.0	307.0	340.7
Volume (thousand tons)	445.0	422.0	468.0	477.0	491.0	522.0	511.9
Petroleum							
Value (million $)	186.0	652.0	792.0	689.0	719.0	544.0	618.3
Volume (thousand tons)	13.7	24.1	22.5	19.9	22.7	20.5	23.5
Other traditional products[a]							
(million $)	343.0	516.0	598.0	597.0	553.0	677.0	523.5
Total traditional products							
(million $)	1,619.0	2,866.0	3,071.0	2,548.0	2,531.0	2,460.0	2,420.8
Total merchandise exports							
f.o.b. (million $)	1,972.0	3,676.0	3,916.0	3,249.0	3,293.0	3,015.0	3,147.1

[a] Includes cotton, sugar, iron, gold, silver, and other metals.
Source: BCRP, Annual Reports, 1984

Table 4.3 Current value of nontraditional exports, 1979–1983 (million US dollars)

Sector	1978	1979	1980	1981	1982	1983
Agriculture	40	75	72	61	70	56
Textiles	103	247	224	234	281	186
Fish	52	104	117	107	98	80
Chemicals	51	76	90	81	65	45
Metal machines	35	67	58	59	50	43
Metallurgy	36	82	82	48	71	55
Nonmetallic minerals		53	58	46	34	17
Others	36	106	144	65	93	73
Total	353	810	845	701	762	555

Source: BCRP, 1983

Table 4.4 Current value of imports by type of product, 1978–1984 (million US dollars)

Item	1978	1979	1980	1981	1982	1983	1984
Consumer goods	191.5	322.0	654.0	603.0	761.0	613.0	543.8
Intermediate products	600.0	738.0	905.0	1,376.0	1,024.0	732.0	949.0
Capital goods	450.0	625.0	1,087.0	1,454.0	1,411.0	900.0	771.0
Public sector	247.0	257.0	426.0	511.0	518.0	457.0	400.0
Private sector	203.0	368.0	661.0	943.0	893.0	443.0	371.0
Other imports	378.0	269.0	444.0	369.0	525.0	447.0	165.0
Total	1,619.5	1,954.0	3,090.0	3,802.0	3,721.0	2,692.0	2,428.0

Source: BCRP, Annual Report, 1984

From here on, the picture changes. The import surge initially triggered by the trade liberalization policies of 1980 was not paralleled by a similar performance of exports; on the contrary, exports and the trade balance tended to deteriorate during the 1980s.

Export performance for both traditional and nontraditional exports began to deteriorate in 1981 – the year after the 1980 tariff reductions. For traditional exports this decline should be attributed mainly to lower international prices. The Banco Central de la Reserva del Perú (1983, table 36) has estimated that if prices had remained at the 1980 level the value of traditional exports during 1981 would have been US$540 million higher than it actually was.) The worsening export performance of nontraditional exports, however, can be ascribed to a variety of causes. First, the real effective exchange rate for nontraditional exports declined sharply in 1981 as a result of a decline in the real exchange rate and of a reduction in export incentives (CERTEX) (see chapter 3). Second, since, with the exception of textiles and fish, nontraditional exports are generally marginal activities for firms producing them, expansionary policies such as those followed during 1981 and 1982 tend to reduce the relative rate of return of selling abroad.[1] The recessionary conditions in the world economy, particularly in neighboring Latin American countries, are also likely to have injured these exports (chapter 3). Finally, the natural disasters of 1983 must bear substantial blame for the significant reduction in the value of exports during that year: in 1983, because of the ocean current El Niño, various parts of the country were affected by floods and droughts; changes in ocean currents also affected the fishing industry. During 1983 the decreases in output of the export-oriented sectors most affected by natural disasters were as follows: agriculture, 9.6 percent; fishing, 35.5 percent; mining, 7.7 percent.

[1] The role of the real effective exchange rate and capacity utilization variables in explaining nontraditional exports is investigated econometrically in Schydlowsky, Hunt, and Mezzera (1983).

In contrast, imports increased rapidly after the trade liberalization policies. The dismantling of nontariff barriers during 1979 was accompanied by a surge in imports from US$1,954 million to US$3,090 million in 1980. Imports continued to increase after the tariff reduction of 1980, reaching a peak of US$3,802 million during 1981. Since 1981 the value of imports has declined systematically. This should be attributed to higher import barriers, recessionary conditions of the domestic economy, and the real devaluation that took place after 1981.

The 1981 rise in imports was mostly in manufactured goods, many of them consumer products that had been prohibited for years. In current US dollars, these imports increased by 42 percent. Table 4.5 shows that during

Table 4.5 Import penetration ratios m of manufacturing industries, 1980 and 1981

ISIC industry and name	m, 1980	m, 1981
311 Food manufacturing	0.221	0.242
312 Food manufacturing	0.019	0.026
313 Beverage industries	0.047	0.060
314 Tobacco manufactures	0.000	0.001
321 Manufacture of textiles	0.037	0.065
322 Manufacture of wearing apparel, except footwear	0.009	0.030
323 Manufacture of leather and products of leather, leather substitutes, and fur, except footwear and wearing apparel	0.010	0.026
324 Manufacture of footwear, except vulcanized or molded rubber or plastic footwear	0.002	0.010
331 Manufacture of wood and cork products, except furniture	0.077	0.148
332 Manufacture of furniture and fixtures, except primarily of metal	0.072	0.052
341 Manufacture of paper and paper products	0.190	0.143
342 Printing, publishing, and allied industries	0.133	0.133
351 Manufacture of industrial chemicals	1.144	1.244
352 Manufacture of other chemical products	0.137	0.111
353 Petroleum refineries	0.065	0.050
354 Manufacture of miscellaneous products of petroleum and coal	4.637	4.291
355 Manufacture of rubber products	0.392	0.512
356 Manufacture of plastic products not elsewhere classified	0.024	0.041
361 Manufacture of poetry, china, and earthenware	0.170	0.202
362 Manufacture of glass and glass products	0.306	0.375
369 Manufacture of other nonmetallic mineral products	0.073	0.107
371 Iron and steel basic industries	0.619	0.913
372 Nonferrous metal basic industries	0.046	0.052
381 Manufacture of fabricated metal products, except machinery and equipment	0.235	0.528
382 Manufacture of machinery except electrical	3.244	4.808
383 Manufacture of electrical machinery apparatus, appliances, and supplies	0.647	1.092
384 Manufacture of transport equipment	0.855	1.373
385 Manufacture of professional, scientific, measuring, and controlling equipment not elsewhere classified, and of photographic and optical goods	2.005	2.881
390 Other manufacturing industries	0.405	0.501

Source: based on data provided by Vice Ministry of Commerce and Ministry of Industry

1981 increases in import penetration ratios – the ratio of the tariff-inclusive value of imports to gross value of production – were general among three-digit ISIC industries. As will be shown, higher import penetration ratios were accompanied by negative effects on manufacturing output and profits.

In the aggregate the higher value of imports does not appear to have affected macroeconomic performance significantly. Some growth was recorded between 1980 and 1982 (see table 4.1) although this can be attributed, in part, to expansionary government policies.[2] At a sectoral level, agricultural growth was higher than aggregate growth, while growth of the mining sector was lower than average. The decline in manufacturing output was slight during 1981 and became more important in 1982. We shall show that in 1981 the decline in manufacturing output was positively correlated with higher import competition. Finally, between 1978 and 1982 the open unemployment rate remained practically constant, but it increased in the nonagriculture sector.

In summary, after 1980 – the years when lower import barriers prevailed – Perú's export performance did not improve; however, trade liberalization was accompanied by an upsurge in imports which, as we shall see, induced reduced output performance of manufactures. Since trade liberalization was introduced in the context of expansionary government policies,[3] it is difficult to disentangle the effects on employment and output performance of trade policies from those of macroeconomic policies. Whatever the precise causes, and despite the fact that no major structural change has occurred which can be blamed for the economy's problems, the reaction to mounting current account deficits and a new balance-of-payments crisis has been a return to inward looking policies.

[2] The following comments exclude 1983, when the economy suffered the consequences of adverse climatic conditions, and 1984, when policymakers once again implemented inward-oriented policies.

[3] An attempt to explain the trend in the real trade balance TB* during the period 1960 to 1983 resulted in the following regression equation:

$$TB^* = -3{,}557.1 + 11.0RER + 12.0TOT + 136.7(FD/GDP) - 26.9IP$$
$$(-3.49) \quad (3.88) \quad (2.17) \quad (4.91) \quad (-1.19)$$

$$R^{-2} = 0.63D - W = 1.23$$

where RER is the real exchange rate, TOT is the terms-of-trade index, FD/GDP is the fiscal deficit as a proportion of GDP, IP is the index of protection (chapter 1), and DW is the Durbin–Watson coefficient. Finally, exports and imports are measured in millions of 1980 US dollars. As can be seen, all variables have the expected sign and, except for the index of protection, the t statistics show that they are significant at usual confidence levels. The strong influence of the relative fiscal deficit on the trade balance is interesting. *Ceteris paribus*, a ratio of fiscal deficit to GDP of − 1 percent will result in a decline of US$137 million (1980 US dollars) in the trade balance.

A Political Economy Interpretation of Perú's Experience

In this section we suggest some explanations for the reversal of Perú's liberalization policy. Clearly, after so short time, any such attempt lacks historical perspective and must therefore be incomplete; however, some useful inferences may be derived by fitting together the various pieces of available evidence.

The accompanying policies to a trade liberalization should attempt to minimize the adjustment costs that must be incurred while the economy is undergoing the reallocation of resources necessitated by the new structure of incentives. At the same time, the goals of the macropolicies should be to insure maximum stability while avoiding balance-of-payments problems: open-trade policies will clearly be more resilient if the economy is not faced by an important devaluation and/or a reintroduction of import barriers to solve a payments imbalance.

The impetus to growth expected from trade liberalization will come fundamentally from exportables industries. In this sense, by definition, policies will result in trade liberalization and increased growth of exportables industries only if there is a relative price movement in favor of these industries. For this to occur, not only should trade barriers be reduced, but also macro-policies should help to insure that the relative price shift in favor of exportables industries take place; that is, it is essential for the real exchange rate to provide adequate profitability for efficient exports to expand.

Further, as emphasized, trade liberalization policies will not be successful unless factor market rigidities are eliminated. Otherwise, factor market policies will obstruct the reallocation of resources predicated by the new trade policies.

Certain characteristics of accompanying policies are indispensable if a trade liberalization is to succeed. These were unfortunately missing from the policies that accompanied Perú's reduction of trade barriers. At this juncture, two questions arise. First, what were the deficiencies of these accompanying policies? Second, why were they not corrected in time?

The Behavior of Real Effective Exchange Rates and Capital Inflows

The decline in the US dollar real exchange rate[4] that accompanied the reduction of import barriers during 1979 and 1980 was the exact opposite of

[4] Recall that in this case study the real exchange rate is defined as the nominal exchange rate multiplied by the ratio of the foreign to the domestic price index. Therefore an increase in this variable is interpreted as a real devaluation while a decline is an appreciation of the domestic currency.

the real devaluation that would be expected to follow a trade liberalization. Why were policymakers in the Banco Central de la Reserva del Perú inclined to devalue at a slower rate than that predicated by inflation differentials?

First, the stabilization program introduced in 1978 had already resulted in an important real devaluation. This devaluation plus a significant improvement in the terms of trade led to a record current account surplus in 1979 (table 4.1). The resulting fast growth of foreign exchange reserves was a signal in favor of a lower real exchange rate. Another alternative to appreciating the domestic currency would have been a faster liberalization of imports. While this alternative was considered by some members of the economic cabinet, it never had the necessary political support. Other alternatives would have been to repay part of the foreign debt and to sterilize foreign exchange inflows.

The policy of devaluing at a lower rate than inflation rate differentials continued during 1981 when there was perhaps less cause for it: some statistics indicate that the Banco Central de la Reserva del Perú should have followed more aggressive exchange rate policies. They show a significant reduction in the terms of trade and also increasing fiscal deficits (table 4.1). Another occurrence in favor of a higher real exchange rate was the important reduction of fiscal incentives for nontraditional exports (CERTEX) that had been implemented in 1981 (chapter 3). In theory, this policy should have been compensated for by a somewhat higher exchange rate.

Allowing the domestic currency to appreciate was an error that damaged Perú's export and balance-of-payments performance. This occurred in an economy where price responses had been severely damaged after 20 years of price intervention and distortionary policies, and at a time when export performance was crucial for showing some benefits from the trade liberalization policies and rallying some support for them.

After 1981, the rate of devaluation was higher than the rate of inflation, and as a consequence the real exchange rate began moving toward more appropriate values. Export behavior does not appear to have responded to this higher real exchange rate, however. There are probably two reasons for this. First, the real devaluation of 1982 was not very significant on average, and in any case only began towards the end of that year. Meanwhile, persistent expansionary government policies were increasing domestic demand, which in turn reduced incentives to export nontraditional products. Finally, the trade output performance of 1983 was dominated by the natural disasters of that year.

The instability of the real exchange rate as defined in table 4.1 was the major determinant of the instability in real effective exchange rates. These are presented in table 4.6 by broad categories of traded goods including

Table 4.6 Real effective exchange rate of import and export goods, 1978–1984 (index base, 1979 = 100)

| Year | Imports | Exports | |
		Traditional	Nontraditional
1978	122.2	76.3	103.8
1979	100.0	100.0	100.0
1980	88.4	98.3	91.7
1981	79.1	71.6	76.5
1982	83.5	64.3	78.4
1983	96.9	79.5	87.7
1984	111.8	74.8	92.1

Some of the variables used in the estimation of effective exchange rates are presented in table 4.7.

Table 4.7 Variables used in the estimation of real effective exchange rates, 1978–1984

| | 1 | 2 | 3 | 4 | 5 | 6 | 9 |
Year	Nominal exchange rate	International price of exportables	CPI, Perú[a]	US WPI[a]	Simple average tariff rate (%)	Weighted average export tax rate (%)	CERTEX rate (%)
1978	156.3	0.65	0.60	0.89	66.0	17.6	27.2
1979	224.7	1.00	1.00	1.00	39.0	7.4	26.3
1980	288.9	1.22	1.59	1.14	34.0	13.9	25.4
1981	422.3	1.03	2.79	1.25	32.0	10.8	15.2
1982	697.6	0.88	4.59	1.27	36.0	6.7	15.2
1983	1,628.6	0.94	9.69	1.29	40.0	2.4	15.2
1984	3,467.0	0.86	20.28	1.32	50.0	1.0	15.2

WPI, wholesale price index.
[a] Base year is 1979.
Source: columns 1, 2, 3, and 5 Banco Central de la Reserva del Perú; column 4, IMF, *International Finance Statistics*; column 7, Schydlowsky et al., 1983, II–14

imports, traditional exports, and nontraditional exports. The following are the equations used for estimating these variables (table 4.7).

1   The real effective exchange rate for imports (REERM) is REERM = $RER_m(1 + t)$, where RER_m is the real exchange rate for imports defined as the nominal exchange rate multiplied by the ratio of the US wholesale price index to Perú's CPI and t is the average legal import tariff rate.

2   The real effective exchange rate for traditional exports (REERTX) is REERTX = $RER_{tx}(1 - t^*)$, where RER_{tx} is the real exchange rate for traditional exports defined as the nominal exchange rate multiplied by the ratio of Perú's export prices to its CPI and t^* is the ratio of export tax collections to the value of traditional exports.

3   The real effective exchange rate for nontraditional exports (REERNX) is REERNX = $RER_{nx}(1 + s)$ where RER_{nx} is the real exchange rate for nontraditional exports defined in the same way as the real exchange rate for imports and s is the legal export subsidy rate. Only the CERTEX incentive has been considered.

The increasing overvaluation of the domestic currency between 1978 and 1981 and the reduction in import duties resulted in a significant decline of the real effective exchange rate for imports. Since then this variable has been increasing. This is explained by the real devaluation and also by the increase in import duties that have taken place since 1981.

Table 4.6 also shows that the real effective exchange rate for nontraditional exports declined significantly between 1978 and 1981. A major determinant of these reductions was the changes introduced to the CERTEX incentive during 1981 (see chapter 3).

The picture of the real effective exchange rate for traditional exports is different. Between 1978 and 1982 the reduction in average export tax rates was greater than the reduction in the real exchange rate for traditional exports and therefore the decline in the real effective exchange rate for traditional exports was less pronounced. In any case, the clear message of table 4.6 is that after 1980 the real effective exchange rate for traditional exports declined significantly. In this instance, the consequences of domestic policies were compounded by a substantial reduction in the international prices of Perú's exportables.

In view of persistent current account deficits since 1980 (table 4.1) the accompanying exchange rate policies could only be sustained by foreign capital inflows. The use of these inflows to finance budget deficits and ambitious public projects, as well as to satisfy private demands for foreign currency to fill the growing gap between interest rates on deposits in soles and in US dollars, intensified after 1982 when the devaluation rate exceeded the inflation rate. As a consequence, the relative rate of return of bank deposits in foreign currency increased. This process led to an important "dollarization" of the economy.[5] Further, the debt problem was aggravated *pari passu* by the extent to which capital inflows financed

---

[5] Nominal interest rates on deposits in soles were systematically below the CPI inflation rate. After 1980, the real return on deposits in US dollars was high, because the international interest rates were high and also because the rate of devaluation was higher than the rate of inflation. See Hanson and Neal (1984).

capital flight. Finally, these inflows allowed policymakers to postpone more aggressive devaluation policies, which in turn harmed the trade liberalization policies.

To summarize, during the years when more open trade policies were in place, the government of Perú followed highly expansionary macropolicies. Much of the fiscal deficit between 1980 and 1984 (7.7 percent of GDP) is attributable to increased government expenditures (table 4.1), including higher public investment which, as a proportion of GDP, increased from 2.6 percent in 1979 to 6.0 percent during 1982 and 1983. Expansionary fiscal policies had several negative effects. First, these deficits were partly financed by domestic borrowing and to this extent crowded out the private sector. Second, the inflationary trend was exacerbated by excess demand pressures, and the inflation rate increased significantly during the liberalization years. Finally, taxation policies became unstable, and tax rates were often changed as more tax revenues were sought. Capital inflows and unstable macropolicies were important determinants of the erratic behavior of the real exchange rate. Together, the resulting macro and real exchange rate performances in large part explain why the trade liberalization policies could not be sustained.

Factor Market Distortions, Capital Intensity, and Labor Market Rigidities

No country is characterized by perfectly competitive factor markets but, by any standards, those present during Perú's liberalization episode must be accounted among the worst. Land, capital, and labor markets were all hamstrung by government interference.

In the first place, most productive agricultural land is managed by land reform cooperatives. As a consequence, markets for the best land are practically nonexistent. It seems unlikely, therefore (though this is speculative), that the benefits from the productive opportunities in the agricultural sector potentially opened by the trade liberalization policies were fully reaped.

In the second place, while direct government interventions in the allocation of imported capital goods through discretionary import licensing were replaced by *ad valorem* tariffs, these tariffs were nonetheless lower than the tariffs protecting domestically produced goods. In many cases – particularly in the agricultural and mining sectors – these capital goods could be imported free of tariffs (chapter 2). The incentives for over-investing remained high not only because of the tariff structure and the currency overvaluation but also because of fiscal incentives, which continued to be conferred irrespective of productivity.

The characteristics of the tariff structure, the appreciation of the currency, and the fiscal incentives for investment reduced the cost of capital goods below opportunity costs. The ensuing signals must have impeded the creation of employment opportunities. Two indicators are worth mentioning. First, between 1978 and 1982, real gross domestic investment increased at an average annual growth rate of 15.6 percent (table 1.8). Much of this investment was in imports of capital goods, whose proportion in total imports increased from 27 percent in 1978 to 38 percent during 1981 and 1982 (table 1.12). Meanwhile, employment was increasing, overall, more slowly than investment. Consider, secondly, the indices in table 4.6 of output, investment, and employment in the formal manufacturing sector (that is, in manufacturing enterprises that presumably reap the costs and benefits of the structure of policy distortions). We identify this sector with the group of manufacturing firms included in the Annual Survey of Manufactures undertaken by the Ministry of Industry. The figures are again illustrative. They show that during 1981 the rate of accumulation of fixed assets was 9.1 percent. Also, during 1978–81, the simple average growth rates of total employment, real fixed assets, and real output were 1.3 percent, 7.6 percent, and 2.5 percent respectively. Clearly, growth of investment in the manufacturing sector has outstripped that of employment, which, in turn, has been outstripped by the growth of the urban labor force. Finally, note that the factor inputs have grown more rapidly than output, that is, total factor productivity has declined.

Another issue is whether the rigidity inherent in the Labor Stability Law discussed in chapter 1 has hampered the capacity of firms to adjust to an important change in policy incentives. Import substitute firms, which are expected to contract as a consequence of trade liberalization policies, are particularly vulnerable to the problems and costs of adjustment entailed by this law. Most of these firms are in the manufacturing sector, and unfortunately it is precisely in manufacturing industries that an important number of stable workers are employed and where this law is enforced.

We have developed a simple test to analyze the short-run reactions of formal manufacturing firms to increased import competition. The null hypothesis postulates that increased import competition is negatively correlated with activity levels, and therefore with the use of productive factors.

The statistics used are taken from cross-section data on 29 manufacturing industries (three digits of the ISIC) for 1980 and 1981 (the last year for which these statistics were available at the time of writing). The data for 1981 are the basis for assessing the short-run reactions of manufacturing industries to the trade liberalization measures of September 1980.

Changes in the degree of import competition are measured by percentage changes in import penetration ratio m, which is defined as the ratio of the tariff-inclusive value of imports to the gross value of production. We use 1980 as the reference year; therefore, this variable is measured as

$m = (m_{81} - m_{80})/m_{80}$.[6] According to the estimates of import penetration ratios for 1980 and 1981 in table 4.5, the eight manufacturing industries with highest m were footwear (324), wearing apparel (322), leather and leather products (323), metal products (381), tobacco (314), wood and cork products (331), textiles (321), and electrical machinery (383). In 1980 these industries accounted for 28 percent and 37 percent of the formal manufacturing value added and employment respectively. Historically, these industries have been particularly protected by the trade regime. In fact, table 4.5 shows that in five of the industries (footwear, wearing apparel, leather and leather products, tobacco, and textiles) the import penetration ratios in 1980 were lower than 4 percent. Therefore the changes in m between 1980 and 1981 are quite consistent with evidence presented in chapter 2 on the Peruvian structure of protection and how changes in this structure, as a consequence of the reduction of trade barriers implemented during 1979 and 1980, might have affected the pattern of imports.

The correlation coefficients between m and behavioral variables of Perú's manufacturing sector are presented in table 4.8. These variables refer to output, factor use, factor returns, and factor shares. All variables are measured as percentage changes between 1980 and 1981, using 1980 as the base year (see tables 4.9 and 4.10).

The correlation coefficients between m and indicators of output and factor use variables have the expected negative sign, that is, changes in import penetration ratios are inversely correlated with changes in output and factor use. Nevertheless, while the relationship of m with output variables is significant at the 1 percent confidence level, the correlation coefficients of m with indicators of factor use are not significant.

---

6 Ideally, we would like to have a perfect measure of changes in competitive imports faced by different industrial sectors before and after the implementation of trade liberalization policies. It is competitive imports that are expected to display the economic reaction that our correlations seek to identify. However, it is extremely difficult to measure competitive imports, especially in an economy that has been closed for many years. We assume that changes in the level of imports in any given manufacturing sector are a proxy for changes in the level of competitive imports. This should be particularly true during a trade liberalization episode where changes in competitive imports presumably explain the bulk of changes in total imports. One caveat should be mentioned. Our measure of import penetration ratio has the shortcoming that imports for each manufacturing sector are measured at an aggregate level while economic variables, including gross value of production, are measured only for the formal manufacturing sector (enterprises employing more than five workers). Nevertheless, we do not expect the estimated correlation coefficients to be biased in any specific direction, given that our independent variable is changes in import penetration ratios and that there is no reason to presume that there was a systematic change in the estimates of the underlying ratios between 1980 and 1981.

Table 4.8 Rank correlation coefficient between m and changes in industry-specific variables of the manufacturing sector between 1980 and 1981

Variable	Correlation coefficient
1 Output	
1.1 Gross value of production	− 0.568*
1.2 Gross value added	− 0.519*
2 Factor use	
2.1 Total employment	− 0.111
2.2 Blue collar (obrero)	− 0.169
2.3 Investment[a]	
3 Factor return	
3.1 Average labor income	− 0.169
3.2 Average salaries[b]	− 0.085
3.3 Profit rate (gross margins/sales)	− 0.324**
4 Factor share	
4.1 Net capital margin/gross value added	− 0.318**

*, **, correlation coefficients that are significant at the 1 percent and 5 percent confidence levels respectively.

[a] Investment is measured in gross terms and includes machinery, equipment, and construction.

[b] Gross margin is measured as the difference between gross value added and (a) the wage bill, (b) depreciation, and (c) taxes. Net margins also exclude depreciation.

Bearing in mind the limitations of the data and the relatively high degree of aggregation of the analysis, these correlation coefficients show a low short-run adjustment response in the use of factors to increased import competition. There are two hypothetical reasons for this behavior: (a) formal manufacturing enterprises faced rigidities in labor markets as a consequence of strict enforcement of the Labor Stability Law; (b) entrepreneurs did not believe that the trade liberalization policies would last and therefore concluded that it was less profitable in the long run to adjust their productive processes to the new structure of incentives than to direct their energies toward resisting trade liberalization policies.

In a sense, the two hypotheses are not independent. There is no chance that a trade liberalization policy will be successful in the presence of rigid factor markets. At the same time, political resistance to liberal trade policies will logically be greater the lower is the capacity of traditionally protected entrepreneurs to adjust their productive process to the new conditions. The reason is simple. The losses suffered by these entrepreneurs increase whenever they are unable to introduce necessary changes in resource allocation to meet foreign competition.

In fact, table 4.8 shows a statistically significant negative correlation between m and changes in profit rates and gross capital margins; that is, on average, the higher the change in import penetration during 1981 was, the more important was the reduction in profitability. Obviously, if entrepreneurs had adjusted their employment levels to the new structure of incentives, the losses would have been smaller.

Trade Policy Treatment of Government-owned Industries

Liberalization should be viewed as a social enterprise. In this sense, the public as well as the private sector should face and adjust to the challenges of increased competition. The available evidence shows that the government was unable or unwilling to meet this challenge successfully. This is documented, among other ways, by noting that during the trade liberalization years the government increased import barriers for those groups of import-competing products produced by public enterprises. The salient example is the steel industry.

Historically, Sider-Perú has been a state-owned monopolistic producer of steel products. The evidence shows that in recent years the domestic prices of steel products have been on average twice as high as the international prices (see Saint Pol and Vega Castro, 1985). In September 1980 the steel industry was also affected by reduced tariff protection. (At that time, no steel product was protected by an *ad valorem* tariff rate higher than 60 percent.) Increased import penetration triggered opposition from the managers of this enterprise, and in April 1981 a regime of prior import licenses was reintroduced for some steel products. This tailor-made import barrier was soon extended to other steel products and imports declined from US$103.6 million in 1981 to US$45.3 million in 1982 (BCRP, 1983, annex 4).

The custom-designed trade policy for the steel industry is only one among several illustrations of the government's lack of conviction about its own trade policies. In Perú, the public sector also owns and controls many other industries including mining, paper, petroleum, energy, water supply, finance, and transportation. Most of these goods and services are produced by inefficient firms who historically have held monopoly positions in the Peruvian economy. During the 1980s, there was never any commitment to increase the productive and economic efficiency of these enterprises, nor was any privatization effort undertaken. Obviously, the unpredictable and high protection policy maintained for many government-owned intermediate and service industries compounded the adjustment problems of the private sector. Most importantly, this behavior shows that the government did not interpret liberalization as a social enterprise.

Table 4.9 Industry-specific manufacturing data, 1980[a]

ISIC industry and name	Imports	Gross value of production	Gross value added	Wages and salaries	Salaries	Investment	Net capital income	Value of sales	Total employment	Blue collar (obrero)
311 Food manufacturing	303.2	396,542	131,221	26,463	16,616	12,390	76,977	345,182	34,352	24,628
312 Food manufacturing	6.6	100,224	26,618	4,412	1,922	2,654	17,588	111,524	5,558	3,192
313 Beverage industries	28.2	172,558	105,393	11,934	5,324	12,955	40,080	119,349	12,275	7,200
314 Tobacco manufactures	0.07	28,035	20,759	1,013	444	85	1,031	9,475	854	548
321 Manufacture of textiles	36.6	288,618	132,390	26,977	17,864	38,711	63,018	226,904	35,515	26,070
322 Manufacture of wearing apparel, except footwear	2.2	70,749	26,825	6,797	4,368	2,060	14,240	54,423	15,082	11,267
323 Manufacture of leather and products of leather, leather substitutes, and fur, except footwear and wearing apparel	0.9	24,291	8,422	2,185	1,479	1,255	4,587	18,858	3,686	2,757
324 Manufacture of footwear, except vulcanized or molded rubber or plastic footwear	0.2	32,299	16,060	4,060	2,916	619	7,424	24,749	7,124	5,349
331 Manufacture of wood and wood and cork products, except furniture	9.8	36,629	15,901	4,995	3,243	4,250	6,649	33,031	10,124	7,631
332 Manufacture of furniture and fixtures, except primarily of metal	4.4	17,516	8,032	3,185	2,142	364	2,063	14,091	6,667	4,976
341 Manufacture of paper and paper products	63.1	95,956	29,580	7,612	4,090	5,452	14,394	82,680	7,525	4,974
342 Printing, publishing, and allied industries	28.3	50,757	21,773	8,501	4,152	3,357	8,904	47,003	10,774	5,728
351 Manufacture of industrial chemicals	478.2	121,050	51,250	8,882	4,323	88,788	30,811	100,014	8,379	4,952
352 Manufacture of other chemical products	90.8	191,781	73,055	16,783	5,379	5,563	34,580	166,118	17,393	8,278
353 Petroleum refineries	48.7	217,159	67,344	3,907	793	389	20,973	185,099	2,780	623
354 Manufacture of miscellaneous products of petroleum and coal	21.6	1,350	510	113	64	203	263	1,164	140	94

355 Manufacture of rubber products	48.0	35,508	14,234	3,349	2,028	2,423	6,450	31,735	3,263	2,284
356 Manufacture of plastic products not elsewhere classified	6.8	80,138	33,302	7,163	4,154	5,644	16,337	69,548	9,236	6,482
361 Manufacture of pottery, china, and earthenware	4.6	7,465	4,738	1,300	1,020	466	1,765	6,664	1,725	14524
362 Manufacture of glass and glass products	20.6	19,490	9,086	3,348	2,552	2,067	2,978	15,973	4,742	3,922
369 Manufacture of other nonmetallic mineral products	18.5	72,911	28,240	7,713	4,711	2,449	11,617	66,274	10,281	7,644
371 Iron and steel basic industries	221.5	103,648	27,031	10,662	5,353	3,796	5,503	88,159	8,041	4,853
372 Nonferrous metal basic industries	42.3	262,905	91,587	2,396	1,785	1,622	86,499	231,917	2,744	2,217
381 Manufacture of fabricated metal products, except machinery and equipment	102.3	125,796	49,067	13,676	8,281	7,802	19,225	114,023	19,506	13,952
382 Manufacture of machinery except electrical	766.8	68,462	28,035	8,120	4,704	2,469	13,158	60,346	9,643	6,330
383 Manufacture of electrical machinery apparatus, appliances, and supplies	264.7	118,388	50,853	9,673	4,799	3,012	29,054	99,128	11,024	6,888
384 Manufacture of transport equipment	401.5	136,032	41,881	9,496	4,889	3,773	24,186	121,801	11,685	7,504
385 Manufacture of professional, scientific, measuring, and controlling equipment not elsewhere classified, and of photographic and optical goods	60.7	8,764	3,727	1,303	492	655	1,350	7,587	1,549	848
390 Other manufacturing industries	35.5	25,360	11,406	2,850	1,346	1,817	5,354	22,327	4,476	2,760

a Variables are in millions of soles except for employment data which are in thousands of persons.

Source: tabulations from the Annual Survey of Manufactures provided by Ministry of Industry. Commerce. Trade. and Integration

Table 4.10 Industry-specific manufacturing data, 1981[a]

ISIC industry and name	Imports	Gross value of production	Gross value added	Wages and salaries	Salaries	Investment	Net capital income	Value of sales	Total employment	Blue collar (obrero)
311 Food manufacturing	429.0	749,666	223,312	42,230	25,879	25,836	134,822	711,344	28,280	20,455
312 Food manufacturing	13.3	212,773	57,574	7,040	3,358	5,941	42,733	232,639	4,938	3,062
313 Beverage industries	41.7	297,258	172,374	21,698	9,625	30,986	64,694	210,250	10,871	6,931
314 Tobacco manufactures	0.2	51,028	39,876	1,958	981	709	4,356	17,533	999	677
321 Manufacture of textiles	54.7	356,160	142,613	40,017	26,017	33,909	51,355	288,674	31,124	23,631
322 Manufacture of wearing apparel, except footwear	5.9	83,507	32,392	10,155	6,745	1,450	14,374	66,497	10,832	8,164
323 Manufacture of leather and products of leather, leather substitutes, and fur, except footwear and wearing apparel	1.9	31,340	10,744	3,684	2,350	1,534	4,188	25,818	3,220	2,355
324 Manufacture of footwear, except vulcanized or molded rubber or plastic footwear	1.0	40,466	23,018	1,610	5,324	2,273	8,476	31,972	6,331	4,643
331 Manufacture of wood and wood and cork products, except furniture	1.0	40,466	23,018	1,610	5,324	2,273	8,476	31,972	6,331	4,643
332 Manufacture of furniture and fixtures, except primarily of metal	19.9	56,953	20,666	6,853	4,950	4,801	8,083	55,116	6,826	5,252
341 Manufacture of paper and paper products	7.3	58,710	28,179	5,360	3,399	4,251	16,538	51,293	4,533	3,347
342 Printing, publishing, and allied industries	54.2	160,328	52,887	13,302	6,915	8,394	24,593	125,929	7,097	4,610
351 Manufacture of industrial chemicals	33.1	105,459	51,839	6,895	8,006	11,405	25,225	98,089	8,576	4,758
352 Manufacture of other chemical products	486.5	165,557	79,888	15,844	7,774	30,286	45,608	158,257	7,803	4,815
353 Petroleum refineries	101.0	384,662	168,825	28,619	8,927	9,151	106,344	335,876	16,430	7,783
354 Manufacture of miscellaneous products of petroleum and coal	63.2	533,260	109,774	15,576	2,315	4,618	18,202	449,696	2,629	699
	21.7	2,145	837	152	101	78	507	1,962	100	71

355 Manufacture of rubber products	71.9	59,373	27,725	6,303	3,252	2,471	14,114	54,408	3,417	2,165
356 Manufacture of plastic products not elsewhere classified	11.4	117,435	47,083	11,274	6,190	12,963	20,733	102,150	7,771	5,368
361 Manufacture of pottery, china, and earthenware	6.2	13,048	7,745	2,316	1,806	998	2,785	10,642	1,555	1,291
362 Manufacture of glass and glass products	28.1	31,752	13,579	4,663	3,484	5,499	4,272	26,701	4,069	3,334
369 Manufacture of other nonmetallic mineral products	26.7	105,795	40,637	11,474	7,158	9,408	17,230	96,358	8,195	6,309
371 Iron and steel basic industries	313.1	145,252	64,943	19,147	9,146	11,081	27,222	129,098	7,516	4,286
372 Nonferrous metal basic industries	38.3	309,560	90,259	6,522	4,947	2,465	75,660	320,708	3,869	3,194
381 Manufacture of fabricated metal products, except machinery and equipment	212.3	170,300	63,047	18,738	11,518	9,830	25,861	155,124	14,490	10,769
382 Manufacture of machinery except electrical	1,094.9	96,424	44,608	12,378	7,475	4,645	21,717	88,261	8,428	5,586
383 Manufacture of electrical machinery apparatus, appliances, and supplies	425.7	165,076	71,822	14,607	7,108	5,808	40,577	135,655	9,246	5,579
384 Manufacture of transport equipment	756.7	233,332	68,385	15,611	7,725	7,966	38,025	242,970	10,160	6,500
385 Manufacture of professional, scientific, measuring, and controlling equipment not elsewhere classified, and of photographic and optical goods	91.2	134,004	5,636	981	628	754	2,301	11,239	1,230	731
390 Other manufacturing industries	46.4	39,234	15,848	4,148	1,681	1,983	7,527	32,045	3,480	1,892

[a] Variables are in millions of soles except for employment data which are in thousands of persons.

Source: tabulations from the Annual Survey of Manufactures provided by Ministry of Industry, Commerce, Trade, and Integration

Why Were Trade Liberalization Policies Introduced?

One inference from the previous analysis is that in Perú the political commitment to trade liberalization policies was never strong. The intriguing question then is why these trade liberalization policies were introduced at all.

The answer is intimately related to the character of Perú's policymaking institutions. The process of forming policy is fragmented in different government agencies, and policy instruments are assigned among them approximately as follows.

1 The Banco Central de la Reserva del Perú manages monetary instruments and has a monopoly power over exchange rate and interest rate policy. In fact, the President of the Banco Central de la Reserva del Perú cannot be removed without Congressional approval.[7]

2 The Ministry of Labor manages labor disputes and the Labor Stability Law, and is consequently an important arbiter of the degree of mobility in the formal market.

3 The Ministry of Economy and Finance has limited control on tax policy, which is largely determined by political considerations. As a result, the fiscal deficit is quite difficult to control.

4 The Vice Minister of Commerce is responsible for managing trade policy. Liberalization was introduced in 1980 when this agency was shifted from the Ministry of Industry – which traditionally defends the interests of import substitute industries – to the Ministry of Economy (see chapter 1).

5 Finally, the Ministry of Industry controls fiscal incentives for investment, and import duty exonerations.

In light of these characteristics, the answer to the question that has been posed becomes clear. Trade barriers were reduced simply because the group of policymakers who became responsible for managing the policy instruments assigned to the Vice Minister of Commerce agreed that an appropriate course of action for Perú was to liberalize trade. Institutional compartmentalization meant, unfortunately, that these ideas never spread to the rest of the government, and therefore political commitment towards open trade policies was never universal or strong; the institutional structure was an inappropriate foundation for trade liberalization measures. In our view, it is precisely for this reason that many policy-induced distortions and macropolicy instability have persisted during the 1980s.

---

[7] In spite of his wishes President Belaúnde could not remove the President of the Banco Central de la Reserva del Perú whom he appointed at the beginning of his mandate.

Impact of Trade Liberalization Policies on the Government Budget

The impact of trade liberalization policies on the government budget is a complicated issue. There are various dimensions to the problem. First there is the dynamic issue of differential rates of economic growth associated with alternative trade strategies. One of the messages of chapter 1 was that increasing policy-induced distortions, including trade barriers, had reduced long-run economic growth. If this is so, an open trade regime would be expected to accelerate growth. In this environment tax revenues would also grow faster and eventually be higher in absolute – though not necessarily in relative – terms than in a closed economy situation. Important as this issue might be, the measurement of the dynamic links between alternative trade policies and the government budget is outside this study's terms of reference.

However, even the short-run static analyses of the links between alternative trade policies and the government budget raise a number of issues. First, it is necessary to know how the shift in import policies affects the average tax rate on imports. In the case of Perú, the presumption is that the average tax rate on imports increased after the introduction of the trade liberalization policies. There are two reasons for this. First, the shift of the trade regime from nontariff barriers to *ad valorem* tariff protection is expected to have a positive impact on import tax revenues, because rents that are captured by the producer under a nontariff barrier system will be transferred to the government under an *ad valorem* import tariff system. Second, a reduction of *ad valorem* tariffs from prohibitively high levels to levels that induce increased imports will surely raise import tax revenues.

Table 4.11 shows that these effects have been substantial in Perú. During 1978, the average incidence of import duties (line G) was 23 percent. From here on, during 1981 and 1982, while the economy was still at the peak of its trade liberalization policies, the ratio increased to 30 percent. During the crisis year of 1983 the ratio declined to 25 percent and it increased again during 1984.

Focusing on the years between 1980 and 1982, and using as a benchmark the average import tax incidence of 23 percent observed during 1978 and 1979, the increase in the average incidence of import duties was approximately equivalent to US$124 million during 1980, US$266 million during 1981, and US$260 million during 1982. Therefore, during 1981 and 1982, the shift in trade policies increased import tax revenues by approximately US$526 million.

We have argued in chapter 3 that the reduction in import barriers was accompanied by lower export subsidies to nontraditional exports. This was a second route by which the shift in trade policies helped to alleviate the

Table 4.11 Behavior of import duties during trade liberalization, 1978–1984 (million US dollars)

Variable	1978	1979	1980	1981	1982	1983	1984
A Import duties	249	303	547	760	681	438	513
B Sales taxes on imported goods	128	141	241	386	452	234	196
C Total tax revenue from import goods	377	444	788	1,146	1,133	672	709
D Row C divided by fiscal revenue	0.22	0.22	0.19	0.22	0.33	0.30	0.31
E Imports	1,620	1,954	3,090	3,802	3,721	2,722	2,429
F Tax ratio[a]	0.035	0.032	0.045	0.057	0.056	0.041	0.042
G Incidence of import duties (row C over row E)	0.23	0.23	0.27	0.30	0.30	0.25	0.29

[a] Ratio of tax collections to GDP.
Source: based on statistics provided by Banco Central de la Reserva del Perú.

budget situation. In January 1981 the CERTEX incentive for nontraditional exports was reduced. As a consequence, the average subsidy rate granted by this investment declined from 25 percent to 15 percent. These 10 percentage points allowed a reduction in subsidies granted to nontraditional exports of US$70 million in 1981 and US$76 million in 1982.

However, there are also several reasons why a trade liberalization could result in lower tax collection, increased government expenditures, or both. In Perú these factors are related to export taxation, lower domestic activity, and increased government subsidies.

First the average export tax rate declined from 13.9 percent in 1980 to 10.8 percent and 6.7 percent during 1981 and 1982 respectively (table 3.5). Had the average export tax rate remained unchanged at the 1980 level, export tax collections during 1981 and 1982 would have been US$79 million and US$182 million higher than they were.[8]

Lower import barriers and increased import competition are expected to have a negative impact on highly protected sectors. In turn, lower levels of activity in import substitution industries are expected to result in lower tax revenues. On the other hand, lower import and export barriers are expected to trigger output expansion of exportables industries. Unfortunately, measuring the fiscal repercussions of these consequences is extremely difficult. In view of data availability, we will focus attention on the tax effects associated with the short-run performance of import substitution industries. To some extent our figures for the fiscal gains of trade liberalization policies must be underestimates, and perhaps by a substantial margin, since the agricultural sector expanded rapidly during 1981 and 1982 (table 4.1) and part of this expansion can reasonably be linked to the trade liberalization policies.

I have assumed that on average manufacturing is the import substitution sector in Perú. We focus attention on the formal enterprises within manufacturing (those covered by the Annual Survey of Manufactures undertaken by the Ministry of Industry) since it is this group which pays taxes. The survey shows that during 1980 and 1981 – the last year for which there are data – tax payments as a proportion of value added by formal manufacturing industries was 20 percent. At the same time, the data show that during 1981 the value added by the firms included in the Annual Survey of Manufactures was practically the same as the figure recorded for 1980. It follows that virtually the same amount of internal taxes was paid by the formal manufacturing sector during 1981 as in 1980. Obviously, this should largely be attributed to the expansionary policies of 1981.

---

[8] These figures are estimated from the difference between average 1980 and average 1981–2 export tax revenues due to the value of traditional exports observed in these years. Obviously, the analysis presented in this section disregarded the effects that changes in trade taxes have on the structure of trade flows.

Summing up, we have estimated that during 1981 and 1982 the 1979 and 1980 trade liberalization policies had a positive impact of US$411 million on treasury revenues (this is obtained by adding US$526 million of increased import tax revenues to US$146 million of lower export subsidies and subtracting US$261 million of lower export tax revenues). At the same time, tax payments made by the formal import substitution industries remained relatively unchanged. Unfortunately, there is no reliable information by which to gauge the effect on the tax payments made by exportables industries. In any case, these are presumed to have increased, and to this extent our figures underestimate the net fiscal revenue effects of the trade liberalization policies.

Short-run Costs and Benefits

It seems evident that, for Perú, the expected gains from shifting toward more liberal and outward-oriented policies are quite impressive, but unfortunately the political economy at the time of liberalization was not appropriate for sustaining a more open trade regime.

One important question that still remains is whether the short-run costs associated with the trade liberalization policies were higher or lower than the benefits. It is hard to answer this question convincingly, partly because there is no straightforward way of separating the unemployment costs of trade liberalization from those attributable to other policies, particularly in a changing macroeconomic situation, and partly because data on this issue are in any case usually unavailable. For example, a shift from nontariff barriers – including discretionary import licensing – to *ad valorem* tariff protection is expected to provide several benefits: greater transparency of administrative procedures; reduced uncertainty and paperwork; reduced bureaucratic costs associated with trade controls; and hopefully lower welfare losses associated with rent-seeking activities. In a country like Perú, such short-run benefits might be substantial, but unfortunately it is not easy to estimate them. The structure and characteristics of labor markets in Perú further complicate analysis of the evolution of aggregate employment and its relationship with the trade liberalization process, mainly because of the existence of a large informal sector which, according to some estimates, represents around 50 percent of the country's labor force (Vega Castro, 1984).

Despite these shortcomings, there are enough indicators from the data to attempt some analysis of the effects that the trade liberalization policies are likely to have had on (a) unemployment and (b) consumer welfare.

Unemployment

Between 1979 and 1982, when the annual growth rate of imports was 15.4 percent, the rate of open unemployment decreased slightly from 7.1 percent in 1979 to 7.0 percent in 1980, to 6.8 percent in 1981, and to 7.0 percent in 1982 (table 1.17). The underemployment rate also decreased from 51.4 percent in 1979 to 49.9 percent in 1982. This behavior of the labor market could be attributed, at least in part, to the expansionary policies of the early 1980s.

Although trade liberalization does not appear to have had an important impact on the broad characteristics of the labor market, it appears to have had an impact on the employment of the manufacturing sector, in which import competition had significantly increased as a result of the 1979–80 trade policies.

The data from the two sources of information on industrial employment in Perú differ. According to the Ministry of Labor, industrial employment increased during 1981 and declined only slightly in 1982, whereas the data from the Ministry of Industry show an important reduction of manufacturing employment during 1981. The source of this discrepancy remains unclear. One reason could be coverage: the data from the Ministry of Labor are based on surveys made on industrial firms located in Lima and employing 50 or more workers; the Ministry of Industry statistics provide information for firms all over the country with five or more workers.

If the size of enterprise accounts for the different behavior of manufacturing employment, then the conclusion is that in terms of employment levels relatively small firms were better able to adjust their workforce to increased import competition. This is compatible with the presumption that labor stability regulations are presumed to be enforced more rigorously on large manufacturing enterprises.

Our estimation of the employment costs of the trade liberalization policies is based primarily on Ministry of Industry figures, on the assumption that, because of their coverage, they are more representative. Table 4.12 shows estimates of manufacturing employment. Unfortunately, at the time of writing, the series only reached 1981. The figures show that, compared with the peak year of 1980, during 1981 manufacturing employment had declined by 15 percent.

Following the methodology suggested in the analytical framework we will assume that the loss of national product attributable to increased unemployment of labor is proportional to the average product per worker. During 1980, the average product per worker in the manufacturing sector was US$14,156. Therefore, during 1981 the output loss attributable to liberalization was US$596 million. This represented around 3 percent of GDP during that year.

Table **4.12** Employment in the
formal manufacturing sector,
1978–1984

Year	Number of workers
1978	258,283
1979	266,882
1980	276,143
1981	234,015

Source: Annual Survey of
Manufactures

There is an important reason why this figure might be overestimated. An implicit assumption behind the estimates is that the manufacturing labor that became unemployed did not find a job. This might lead to a gross overestimation of the loss attributable to short-run unemployment, particularly in view of the declining economy-wide unemployment and underemployment rates during 1981. Moreover, it might have been relatively easy for some of these workers to find a job in some informal activity.

Even if all this were not the case, it is not necessarily true that other factors that were combined with labor also became unemployed. Obviously, the loss would be smaller if these other factors continued to operate.

A final reason why the figure might be overestimated is that we have used 1980 as the reference year. In the Annual Survey of Manufactures, this year shows the highest level of manufacturing employment. Therefore our estimates of labor unemployment would have been smaller if a different reference period had been used.

Consumer Welfare

Trade theory shows how in the long run trade liberalization results in net welfare gains, some of which are appropriated by the consumer. This is another reason why the short-run costs of the 1979–80 policies could have been smaller than those presented. Unfortunately, available data do not allow a precise assessment of the short-run consumer gains. Nevertheless, some comments may be useful.

Available estimates show that the potential gains for Peruvian consumers of the adoption of trade liberalization policies are quite impressive. Cebrecos and Vega Castro (1979) have analyzed figures on consumer prices for 112 products collected by the Programa de Estudios Conjuntos para la Integración Económica Latino-Americana (ECIEL). These prices were collected during 1973 for a group of Latin American countries. It should be mentioned that the ECIEL work program strongly emphasized product homogeneity in its selection of sample products, since a major goal of the research was to make cross-country comparisons of price differentials.

These estimates have two major drawbacks, however. First, the study only includes Latin American countries, and therefore price comparisons cannot be made with international trade prices. In the second place, the focus on consumer prices means that differential trade margins and tax structures somewhat obscure the interpretation of the protection effects of estimated price differences. Nevertheless, Cebrecos and Vega Castro (1979) argue that trade margins and tax structures were not very different at that time across the sample of countries.[9]

The countries in the sample include Bolivia, Brazil, Colombia, Ecuador, Mexico, Perú, and Venezuela. The aggregate findings of the study reported by Cebrecos and Vega Castro (1979) show that Colombia was the country with the lowest recorded consumer prices on a higher number of products. These represented 39.5 percent of the product sample. However, Perú was the country showing the lowest number of products (4.4 percent of the product sample) having this characteristic.

Table 4.13 presents estimates of legal rates of protection and price differentials for individual products. Column 1 shows one plus legal tariff rates that prevailed in 1973. Column 2 is the ratio of consumer prices in Perú to the Latin American country where the price was lowest. Some

Table 4.13 Product-level protection estimates, 1973–1983

Product	One plus legal tariff	Ratio of Perú's prices to lowest prices in other Latin American countries[*]
1 Ham	2.20	2.27
2 Mortadella	2.20	1.50
3 Canned tuna	2.00	1.50
4 Canned sardines	2.10	2.57
5 Shrimp	1.83	1.57
6 Evaporated milk	1.00	[b]
7 Butter	1.37	1.37
8 Cheese	1.99	2.37
9 Cornflour	2.07	2.88
10 Corn starch	1.81	1.75
11 Noodles	2.16	[b]
12 Barley	1.27	1.28
13 Canned peaches	2.62	2.44
14 Canned pineapple	2.73	1.55
15 Tomato sauce	2.34	3.54

[9] Cebrecos and Vega Castro (1979) refer to previous work by Cebrecos and Zolezzi on this subject. It is likely that the major differences across countries are to be found in foodstuffs, beverages, and tobacco. Tax rates, as well as the effects of price controls, on these products are likely to diverge between countries.

16 Canned peas	2.62	1.92
17 Margarine	1.49	1.11
18 Vegetable lard	1.79	b
19 Animal lard	1.56	b
20 Vegetable oil	1.45	1.09
21 Powdered soup	2.31	3.76
22 Vinegar	2.34	3.33
23 Soda water	2.05	2.67
24 Mineral water	2.05	2.67
25 Wine in bottle	2.96	1.21
26 Beer	3.34	3.20
27 Instant coffee	2.14	1.49
28 Tea	1.95	1.31
29 Powdered chocolate	3.46	4.17
30 Cigarettes	4.93	3.50
31 Men's slacks	3.93	1.67
32 Working slacks	3.93	2.25
33 Shirts	3.73	3.11
34 Underwear	5.49	2.60
35 Undershirts	5.49	2.97
36 Footwear	5.67	1.44
37 Poplin	2.74	2.37
38 Dacron	2.74	5.57
39 Flannel	2.74	b
40 Women's slacks	6.93	1.42
41 Girls' blouses	3.92	2.26
42 Panties	4.03	1.83
43 Brassieres	2.79	4.06
44 Nylon socks	4.03	1.60
45 Girls' sweaters	3.64	1.61
46 Cotton blouses	2.55	1.85
47 Corduroy	2.55	3.76
48 Other wearing apparel	2.47	2.18
49 Other wearing apparel	2.55	2.77
50 Sheets	4.39	1.97
51 Towels	4.39	3.89
52 Blankets	2.72	1.43
53 Men's footwear	3.39	1.27
54 Women's footwear, high	3.39	1.52
55 Women's footwear, low	3.38	1.64
56 Tennis shoes	1.95	3.57
57 Matches	2.30	2.00
58 Soup plates	2.43	1.55
59 Glasses	2.22	4.10
60 Spoons	2.13	1.63
61 Pressure cookers	1.89	2.91
62 Aluminium saucepans	1.89	2.10
63 Metallic wool	2.31	3.51
64 Tires	1.75	2.06
65 Spark plugs	1.62	1.44
66 Batteries	1.88	1.34

67 Electric refrigerators	1.84	1.06
68 Gas kitchens	2.00	1.39
69 Washers	1.81	2.35
70 Sewing machines	1.62	1.90
71 Electric irons	1.95	1.28
72 Electric mixers	1.93	5.53
73 Table radios	2.17	6.37
74 Portable radios	2.17	1.89
75 Portable televisions	2.25	2.07
76 Laundry soap	2.21	1.07
77 Detergents	2.09	1.12
78 Toilet paper	1.93	1.25
79 Electric bulbs	1.74	2.12
80 Insecticides	1.45	2.82
81 Talcum powder	1.77	8.29
82 Bath soap	2.40	1.64
83 Shaving cream	2.38	5.30
84 Toothpaste	2.65	2.04
85 Sanitary napkins	1.93	1.29
86 Sulfanumedin	1.43	2.38
87 Aspirin	1.47	3.40
88 Rubbing alcohol	1.91	4.28
89 Absorbent cotton	1.46	1.59
90 Vitamin C	1.33	2.54
91 School notebooks	1.92	1.79
92 Popular books	0.00	5.05
93 Pens	2.04	1.83
94 Locker ball	1.81	2.07
95 Prepared wood	2.49	2.19
96 Trucks	1.32	1.89
97 Pick-ups	1.42	1.54
98 Cars	2.32	1.79
99 Motorcycles	1.69	1.29
100 Bicycles	1.73	1.40
101 Three-speed bicycles	1.73	1.40
102 Telephones	1.44	1.34
103 Plows	1.32	3.99
104 Cement mixers	1.42	5.19
105 Centrifuge pumps	1.43	1.40
106 Air compressors	1.32	3.16
107 Electrical motors	1.53	2.49
108 Welders	1.42	1.46
109 Transformers	1.67	2.24
110 Voltmeters	1.43	2.86
111 Hand drills	1.42	2.22
112 File cabinets	1.80	1.20

[a] Perú's prices lower than in other countries.
[b] Official exchange rates were used to convert domestic-currency-denominated prices into dollar figures.
Source: from data presented in Cebrecos and Vega Castro, 1979

comments are in order. First, at a disaggregated level, column 1 reflects previous findings, reported in chapter 2, that consumer goods such as clothing (women's slacks, underwear, and undershirts) were relatively protected by the legal tariff structure. Figures in this first column also show a wide dispersion in legal protection rates. Second, the figures in column 2 show that Perú had lower consumer prices than its Latin American neighbors in *only* five products in the sample (of which three were foodstuffs which, as mentioned, could have been affected by price controls at the time). At the other extreme, in 55 out of 112 products in the sample, Peruvian consumers were paying *more than double* the prices of the most "efficient Latin American country."

We have already discussed various dimensions of the costs that the Peruvian trade regime of the 1970s was imposing on its economy. These figures show that, even by Latin American standards, Perú's policies have resulted in significant consumer price distortions. On average, consumers in Perú paid 137 percent more than their Latin American neighbors.

Clearly, the potential gains for Perú's consumers from trade liberalization policies appear to be considerable. The extent to which consumers actually reaped the gains of the 1979–80 import liberalization policies depends on how fast prices of protected domestic products declined. A precise analysis of this issue is not possible with the available data. Nevertheless, the behavior of relatively aggregate price statistics show that in the short run consumers were able to reap some of the gains from a more open trade regime.

Table 4.14 shows the quarterly behavior of different components of the CPI. The products in this index was reclassified by the Banco Central de la Reserva del Perú into three groups: controlled, nontradeables, and tradeables. The two bottom lines show accumulated inflation during the period when the economy was more open (1980, quarter III, to 1982, quarter IV) and when the economy was being closed (1983, quarter I, to 1984, quarter III) to international trade.

The figures show that, during the first period, accumulated inflation of tradeables (a majority of which are import competing) increased less than the aggregate index, particularly in relation to nontradeables. Especially interesting are the prices of textiles and footwear products, which increased much more slowly than the average CPI.

However, when trade policies began to be reversed, particularly in 1984, the price behavior of tradeables was not very different from that recorded for the aggregate index.

Though far from conclusive this evidence certainly suggests that trade liberalization led to consumer gains. Unfortunately, it is still not known whether gains exceeded the losses that we have recorded. In any case, our analysis suggests that the upper bound estimate of the costs of the

Table 4.14 Quarterly changes of the consumer price index, 1980–1984 (percent)

| | | | Not controlled | | | |
| | | | Tradeables | | | |
Quarter	Total	Controlled	Total	Textiles and shoes	Houseware appliances	Nontradeables
1980 I	13.9	6.0	13.7	17.2	14.2	17.6
II	8.4	0.6	11.7	15.0	12.7	9.3
III	17.1	17.7	20.7	21.6	11.2	14.5
IV	11.2	6.3	12.7	9.0	10.3	12.1
1981 I	24.5	40.9	16.4	13.5	16.6	24.3
II	11.9	11.1	14.6	12.1	12.7	10.5
III	10.8	10.4	10.5	7.8	8.1	11.1
IV	11.9	15.2	9.8	7.6	9.0	11.9
1982 I	15.5	14.0	12.0	11.2	11.4	18.6
II	12.5	15.4	12.0	10.2	17.9	11.6
III	14.0	13.1	10.0	8.9	13.4	17.0
IV	16.7	19.4	15.6	9.6	12.3	16.3
1983 I	27.5	34.9	17.7	9.7	96.4	30.4
II	22.4	33.8	20.8	13.1	23.6	18.3
III	25.7	28.4	25.2	14.5	27.4	24.7
IV	14.7	12.4	25.5	24.4	23.2	9.7
1984 I	24.3	29.2	24.9	18.9	22.4	21.3
II	18.8	23.2	21.6	21.1	20.1	14.5
III	18.0	19.8	17.4	20.9	15.6	17.4
IV	21.3	20.1	25.1	27.6	20.9	19.4
Accumulated						
1980 III to 1982 IV	3.32	3.76	2.91	2.53	2.86	3.45
1983 I to 1984 IV	4.76	5.97	4.98	3.92	4.64	4.10

Source: Consumer price index disaggregation prepared by the research department of Banco Central de la Reserva del Perú

short-run trade liberalization policies was 3 percent of GDP but that it is very likely that the "real" cost was much smaller.

Final Remarks

In this chapter three issues related to Perú's trade liberalization attempt have been analyzed. The first refers to the behavior of the economy following the introduction of trade liberalization policies and analyzes reasons for the reversal. A second issue is the impact of trade liberalization on treasury income. Finally, we provide a discussion of the social costs and benefits associated with the shift in trade policies.

We have concluded that, from an economic viewpoint, the failure of Perú's trade liberalization policies can be attributed to several factors, including expansive fiscal policies, currency overvaluation and unstable real exchange rates, and factor market distortions that prevented high labor mobility. Without these problems, Perú's current account deficits in recent years would have been less important, and therefore the pressures for taking corrective actions by devaluing or by reintroducing import restrictions would have been less compelling.

We have also argued that, within the government, political commitment to the new trade policies was weak. Moreover, because the accompanying policies were not supportive of more open trade policies, export performance did not improve. This in turn must have harmed the ability of the government to rally support for its more open trade policies. Regarding the impact of the trade policy shifts, our estimates show that trade liberalization policies had a positive effect on treasury income. Finally, we have presented an upper estimate of the short-run unemployment costs of trade liberalization policies as equivalent to 3 percent of GDP.

5

Timing and Sequencing of Policy Reforms: Lessons from Perú's Experience

Introduction

In principle, the timing and sequencing of policy reforms are two separate problems. Timing is concerned with when reforms should be initiated and how long the process should take. Sequencing enters the picture once multistage strategy has been adopted, often because the initial situation is characterized by more than one distortion which it has been decided should be sequentially eliminated.

Unfortunately, neither theory nor empirical evidence provides clear directions for choosing among alternative combinations of the timing and sequencing of policy reforms. A persuasive theoretical argument for a one-stroke as opposed to a multistage approach is that new and stable policy signals should minimize the danger of resource misallocation associated with a gradual path. This insight, which comes from the theory that moving to first-best situations is less risky from a welfare point of view than remaining in a second-best world, is limited by the presence of factor immobility, factor specificity, or both. However, the extent to which factor mobility is then itself restricted by policies and institutional barriers remains an empirical question. *A priori* there is no reason to presume that the degree of factor mobility will remain low after policy-induced distortions and institutional rigidities have been eliminated.

Empirical justification for the factor-specificity argument against a one-shot comprehensive liberalization policy is also shaky. In any case, in theory the welfare ranking of policies suggests that protecting the income of factor-specific workers with trade barriers is inferior to, say, the alternative of introducing a subsidy mechanism to compensate for factors displaced by trade.

It is our view that the major obstacles – from an economic viewpoint – to liberalization in Perú are not related to factor specificity but to the inflationary trend of the economy and policy-induced distortions in factor markets. In the next section we review these issues and draw the lessons from Perú's experience.

The analysis would certainly be incomplete if our discussion did not include considerations of the political obstacles to liberalization policies; some of these are therefore highlighted in the subsequent section.

Sequencing of Policy Reforms

Price Stabilization and Exchange Rate Policy

The importance of fiscal discipline and price stability for a trade liberalization policy cannot be sufficiently emphasized. The historical experience of Perú, as well as that of many other developing countries, suggests that high inflation has been accompanied by currency overvaluation and real exchange rate instability. Sooner or later, macroeconomic policies have led to major balance-of-payments difficulties, and experience shows that, when these problems surface, inflation-prone countries have usually been reluctant to implement real devaluation policies. Because of this, the policy package to deal with these problems has often included the imposition of higher trade barriers. The barriers have usually been maintained well after the payment problem has disappeared. This policy behavior has characterized Perú since at least the late 1940s – protectionist policies have been implemented in all balance-of-payments crises since World War II, including the late 1940s and late 1950s, 1967–8, 1975–8, and 1984–5 (see chapter 1).

In principle, a policy could be envisaged that, in the presence of inflation, would stabilize the real exchange rate. However, the likelihood that this could be implemented permanently in an economy with two-digit or three-digit annual inflation, such as Perú's, is minimal. Under inflationary circumstances, the temptation and political pressures to use exchange rate policies for stabilization purposes are strong. This has occurred in Perú as well as in many other countries, with very negative effects.

The most sensible scenario for introducing and maintaining appropriate exchange rate policies is one where the inflation rate is brought down drastically and permanently. Exactly how this should be done is a subject outside the scope of this case study. Nevertheless, some comments relevant to Perú might be useful.

As table 4.1 shows, from 1978 to 1985 the annual inflation rate as measured by the CPI remained above 60 percent. Also, as expected, higher fiscal deficits have been associated with increasing inflation rates. In order to reduce inflation and inflationary expectations, this fiscal deficit needs to be reduced drastically. This can be done by reducing expenditures or increasing revenue; probably, any stabilization program will entail a mix of both, but we would suggest that in Perú reduction of expenditures is paramount.

Government expenditures need to be reduced in the first place simply because they have gone too far. During the late 1960s and early 1970s, these expenditures used to be around 20–30 percent of GDP. Table 4.1 shows that since 1978 these expenditures have grown dramatically and during the early 1980s were standing between 50 and 60 percent of GDP.

The alternative solutions – higher taxes on the private sector, or increasing the prices of goods and services provided by the public sector – could lead to new distortions or worsen the economic costs of the existing distortions. The recent experience of Perú suggests that attempts at raising tax revenues were unsuccessful. For example, tax revenues as a percentage of GDP reached a peak of 17 percent in 1980. Since then, the figure has declined to around 12 percent during 1983 and 1984. This has occurred in a period during which trade liberalization policies have apparently yielded important tax revenues (chapter 4). One explanation for this behavior is that increased tax rates and tax pressures give agents the incentives to shift their undertakings to informal activities.

An additional and probably serious risk in taxing formal activities too heavily is the potential reinforcement of the incentives for capital flight. It should therefore be a goal of the stabilization and liberalization program to boost the confidence of the owners of these activities and induce them to keep the capital at home.

The suggestion of raising the prices of goods and services provided by the public sector might be reasonable when these prices are subsidized, but chapter 4 has shown examples in Perú where public sector enterprises, such as steel and paper, that were producing tradeable goods were unable to adjust to increased import competition. Tailor-made trade policies implied that these enterprises could continue operating only if foreign competition was eliminated. Clearly, many of Perú's public sector enterprises can survive only if the government continues to grant them monopoly positions through trade barriers and other forms of governmental protection.

Finally, there is an important political reason why unproductive public sector expenditures and the importance of the economic activities of the government should be reduced. A truly generalized liberalization attempt cannot coexist for long with important but economically inefficient government activities; trade policy reversals are bound to be the outcome. Inefficient public sector enterprises simply cannot compete with imports. When – as in Perú – the government reintroduces import barriers in favor of these firms, demand for higher protection will come from sectors that must buy their inputs from these protected public sector enterprises. These chain reactions lead us to suggest that the government should consider the social benefits associated with the introduction of deregulation and privatization schemes implemented *pari passu* with trade liberalization policies.

In sum, it is crucial to accompany a trade liberalization policy with realistic exchange rate policies. Since the high and growing inflationary trend during the 1980s was a critical impediment to the implementation of such policies in Perú, a reduction of the budget deficit and of inflationary pressures would seem a prerequisite to the introduction of a successful liberalization attempt. We argue that this reduction of the budget deficit, in Perú at any rate, should be effected mainly through a reduction in government expenditures.

Factor Markets

In addition to its macroeconomic instabilities, the Peruvian economy is riddled with controls and distortions in factor markets. Included in this set are barriers to direct foreign investment, agricultural land holdings by agrarian reform enterprises, and the Labor Stability Law. These controls imply that Perú's economy is operating inside (perhaps well inside) its production possibility frontier. Therefore, dismantling barriers to factor mobility should have positive effects on the allocation of resources, and consequently on national income. For example, barriers to direct foreign investment could be lifted after the trade policy reforms have been implemented. In this way, we minimize the possibilities for inmiserizing growth (Johnson, 1966) and avoid the creation of protected foreign enterprises which at a later date could become powerful interest groups against trade liberlization policies.

Particularly important is the dismantling of the barriers to labor mobility erected by the Labor Stability Law (see chapter 4). This law affects employment in the protected formal manufacturing sector which, though small proportionately (8 percent of the nonagricultural labor force in 1980), will have to make the most substantial adjustments to increased import competition.

The logic of our economic analysis suggests that, in scheduling policy reforms, those affecting factor markets should be introduced early in the process. Otherwise the adjustment costs to the trade policy shift could turn out to be too high for the owners of the capital stock in formal manufacturing enterprises. While it is reasonable to expect some firms in the formal sector to go bankrupt as a result of trade liberalization even in a scenario where factor markets are characterized by high mobility, absence of this mobility would trigger even more failures and adjustment costs. In such circumstances, the inevitable political opposition is likely to be strong enough to prevent an important de-industrialization process from taking place.

Formal manufacturing entrepreneurs, as a general rule, have been highly protected and politically well organized, and as a group are traditionally and temperamentally disposed to resist liberalization policies. However, several of these entrepreneurs, particularly the labor intensive industries such as clothing and footwear, are potentially successful exporters. Once this potential is realized, a natural consistency in favor of the reforms emerges, and the entrenched opposition is correspondingly eroded. In our view, whether this occurs depends to a great extent on whether factor market rigidities can be eliminated.

This line of reasoning does not underscore the important role that will be played by the huge informal sector in a more open economy. Clearly, a significant amount of entrepreneurial talent must have been concentrated on overcoming government controls and regulations and finding profitable opportunities in informal activities. In fact, Saint Pol and Vega Castro (1985) argue that, in sectors such as clothing and footwear, informal activities have put competitive pressure on formal enterprises. Nevertheless, estimates show that most informal activities are located in nontradeables sectors such as commerce (see Vega Castro, 1984). Therefore a policy shift towards more uniformity of incentives and in favor of exportables sectors will pull resources out of protected inefficient formal industries and informal activities in nontradeables. In fact, this is probably the primary pool of resources from which Perú can expect to achieve a high growth, labor intensive, export-oriented, industrialization process.

As export opportunities open up, informal entrepreneurs should become successful producers of tradeable goods, but initially the formal manufacturing activities are the most likely to take the lead in the export drive. For this to be possible, factor mobility, and in particular labor mobility, should be high.

In summary, in Perú the liberalization of factor markets is important not only from a resource allocational point of view but also from a political point of view. These measures are needed even if the economy does not liberalize trade, but they appear to be crucial for a successful trade liberalization policy.

Trade Policies

The magnitude of the trade policy shifts needed to achieve the intended objectives of a reform are naturally determined by the initial circumstances in which the reform is launched. The trade regime in Perú has traditionally been characterized by the use of generalized import licenses to protect domestic producers from foreign competition; this was so during the late 1960s and 1970s and remains so today.

We have argued that, if a trade regime of this sort is accompanied by an unstable macroenvironment, including high and growing inflation rates and factor market rigidities, the introduction of an ambitious trade liberalization is risky and could be costly. Moreover, the prospects for introducing trade liberalization in the future are seriously damaged if earlier attempts are frustrated, because people are likely to attribute failure to the liberalization policies and not – as they should – to the accompanying circumstances. This does not mean that trade policies cannot be improved under inappropriate macropolicies. For example, we believe that the replacement of nontariff barriers by tariffs would yield increased tariff revenues to the treasury while simultaneously making the trade regime more transparent, as indeed actually happened when this reform was implemented in Perú in 1979.

On the export side, we also believe that the 1981 reduction of the CERTEX incentive was a move in the correct direction. Recent research supports the proposition that discretional subsidies to nontraditional exports should be replaced by a free-trade regime for exporters, essentially allowing direct and indirect exporters to import freely the goods necessary to make their export activities profitable in international markets. This suggestion is supported by the growing tendency on the part of the United States to impose CVDs against discriminatory fiscal and financial subsidies that confer benefits on exporters (Finger and Nogués, 1987). This has been the experience of Perú in recent years (chaper 3).

Obviously, the climate for introducing an ambitious trade liberalization will be more propitious if accompanying policies are such that

1 the price level has been stabilized or, at the very least, inflationary forces have been reduced significantly;
2 there is a commitment to maintain a realistic exchange rate policy, and macro policies are such that near balance-of-payments equilibrium is assured;
3 factor markets are functioning competitively and, in particular, there are no institutional barriers to labor mobility; and
4 there are no political uncertainties and the government has a clear political commitment in favor of the policy changes.

These characteristics pave the way for the introduction of important reforms of import and export policies; unfortunately, our analysis in chapter 1 shows that, since the mid-1950s, they have been absent from the political economy scenario of Perú.

Summary

This section has reviewed what in our view are the major barriers to introducing a durable trade liberalization in Perú. Although the analysis has presented the topics in order of priority, it is important to stress the links between policy instruments and targets. When these links are taken into account, the problem of policy sequencing can be viewed in terms of the relative emphasis given to instruments and targets at different stages.

For example, we emphasize that policy in the initial stage should focus on the goal of price stabilization and the establishment of a flexible and realistic exchange rate. The reduction, rationalization, and privatization of inefficient government activities are crucial for achieving these objectives, but trade liberalization policies clearly also have a role to play, for the simple reason that policy-induced distortions in factor and product markets have budgetary impacts. Agricultural pricing policies and the import regime are a case in point with important implications for the government deficit. In Perú, consumption subsidies have resulted in continued deficits equivalent to around 1 percent of GDP (BCRP, *Annual Report*, 1983). A similar deficit has arisen from the commercialization of wheat; in this case, the government holds the monopoly to import wheat and sells to the mills at prices that have been 20–30 percent below border prices.

The import policy has also aggravated the budget deficit. Import barriers implemented with nontariff barriers distribute rents from consumers to producers. A shift of the trade regime to protection through tariffs will increase tariff revenues. While tax revenues derived from economic activities that are displaced by imports might be diminished, in the case of Perú the net effect of the higher tax revenues attributable to the trade policy changes was between 1 and 2 percent of GDP. Finally, import policies were compensated for by discriminatory export subsidies, with obvious budgetary consequences. Summing up, for Perú the reduction of major trade distortions will enhance the likelihood of a successful stabilization program.

Reactions to Changes in Trade Policy: Analysis of the News Media

Our objective in this section is to provide a tentative analysis of the reactions to trade policy shifts that were made public in the news media. The information presented in the newspapers (a) records the public debate on trade policy and (b) both reflects and influences public perceptions of the issues. Codification of the statements in the news media thus allows us to identify the participants in the debate, and to identify the arguments, theories, and quantitative estimates used to defend the participants' positions and to explain the causes of the disruptions and displacements experienced by the Peruvian economy.

The conclusions of our analysis are limited in this instance because, owing to constraints of the scope of this study, we have analyzed only one newspaper among the many sources available. The newspaper selected is *El Comercio*, chosen because its views are slightly more market oriented than those of other existing newspapers. *La Prensa* used to be the major newspaper holding market-oriented views, but this newspaper closed in mid-1984, before the trade policies were reversed.

The results of our codification appear in two prototype tables. Table 5.1 categorizes the speakers in the trade policy debate and records the number of times they favored or opposed more open trade policies; table 5.2 presents the frequency distribution of arguments raised for and against open trade policies.

We have identified the following potential actors in the public debate: the President, cabinet members, leaders of political parties, protected entrepreneurs, labor union leaders, consumers, exporters, and writers of editorials.

The arguments have been classified according to whether or not they favor open trade policies. In turn, arguments that oppose open trade policies have been categorized as "scientific" and openly protectionist. The first group includes arguments such as infant industry, economies of scale, national sovereignty, and diversifications of the production and export structure. Among openly protectionist arguments, we have distinguished

Table 5.1 Individual statements for and against a trade liberalization policy

	For		Against	
Speaker	1980	1984	1980	1984
President	0	0	0	0
Cabinet members	15	1	0	11
Leaders of political parties				
Acción Popular	3	1	0	2
PPC	2	0	1	2
APRA	0	0	1	5
Communist	0	0	0	1
Protected entrepreneurs[a]				
General	0	0	9	3
Sectoral	0	0	0	
Textile	0	0	5	3
Automotive	0	0	1	
Labor union leaders	0	0	0	0
Consumers	1	0	1	0
Exporters	1	0	4[b]	2
Nontradeables	2	1	0	1
Editorial articles	2	0	1	0
Professionals	0	2	3	4
Total	26	5	26	34

[a] The sectoral statement was made by leaders of the textile industry.
[b] Raised by nontraditional exporters
Source: based on articles published in *El Comercio*, various issues

Table 5.2 Arguments for and against protection, 1980 and 1984

Argument	Trade liberalization 1980	Liberalization reversal 1984
In favor of protection		
"Scientific"		
Infant industry	0	0
Economies of scale	0	1
National sovereignty	1	1
Diversification of the production and export		
structure	1	2
Protectionist		
Destruction of productive capacity	9	19
Reduction of job opportunities	11	3
Less than fair trade		
Dumping	8	1
Other forms of predatory pricing, including low		
foreign wages	0	1
Traditional preference for imported goods	0	0
Erroneous accompanying policies		
Factor market imperfections		
Labor market imperfections	12	1
Capital market imperfections	2	1
Land market imperfections	0	0
Fiscal and balance-of-payments motives		
Fiscal and/or balance-of-payments problems	1	5
Inappropriate tax system	15	1
Inappropriate exchange rate policies	2	0
Lack of adjustment policies	3	0
Total	65	36
Against protection		
Consumer benefits	11	0
Increased fiscal income	0	3
Improvement of resource allocation	6	2
Increased employment opportunities	1	0
Increased growth potential through expanded size		
of markets	3	0
Cost competitiveness	5	1
Reduction of inflation	1	0
Total	27	6

Source: based on articles in *El Comercio*, various issues

destruction of existing production and employment structures, imports of less than fair value, and irrational preferences of domestic residents for imported goods.

We have also coded statements in favor of protection that were argued on the basis that the accompanying policies were not supportive of more liberal trade policies. These include factor market imperfections as well as arguments on macro policy.

The analysis covers the periods from August to December 1980 and from August to December 1984. The first period includes the moment when the maximum tariff rate was reduced from 155 percent to 60 percent. The second period includes the increase in tariff escalation and the reintroduction of import prohibitions. The analysis therefore covers two crucial periods in the recent history of Perú's trade policy.

Period of Trade Liberalization

Table 5.1 shows the number of times that different actors made statements for and against trade liberalization. During the months in which trade liberalization policies were implemented, there were 26 statements in favor of these policies and an equal number against them. Several points are of interest. First, the President did not participate in the public debate. This bears out our contention in chapter 2 that trade policies during Belaúnde's government were essentially the responsibility of the economic cabinet members who, as expected, eventually had to defend the policies they were implementing. In fact, of the 26 statements in favor of liberal trade policies, 15 were made by these cabinet members, and in particular by the Secretary of Commerce. This compares with only five statements made by leaders of the parties in power at the time: Acción Popular and PPC.

Second, consumers and efficient exporters, the major beneficiaries of trade liberalization policies, were practically inactive in the debate on trade policies. The introduction of trade liberalization policies does not appear to have generated support from the potentially most important groups of beneficiaries.

Third, as expected, protected entrepreneurs were the most active actors against trade liberalization policies. During the second half of 1980 they made 15 of the 26 statements against these policies. Nine of these statements were made by leaders of the National Society of Industries, the grouping that defends the interests of the protected manufacturing sector. This finding is clearly in line with the patterns that self-interest would predict.

Another point to stress is the relatively numerous statements of exporters against trade liberalization policies. All these statements were made by leaders of ADEX, whose major purpose is to defend the interest of nontraditional exports. As has been shown in chapter 2, several nontraditional exports are made by industries whose domestic markets are highly protected. Therefore it is in this market that producers make most of their profit. Their interest is in protection and they use ADEX to lobby in favor of discretionary export subsidies.

Table 5.2 shows the arguments used in the public debate, and the number of times that each of these arguments was put forward by the actors. There are several points of interest. First, arguments in favor of protection were voiced much more often than arguments in favor of liberal trade policies. During the second half of 1980, arguments were made 65 times in favor of protection as against 27 times in favor of a liberal trade policy. This to a great extent reflects the fact that speakers in favor of protection were more vocal and raised a relatively greater number of arguments than those who spoke in favor of open trade policies.

Also note that the bulk of the arguments put forward in favor of protection were openly protectionist rather than of the "scientific" type. Most often, they argued that more liberal trade policies would destroy existing productive capacity and job opportunities. The existence of dumping practices was also raised as an argument for increased import barriers.

Quite unexpectedly, most attacks against trade liberalization policies were argued on the grounds that the accompanying policies were not supportive of a more open trade regime. In this regard, the actors stressed that the tax system was inadequate and, in particular, that the tax burden was excessive and put enterprises in an unfavorable position to meet the challenges of foreign competition. They also argued, quite frequently, that the Labor Stability Law imposed serious barriers to the adjustment process. These arguments differ from our own (chapter 4) only in that exchange rate policies do not appear to have been the focus of attention. It therefore appears that the public debate – particularly as presented by protected interests – showed a great deal of awareness of the significance of labor market distortions and tax policies, but less awareness of the exchange rate.

Period of Reversal of Trade Liberalization Policies

During the second half of 1984, by contrast with the trade liberalization period, statements against open trade policies considerably outnumbered those defending them: 36 against, as opposed to only six in favor. Among the six, the most relevant in political terms was put forward by the Minister of Economy, but his argument, presented during the 1985 budget debate, was of a fiscal nature: included among the measures introduced into that budget were several import prohibitions, and his opposition to these was based on the argument that they would reduce tax revenues.

The most active opponents of trade liberalization policies in the public debate were cabinet members and leaders of the political parties. Eleven statements were made by cabinet members against trade liberalization policies, most of them by the Minister of Industry who, as mentioned, is in charge of defending the interests of import substitution groups.

Except for one congressman of the ruling party, the other leaders of political parties during this period spoke consistently against trade liberalization policies. By then, even leaders of the government parties (Acción Popular and PPC) were opposing trade liberalization policies. However, the majority of the statements against these policies were made by members of APRA, the party that was democratically elected to govern Perú after July 28, 1985.

Protected entrepreneurs, by contrast with politicians, were virtually silent during this period of reversal of trade liberalization, for the obvious reason that all political leaders including the Minister of Industry were already strongly arguing in their favor. Probably the most interesting point about this period is the paramount importance assumed by the argument that the productive capacity of the Peruvian economy would be destroyed by liberal trade policies.

Conclusion

The evidence of our survey of public opinion, despite its limited coverage, points firmly enough in one direction to allow some general conclusions. Clearly the opponents of open markets have carried the day in the public debate: of the 91 individual statements, 60 were against trade liberalization policies, while the occasions when arguments were put forward in favor of protection (101) far outnumbered the occasions when arguments were made against protection (33). With such clear indications that, politically, trade liberalization policies are regarded as having more costs than benefits, it comes as no surprise that APRA – the party that won the 1985 national elections by approximately 50 percent of the votes – has conspicuously and emphatically stated its opposition to liberal trade policies. Plainly, the evidence of public perceptions gathered from our analysis strengthens the proposition that liberalization ideas, principles, and policy proposals today face enhanced public resistance nourished by nationalistic sentiment which has been reinforced by the failure to shift toward more liberal policies.

The Role of a Safeguard Mechanism

The political economy that prevails at the eve of a liberalization attempt is almost invariably unfavorable to the implementation of these policies simply because liberalization policies shift the distribution of income against the traditionally protected factors. These factors are concentrated on a few monopolistic and oligopolistic firms that are well organized and can therefore mobilize formidable resistance to the introduction of policies that may be more geared to the national welfare than to their own specific interests.

One strategy in dealing with these groups would be to refuse the subsidies they request – in effect to deliver the message "adjust or go bankrupt." This did not happen in Perú and is unlikely to be practicable under a democratic regime. Instead, the government in several instances provided different forms of economic assistance, but in a haphazard way. For example, tariff reductions on nonproduced capital goods were granted to several sectors; nontariff barriers were introduced for steel products; tariff increases benefited the paper industry; and tax deferrals and subsidized credit were provided to several industries including textiles (chapter 2; see also Saint Pol and Vega Castro, 1985).

These import relief measures had two characteristics in common: they were granted to powerful and important industries, and the decisions were taken without regard to the economic costs and benefits.

Given that the government may well eventually provide economic relief to some of the industries affected by the liberalization measures, it might be in the national interest, if Perú decides to implement a comprehensive program of trade liberalization, to introduce a safeguard mechanism. In fact, the right of countries to introduce such mechanisms is included in the GATT.

Creation of a safeguard or escape mechanism has two important political objectives. First, the mechanism will help a political agreement on an initial trade liberalization to be reached. The resistance to liberalization is disarmed by the assurance that protection or other forms of government assistance will be reintroduced when they are really needed. Second, once the trade liberalization policies have been implemented, the safeguard mechanism would sort out those requests for import protection which are consistent with the national interest. Each request should be studied by a competent staff whose recommendations should be published and publicized.

In time this system could be expected to form an institutional basis for making the decision-making process more transparent and less discretional than has been the norm in Perú. Exactly how this mechanism will work is a matter for discussion once agreement on the nature of the global trade regime has been reached. Nevertheless, the following ideas, similar in concept to Australia's Industry Assistance Commission, are suggested.

1   The conclusions of this professional group should be as unbiased as possible. The group should therefore probably not be part of the government office that directly manages the incentives to industry.

2   The mechanism would be all inclusive in the sense of managing requests for import protection attributed to fair as well as unfair import competition. Therefore the group would study requests for import relief that are triggered by, say, "normal" competitive forces that result in a fast surge in competing imports, as well as requests based on the presumption of dumped and subsidized imports. (Recall from the discussion in chapter 4 that this was an important argument that protected entrepreneurs put forward in favor of increased import barriers.)

3   The mechanism should accept requests for import restrictions as well as for reductions in import barriers. That is, everyone should have a voice in the safeguard mechanism. Obviously, this also helps the goal of institutionalizing unbiased procedures.

4   The evaluation of the petitions should be informed by discussion of which groups in society will benefit and which will suffer from the decision. The report should also include an estimate of the economic costs and benefits of the decision. Liberalizing an economy that has been protected for decades will produce significant dislocations. The government should make every possible effort to let the general public know the principles and benefits behind the new policies. This, in our view, is also an important element in rallying support in favor of the new policies.

5   The decisions taken, and the bases on which they were made, should be made public.

6   To ensure that the economic assistance enhances productivity, it should only be given for a limited time.

Final Remarks

On the basis of Perú's experience, in this concluding chapter we have discussed the characteristics of a sequencing of policy reforms that would contribute to the successful introduction of a trade liberalization. First, the importance of stabilization was emphasized. We argued that in Perú price stabilization is unlikely to stick unless government expenditures are reduced. The reduction of these expenditures should be the pillar for achieving a long-lasting price stability. Second, the importance of reducing and eventually eliminating distortions and rigidities in factor markets has been emphasized. We have given both economic and political economy arguments of why, in Perú, the elimination of these controls – particularly those in urban labor markets – is crucial, for promoting the national interest in general and for promoting the likelihood of a successful trade liberalization in particular.

We have also distinguished different trade liberalization policies and emphasized the links that they have and the role that these policies play during a stabilization program.

Finally, the Peruvian experience shows that the commitment of the leadership to the policies is of paramount importance, and that they must win vocal support for the cause in parliamentary and public debate. From this study in general, and our analysis of the public debate in particular, it has been argued that those who introduced the trade liberalization policies received little support from the party in power, no support from consumers and efficient exporters, and outright criticism from APRA, the party that was most likely to win and eventually won the 1985 elections. In fact, the story of the Peruvian economy since World War II (chapter 1) is of a succession of political leaders who have not been able to agree on a stable and predictable set of economic policies. Economic strategies have shifted from socialist planning, to populism, to market oriented and back again. While this process continues, the history of Perú predicts that this country will remain stagnant and underdeveloped.

References

Abusada-Salah, Roberto (1977) "Utilización del capital instalado en el sector industrial peruano." Universidad Católica del Perú, Centro de Investigaciones Sociales Económicas Políticas y Antropológicas (CISEPA), Documento de Trabajo no. 31.

Altimir, Oscar (1982) "The extent of poverty in Latin America." Washington, DC: World Bank, Staff Working Paper no. 522.

BCRP (Banco Central de la Reserva del Perú) (1983) *El Proceso de Liberalización de las Importaciones: Perú, 1979–1982*. Lima, May.

BCRP, *Annual Reports*. various issues.

Bolóña, Carlos (1981) "Tariff policies in Perú 1880–1980." Ph.D. dissertation, University of Oxford, unpublished.

Cebrecos, Rufino and Jorge Vega Castro (1979). "Los efectos de una nueva política de protección en el Perú." Universidad Católica del Perú, CISEPA, Documento de Trabajo no. 40.

Cline, William (1981) "Economic Stabilization in Peru 1975–78." In William Cline and Sidney Weintraub, eds, *Economic Stabilization in Developing Countries*. Washington, DC: Brookings Institution.

Corbo, Vittorio and Patricio Meller (1981) "Alternative trade strategies and employment implications." In Anne O. Krueger, Hal Lary, Terry Monson, and Narongchai Akrasanee, eds, *Trade and Employment in Developing Countries: Individual Studies*, vol. 1, Chicago, IL: University of Chicago Press.

ECLA (Economic Commission for Latin America) (1959) *Análisis y Proyecciones del Desarrollo Económico, VI: El Desarrollo Industrial del Perú*. United Nations, April.

El Comercio (1980 and 1984), various issues.

Finger, J. Michael and Julio Nogués (1987) "International control of subsidies and counter-vailing duties." *World Bank Economic Review*, 1 (4), September, 707–25.

Fitzgerald, Edmund (1976) *The State and Economic Development in Peru since 1968*. Cambridge: Cambridge University Press.

GATT (General Agreement on Tariffs and Trade) (1986) "Agreement on interpretation of Articles VI, XVI, and XXIII of the GATT." Geneva.

Hanson, James A. and Craig R. Neal (1984) "Interest rate policies in selected developing countries, 1970–82." Mimeo. Washington, DC: World Bank.

IMF (International Monetary Fund), *International Financial Statistics*, various issues.

INE (Instituto Nacional de Estadística) (1983) *Cuentas Nacionales del Perú, 1950–1982*. Lima, Perú: República Peruana, INE, Dirección General de Cuentas Nacionales, August.

Johnson, Harry (1966) "Two notes on tariffs, distortions and growth." *Economic Journal*, March.

Krueger, Anne O. (1983) *Trade and Employment in Developing Countries*. Chicago, IL: University of Chicago Press.

McClintock, Cynthia and Abraham Lowenthal, eds (1983) *The Peruvian Experiment Reconsidered*. Princeton, NJ: Princeton University Press.

Nogués, Julio (1983) "Alternative trade strategies and employment in the Argentine manufacturing sector." *World Development*, 11; December, 1029–42.

Nogués, Julio (1986) "An historical perspective of Perú's trade liberalization policies of the 80s." Washington, DC: World Bank Development Research Department, Economics and Research Staff, Discussion Paper no. 168.

Orden, David et al. (1982) "Policies affecting the food and agricultural sector in Perú, 1970–1982: an evaluation and recommendation." Mimeo. US Agency for International Development.

Preeg, Ernest H. (1981) *The Evolution of a Revolution: Perú and Its Relations with the United States, 1968–1980*. Washington, DC: NPA Committee on Changing International Realities.

Saint Pol, Patrick and Jorge Vega Castro (1985) "Additional evidence on the effects of Perú's trade liberalization policies." Mimeo. Washington, DC: World Bank.

Schydlowsky, Daniel, Shane Hunt, and Jaime Mezzera (1983) La Promoción de Exportaciones no tradicionales en el Perú. Lima: Asociación de Exportadores del Perú.

Schydlowsky, Daniel, and Juan J. Wicht (1983) "The anatomy of an economic failure." In Cynthia McClintock and Abraham Lowenthal, eds *The Peruvian Experiment Reconsidered*. Princeton, NJ: Princeton University Press. An extended version of this paper has been published in Spanish: (1979) *Anatomía de un Fracaso Económico, Perú, 1968–1978*. Lima: Universidad del Pacífico.

Thorp, Rosemary (1977) "The Post-import-substitution era: the case of Perú." *World Development*, 5, 125–36.

US Federal Register, "Cotton sheeting and sateen from Perú: final results of administrative review of countervailing duty order." *US Federal Register*, 49 (17), pp. 34, 543.

Vega Castro, Jorge (1984) "El sector informal en Perú." Mimeo.

Webb, Richard (1977) *Government Policy and the Distribution of Income in Peru, 1963–1973*. Cambridge, MA: Harvard University Press.

Westphal, Larry (1982) "Fostering technological mastery of selective infant industry protection." In Moshe Synguin and Simón Teitel, eds, *Trade, Stability, Technology and Equity in Latin America*. New York: Academic Press.

World Bank (1983a) *1983 World Bank Atlas*. Washington, DC: World Bank.

World Bank (1983b) *World Tables*. Washington, DC: Johns Hopkins University Press for the World Bank.

World Bank (1983c) "Peru's manufacturing sector, performance and policy issues." Mimeo.

Index

Abusada–Salah, Roberto, 293, 320
Acción Popular, Perú, 320
ADEX. *See* Asociación de Exportadores (ADEX)
Agrarian reform, Perú, 289–90, 319, 341, 345
Agricultural sector
 Brazil
  discriminatory trade practices against, 32, 59
 Colombia
  contribution to gross output of, 155
  growth of, 157
 Perú
  decline in growth of, 290, 303
  discriminatory pricing policy against, 301, 303, 341
  employment in, 314–15
Alianza para la Revolución Americana (APRA), 319, 320
Altimir, Oscar, 289
Andean Group, 170n, 308n
 role in trade policy of, 323, 325n
 See also Common external tariff (CET)
ANDI. *See* National Association of Industrialists (Asociación Nacional de Industriales: ANDI), Colombia
Antidumping subsidies, 338–40
Apparent import tariff, Colombia. *See* Tariffs
APRA. *See* Alianza para la Revolución Americana (APRA)
Asociación de Exportadores (ADEX), 334, 340
Asociación Latinoamericana de Libre Comercio (ALALC), 170n
Associação dos Exportadores Brasileiros, 37
Associations in Brazil, 37–8
Authoritarian government, Brazil (1964–84), 9, 11–12, 34–7
 short-run changes of, 43–6

Bacha, Edmar L., 101n, 103, 105n
Baer, Werner, 115n
Balance of payments
 Brazil, 16–17
  effect of policy changes on, 21–2, 46–7
  effect on policy of, 21–2, 40–2, 52–6
  as factor in liberalization policy, 40–2, 53–4

Colombia
 effect of crisis in, 160–1
 use of QRs to correct, 173–4
Perú, 287–8
 domestic policy effect on, 282–95
 See also Capital account; Current account
Banco Central, Brazil, 52–3, 69–71, 76–7, 86–7
Banco Central de la Reserva del Perú (BCRP), 294, 337, 350, 361, 385
Banco de la República, Colombia, 173, 175, 180, 189, 194n
Banco do Brasil, 76, 86–7
 CACEX (Carteira de Comércio Exterior) foreign trade division, 18, 38, 54–5, 76, 116
 import–export division of (CEXIM), 16, 17, 18
Banco Industrial, Perú, 337
BCRP. *See* Banco Central de la Reserva del Perú (BCRP)
BEFIEX. *See* Fiscal Benefits for Exporting (BEFIEX)
Belaúnde Terry, Fernando, 287, 288–9, 292, 320, 345, 388
Beltrão, Helio, 46
Bergsman, Joel, 29, 32, 44–5, 50, 51, 84n, 138
Berry, Albert, 256
Black market
 Brazil
  exchange rate in (1964), 59
  as parallel market (*mercado paralelo*), 77
 Colombia
  differential between official rate and, 187
  factors contributing to, 180
Bolóña, Carlos, 282n, 284, 285, 286, 287, 290
Bonelli, Regis, 128, 131
Borrowing, foreign
 Brazil
  effect on capital inflows of public, 72–3
  to finance current account, 52
  laws regulating public, 69–71
  policy for, 68, 69–73
 Colombia
  restrictions for, 195–6
 Perú, 292
 See also Debt, external; Loans, variable rate